D1434414

The Private Pilot's Licence Course

Meteorology
Navigation

The Private Pilot's Licence Course

Meteorology
Navigation
JAR Edition

Jeremy M Pratt

ISBN 1 874783 76

Published by

Airplan Flight Equipment Ltd

First Edition 1996
Reprinted 1996
Reprinted with amendments and revisions 1998

Second edition 2000
Reprinted with amendments and revisions 2001
Reprinted with amendments and revisions 2002

The Private Pilot's Licence Course Navigation and Meteorology

ISBN 1 874783 76

Airplan Flight Equipment Ltd.,
1a Ringway Trading Estate, Shadowmoss Road, Manchester M22 5LH
Tel: 0161 499 0023   Fax: 0161 499 0298
email: enquiries@afeonline.com
www.afeonline.com

contents

Meteorology Introduction

contents

contents

contents

contents

Navigation Introduction

contents

contents

contents

contents

editorial

Acknowledgments

This book would not have been possible without the invaluable assistance of many people and organisations, including:

Air Accident Investigation
    Branch
AIS Headquarters,
    Heathrow
Aviation Picture Library

Civil Aviation Authority:
−   Chart Room
    (especially John
    Gentleman and David
    Smith)
−   Safety Promotion
    Section (especially
    John Thorpe and
    David Hocking)

Camber Publications Ltd
Steve Dickinson
Dundee University
Peggy Follis
Peter R March
Chris Mathews
Météo Montpellier
John Nelson
Rik Payne
Hervé Piedra
John Ross
Gill Stitt
Rob Taylor GDi studio
J M H Thomas
The Times Newspaper
Paul Tomlinson
UK Met. Office:
−   Jill Harmer, Marketing
    Manager
−   Karen Dutton
The UK VFR Flight Guide
Wisconsin Aviation,
    France

AUTHOR: JEREMY M PRATT

Jeremy Pratt took his first flying lesson aged 14, paid for by weekend and holiday jobs at his local airfield cleaning aircraft and working in the hanger. Later he also worked in the air/ground station of the airfield and in the operations department of an air taxi company. He completed his PPL after being awarded an Esso/Air League scholarship and became a flying instructor at the age of 19. Since then he has taught students for the Private Pilots Licence and associated ratings and also applicants for professional flying licences. He has flown as a commercial pilot in a variety of roles and has also flown microlights, gliders and helicopters. He stays current by instructing and flying around Europe for business and pleasure.

He has been Managing Director of Airplan Flight Equipment since 1985, is author of the 'Pilot's Guide' series, the 'Questions and Answers' series; and has also co-authored, compiled and contributed to, a number of aviation books and publications.

TECHNICAL ADVISORS:

Bill Stitt − Chief Flying Instructor of Essex Flying School, Bill has been a flying instructor for over 20 years and is a delegated flight examiner. He has been training instructors for over 15 years and he is married to a flying instructor: their daughter also flies!

Phillip G Mathews − Chief Flying Instructor of Cotswold Aviation Services, Phil has over 10,000 hours experience of flying light aircraft. He gained his PPL at the age of 17 and went on to achieve an ATPL through the 'self-improver' route. Phil also runs his own business teaching applicants for the PPL and IMC rating technical exams and flies as a commercial pilot.

Colin McAllister − Met. Office College Lecturer. Colin was an aviation forecaster in the forces for many years, working at several RAF bases. He then taught meteorology in the RAF for several years, before joining the Met. Office College at Reading. Here he teaches trainee forecasters and also assists on courses for PPLs run by the UK Met. Office.

Meteorology introduction

Meteorology is regarded by many as the most interesting – if most complex – of all the subjects in the PPL course. Perhaps this is because meteorology cannot be learnt 'parrot fashion'; an *understanding* of the basic mechanisms at work is required. These basics are covered in the first chapters of this section. Do work through these chapters carefully, and don't hesitate to go back and re-read anything you are unsure about. A sound understanding of meteorological principles will make the rest of the book that much easier.

Weather **is** fascinating and, as most people have noticed, it is not entirely predictable. Weather systems are driven by complex interactions between many elements. A small change in one of these elements can be enough to influence the weather, be it the slight shift of an ocean current re-routing a major depression or an isolated factory triggering cloud and rain many miles downwind. If you appreciate this inherent unpredictability, you will treat all weather forecasts with a reasonable degree of caution – which is no bad thing. You will also realise that it is difficult to make definitive statements about day-to-day weather, and words like "tend", "may", "can" and "often" appear much more here than in other subjects. Let's be honest – if weather was simplistic and predictable, it wouldn't be half as interesting!

The meteorology section of the PPL course **does not** aim to make you a weather forecaster – we have the Met. Office for that. Instead the meteorological section should equip you to:

1: *interpret weather information* and so make safe planning decisions based on it;

2: *assess the actual weather* occurring, and make sound decisions based on what you see.

And, of course, the better you understand meteorology, the better your judgement will be.

So this book concentrates on the practical aspects of meteorology which affect flight planning and in-flight decisions. To this end we have avoided, where possible, jargon and purely theoretical concepts. Furthermore, sample weather forecasts and weather reports are used extensively to illustrate weather phenomena. The main features of each example are described in the accompanying caption. If you want to fully decode a forecast or report, the necessary information can be found in the chapter entitled 'Aviation Weather Reports & Forecasts'.

Now the standard disclaimer. Throughout this book the pilot, forecaster, met. observer etc. is referred to using the pronoun 'he'. This has been done purely to avoid the unwieldy and repetitive use of "he or she". As usual, I ask for the reader's understanding.

Finally, a sombre note. Weather is a major factor in a large proportion of general-aviation accidents. Dealing with bad weather is all about pilot judgement and virtually nothing to do with flying skill. No amount of piloting ability will make fog less dense, reveal a mountain hidden by cloud, or make the inside of a thunderstorm less turbulent. The root cause of 'weather' accidents is nearly always lack of judgement: either by ignoring or failing to account for forecast bad weather before take-off or by continuing the flight into poor weather, rather than diverting or turning back. The weather is a powerful and ruthless force when it turns against you. Taking it on or "having a go" is merely inviting the inevitable conclusion to a one-sided contest. After-all, weather is just part of nature – and nature always wins, sooner or later. The losers are those pilots who become just another 'weather accident' statistic.

Properties of the Atmosphere

Meteorology

*Properties
of the
Atmosphere*

▶ **Composition and Structure**

▶ **Pressure, Temperature and Density**

▶ **Conversion Of Temperature**

▶ **Revision**

Meteorology

▶Composition and Structure

The atmosphere is a mixture of gases held to the earth by gravity. The approximate proportions of gases in a dry atmosphere are:

78% Nitrogen

21% Oxygen

1% Other gases (argon, krypton, etc.)

The approximate proportion of gases (excluding water vapour) in the atmosphere

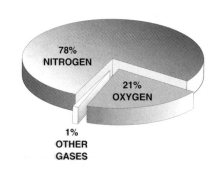

The atmosphere is never completely dry. The amount of water vapour (which is an invisible gas) in the atmosphere varies from close to zero in the cold, dry polar regions to a maximum of around 4% in the hot and humid parts of the world adjacent to tropical seas. Water absorbs and releases energy in the form of heat, and condenses to form clouds, rain, snow and so on. It is the relatively small amount of water in the atmosphere which is responsible for almost all significant weather.

The atmosphere can be divided into layers. The layer closest to the earth and of most interest to the light-aircraft pilot is the *troposphere*. The troposphere extends from the surface upwards to a region known as the *tropopause*. Because the troposphere contains virtually all the water in the atmosphere, this is where most 'weather' – clouds, fog, mist, rain, snow etc. – is to be found, although occasionally a particular weather feature such as the top of a thunderstorm may push upwards through the tropopause.

On average, the troposphere is most shallow over the poles, and deepest over the equator

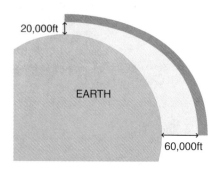

The tropopause marks the 'ceiling' of the troposphere. It is found at levels varying from around 20,000ft over the polar regions to 60,000ft over the equator. In the temperate latitudes, roughly mid-way between the tropics and the poles, the average altitude of the tropopause is around 35,000ft. The tropopause is higher in summer than in winter, and it rises and falls as high-pressure and low-pressure systems move under it.

The lowest three layers of the atmosphere, which are of the most interest to pilots

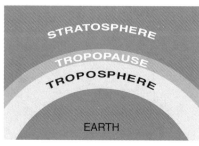

Above the tropopause is the *stratosphere*. Because the tropopause effectively acts as a lid, keeping most of the water vapour – and so virtually all weather – in the troposphere, there is less here to interest pilots apart from certain types of wind, of which more later. The stratosphere extends from the tropopause to an average height of about 20 miles (120,000ft) above the surface.

▶ Pressure, Temperature and Density

Pressure, temperature and density are the main physical properties of a gas, or any mixture of gases such as the atmosphere. The interplay between these three parameters largely determines the behaviour of the atmosphere. A good knowledge of how they interact is the key to understanding meteorology.

The atmosphere acts very much like an ocean; it is constantly in motion and has ebbs and flows, currents and temperature variations. Living on earth's surface, we are at the bottom of this ocean and are subject to the enormous pressure of the atmosphere bearing down on us. Of course it doesn't *feel* like an enormous pressure because we have evolved with the atmosphere pretty much the way it is now; in fact we rely on the intense pressure to be able to breathe. Nevertheless, the weight of air at the surface is something like one tonne per square metre. Higher in the atmosphere there is less weight of air pressing down, and hence less pressure.

The pressure of a gas can be expressed in several different units. In aviation the most common unit is the *millibar* (abbreviated to mb) although this is gradually being replaced by the *hectopascal* (hPa). Thankfully, one millibar equals one hectopascal so the only real difference is one of terminology. In the UK "millibar" is being retained as standard RT phraseology for the foreseeable future, but don't be surprised to come across "hectopascal" elsewhere. Throughout this book pressure will be referred to in mb/hPa.

The other well-known unit of pressure measurement is *inches of mercury*, as employed on the dials of household barometers but also used for aviation purposes in some countries, notably North America. Many flight guides carry a conversion table between millibars/hectopascals and inches of mercury.

Just to make life interesting, some Eastern European countries express pressure in millimetres of mercury...

The reduction of pressure with height does not take place at a constant rate. At the surface, pressure reduces at about one millibar per 27ft. By 20,000ft the rate of pressure reduction is about one millibar per 50ft, and by 30,000ft it is about one millibar per 75ft.

300mb — 30,000ft

500mb — 20,000ft
700mb
850mb — 10,000ft
5,000ft

Pressure decreases with increasing altitude

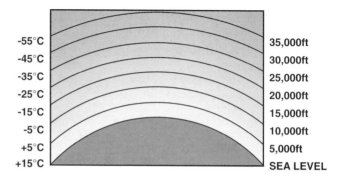

-55°C	35,000ft
-45°C	30,000ft
-35°C	25,000ft
-25°C	20,000ft
-15°C	15,000ft
-5°C	10,000ft
+5°C	5,000ft
+15°C	SEA LEVEL

Temperature usually decreases with increasing altitude. Depicted here are the 'standard' temperatures at various altitudes

Temperature also varies throughout the atmosphere, and under normal circumstances it decreases with height. In the troposphere, the average rate of temperature change is about 2°C for every 1000ft of altitude change. So if the surface temperature is +15°C, the temperature at 10,000ft on an average day would be -5°C. The rate of temperature change through the atmosphere is known as the *lapse rate*. The reduction in temperature continues up to the tropopause, above which the temperature is assumed to remain constant regardless of altitude. So there is no lapse rate in the stratosphere.

Other things being equal, the density of a gas reduces as its pressure is reduced. However, its density increases as temperature is reduced. If this sounds vaguely familiar to those who underwent school physics, it is one expression of Boyle's Law. In an aviation context, it immediately leads to a conundrum. We know from observation that the density of the atmosphere is less at altitude than at the surface. It has just been stated that reduced pressure will reduce the density, but a reduction in temperature implies an *increase* in density. Can these both be right? The answer is yes, because the change in pressure has a more marked effect on density than the change in temperature.

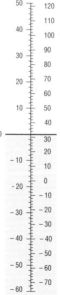

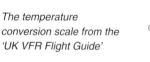

The temperature conversion scale from the 'UK VFR Flight Guide'

►Conversion of Temperature

Throughout this book temperature is referred to in terms of *degrees Celsius,* which is the most commonly used unit in aviation and is the same thing as "degrees Centigrade". Temperature can also be referred in degrees Fahrenheit, reference to which remains common in the UK and elsewhere. To convert from Celsius to Fahrenheit there are a couple of methods:

To convert °C to °F divide by 5, multiply by 9 and add 32;

e.g. 15°C : ÷ 5 (= 3); x 9 (= 27) + 32 = 59°F

To convert °F to °C subtract 32; divide by 9, multiply by 5;

e.g. 59°F : - 32 (= 27); ÷ 9 (= 3); X 5 = 15°C

There is a quicker, if slightly less accurate, rule of thumb. Start from the basis that 10°C = 50°F. Thereafter allow 9°F for each 5°C;

for example, 20°C = 68°F.

Obviously this rule can be used in reverse;

40°F = 4°C.

Properties of the Atmosphere

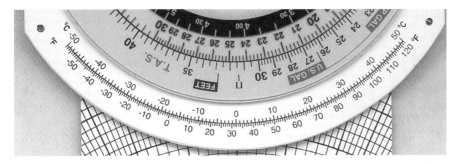

The temperature conversion scale on an ARC-1 flight computer

If this is rather too much mental arithmetic, graphs and conversion tables (such as that on a flight computer) are usually widely available. For most of us non-mathematicians these give a rather better chance of arriving at an accurate answer!

▶Revision

Revision questions are printed at the end of each chapter in this book. The aim of the revision questions is to enable you to test your knowledge of the chapter subject, and to help you retain the principal elements of each subject.

Attempt the revision questions once you are satisfied that you have understood and learnt the main points of each chapter. You should aim for a 'success' rate of around 80%.

1   What is the approximate proportion of oxygen in the dry atmosphere?

2   What is the name of the layer of the atmosphere between the troposphere and the stratosphere?

3   How does density vary with temperature (assuming pressure remains constant)?

4   What is the approximate vertical distance represented by a change in pressure of 1mb near the surface?

5   10mb = how many hPa?

6   The temperature at the surface is +5°C. At 5000ft the temperature is -10°C. What is the lapse rate?

7   Given a surface temperature of +80°F, and a lapse rate of 3°C per 1000ft, what temperature would you expect at 10,000ft?

Answers at page MET 181

The Motion of the Atmosphere

Meteorology

*The Motion
of the
Atmosphere*

▶ Heating of the Atmosphere

▶ Measurement of Pressure

▶ Pressure Gradient

▶ Coriolis Force, Geostrophic Wind

▶ Measurement of Wind

▶ Variation of Wind Velocity with Altitude

▶ Local Winds

▶ Diurnal Variation of Wind Velocity

▶ Turbulence and Windshear

▶ Depressions and Anticyclones

▶ Revision

Meteorology

▶ **Heating of the Atmosphere**

Despite the sub-heading, the first point to grasp is that the atmosphere itself acquires virtually no heat energy directly from the sun. To all intents and purposes it is transparent to solar radiation. Radiation from the sun heats up the earth's surface, and the fact that this heating is not uniform across the planet has some profound meteorological consequences.

Because of a combination of factors, including the virtually spherical shape of the earth, solar energy is more concentrated in tropical areas than in polar regions. So at the tropics the surface gains a lot of energy from the sun and becomes heated. Some of this heat is transferred to the atmosphere, and in effect the atmosphere is warmed from below. At the poles, the energy from the sun is spread over a much wider area and the surface remains cold. Hence the air in the vicinity of the poles is cold. Furthermore, the earth is tilted on its axis. This causes the northern and southern hemispheres to receive varying concentrations of solar energy according to the position of the earth in its orbit around the sun. This is the reason why summer occurs in the northern hemisphere when it is winter in the southern hemisphere and *vice versa*.

The sun's energy is far more concentrated near the equator than near the poles. This is the principal reason why surface temperatures are warmer at the equator than at the poles

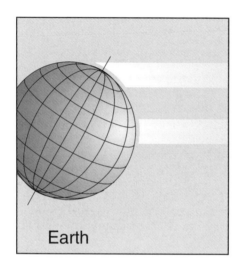

Earth

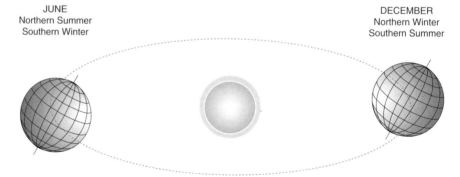

JUNE
Northern Summer
Southern Winter

DECEMBER
Northern Winter
Southern Summer

The earth's orbit around the sun determines the seasons

If this was all there was to surface heating, there would be a uncomplicated circulation of air over the planet. Air at the tropics would be warmed from below by the hot surface. So it would become less dense than surrounding air and start to rise, eventually spreading out to the north and south. At the same time, the very cold ground in the polar regions would be cooling the air, increasing its density at the surface. The net result of this at the earth's surface would be areas of high pressure at the poles and low pressure in the tropics. Air moves from high pressure to low pressure. So the flow at the surface (the surface wind, if you like) would be directly from the poles to the tropics.

In actual fact, a number of factors modify this simple model. For one thing, different types of surface have different heating properties. Land tends to heat quickly and cool quickly, and is capable of changing from cold to hot and back in a matter of hours. Water changes temperature far more slowly. The cycle of heating and cooling of the oceans can be measured in months, so there is often a relatively high sea temperature long after the summer (and therefore the strongest solar heating) has ended. Conversely, having cooled through the winter, it will be well into the late spring before sea temperatures rise significantly.

Accepting that there are complicating factors, however, the basic principle is simple. The uneven heating of the earth's surface creates areas of high and low pressure, and the flow of air from high pressure to low pressure is *wind*.

▶ Measurement of Pressure

From what has been said, you will not be surprised to learn that a knowledge of pressure distribution is of prime importance to pilots and meteorologists. For this reason, meteorological stations measure the atmospheric pressure at the surface, which immediately raises a complicating factor – the observing points are all at different elevations, i.e. different altitudes above sea level. For example, RAF Valley is 37ft AMSL, whereas Biggin Hill is about 600ft AMSL. The difference in elevation amounts to a pressure differential of around 21mb (if 27ft = 1mb, approximately). So the direct plotting of surface pressure measurements would be pointless, because at each place pressure is being measured from a different datum (that is, at a different elevation). To give a uniform datum, the observed pressure is increased using a standard formula to calculate what the pressure *would be* if the station was at sea level. In this way a chart of observed pressures can be drawn in which all figures are based on a common sea-level datum.

A basic plot of sea level pressures (QNHs)

Once these pressure measurements are plotted on a chart, lines are drawn joining points of equal sea-level pressure. These lines are known as *isobars*. Isobars can be likened to the contour lines of a map. Just as contour lines indicate high ground, valleys, plains, steep gradients and so on, isobars indicate areas of high pressure, low pressure, pressure gradients and the like.

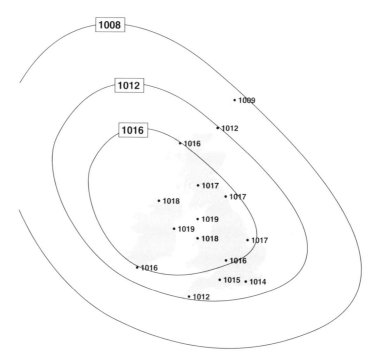

Isobars drawn in around pressure plots. Isobars are lines joining places of equal sea-level pressure

▶Pressure Gradient

Air flows down a pressure gradient – from high pressure to low pressure – just as water will run from the top of a hill into a valley. The steeper the slope of the ground, the closer together the contour lines will be on a map. And the steeper the ground, the faster water flows down the slope. Isobars work in just the same way. Isobars close together indicate a steep pressure gradient, which means a large change in pressure over a short distance; the closer together the isobars, the steeper the pressure gradient and the stronger the wind. Conversely a 'slack' pressure gradient (widely spaced isobars) indicates light winds. The relationship between isobar spacing and wind strength is easy to formulate, and with a little practice wind strength can quite easily be estimated from the isobar spacing on a weather chart where a wind scale is printed on the chart.

Air flows down the pressure gradient, from high to low, just as water flows down a surface gradient

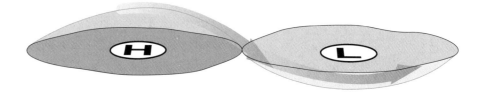

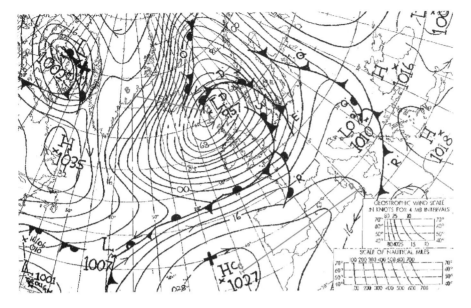

The line A-B is across a steep pressure-gradient – implying strong winds. The line C-D is across a slack pressure-gradient – implying weak winds. Across the UK is a typical spring gale, with low pressure to the north of the UK and closely packed isobars across the country which brought surface winds in excess of 40 knots to Scotland and northern England

▶ Coriolis Force, Geostrophic Wind

From the foregoing, you might expect that air flows directly from high pressure to low pressure. In fact, due to something called the *Coriolis force*, its behaviour is slightly different.

Coriolis force is a consequence of the rotation of the earth on its axis. Imagine trying to draw a straight line out from the centre of a rotating disc. Although you are moving the pencil in a straight line, the resulting drawn line is curved due to the rotation of the disc. Coriolis force acts in much the same way on a moving particle. In the northern hemisphere the force acts at 90° to the right of the moving particle, whereas in the southern hemisphere it acts at 90° to the left. Coriolis force is strongest at the poles and zero at the equator. The faster the particle is moving, the greater the effect the Coriolis force has on it.

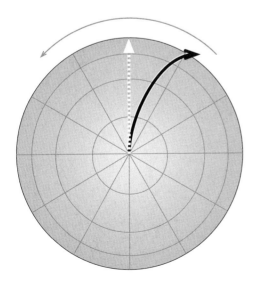

EARTH
Seen from above the north pole (with direction of motion).
Dotted line is imaginary track, solid line is actual track.

The deflection of a moving air particle by Coriolis force as seen from above the north pole

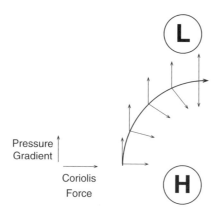

The path of a moving air particle. In this case it is deflected to the right (in the northern hemisphere) until pressure-gradient force and Coriolis force are balanced

So when air begins to move as a consequence of a pressure-gradient, it is deflected (to the right in the northern hemisphere) by the Coriolis force. This deflection 'curves' the path of the air particles. The flow of air may be sufficiently deflected for the pressure-gradient force and the Coriolis force to be exactly balanced. When the air is flowing along straight, parallel isobars, the resulting wind is known as the *geostrophic wind*.

Where isobars are curved (such as those around an area of high or low pressure) the resulting wind can be referred to as the *gradient wind*. A detailed examination of the processes behind gradient wind is (thankfully) outside the scope of the PPL course. However, one practical feature of gradient wind is that for the **same isobar spacing**, wind speeds around an area of low pressure are often less than wind speeds around a high-pressure area.

▶ Measurement of Wind

Wind is always measured and forecast as a **velocity**, which means that wind direction and wind speed are always quoted together.

The wind direction is the direction *from* which the wind is blowing. Weather forecasts and reports usually refer to the wind direction in degrees true, although wind direction given by radio from an ATSU is usually in degrees magnetic.

Wind speed is measured by an anemometer, and normally reported in knots (nautical miles per hour, abbreviated to KT) although it can also be expressed in metres per second (MPS) or, more rarely, kilometres per hour (KMH). Although the knot is the standard unit in aviation for measuring wind speed in most parts of the world, metres per second are often used in eastern Europe. A rule-of-thumb conversion is simple; double the metres per second figure to obtain the speed in knots. Hence a wind speed of 10MPS is about 20KT.

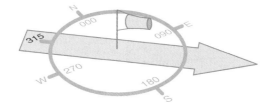

The measurement of wind velocity

Wind velocity northwest (315°) at 20knots

As mentioned, wind direction and speed are reported together as a wind velocity. So a wind blowing from 315 degrees at a speed of 20 knots might be reported verbally as "315 at 20", which could be written as "315/20KT" or just "31520KT".

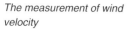

EGNH 190550 190550Z 31010KT CAVOK 15/10 Q1021=

The reporting of surface wind velocity. 'EGNH' is the ICAO code for Blackpool airport in the UK (all UK airfield ICAO codes start with 'EG'). The METAR (actual report) from Blackpool at 0550 UTC (Z) on the 19th day of the month gives the surface wind as being from a direction of 310° true, with a wind speed of 10 knots

EGPD 190550 100550Z 32007KT 310V010 9999 SCT005
BKN020 12/12 Q1025 =

A METAR (actual report) from EGPD – Aberdeen – at 0550 UTC. The surface wind is from 320° at 7 knots, although the direction is varying from 310° to 010°

When a wind direction changes, its direction in terms of degrees will either increase or decrease. When the wind direction *increases* clockwise (e.g. from 315° to 080°) it is said to have *veered*. When the direction *decreases* anti-clockwise (e.g. from 315° to 270°) it is said to have *backed*. One way to memorise this is to think of wind direction that has changed anti-clockwise – **backwards** – as having **backed.**

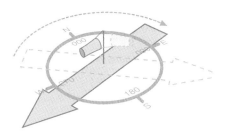

The wind has veered

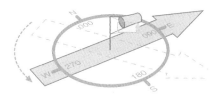

The wind has backed

LEFT> A veering of wind direction

RIGHT> A backing of wind direction

▶Variation of Wind Velocity with Altitude

The wind velocity at 2000ft is often referred to as the "free wind" since it is assumed to be free of the effects of contact with the surface. This raises the obvious question of what are the effects of contact with the surface? Where air flows over the earth's surface, friction reduces its speed. As speed decreases, the effect of Coriolis force is reduced and the wind direction backs (in the northern hemisphere). The change in wind velocity is greatest over the land, whose irregular surface and obstructions reduce wind speeds the most, and least over a smooth sea which causes little friction.

Over the sea, the difference between the surface wind and the 2000ft wind will amount to a decrease in speed of about 20% and a backing of about 10°. So a 2000ft wind of 270/20 might be associated with a surface wind of 260/16. Over the

An average change in w/v over a calm sea, from the 'free' wind of 270/20 at 2000ft to the surface wind of 260/16

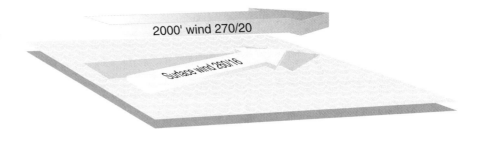

An average change in w/v over land, from the 'free' wind of 270/20 at 2000ft to the surface wind of 240/10

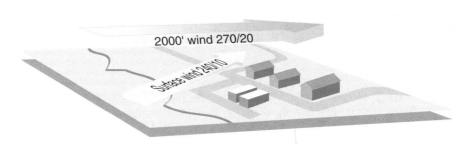

land, where friction is increased, the reduction in speed is much greater – nearer 50% – and therefore the backing in direction is more marked at about 30°. In this case a 2000ft wind of 270/20 would suggest a surface wind of 240/10.

The layer of atmosphere through which this change occurs is known as the *friction layer*. The type of surface and wind speed affects the thickness of the friction layer. Over the sea in light winds, the friction layer may be as little as 500ft thick. Over an irregular land surface during strong winds, the friction layer could be more like 5000ft thick – i.e. the effects of surface friction will be evident up to 5000ft or so. This is one reason why one sometimes has to climb surprisingly high to find smooth air on a blustery day.

Decreasing wind speed through the friction layer

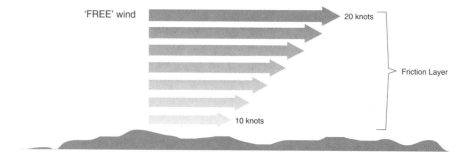

```
50N 0230E
24    250    25    -30
18    240    20    -17
10    220    15    -03
05    210    20    +06
02    190    25    +11
01    180    20    +12
```

The forecast w/v and temperatures at various levels over a fixed point (in this case 50N 0230E) taken from a METFORM 214 chart. For example, at 5000ft altitude the w/v is forecast to be 210° true at 20 knots, with a temperature of +6°C

▶Local Winds

We've already seen that uneven surface heating and the consequent pressure distribution results in wind flow over large areas. However, smaller-scale variations of temperature and pressure also cause more localised winds.

Coming back to surface heating, you will appreciate that there is a daily temperature cycle. This results from the simple fact that when the sun sets at night, the surface stops warming up. So night-time temperatures are generally lower than day-time temperatures. If all other factors (cloud cover, weather, air mass etc.) are equal, the lowest temperature at the surface occurs just before dawn and the highest temperature just after midday. This daily cycle is known as *diurnal variation*.

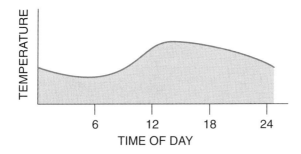

The average diurnal variation of temperature

Sea breezes are caused by the diurnal variation of temperature and the different heating properties of land and sea. Imagine a cloudless summer's morning at the beach; there is a slack pressure-gradient, so winds are light. The land is quickly heated by the sun and is soon warming the air over it, whereas the air over the colder sea remains cool. Air over the land warms, becomes less dense and rises, spreading out (diverging) at about 1000ft above the surface. Over the sea, however, the cooler air is more dense and tends to descend (subsiding). The net effect is that by the early afternoon there is a higher pressure over the sea than over the land. The result? Air flows across the pressure-gradient, from high to low, causing a *sea breeze* – a cool breeze blowing towards the land from the sea.

On a clear summer's day surface heating causes the air over the land to be warmer (and less dense) than the air over the sea. The difference in air density leads to a pressure differential – high pressure at the surface over the sea and low pressure over the land

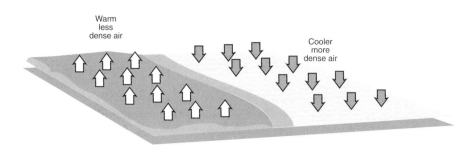

Air flows across the pressure gradient, from high to low, creating a cool breeze from the sea – a sea breeze

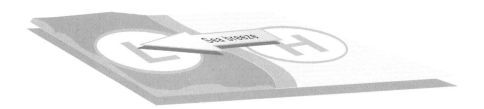

Initially the breeze blows at 90° to the coast, although in time the Coriolis force may veer the wind flow (by 30° or more) and cause it to blow at an angle to the coastline. Sea breezes are not normally found above 1000ft and are seldom stronger than 10kts. Initially a sea breeze will be confined to the coast, although by late afternoon it can spread as much as 20-30 miles inland.

At night the situation is reversed. The land cools rapidly and is soon colder than the sea. The pressure-gradient and so the flow of air is reversed, and an off-shore breeze blows from the land to the sea. This is known – unsurprisingly – as a *land breeze*.

On a clear night, the land cools more rapidly than the sea leading to cooler, denser air over the land than over the sea. The resulting pressure differential – high pressure over the land and low pressure over the sea – causes a land breeze

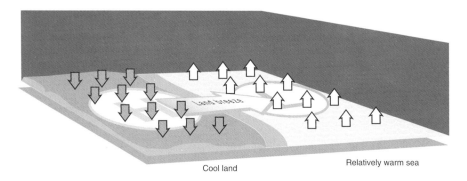

The Motion of the Atmosphere

Diurnal temperature variation is also responsible for up-slope and down-slope winds found in mountainous areas. During a clear night the land cools rapidly, so the layer of air next to the surface is also cooled – making it more dense than the surrounding air. Gravity takes effect and the dense air starts to flow down the slope. The result is a *katabatic wind,* and in some particularly mountainous areas it can reach gale-force strength. Where this wind is regularly experienced, it is often given a local name – such as the 'bora' in the Adriatic. Such winds can be difficult to forecast and can often set in with little or no warning. They are a good example of where local knowledge can be invaluable to the forecaster and pilot alike.

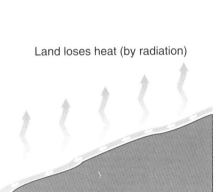

Land loses heat (by radiation)

Layer of cool, dense air – flows down the slope, drawn by gravity

On a clear night the surface loses heat to space. The air next to the surface becomes cooler (and denser) and if there is a slope, it will flow down it – creating a katabatic wind

The reverse effect, an up-slope wind, may occur on sunny days when the air next to the surface is warmed by the warm land on sun-facing slopes. The resulting wind is less strong (because it is flowing against gravity) and is known as an *anabatic wind.*

▶Diurnal Variation of Wind Velocity

The diurnal temperature cycle also causes a more general daily variation of wind, which is governed by surface type.

The sea tends to heat and cool slowly. Because of this, there is little change in surface heating over the sea, and little change in the friction layer by day or night. Over land, the picture is slightly different. The surface heats and cools quickly. By day, surface heating causes convection ("thermals" of rising and descending air, the former much sought after by glider pilots) which increases mixing in the atmosphere. The result is that by day the surface wind veers, increases in strength and becomes more gusty as more of the faster-moving upper wind is mixed into the friction layer. By night, the processes reverse and mixing decreases. Surface winds tend to back, decrease and become more steady.

By day, convection increases 'mixing' in the friction layer, making the surface wind stronger and more gusty

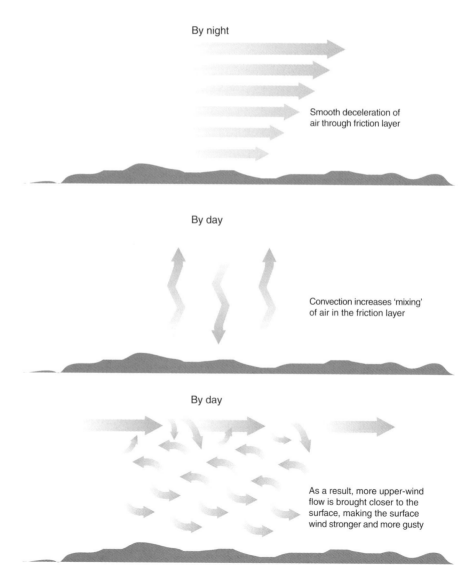

By night

Smooth deceleration of air through friction layer

By day

Convection increases 'mixing' of air in the friction layer

By day

As a result, more upper-wind flow is brought closer to the surface, making the surface wind stronger and more gusty

▶ Turbulence and Windshear

Low-level turbulence can be caused by airflow over and around ground features and obstructions. You can visualise the effect as being rather like that of water flowing over rocks and pebbles on a beach. Downwind of an obstruction or high terrain, the turbulence can be quite pronounced. The stronger the wind and the bigger the obstruction, the greater the chance of turbulence developing.

Turbulent air is often found downwind of an obstruction, sometimes even in light wind conditions and in the lee of a small hill

A change in wind velocity with a change in height is known as *windshear*, sometimes also referred to (by pilots if not meteorologists) as the *wind gradient*. Windshear can involve a change in wind direction, a change in wind speed or a change in both simultaneously.

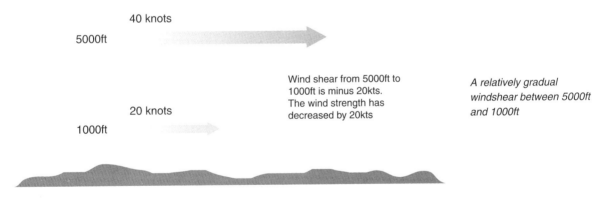

40 knots

5000ft

20 knots

1000ft

Wind shear from 5000ft to 1000ft is minus 20kts. The wind strength has decreased by 20kts

A relatively gradual windshear between 5000ft and 1000ft

Low-level windshear and turbulence can be associated with thunderstorms, temperature inversions (*q.v.*) or a strong wind blowing over a surface obstruction, and can present a serious hazard to aircraft. Both are looked at in more detail later in this book.

Meteorology

▶Depressions and Anticyclones

Before leaving the subject of pressure distribution, a little more terminology. A roughly circular area of high pressure is called an *anticyclone*, and has a clockwise wind flowing around it in the northern hemisphere. Where an area of high pressure is elongated, it is often referred to as a *ridge*. An area of low pressure is called a *depression* and has an anti-clockwise flow in the northern hemisphere. An elongated area of low pressure is often referred to as a *trough,* although this word is also used in another context as will be seen later. An area of little or no pressure-gradient between anticyclones and depressions is known as a *col*.

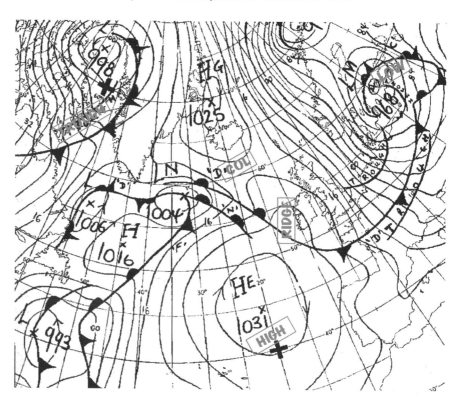

Areas of high and low pressure as seen on a North Atlantic surface pressure chart

When you look at the isobars on a met. chart, you can assume that the wind at around 2000ft will be following the direction of the isobars, and that the strength is indicated by the isobar spacing. Remembering that in the northern hemisphere air

Air follows isobars anti-clockwise around a low-pressure area and clockwise around a high-pressure area, in the northern hemisphere

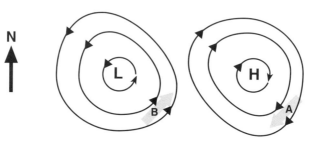

B: 'Free' wind direction approx

A: 'Free' wind direction approx 060°

flows clockwise around the high- pressure areas, and anti-clockwise around low-pressure areas, a simple rule known as *Buys Ballot's Law* becomes apparent. This states that **in the northern hemisphere, if you stand with your back to the wind, the low-pressure area is on your left**.

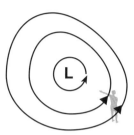

Buys Ballot's
Law

In the northern hemisphere if you stand with your back to the wind, the low-pressure area is on your left

▶Revision

8 What is an isobar?

9 Which of the two points below will be experiencing the higher wind speed?

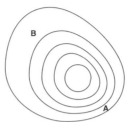

10 In a weather forecast, how is wind direction normally measured?

11 Just before take-off you are given the surface wind by radio from the ATSU. Will it be a true or magnetic direction?

12 Wind direction changes (the shortest way) from 340° to 010°. How can this change be described?

13 Given a 2000ft wind of 090/30, estimate the daytime surface wind over land (assuming frictional effects only).

14 With a coastline running north/south, with the sea to the east side, what wind direction would you expect mid-afternoon when a sea breeze has become established?

15 In the early morning, the surface wind at an airfield is steady at 180/05. How would you expect this wind velocity to change on a summer day, assuming that all other factors – pressure-gradient, cloud cover, etc. – remain constant?

16 In the diagram below (representing the northern hemisphere), which is the area of low pressure?

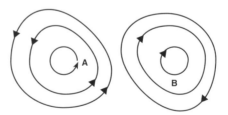

Answers at page MET 181

Pressure and Altimetry

Meteorology

*Pressure
and
Altimetry*

Meteorology

▶ Measurement of Pressure

A meteorologist measures pressure using a *sensitive barometer*, which usually gives the observed pressure in millibars/hectopascals or inches of mercury. Every aircraft also carries a sensitive barometer – it is called an *altimeter*. The altimeter is an aneroid barometer consisting of a set of metal 'bellows' that have been partially evacuated and sealed. As pressure rises and falls the bellows expand and contract. This movement is measured, calibrated, and displayed on the altimeter face in terms of vertical distance.

This raises an important point, which is worth emphasising. An altimeter does **not** display true vertical distance above the surface. An altimeter is merely a barometer that displays the actual (static) pressure in the form of *distance above a selected datum*.

Imagine for a moment that we are at the seaside at Newlyn, Cornwall (as it happens, the sea level at Newlyn is the datum used for calculating UK Mean Sea Level). We have an altimeter with us and set the sub-scale to the observed pressure, which is 1000mb. This is QNH, the pressure at sea level. And because we are at sea level, the altimeter should read zero. We can of course invert the process if we don't happen to know the observed pressure; we simply set the altimeter to the altitude (in this case zero) and take the reading at the sub-scale.

So the altimeter is set to QNH and will henceforth indicate *altitude* above mean sea level. Now we take the altimeter the short distance to the airfield at Land's End. A flight guide or aeronautical chart will tell us that Land's End airfield has an elevation (its vertical distance above sea level) of 401ft. In what are called "standard atmospheric conditions" *(q.v.)* the altimeter will now be measuring a pressure of about 985mb and displays this as a reading of around 401ft – in other words the elevation (or altitude) of Land's End airfield.

If we change the altimeter sub-scale setting to 985mb, the altimeter should now read zero. This is because we have now set it to the airfield QFE, and it is reading *height* above a datum – which in this case is Land's End airfield.

With the altimeter set to 985, it reads vertical distance above the 985mb pressure level.

With the altimeter set to 1000, it reads vertical distance above the 1000mb pressure level.

The altimeter reads vertical distance above the pressure level set on the sub-scale

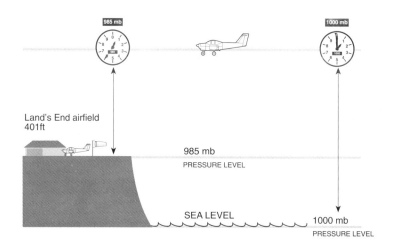

Land's End airfield
401ft

985 mb
PRESSURE LEVEL

SEA LEVEL

1000 mb
PRESSURE LEVEL

Pressure and Altimetry

The whole point of this theoretical jaunt is to demonstrate the fallibility of the altimeter. Taking our aircraft's instrumentation to the seaside before we go flying is not likely to be a practical proposition for most of us; we must rely on the reported QNH at an airfield to tell us the sea-level pressure. But if pressure is reported wrongly to us, or if we set the wrong pressure on the altimeter sub-scale, the altimeter is no longer giving an accurate reading. This is why it is **vital** to use the correct setting on the altimeter sub-scale, and to remember that **the altimeter can only indicate the vertical distance above whatever datum the pilot has selected.**

▶ Altimetry

The finer points of altimeter setting are covered in PPL 2 (Air Law, Operational Procedures and Communications) but as a refresher, there are three standard altimeter datums:

Altitude

QNH is set on the altimeter sub-scale, and altitude above mean sea level is indicated.

Height

QFE is set on the altimeter sub-scale, and height above a set datum (usually an airfield) is indicated.

Flight Level (QNE)

1013 mb/hPa or 29·92 inches of mercury is set on the altimeter sub-scale, and the Flight Level above this pressure level is indicated.

It is obviously of vital importance to be *absolutely clear* which datum is being used, and to set the correct pressure setting on the altimeter sub-scale. And bear in mind that by flying at a constant indicated altitude, we are in fact following a level of constant pressure. So the altimeter setting needs to be periodically updated during a flight.

It's a nice summer day, so let's return to the beach at Newlyn with our altimeter. Obviously the observed pressure at sea level at Newlyn is a perfectly good sub-scale reference if we decide to fly in southern Cornwall. However, if we become adventurous and want to fly further afield, the value of the pressure at Newlyn becomes of less and less use to us.

Imagine a situation where there is a strong pressure-gradient across the UK. The sea-level pressure (QNH) around the Newlyn area is 1002mb, and a pilot is planning to fly from there to Kirkwall in the Orkneys where the QNH is 969mb. Being a busy man, and not really having time for proper flight planning, this gentleman draws a straight line from Land's End to Kirkwall; he notes that the highest bit of ground *en route* is at about 4200ft and decides that at 5000ft he is not going to hit anything or anyone. After take-off our intrepid aviator climbs to 5000ft, sets the autopilot to 'Altitude Hold' and heads north or thereabouts.

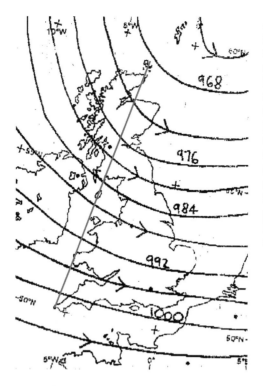

Pressure distribution across the UK on the day of the imaginary flight from Land's End to Kirkwall

As a working average, 1mb of pressure change can be taken to equal a 30ft change in height, up to about 10,000ft altitude. So at an indicated 5000ft, the aircraft will this day be at a pressure level of about 835mb; that is 1002 – (5000ft ÷ 30ft per mb). As long as the aircraft stays at the pressure level of 835mb, the altimeter will read 5000ft. The problem arises if the altimeter setting is not updated. Flying towards an area of low pressure, the 835mb pressure level is lowering, coming closer to the surface.

Let's assume that our hero is not updating the altimeter setting, perhaps because he's too busy fiddling with his new GPS receiver. As he passes abeam Snowdonia, where the QNH is about 990mb, the 835mb pressure level is about 4640ft above sea level (the difference between the actual QNH and that set on the altimeter is 12mb x 30ft = 360ft) even though the altimeter still reads 5000ft. Our pilot is still over the sea, and he is still more than 1000ft higher than the highest point in Snowdonia. So far his luck is holding. By the time he is passing over the Isle of Man, where the QNH is about 986mb, the aircraft is down to 4520ft AMSL – with the altimeter still happily reading 5000ft. The highest point on the Isle of Man is about 2200ft AMSL, so our man is still in luck, but he is getting lower and lower all the time. Mind you, the altimeter is still reading 5000ft. So everything must be all right, mustn't it?

Flying towards an area of low pressure, an aircraft flying at a constant indicated altitude on a fixed altimeter setting will in fact be descending

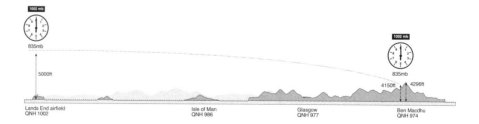

If our aviator was thinking, the alarm bells might be ringing by now. The aircraft is certain to be experiencing right drift (if the pilot didn't correct for the wind, the aircraft would drift to the right of track); so think for a moment what this means. Remembering Buys Ballot's law, when standing with your back to the wind, the

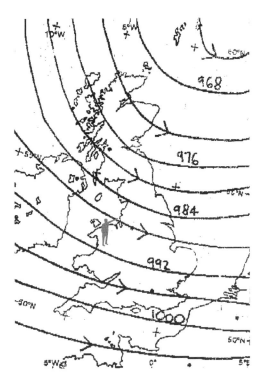

low pressure is on your left. Superimpose that picture over the aircraft's track and even without a weather chart, you can see that the aircraft is flying towards an area of low pressure. But of course, our pilot isn't thinking.

He will make it over the Scottish border, but passing between Glasgow and Edinburgh (where the QNH is about 977mb) he will now be down to about 4250ft. However, glancing up from his GPS for a moment, he sees 5000ft indicated on the altimeter and is perfectly content. And why not? The altimeter is working just fine. It is indicating that the aircraft is 5000ft above the 1002mb pressure level, which is true. There's just one small point; by now the theoretical 1002mb pressure level is some way below ground. The flight is likely to terminate rather violently in the Cairngorms,

A practical illustration of Buys Ballots's Law

probably on the southern slope of Ben Macdui just below the summit (which is at 4296ft). This very beautiful – if somewhat desolate – spot is five miles from the nearest road and an inconvenient 117 nautical miles short of Kirkwall. The accident investigator will note that the crash site is about 4150ft above sea level. He will also note that the altimeter was reading 5000ft at impact...

In case you're thinking that this is an extreme example, be advised that it is not. The pressure-gradient mentioned is by no means exceptional, and something like it occurs on average two or three times a year in the UK. You could argue that in this sort of steep pressure-gradient, bringing as it did surface winds in excess of 45 knots, our aviator had no business being airborne anyway – and you might have a good point. Nevertheless, you can imagine that on a long-distance flight, even a less steep pressure-gradient will lead to significant inaccuracies in altimeter reading if the pressure setting is not updated regularly. If flying from a high-pressure area to a low-pressure area the altimeter will **over-read** and indicate that the aircraft is higher than it actually is, unless the sub-scale setting is regularly updated.

Hence **high to low, down you go**.

An incorrect altimeter reading caused by having the wrong sub-scale setting selected is sometimes called '*barometric error*'.

In the above example we have concentrated on altimeter error caused by flying between areas of different *pressure*. A similar error occurs if flying between areas of different *temperature*. Warm air is less dense than cold air. So if we have two columns of atmosphere containing a fixed amount of air, the warm column will be taller than the cold column even if they both have the same surface pressure. It follows that the same pressure level will be higher in the warm air than the cold air.

An altimeter is calibrated to a 'standard' set of atmospheric conditions known as the *International Standard Atmosphere* or ISA. Two of the properties of the ISA are a sea-level temperature of +15°C and a temperature lapse rate of approximately 2°C per 1000ft. So in air which is warmer than standard, the altimeter will **under-read** and the aircraft is **higher** than indicated. In air which is colder than standard, the altimeter will **over-read** and the aircraft is **lower** than indicated.

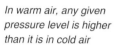

In warm air, any given pressure level is higher than it is in cold air

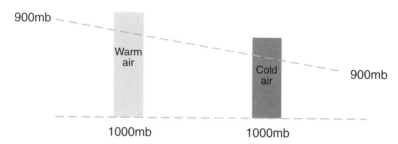

Going back to our original example, assume a sea-level temperature at Land's End of +20°C (warmer than ISA) and a sea-level temperature of 0°C at Kirkwall (colder than ISA) – unlikely, but not impossible. We will also assume that our hero has learnt the error of his ways and is using the correct altimeter settings this time. At 5000ft indicated over Land's End, his true altitude (allowing for temperature error) will be around 5100ft. By the time he reaches the Orkneys, 5000ft indicated will be about 4700ft true altitude. Clearly this is still an error, but one which is nowhere near as marked as the barometric error; the effect of temperature on altimeter reading is much less pronounced than the effect of pressure change. Nevertheless, you should now appreciate that the altimeter is subject to a number of errors – hence the need for sensible margins when calculating safety altitudes. The subject of temperature and the calculation of true altitude is covered in the 'Navigation' section.

Transition Altitude

In talking about pressure variation and altimeter settings, a short review of transition altitude, layer and level is in order. This is the vertical distance at which a transition can be made between a QNH pressure setting and the 'standard' altimeter setting of 1013mb/hPa – this standard setting is sometimes known (mostly to the met. office) as QNE.

The transition altitude is the altitude above which the altimeter can be set to 1013 so that the altimeter reads Flight Levels. In most countries there is a standard transition altitude outside controlled airspace: in the UK this altitude is 3000ft. Inside controlled airspace around certain aerodromes there may be different transition altitudes and these are listed in the AIP. The transition level is the lowest available flight level **above** the transition altitude. The actual transition level on any given day will depend on the actual pressure setting because if the QNH is significantly less than standard, an aircraft might have to descend below the transition altitude to find the appropriate Flight Level - which is not permitted. Remember, the transition level is the lowest available flight level **above** the transition altitude. If you unclear about why the actual transition level varies day-to-day, now is a good time to revise 'Transition Level' in PPL2 Air Law and the preceding part of this chapter. Finally, the layer between the transition altitude and the transition level is called (unsurprisingly) the transition layer.

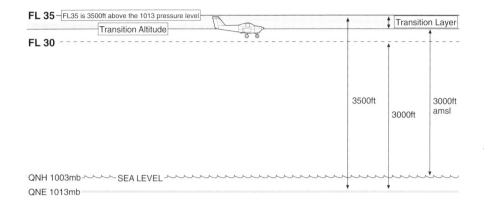

On this day the QNH is 1003, i.e. 10mb/hPa or 300ft less than the standard setting of 1013. FL30 is below the transition altitude of 3000ft, so is unavailable. Therefore the transition level just now is FL35 and the transition layer is 200ft thick.

▶ Pressure Altitude and Density Altitude

Pressure altitude is simply the altimeter reading when the subscale is set to the standard (International Standard Atmosphere) setting of 1013. You will realise that a Flight Level is therefore just the pressure altitude with the last two numbers removed: so FL35 is 3500ft pressure altitude.

Density altitude is a concept often used in relation to aircraft performance. In essence, the density altitude is found by first converting the actual altitude to a pressure altitude (that is, calculating any pressure variance from ISA conditions). The pressure altitude is then further corrected for any temperature variation from ISA. The result is the 'ISA' altitude that would have the same density as the actual elevation at the prevailing pressure and temperature. This becomes important in particular when a combination of low pressure and high temperature mean that the density altitude is significantly higher than the actual altitude. For example, imagine that you are about to take-off from a runway that has an elevation of 500ft above sea level, but the QNH is 986mb and the temperature is +30°C. You might expect the aeroplane to perform almost as well as at sea level, but in fact the density altitude is closer to 4000ft and the aeroplane will perform accordingly. The concept of density altitude in relation to aircraft performance is explored more fully in PPL 4.

▶Revision

17 What is the datum when QNH is set on an altimeter?

18 If an altimeter reads zero when on the ground at an airfield, what datum is set on the altimeter sub-scale?

19 An airfield QNH is 1015mb/hPa and it has an elevation of 360ft. What (approximately) will the QFE be, assuming 30ft per millibar?

20 An aircraft is experiencing right drift (the wind is from the left). If the altimeter setting is not updated, will the altimeter start to under-read or over-read?

Answers at page MET 181

Humidity and Stability

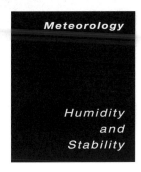

Meteorology

*Humidity
and
Stability*

▶ Humidity

▶ Change of State

▶ Temperature Lapse Rate

▶ Atmospheric Stability

▶ Temperature Inversion

▶ Revision

Meteorology

▶ Humidity

Having looked in some detail at two of the principal properties of the atmosphere – temperature and pressure – we can look at the third major property. This is *water content*, and it is largely responsible for weather.

The amount of water vapour in the atmosphere is referred to as *absolute humidity*. Water vapour is an invisible gas, which is present to a certain degree at all places in the atmosphere. The greater the proportion of water vapour in the atmosphere, the higher the humidity.

A given quantity of air can contain a certain amount of water as invisible water vapour. The proportion of water vapour which a 'parcel' of air can hold varies with a number of factors, principally temperature. Warm air can hold more water vapour than cold air at the same pressure. By way of illustration, at 0°C a kilogram of air can hold up to 4gm of water vapour. At 15°C a kilogram of air can hold up to 10gm of water vapour, and at 30°C it can hold up to 27gm.

As a parcel of air is cooled, the amount of water content it can hold as a gas decreases

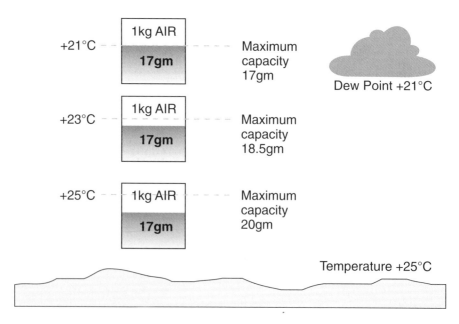

The question is, what happens when there is too much water vapour for the air to hold? Imagine a 1kg parcel of air at the surface, with a temperature of 25°C. It is holding 17gm of water. Now let's set this parcel of air rising. As it rises, it expands and cools. As it cools, the amount of water vapour it can hold decreases. Eventually (at about 21°C in standard atmospheric conditions) the parcel reaches the limit of its ability to hold its water content as water vapour. At this temperature it is holding all the water vapour it possibly can, and is said to be *saturated*. If the parcel of air is cooled any further, the water vapour will begin to condense into liquid and become visible as water droplets. The result is *cloud*.

The temperature at which the air becomes saturated (i.e. it is holding the maximum water vapour possible without it condensing into water droplets) is known as the *dew point*. Dew point is measured in meteorological observations and reported in actual weather reports.

Humidity and Stability

A little thought suggests that the relationship of dew-point temperature to actual temperature gives a good indication of the percentage of water vapour in the air. Where there is a large gap between temperature and dew point, the air is obviously quite dry. So it will have to be cooled a long way, or a lot of moisture added to it, for condensation to occur and clouds to form. A wide temperature/dew point spread implies a high cloud base, or no cloud at all.

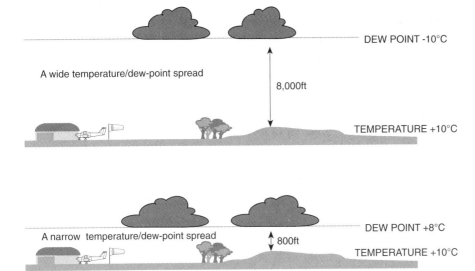

TOP> A wide temperature/dew-point spread implies relatively dry air, and high cloud (if any)

BOTTOM> A narrow temperature/dew-point spread implies moist air. and low cloud or fog

If there is a small gap between temperature and dew point, the air is obviously much closer to saturation. Just a small reduction in temperature or a little additional moisture could cause condensation and thus cloud formation. A narrow temperature/dew point spread implies the possibility of low cloud or even fog.

```
EGKK 211050 211050Z 05012KT 020V090 CAVOK 25/03
Q1020 NOSIG=
```

A METAR (actual report) from EGKK (London Gatwick) at 1050 UTC. The temperature is +25°C, the dew point is +3°C. This wide temperature/dew-point spread means that the air is fairly dry, and in fact there was no cloud at all

```
EGCC 211150 211150Z 24005KT 2000 DZ SCT001 BKN003
07/06
Q1004=
```

A METAR (actual report) from EGCC (Manchester) at 1150 UTC. The temperature/dew-point spread is just 1°C, implying a humid atmosphere. In fact there was drizzle and cloud down to 100ft above ground level

Meteorology

The view across Manchester Airport at the time of the 11.50 METAR report. The control tower (134ft AGL) is just in the cloud base

The percentage of water vapour a parcel of air *is holding*, compared to the amount it *could hold* before becoming saturated, is known as the *relative humidity*. In other words if a parcel of air contains half the water vapour it could hold before becoming saturated, the relative humidity (RH) is 50%. If air is saturated the relative humidity is 100%, because the air is holding all the water vapour it can before condensation will begin. Remember in this context that warm air can hold more water vapour than cold air. So warm air with 90% relative humidity contains more moisture than cold air with 90% relative humidity. The weather information given to pilots does not include the RH, but RH is of great interest to meteorologists in forecasting weather. In computer forecasting models, the three most important atmospheric measurements are those of pressure, temperature and humidity.

The higher the relative humidity (RH) of a parcel of air, the closer it is to saturation. At 100% RH the air is saturated

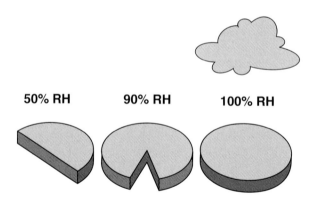

50% RH   **90% RH**   **100% RH**

A final point for now regarding humidity. Water vapour is less dense than dry air. Therefore **moist air** (high humidity) **is less dense than dry air** (low humidity).

▶Change of State

We have already looked at water which exists in the atmosphere as droplets or as a gas. In accordance with the usual laws of physics, water can exist in the atmosphere in three states – as a solid (ice), a liquid (water droplets) or a gas (water vapour).

Whenever water changes state, an exchange of heat energy takes place. For water to change state from solid to liquid, or from liquid to gas, it needs energy. This comes in the form of heat, which is absorbed from the surrounding air. As the air loses its energy, it is cooled. The popular terms to describe the changes of state are:

Solid - (*Melting*) - Liquid - (*Evaporation*) - Gas

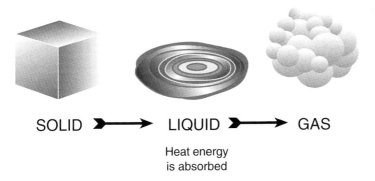

When the reverse process takes place, i.e. when water changes state from gas to liquid or from liquid to solid, it gives up energy – heat is released and the surrounding air is warmed. The popular terms to describe the changes of state are:

Gas - (*Condensation*) - Liquid - (*Freezing*) - Solid

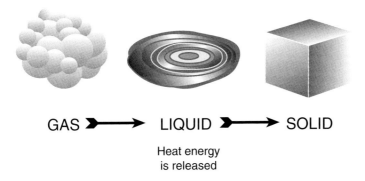

For completeness, it should be added that water can also change directly from gas to solid or from solid to gas. These processes are known as *sublimation* in the USA. In the UK a change of state solid to gas is called sublimation, but a change of state from gas to solid is called *deposition*.

The heat exchange involved in the change of state may be felt if you accidentally spill AVGAS or some other volatile liquid on to your hand. The liquid evaporates into vapour and the heat energy is absorbed from your skin, which makes the affected area feel cold.

▶ Temperature Lapse Rate

Temperature lapse rate is the rate at which temperature changes with a change in height. An average figure of 2°C per 1000ft has been used so far in this book. However, it is necessary to appreciate that the lapse rate is variable and changes all the time according to atmospheric conditions.

A knowledge of the actual temperatures throughout the atmosphere is important to weather forecasters. To collect this information radiosonde balloons are launched which transmit various items of information, including temperature, as they climb through the atmosphere. Armed with this data, a forecaster can see the *actual* rate of temperature change with height – commonly referred to as the *Environmental Lapse Rate* (ELR). The ELR is then compared with average lapse rates for air that is moving vertically.

When dry air rises, its lapse rate is taken to be around 3°C per 1000ft. This value is sometimes called the *Dry Adiabatic Lapse Rate* (DALR).

When saturated air rises its lapse rate is less than this, because as water vapour condenses into liquid droplets heat energy is released. This retards the rate of cooling, and rising saturated air cools at around 1·5°C per 1000ft. This is sometimes called the *Saturated Adiabatic Lapse Rate* (SALR).

By comparing the actual temperature profile of the atmosphere (the ELR) with the DALR and SALR of rising air, a forecaster can make assumptions about the stability of the atmosphere.

▶ Atmospheric Stability

The *stability* of the atmosphere is a major factor in dictating the weather. Stability describes the tendency of the air to resist vertical motion.

Stable air resists vertical motion. If air in a stable atmosphere is displaced vertically, it will return to its original level.

Unstable air does not resist vertical motion. If unstable air is displaced vertically, it may well continue to move – forming vertical air currents.

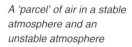

A 'parcel' of air in a stable atmosphere and an unstable atmosphere

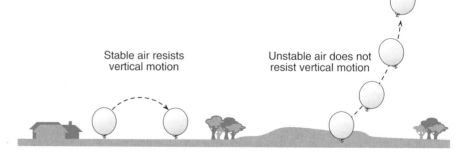

Stable air resists vertical motion

Unstable air does not resist vertical motion

As before, in this sense the atmosphere can be likened to an ocean. A calm ocean has little vertical movement, just like stable air. A rough ocean can have enormous vertical movement, just like unstable air.

Humidity and Stability

A stable atmosphere

An unstable atmosphere

A stable atmosphere is like a calm sea, and unstable atmosphere is like a rough sea

Temperature and humidity have a marked effect on atmospheric stability. Imagine a sunny summer day over land. Over a 'hot spot' – a town or factory, for example – a parcel of quite dry air is heated above the temperature of the surrounding air. Being less dense, it is buoyant and so starts to rise. As it rises its lapse rate is 3°C per 1000ft (i.e. the DALR). Meanwhile the surrounding air is cooling at an actual lapse rate (the ELR) of about 2°C per 1000ft. As long as the rising air is warmer (and less dense) than the surrounding air, it will keep rising:

Level	'Parcel' Temp.	Environmental Temp.
5000ft	+10°C	+10°C
4000ft	+13°C	+12°C
3000ft	+16°C	+14°C
2000ft	+19°C	+16°C
1000ft	+22°C	+18°C
Ground	+25°C	+20°C

At 5000ft the parcel of air reaches the same temperature as the surrounding air. It therefore loses its buoyancy and stops rising.

This example refers to a shallow layer of instability caused by convection. However, the atmosphere can be unstable (or stable) through a much greater depth. Stability is generally affected by heating or cooling of the atmosphere by the surface. Heating from below tends to make the atmosphere unstable. An unstable atmosphere is characterised by 'choppy' flying conditions, and convective clouds with vertical development possibly giving heavy showers, but good visibility outside these showers. Cooling from below tends to make the atmosphere stable. A stable atmosphere usually means smooth flying conditions. Any cloud tends to be flat and layer-type covering large areas. Any precipitation (rain, snow, drizzle etc.) lasts for a long time and visibility can be quite poor.

LEFT> Extensive layered cloud in a stable atmosphere

RIGHT> Vertical 'heaped' cloud in an unstable atmosphere

▶Temperature Inversion

So far we have considered a 'standard' temperature profile, where the atmosphere is cooler at altitude. However, temperature does not always decrease with increasing height; sometimes it can do precisely the opposite. This situation is known as a *temperature inversion* (the Environmental Lapse Rate is inverted) of which more later.

A temperature inversion

+8°C
+9°C
+10°C
+11°C
+10°C
+9°C   The inversion layer
+8°C
+7°C

▶Revision

21 What is dew point?

22 Imagine two parcels of air, both at 15°C. One has a relative humidity of 30%, the other a relative humidity of 90%. Which will have the higher dew-point temperature, and why?

23 Imagine two parcels of air, both with a relative humidity of 90%. One has a temperature of +25°C, the other a temperature of +10°C. Which has the greater moisture content?

24 Does a change of state directly from solid to gas absorb or release heat energy?

Answers at page MET 181

The International Standard Atmosphere

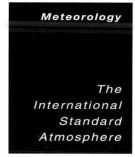

Exercise

Meteorology

*The
International
Standard
Atmosphere*

▶ The Need for the International Standard Atmosphere

The atmosphere behaves much like a fluid in many ways. Its basic parameters of temperature, density and pressure are constantly changing at any one location. This could make life very difficult for those who need a constant calibration to work to – for example instrument manufacturers, aircraft designers and so on. To overcome this problem, an 'average' set of atmospheric conditions, known as the *International Standard Atmosphere* (ISA) has been established.

▶ The Parameters of the ISA

The basic parameters of the ISA are quite simple. At sea level, the following conditions apply:

Temperature   +15° C.

Pressure   1013·25 mb/hPa (29·92inHg or 760mmHg).

Temperature Lapse Rate   1·98°C/1000ft. The temperature decreases at this rate until 36,090ft, above which it remains at a constant -56·5 °C.

Given an ISA sea-level air temperature of +15 °C and a lapse rate of 1·98°C/1000ft, the ISA temperature at any altitude up to 36,090ft can be calculated. You might find it listed in a table, such as:

Sea Level	15°C
2000ft	11°C
4000ft	7°C
6000ft	3°C
8000ft	-1°C
10,000ft	-5°C

However, using a rounded figure of 2°C/1000ft, calculation of ISA temperature at altitude is not a difficult calculation even for a non-mathematician!

Of course, real conditions are invariably different from those of the ISA. If the actual air temperature (sometimes referred to as *Outside Air Temperature* or OAT) at 3000ft is +10°C, whereas the ISA temperature at 3000ft is +9°C, the actual temperature can be described as "ISA +1". Performance tables for an aircraft may be marked "ISA, ISA +10°C, ISA –10°C" etc. OAT can also be a limitation in a flight manual e.g. "Flight in conditions beyond ISA +30°C not permitted".

The difference between ISA conditions and the ambient (actual) conditions can have a marked effect on aircraft performance and the accuracy of aircraft instruments. By way of illustration, imagine an average light aircraft which, at gross weight and ISA sea-level conditions, has a take-off distance of 650m. Take that same aircraft to Denver in the USA, (elevation 5600ft) when the temperature is +25°C, and its take-off distance required is likely to be around 1100m!

The International Standard Atmosphere

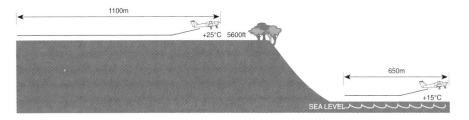

Increased altitude usually means reduced density, which reduces aircraft performance

The effect of atmospheric conditions on aircraft performance is looked at in more detail in PPL4.

▶ Revision

25 In ISA conditions, what would be the temperature at 15,000ft?

26 What altitude (to the nearest 1000ft) has a temperature of +5°C in the ISA, and what would the pressure be at that level (assuming 30ft per mb)?

27 The actual temperature at 11,000ft is referred to as "ISA - 4". What is the actual temperature?

28 What is the sea-level pressure (in hectopascals) in the ISA?

Answers at page MET 181

Clouds and Precipitation

Meteorology

*Clouds
and
Precipitation*

Meteorology

▶Formation of Clouds

Cloud is formed when air is cooled below its dew-point temperature and water vapour condenses into water droplets or ice particles.

Strictly speaking, for condensation to occur there have to be some form of *condensation nuclei* (also sometimes known as *hygroscopic nuclei*) present, such as microscopic particles of dust, smoke, salt etc, on to which water vapour can condense. In reality, such nuclei exist just about everywhere in the atmosphere, although they tend to be more concentrated around industrialised and built-up areas. So in practical terms the principal factors in cloud formation are humidity and the cooling process.

There are several different ways in which air can be cooled. Clouds are commonly formed by some sort of lifting action, which causes the rising air to expand and cool. *Convection* is just such an action, usually caused by part of the surface heating more quickly than its surroundings. This generates a rising parcel of air.

Typical 'fair weather' cumulus – formed by weak convective currents – seen here over Dallas Fort-Worth airport

Once the rising air passes through the dew-point temperature, heaped and lumpy cloud known as *cumulus* is formed. Small cumulus (or, for the linguistic purists, cumuli) may form due to unequal surface heating even in a stable atmosphere. In this case they do not grow to any great vertical extent, are well spaced and are often called "fair-weather" cumulus. If you know the temperature and dew point it is relatively simple to estimate the height at which convective cumulus cloud will form (the lowest level of a cloud is known as the *cloud base*). Just take the difference (in °C) between the surface temperature and the dew point, and multiply by 400. The result is an approximate cloud base (in feet) for convective cloud. For example, the temperature on the day this was written is +12°C and the dew point is +6°C. The difference between temperature and dew point is 6 °C. 6 x 400 gives 2400ft. And there you have a forecast cloud base – looking out of the window suggests that it's about right. Needless to say, weather forecasting is not usually so simple and even this rough and ready calculation is subject to all sorts of caveats and exceptions if you look into it in enough detail. Let's move on instead.

Clouds forming by convection where the surface temperature is +12°C and the dew point is +6°C. This implies a cloud base of about 2400 feet above the surface

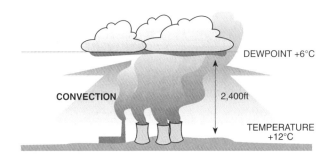

DEWPOINT +6°C

CONVECTION 2,400ft

TEMPERATURE +12°C

Clouds and Precipitation

Where air rises over a very large area (for instance where two differing air masses meet – as discussed later) the lifting action can also form clouds. Where the slope between these air masses is gentle, clouds of great horizontal extent may form (often of a type known as *stratus*) and these indicate a stable atmosphere. In contrast, where the slope between the air masses is steeper, large cumulus clouds of great vertical extent may form. These indicate an unstable atmosphere.

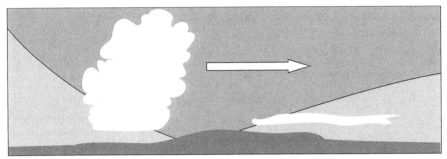

Cloud often forms where differing air masses meet

Here the sharp under-cutting of a warmer airmass by a cooler one is causing vertical, cumulus-type clouds to form.

Here a warm airmass is gently overflowing a cooler airmass. The gentle lifting action is forming layer-type clouds.

Air is also forced to rise if it meets an obstruction such as a mountain range. This type of lifting action is known as *orographic ascent* or *orographic uplift*. In a stable atmosphere, orographic lifting will cause layered clouds to form. In an unstable atmosphere, cumulus clouds are more likely. The subject of cloud and weather over mountainous areas is covered later in this book.

LEFT> Cumulus clouds being formed by orographic lifting

RIGHT> Layered cloud forming orographically over the high ground of Kintyre as moist air from over the sea is forced to rise over the hills

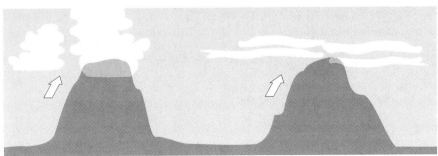

If clouds are formed by orographic lifting, the type of cloud is usually dictated by the stability of the air

UNSTABLE ATMOSPHERE
Orographic lifting causes vertical, cumulus-type clouds to form.

STABLE ATMOSPHERE
Orographic lifting causes layer-type cloud to form.

Relatively warm air flowing over snow-covered ground causing extensive stratus-type cloud to form by advection

As well as cooling by lifting, air can be cooled by the surface over which it is flowing – for example, warm air flowing over a cool surface. If the air is cooled enough, low cloud or even fog can form. The process whereby air can be cooled in this way is known as *advection*.

Clouds can also be formed by turbulent mixing between atmospheric layers above and below the level of the dew-point temperature. Such mixing may be caused by rough terrain (which can produce turbulence) or by deepening of the friction layer caused by surface heating. The cloud formed may be of the stratus

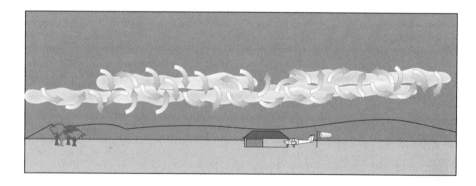

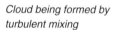

Cloud being formed by turbulent mixing

type, although if it is more broken or fractured it may be more like the form usually known as *stratocumulus*. The formation of cloud in this way is difficult to forecast, relying as it does on a number of delicately balanced factors. Summer mornings can see the formation of turbulence cloud. Typically, after a night with clear skies, the rising sun heats the surface and with a light wind (around 10-15kts) the atmosphere is "stirred up", leading to just the sort of mixing action which causes turbulence cloud to form. In the spring and summer, such cloud is usually dispersed as the sun's solar energy becomes stronger during the morning. However, more than one early-morning aviator has been caught out by an unforecast bank of low stratus cloud formed in this way. Turbulence cloud can also form around the level of a temperature inversion caused by a persistent anticyclone in winter. This unbroken layer of turbulence cloud often persists for days or weeks, leading to so-called winter "anticyclonic gloom" (which describes both weather and the mood it produces!).

Clouds and Precipitation

0830 (Local). Typical morning turbulence cloud, with a cloud base of about 1000ft. The temperature is +13°C, the dew point is +9°C

LEFT> 0930 (Local). Surface heating has begun to break up the cloud. The cloud base is now 1300ft. Temperature is +16°C, dew point is +11°C

RIGHT> 1000 (Local). The low cloud has mostly dissipated; the cloud base is 2500ft. Temperature is +18°C, dew point is +11°C

Finally, cloud can form in areas of convergence where two differing air masses meet. This convergence can be a widespread effect, or can be as localised as a prevailing offshore air flow meeting an incoming sea breeze. Where cumulus clouds are formed by convergence, they may form a 'street' – a long line that can stretch for hundreds of miles downwind. These are much sought-after by competition glider pilots, so it is worth keeping a very sharp lookout for gliders under a cloud street.

GENERAL AIRFLOW   SEA BREEZE

SEA LEVEL

Convergence normally forms cumulus-type clouds

*Small lines of cumulus
'cloud streets' over Kent*

▶ Clouds Types and Classifications

Each type of cloud can be classified according to its characteristics and level. It is important to understand these classifications so that you can visualise cloud type from a weather forecast or report, and correctly describe the clouds you see.

Two basic cloud classifications have already been discussed; vertical cumulus-type and horizontal stratus-type clouds. Each cloud type can be further classified by its approximate level.

Low Cloud

6500ft and below. This has no particular level classification and is known simply by type e.g. *stratus, cumulus* etc.

Medium Cloud

6500ft to 23,000ft. Cloud types have the prefix *alto,* e.g. *alto cumulus.*

High Cloud

16,500ft to 45,000ft. Cloud types are 'cirriform' e.g. *cirrostratus*, or can be simple *cirrus* cloud

Bear in mind that the levels quoted are not arbitrary cut-off points but are indicative of the approximate altitudes in temperate latitudes (i.e. between about 30° & 60° of latitude). In polar regions the levels are lower; in tropical areas they are higher.

Clouds giving precipitation may also carry the prefix *nimbo* or the suffix *nimbus*, meaning rain-bearing; e.g. *nimbostratus* and *cumulonimbus.*

Clouds of large vertical extent, such as cumulonimbus or nimbostratus, can extend from the low level through the medium level and – in the case of large cumulonimbus – right into the high level and occasionally through the tropopause.

Clouds and Precipitation

Here is the basic classification of cloud types:

Stratus (ST)

A grey sheet-like layer of cloud often covering the whole sky. The base can be very low – indeed, right down to ground level – and visibility can be poor over large areas. Due to the stable nature of stratus, it contains little or no turbulence.

Low stratus cloud

Cumulus (CU)

A well-defined cloud with varying vertical extent. Usually detached, although can be embedded within other cloud. The vertical currents inside the cloud can be very strong, and a developing cumulus is capable of rapid vertical growth. Large cumulus clouds often contain turbulence and are a sign of instability in the atmosphere. Outside cumulus, visibility is often good.

Cumulus clouds (with high cirrus above)

Stratocumulus (SC)

A hybrid cloud type capable of taking several forms. It can be produced by cumulus collapsing and spreading out; by turbulent mixing; or by orographic lifting. White or greyish in appearance, stratocumulus can be present in large patches or a uniform layer. It is fair to say that stratocumulus can be something of a catch-all term used to indicate cloud that is neither strictly cumuliform nor stratiform.

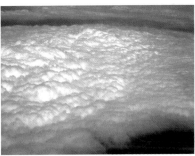

Extensive stratocumulus cloud seen from above

Nimbostratus (NS)

Thick, dark-grey layered cloud with an indistinct base, producing precipitation over a wide area. Often formed in a stable atmosphere containing a lot of moisture. Nimbostratus cloud is often associated with warm fronts (*q.v.*) and can bring prolonged and heavy precipitation.

Nimbostratus cloud

Altostratus (AS)

Flat, layer clouds which are usually light grey or white. Possibly thick enough to produce some precipitation but little turbulence. Distinguishable from nimbostratus by having a clearly defined base and tending to be less thick.

Altostratus cloud heralding an approaching warm front

Altocumulus clouds. The streaks below the cloud are 'virga' - rain or snow falling from cloud but evaporating before reaching the ground

Altocumulus (AC)

Grey or white patches of rolled or bubble cloud, possibly producing some precipitation.

Cirrus cloud over the Alps

Cirrus (CI)

Thin, wispy clouds composed almost entirely of ice crystals (as are all cirro-type clouds). They move across the sky with little change of form or shape and contain little moisture or turbulence.

A thin veil of cirrostratus cloud

Cirrostratus (CS)

A transparent veil of high cloud. Produces a halo effect around the sun or moon. Indicative of an approaching 'front' (*q.v.*).

Cirrocumulus cloud and a persistent contrail from a high-flying aircraft

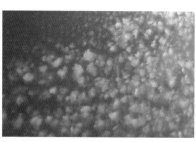

Cirrocumulus (CC)

Not a common type of cloud; caused by shallow convection currents at high altitude and so containing some turbulence. Consists of regular flakes or ripples, and sometimes produces a visual effect known as a "mackerel sky".

A 'classic' cumulonimbus cloud, near Portsmouth

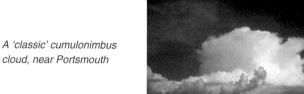

Cumulonimbus (CB)

Cloud type associated with thunderstorms. Great vertical extent, often with a base relatively near the surface and a top at the tropopause (where the distinctive 'anvil' forms). A cumulonimbus can contain several major hazards such as turbulence, windshear, intense precipitation, lightning etc. and should be avoided if at all possible.

▶ Cloud Types and State of the Atmosphere

Clouds are the most obvious visual clue to the state of the atmosphere. After a little practice, a pilot with some basic meteorological knowledge can learn a lot from observing cloud formations and how they are changing. Specific details are covered in more depth in the following chapters, but here are a few general pointers:

Large cumulus-type clouds are generated by strong vertical currents (often convective) and as such indicate an unstable atmosphere. The taller the cumulus clouds, the greater the atmospheric instability. Extensive cumulus clouds, including those which produce rain, indicate the sort of conditions which TV weather forecasters like to describe as "changeable". There can be brilliant sunshine and excellent visibility; then with almost no notice the sun is blotted out by a large cumulus and it may rain heavily. A few minutes later the rain has cleared and it is sunny again. Flight in and around such clouds tends to involve varying degrees of turbulence.

An isolated cumulonimbus cloud bringing a short-lived shower, as seen off Jersey

Stratus-type clouds indicate settled weather and a more stable atmosphere. Such cloud is likely to cover a wide area: if it starts to rain, it is likely to continue raining for some time. Flying conditions in and above such clouds tend to be smooth.

Extensive layered cloud seen over the North Sea. The cloud, and any precipitation, will cover a large area

From the ground, clouds can also indicate the wind direction. Obviously the wind direction indicated by the clouds is the wind direction at altitude, which will **not** be the same as the surface wind. Clouds at different levels may move in different directions, indicating the differing wind velocities through the atmosphere. However, you will have to study the sky carefully and for some time to distinguish this.

Once airborne it is pretty well impossible to gauge the movement of clouds by direct observation, although in the right conditions the movement of cloud shadows over the ground can – with luck – indicate the wind velocity.

▶Reporting Cloud Types and Amounts

Area forecasts (such as the UK METFORM 215 low-level forecast) indicate cloud type, using the abbreviations already noted. Aerodrome observations such as METARs (reports of actual weather) and aerodrome forecasts (TAFs) do not record cloud type unless it is a towering cumulus (TCU) or cumulonimbus (CB).

Cloud amount can be described in one of two ways:

Cloud cover can be expressed in units called *oktas*, which are eighths. The range is from one okta (one-eighth), meaning that one-eighth of the total sky is covered by cloud, to eight oktas (eight-eighths), meaning that the whole sky is completely covered by cloud.

```
ZONE 3 GEN 12KM RA 4-7/8SC 1500/3000
                    5-8/8AC 8000/16000
```

Forecasting cloud: a line from a METFORM 215 forecast predicting 12 kilometres visibility, rain, 4 to 7 oktas of stratocumulus cloud base 1500ft, tops 3000ft amsl and 5 to 8 oktas altocumulus base 8000ft, tops 16,000ft amsl

Alternatively, a simplified three-grade classification of cloud amount may be used:

Classification	Abbreviation	Amount in Oktas
Few	FEW	1 to 2 oktas
Scattered	SCT	3 to 4 oktas.
Broken	BKN	5 to 7 oktas.
Overcast	OVC	8 oktas.

This simpler classification is the one used in METARs and TAFs. Do bear in mind that a cloud amount given in an actual weather report has been measured from a fixed point and may not correspond exactly with in-flight conditions. Imagine a met. observer faced with reporting a situation where the northern half of the sky is completely covered by cloud but the southern half of the sky is absolutely clear of cloud. This situation would be reported as "4 oktas of cloud (scattered)". However, flying to the north of the observer you would encounter total cloud cover.

```
EGPK 251450 251450Z 18018G30KT 140V210 9999 -RA
SCT008 BKN020 OVC080 07/05 Q0992 =
```

Reporting cloud: a METAR (actual report) from EGPK (Prestwick) at 1450 UTC. There is a scattered (3-4 oktas) cloud base at 800ft above aerodrome level, a broken (5-7 oktas) cloud base at 2000ft and an overcast (8 oktas) cloud base at 8000ft

Clouds and Precipitation

LEFT> 1 to 2 oktas of cumulus cloud over Texas, permitting good sight of the ground

RIGHT> Broken stratocumulus giving intermittent sight of the ground

BOTTOM> 7 oktas of stratocumulus – just an occasional break in the cloud. To get a better view of the ground, climb higher above the cloud layer

The cloud coverage is 4 oktas, because that is the total amount of sky covered by cloud from the observer's standpoint. Nevertheless, to the north of the observer there is total cloud cover

▶ Precipitation

Precipitation consists of particles falling from cloud. In weather reports and forecasts the type of precipitation will be defined, e.g. rain, drizzle, snow, hail and so on.

As a general rule, anything other than the lightest precipitation (such as drizzle) implies cloud at least 4000ft thick. Heavier precipitation implies thicker cloud.

Precipitation from stratiform-type clouds tends to be light: drizzle, light rain, light snow, etc. This is because such clouds have comparatively weak vertical currents and can only support very lightweight particles before they become heavy enough to fall out of the cloud. Cumuliform clouds have considerably stronger vertical currents and can support particles which can become a good deal heavier before falling from the cloud. So precipitation from cumulus clouds can be moderate or heavy. Indeed, precipitation from a cumulonimbus cloud can be in the form of *hail*. Hailstones weighing up to 1lb (0·45kg) have been recorded in Europe – heavy precipitation indeed! In met. reports and forecasts, precipitation is classified as follows:

Drizzle (DZ)

Light liquid precipitation whose drops are too small to constitute rain. Generally falls from stratus and stratocumulus clouds.

Rain (RA)

Liquid precipitation with a larger droplet size than drizzle. Rain in different intensities (slight, moderate, heavy) can fall from many different types of cloud.

Snow (SN)

Precipitation in the form of ice crystals. As a rule, snow only reaches the ground if the surface temperature is +4°C or below. The notion that it can be too cold to snow has no basis in fact, although the heaviest falls of snow are usually associated with temperatures of around 0°C (freezing).

Snow Grains (SG)

These are small ice particles, the frozen equivalent of drizzle.

Hail (GR)

Hard ice stones generated in well-developed cumulonimbus clouds. In the UK and Western Europe, hail is mostly a spring or summer occurrence. Met. reports may also refer to small hail (GS).

There are two other types of precipitation, less common in Europe:

Ice Pellets (PE)

Pellets of clear ice, which tend to fall from thick layered clouds such as nimbostratus.

Diamond Dust (IC)

Nothing to do with real diamonds, alas, "diamond dust" consists of tiny ice crystals that appear to be suspended in the air and which fall from clear skies in calm arctic conditions. Diamond dust is almost unknown outside the extreme north of Europe.

The precipitation described in a met. report relates to what is actually reaching the ground. It is not uncommon for one type of precipitation (e.g. snow) to fall from a cloud but for it to melt *en route* to the surface and so become rain.

Sometimes rain can fall from a medium-level cloud, but evaporate before reaching the surface. This is characterised by streaks below the cloud, known as *virga*.

Note that the term *sleet* is not universally recognised. In the UK, 'sleet' means rain and snow or snow melting to form rain. In the USA, sleet more often means ice pellets or similar precipitation. To avoid confusion, the term is not used in international weather communications. What is known in the UK as sleet will be described as rain and snow (RASN).

Clouds and Precipitation

In METARs and TAFs the intensity of the precipitation will be given:

-	=	slight
No indication	=	moderate
+	=	heavy

For example:

-RA	Slight rain
SN	Moderate snow
+GR	Heavy hail

With a little awareness, the type of precipitation being reported can give clues to other weather factors. For example, drizzle is usually associated with low cloud, poor visibility and high humidity. These add up to poor flying conditions and an increased chance of carburettor icing. Rain (especially if it is heavy) will adversely affect the runway surface, particularly if it is a grass runway. You will not be surprised to know that aircraft controllability is more difficult on a wet runway, so be particularly cautious if there is also a crosswind present. **A wet grass runway will also significantly lengthen the take-off and landing distance.** Falling snow reduces visibility dramatically, and snow on the ground will have an obvious effect on surface movements. If lying snow is not removed from the runway and taxiways, aircraft operations may not be possible. In VOLMET reports (described in the 'Aviation Weather Reports and Forecasts' chapter), a UK airfield closed due to snow is described as 'SNOCLO'.

```
Zone 3   GEN  20KM  NIL        1-4/8CUSC 2500/5000
                                5-7/8AC 12000/16000
ISOL SOUTH  3000M  HEAVY RA  8/8LYR 500/20000
                             + EMBD CB 2000/30000
```

A section from a METFORM 215 forecast. The first section forecasts the visibility at generally 20km in nil precipitation/weather with a cloud base of 1 to 4 oktas of cumulus and stratocumulus at 2500 feet amsl, tops 5000ft; and 5 to 7 oktas of altocumulus 12,000ft to 16,000ft. The second section forecasts that in isolated areas in the south of zone 3 the visibility will fall to 3000m in heavy rain, 8 oktas of cloud with a cloud base of 500ft and tops of 20,000ft. Note 'EMBD CB' – embedded cumulonimbus – base 2000ft, tops 30,000ft. CBs embedded in other cloud are extremely dangerous because the pilot is not able to see and avoid them

▶ Revision

29 What type of cloud can be formed by convection in an unstable atmosphere?

30 Describe the cloud type illustrated below.

31 Describe at least two of the cloud types visible in the photograph below (the island is Ailsa Craig, off the Ayrshire coast), and the approximate amount of cloud cover of the highest cloud.

32 What is the cloud type illustrated below and which serious weather hazard might be found in it?

33 What classification is given to cloud cover of 8 oktas?

34 What is the classification of heavy snow?

35 Decode the following cloud and precipitation report:

SCT CB   +RA

Answers at page MET 182

Visibility

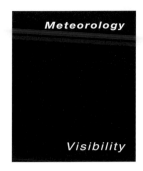

Meteorology

Visibility

▶ Definitions and Measurement

▶ Haze, Smoke, Dust and Sand

▶ Fog and Mist

▶ Visibility in Precipitation

▶ Revision

Meteorology

▶ Definitions and Measurement

Clear air: what a nice idea. Unfortunately, in many parts of the world the air is anything but clear most of the time. The transparency of the air can be reduced by all sorts of particles in the atmosphere: water droplets (such as clouds), precipitation, sand, smoke, haze, etc.

Visibility is one of those meteorological factors that affects aviation far more than other forms of transport. It is not unusual for an inexperienced student pilot to arrive at an airfield ready to fly, convinced that the blue sky means perfect flying conditions. Only when looking some distance away does he realise just how poor the horizontal visibility is. You only have to fly once in a visibility of 4000m or thereabouts – which is not at all uncommon on an English anticyclonic summer or autumn day – to realise how much more difficult visual flying is in such conditions. Indeed, flying in this sort of visibility in haze has been likened to flying around inside a dirty goldfish bowl, which describes the view well.

There are two definitions of visibility which affect the pilot. *Flight visibility* is the visibility forward from the flight deck of an aircraft. Look straight ahead in flight and the distance you can see is the flight visibility. It is flight visibility that is used in determining the limitations of VFR flight and licence privileges (see the Air Law section of PPL 2) but the definition does have its subtleties. If you are flying straight towards a cloud (clouds are mostly not transparent) the distance to it is the flight visibility. Even if it is the only cloud in the sky and visibility is 100km everywhere else, your flight visibility is 500m if the cloud is 500m ahead of you.

The difference between flight visibility and meteorological visibility

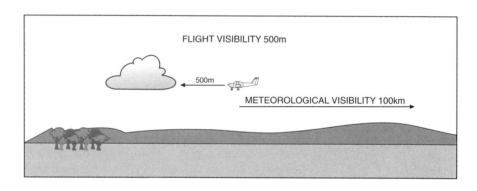

FLIGHT VISIBILITY 500m

500m

METEOROLOGICAL VISIBILITY 100km

Meteorological visibility (sometimes called "met. vis"), is the visibility as reported in an actual weather report (METAR, also sometimes called an 'actual') or forecast in a TAF, AIRMET or METFORM. It is defined as the greatest horizontal distance at which a suitable object can be recognised. In Europe, visibility is reported in metres or kilometres. In the UK, and indeed in most countries world-wide, it is the lowest visibility that is reported. If there are significant variations in visibility in different directions, these may be reported but not forecast.

In TAFs and METARs, a visibility of 10km or more may be given as '9999' (often spoken as "all the nines" or "more than 10 kilometres" or "10 plus").

A met. observer measures visibility by viewing objects or landmarks at a known distance from the observing point; for example, a ridge with trees at 1800m, a church spire at 3000m, a power line at 5km and a hill at 12km. Visibility at night is measured by viewing lights of a known intensity through an optical instrument equipped with a range of filters.

In low-visibility conditions an RVR (Runway Visual Range) may be reported, but not forecast, for the runway in use. RVR is generally reported only when visibility falls below 1500m, which pretty much rules out VFR flight and takes one into the realm of IFR flights and approaches at suitably equipped airports.

It is worth remembering that quite often the horizontal visibility at ground level is better than the airborne visibility.

▶ Haze, Smoke, Dust and Sand

When visibility is reduced by smoke or particles of solid matter, a number of different descriptions can be used to describe the weather phenomenon. Collectively, they are known to the Met. Office (who must have a bigger dictionary than pilots) as *obscuration.*

Haze (HZ)

Haze is often used as a catch-all description of smoke and dust in the atmosphere and is frequently associated with anticyclonic conditions. The subsiding (sinking) air of an anticyclone tends to encourage one or more temperature inversions to form. An inversion acts as a "lid" in the atmosphere, forming a haze layer which usually reaches from the surface to the level of the inversion. The longer the anticyclone persists, the worse the visibility becomes as smoke and other pollutants are pumped into the atmosphere and trapped under the inversion. The top of the haze layer (usually at the inversion) is often sharply defined and flying conditions above it are usually clear and smooth. However, flight in and above haze has a couple of potential traps for the unwary.

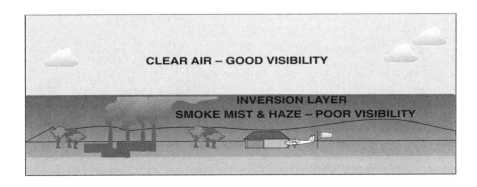

A strong inversion can act as a 'lid', trapping smoke, dust, haze, mist and even fog and cloud in the inversion layer

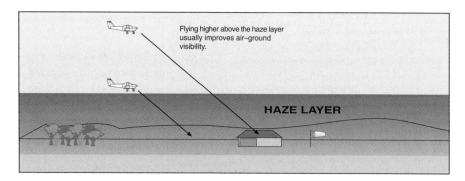

Flying higher above a haze layer normally improves air-to-ground visibility

Air-to-ground visibility above a haze layer may be reasonable and can often be improved by flying higher above the haze. However, visibility within the haze layer may be markedly worse if the slant (oblique) range through the haze layer is increased. It is quite possible to arrive overhead an airfield and be able to see it clearly when looking vertically down through the haze layer. However, as the aircraft descends into the haze, you have to look obliquely through a much greater thickness of the layer and you may well lose sight of the airfield.

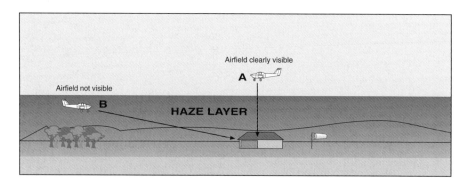

Directly overhead the airfield, pilot A is looking straight down through only a shallow layer of haze, and the airfield is clearly visible. Pilot B is looking through a much greater thickness of haze, and cannot see the airfield

Visibility in haze tends to be much worse when looking into the sun. This can be a particular problem if, for instance, you are approaching a westerly runway in the late afternoon when the glare of the low sun and the haze combine to reduce visibility significantly.

*LEFT> Visibility **into** sun in haze*

RIGHT> Visibility from the same place looking 'down sun'

Visibility

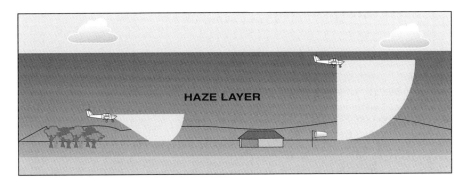

Within a haze layer, flying lower will improve air to ground visibility – but watch out for obstructions!

Within haze layers there may also be quite pronounced local variations in visibility. Visibility near the top of a haze layer is often worse than visibility lower down. Where cumulus clouds have formed at the top of the layer, the visibility directly under these clouds can be significantly worse than elsewhere – due in part to the increased humidity. In these conditions it is better to avoid such areas, either by flying lower if it is safe to do so or by flying around the cloud bases.

When clouds form at the top of the haze layer, visibility directly beneath cloud is often especially bad

The top of this winter haze layer is clearly visible, with patches of stratocumulus forming at the top of the inversion

Once haze has formed, it tends to persist and gradually worsen until a weather system such as an active depression moves through and clears the atmosphere.

Smoke (FU)

Smoke from industrial, domestic or natural fires obviously reduces visibility downwind of the source. In general terms, light winds mean that smoke does not disperse easily; an inversion will also prevent the dispersal of smoke. The reduction in visibility is usually worse downwind of concentrated industrial areas, and during winter anticyclonic conditions.

Smoke reduces visibility downwind of the source

Dust (DU) and Sand (SA)

To a meteorologist, these two phenomena are differentiated by the particle size (dust particles being smaller) and are not confined to desert areas. Dust can reach Europe in the summer, when the airflow is directly from north Africa. Visibility can be significantly reduced; if it rains, dust particles can be 'washed out' in the raindrops causing "coloured rain".

Blowing dust or sand can occasionally affect an airfield during strong wind conditions, especially in the case of a coastal airfield near extensive sand dunes. Coastal areas can also be affected by sea spray, which reduces visibility in strong winds. However, since the wind needs to be at least severe-gale strength for this to happen (Force 9, which implies 41 to 47 knots mean speed and gusts up to 60 knots), reduced visibility is not likely to be the pilot's biggest concern at the time!

▶ Fog and Mist

The terms *fog* (FG) and *mist* (BR) describe conditions when visibility is reduced by water droplets. Mist describes a visibility of 3000 to 1000m; fog is used to describe a visibility of less than 1000m.

An understanding of the formation of fog, which is essentially cloud at ground level, is of great importance to the pilot. By definition, any fog will disrupt aircraft operations – and particularly thick fog can close even a major international airport to all aircraft except those fitted with sophisticated equipment and certified for automatic landings. The two most common types of fog in Europe are *advection fog* and *radiation fog*. Both are caused by moist air being cooled below its dew point by contact with a cold surface.

Visibility

LAND

SEA LEVEL

Thick advection fog over the sea and coastal areas.
Further inland the fog may break and lift into low cloud.

Advection fog blowing inland, rising to form low cloud, and eventually breaking up

Advection fog is a widespread sheet of fog produced when warm moist air flows over a cooler surface. Advection fog can form over the sea in winter months when warm air from the south is cooled below its dew point by the cold sea. An onshore breeze can carry such fog over land, and advection fog particularly affects south

Advection fog and low stratus over Lake Bodensee (between Germany and Switzerland). A number of aircraft have been lost after suddenly encountering low cloud and fog on the approach to nearby Friedrichshafen airport

Wales, south-west England and north-west France in the winter and spring when a south-westerly wind is blowing. Advection fog forming over the sea (sometimes called *sea fog*) can persist even in strong winds, unlike advection fog over the land which tends to be dispersed by strong winds. For example, in the Channel Islands thick fog combined with 40-knot winds is by no means rare! Advection fog can form over the land in winter when a relatively warm airflow (again usually from the south-west) passes over cold ground, perhaps with lying or thawing snow. The melting snow cools the air whilst adding moisture to it and widespread fog can form readily, often moving as a band at the leading edge of the warmer air.

Advection fog over the sea is worst during the spring and summer; over land it tends to be quickly dispersed by daytime heating and should not persist too far inland, although poor visibility and low cloud may be a problem just inland of the coast. That said, low cloud and advection fog can penetrate quite far inland overnight, particularly along river valleys. Thus airfields in valleys (such as Edinburgh and

Advection fog forming over lying snow, central France

Teesside in the UK) can be particularly vulnerable to low stratus and fog moving in from the sea, which reaches them earlier than other airfields and stays longer.

Advection fog from the sea coming ashore near Holyhead, Anglesey. Here the fog is dissipating as soon as it passes over the land

Advection fog over the sea does not vary between day and night, and will simply persist until a different airflow arrives. By its nature, this type of fog is relatively simple to predict and should not catch out a pilot who has been checking forecasts and actuals.

Radiation fog, on the other hand, is far less predictable. Radiation fog forms only over land and is caused by surface cooling at night. On a clear night the ground loses heat to space, a process known as *radiation* (hence the term 'radiation fog'). A sky which is cloud-free or nearly so is important in this connection because cloud tends to act as an insulator, retaining warmth during an overcast night.

If the surface is cooling, the layer of air next to the surface will be cooled by contact with it. Once this cooling process is under way, the moisture content of the air is all-important. The greater the moisture content of the air – or, if you prefer, the higher its relative humidity – the more easily the air will reach saturation. When conditions are favourable for the formation of radiation fog, this is why you will often find meteorologists and experienced pilots watching the temperature and dew point closely. The closer they become (the narrower the temperature/dew-point spread) the greater the likelihood of radiation fog. As a rule, once the temperature/dew-point spread is less than 2°C and narrowing, fog or very low cloud is imminent.

The final factor in the formation of radiation fog is the wind. Light winds – anywhere between about 2 and 8 knots – are ideal for the creation of radiation fog. In the event of less than 2 knots wind speed, a heavy dew will probably form instead of fog (although occasionally fog may form even in calm conditions). Much more than 10 knots wind speed and the increased mixing in the atmosphere will form low cloud rather than ground-based fog.

Visibility

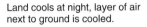

Land cools at night, layer of air next to ground is cooled.

Air is cooled to near dewpoint. The more moist the air, the closer it is to condensation.

Light wind, or heating at sunrise, mixes atmosphere causing condensation at ground level.

The ground 'radiating' heat on a clear night, cooling the air in contact with the surface. The cooling of the air brings it close to saturation, especially if it already has a high relative humidity. A light wind provides the ideal mixing action to form thick fog

To summarise, the three principal factors for the formation of radiation fog are:

- Little or no cloud at night and cooling by radiation.
- High relative humidity.
- Light winds, ideally 2-8 knots.

Radiation fog may start to appear around sunset, but statistically it is most likely to occur in the early hours and around dawn. The most common time of year for the occurrence of radiation fog in Europe is the late autumn, when the diurnal variation of temperature is greatest, although the spring sees a lesser peak in fog occurrence. An anticyclone or ridge (or possibly a col) brings clear skies and light winds, and southerly or south-westerly winds tend to be associated with air with the highest relative humidity. But it must be stressed that none of these can be taken as absolutes.

A tall mast showing through a shallow layer of fog

EGSS 130620 130620Z 35007KT 0100 R05/0250 FG VV/// 07/07 Q1028=

A METAR of fog conditions. It is 13th October, and an area of high pressure is settled over the UK. At London-Stansted (EGSS) at 0620 UTC there is a light wind from the north, a visibility of 100m and a Runway Visual Range (RVR) on runway 05 of 250m in fog. There is no vertical visibility (presumably due to the fog) so the observer cannot assess cloud cover. The temperature is +7°C, the dew point is also +7°C.

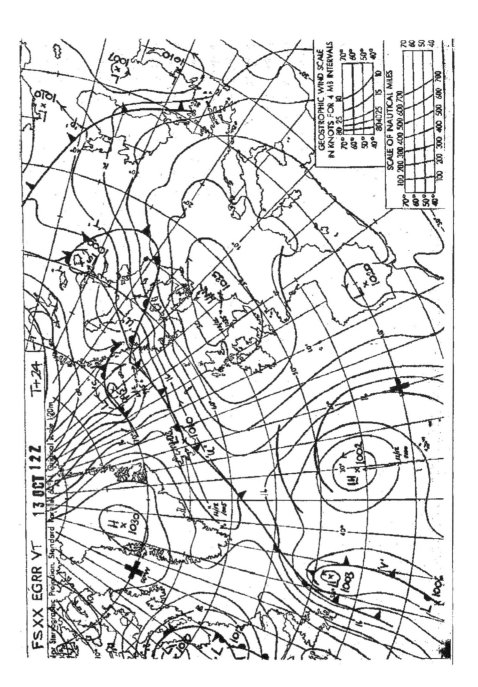

A North Atlantic Surface
'Synoptic' chart, showing
high pressure centred
over Europe in mid-
October – ideal conditions
for radiation fog

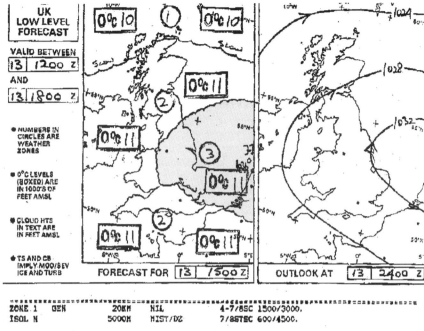

<pre>
==
ZONE 1   GEN   20KM   NIL   4-7/8SC 1500/3000.
ISOL N   5000M   MIST/DZ   7/8STSC 600/4500.

                                            CLD ON HILLS. OCNL MOD TURB BLW 6000 OVER
                                            SHETLAND. MTW, MAX VSP 400FPM NEAR 5000.

ZONE 2   GEN   15KM   NIL   0-3/8CUSC 3000/6000.
OCNL, MAINLY S   5000M   MIST/HAZE 1-5/8STSC 1500/4000.
OCNL NEAR BOUNDARY   2000M   MIST   4-6/8STSC 600/2000.
      ZONE 3

                                            CLD ON HILLS. MOD TURB IN CLD.

ZONE 3   GEN   4000M   MIST   4-7/8STSC 1200/2500.
ISOL LAND, MAINLY   500M   FOG   5-8/8ST 100/1500.
   CONTINENT
OCNL, MAINLY E & S   8KM   HAZE   0-3/8SC 2000/2500.

                                            CLD ON HILLS.

OUTLOOK UNTIL 132400Z: MIST, PATCHY FOG AND LOW CLD BEC MORE WDSPR IN ZONES 2 AND 3.   ⬅
</pre>

A METFORM 215 forecast the same day. Fog conditions are forecast in Zone 3. Note also that mist, fog and low cloud are expected to become widespread towards 2400 UTC - i.e. after nightfall

It is the fine balance of atmospheric conditions capable of causing radiation fog that often make it so unpredictable. During a particularly calm night, little or no fog may form. However, at sunrise the heating of the surface – leading to convection currents which stir up the atmosphere – can cause enough mixing for thick fog to form rapidly just after dawn. Just the thing to catch out the early-morning aviator!

Early-morning radiation fog lingering in a valley in Germany

Terrain can also have a marked effect on the formation of radiation fog. It tends to form earliest, and last longest, in valleys. Here the cold air sinks (katabatically) to the valley floor at night, where there may be a river or lake to increase the relative humidity. Once the sun rises in the morning, the valley may stay in shadow for longer, denying the sun's heat the chance to disperse the fog. However, an airfield on a hill is not guaranteed to stay fog-free. Fog may form below the airfield, leaving it in the clear – especially at night. However after dawn, the fog may be warmed and lift to cover the airfield, just as everywhere else is becoming clear of fog!

A katabatic wind can bring cold air to the bottom of a valley, where fog forms

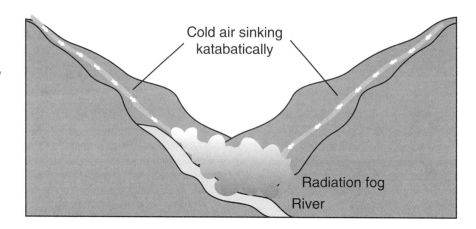

Cold air sinking katabatically

Radiation fog

River

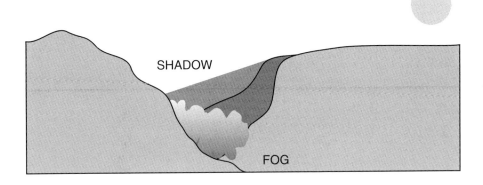

Fog often persists in a deep valley, especially if it stays in shadow for some time

Fog lying in a valley – as seen here in South Wales

Removal of radiation fog (or 'burning-off', as pilots and meteorologists often describe it) usually takes place by courtesy of the sun, which raises the ground temperature, thus heating the fog and removing it. It follows that radiation fog in the summer (which is quite rare) tends to be quickly dissipated by the strong sun. In winter the sun may not be strong enough to disperse the fog completely, which may then linger in places throughout the daylight hours and then become widespread again at night. This is especially irritating if it happens on and around an airfield, and it can persist for several days. Radiation fog can be cleared by strengthening winds, which initially lift the fog into a layer of low stratus before breaking it up.

Extensive radiation fog covering the English midlands on a September morning. The marked inversion is evident at the top of the fog layer

Fog patches can move around unpredictably, leaving some parts of an airfield clear, but others with a visibility of a few hundred metres or less

EGPH 030634Z 030716 23003KT 0400 FG BKN002 TEMPO 0709 3000 BR
NSC BECMG 0810 7000 SCT006 BECMG 1012 CAVOK=

A TAF forecasting a fog clearance:

1   EGPH 030634Z 030716 23003KT 0400 FG BKN002

A TAF (forecast) for Edinburgh (EGPH), issued at 0634 UTC (Z) on the 3rd, for the period 0700 to 1600 UTC on the 3rd. The forecast period begins with a visibility of 400m in fog, and a broken cloud base 200ft above aerodrome level.

2   TEMPO 0709 3000 BR NSC

Temporarily (for short periods) between 0700 to 0900 UTC the visibility is forecast to increase to 3000m in mist, with No Significant Cloud.

3   BECMG 0810 7000 SCT006

The weather is forecast to become (BECMG) during 0800 to 1000 UTC 7000m visibility with a scattered cloud base at 600ft – this is the fog lifting and breaking into low cloud.

4   BECMG 1012 CAVOK=

Now the really interesting bit for a VFR pilot; BECOMING 1000 to 1200 UTC, CAVOK. CAVOK (Ceiling And Visibility OK) means in essence no cloud below 5000ft and visibility 10km or more. However, remember that this is just a forecast and needs to be treated with caution. It is not a guarantee that the fog will clear at the appointed hour. If you are flying to Edinburgh you should have lots of reserve fuel, up-to-date weather reports and forecasts for the area, and several fog-free alternates planned.

Visibility

The clearance of fog is one of those topics that tends to cause a degree of mild acrimony between weather forecasters and pilots, basically because it is very difficult for a forecaster to get the timing of the clearance correct. The forecasting of fog clearance is based on a precise knowledge of the conditions throughout the atmosphere at each place where fog has formed. Unfortunately this information can never be fully available to the forecaster, so he has to make an educated guess of the time at which the fog will clear. It might be over-active aviators' imagination or a statistical freak, but most pilots would agree that the forecast times of fog clearance are more often than not over-optimistic. Regrettably it is not uncommon for the predicted clearance time to be mysteriously put back with each new forecast as the fog fails to oblige by disappearing when it was supposed to. Think of a forecast with a predicted fog clearance time as like a cigarette packet – it should carry a prominent health warning! If you are relying on a forecast fog clearance to reach an airfield, remember that the clearance may not happen at all, let alone at the forecast time. Fog clearance also varies in different areas. If you fly to an airfield without met. facilities, you cannot assume it will be fog-free just because a nearby airport is clear. A quirk of the local terrain (maybe your destination airfield is in a valley or next to a lake) could easily leave your destination fog-bound. Caution is the watchword in these conditions. Carry plenty of reserve fuel and have lots of fog-free alternates planned.

Apart from the two principal types of fog, there are a few others – more rare but worth mentioning.

Steaming fog forms above water when the air is much cooler than the water. It is a phenomenon sometimes seen when a water-covered road steams in sunshine – or if you put a bowl of warm water into a refrigerator. Although relatively rare in most of Europe, it can form quite easily in the Norwegian fjords. It is common in polar and arctic regions and is also known as "arctic sea smoke" or "frost smoke".

Frontal fog occasionally forms just ahead of a warm or occluded front (described in the frontal depressions chapter), either as the cloud comes down to ground level or if the air becomes saturated by continuous rain.

Intense rain (such as that ahead of a front) can saturate the air, forming low cloud or even fog

Intense precipitation ahead of a warm front leading to the formation of additional low cloud and fog.

Finally, one misleading term to be wary of is *hill fog*. In the past this was used simply to describe cloud covering high ground. The preferred terminology for this condition is now "cloud covering the hills".

▶Visibility in Precipitation

Any precipitation will reduce visibility to a certain extent. Slight or moderate rain tends not to reduce visibility greatly, but a very heavy downpour such as that associated with a thunderstorm may reduce visibility down to 1000m or less. *Drizzle* is associated with low cloud and high relative humidity. As such, drizzle nearly always means visibility of less than 3000m .

Hail and sleet cause a marked reduction in visibility. However, each is a hazard in its own right (airframe damage can result from hail, and icing can take place in sleet) and proficient VFR pilots will avoid such precipitation anyway.

Falling snow has a dramatic affect on visibility. Even a moderate snow shower can reduce visibility to 1000m or less; fly into falling snow and all visual reference will quickly be lost. In heavy snow, visibilities of less than 200m are quite common. Even on the ground, you could easily get lost at your home airfield! Here again, flight into a snowstorm is not something to be lightly undertaken by a VFR pilot.

Even moderate snow dramatically reduces visibility, often to less than a kilometre

In very cold conditions, lying snow can be raised by strong winds. Such a phenomenon is described as "drifting snow" (DRSN) if it remains within 2m of the ground or "blowing snow" (BLSN) if it extends above 2m.

▶Revision

36 What is indicated by "9999" in a TAF?

37 What sort of pressure system is most likely to lead to haze or smoke conditions?

38 Which of the aircraft below has the best chance of seeing the airfield?

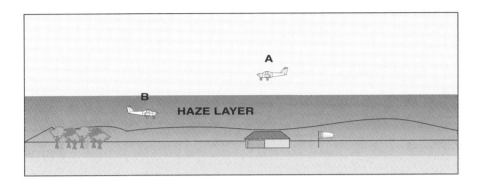

39 What type of fog may form when warm air moves over a cold surface?

40 What three conditions are most likely to lead to the formation of radiation fog?

41 What visibility is suggested by the forecast "0700 FG"?

42 What type of precipitation causes the greatest reduction in visibility?

Answers at page MET 182

Air Masses

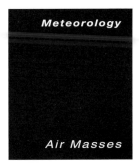

Meteorology

▶ Origin and Classification of Air Masses

An *air mass* is a large body of air with very similar values of temperature and humidity over an extensive area. An air mass gains this property when a large quantity of slow-moving air remains over a particular region for a period of several days or weeks. Once the air mass leaves its 'source' region, meteorologists can predict the type of weather it will bring with it. This will depend on the original characteristics of the air, the route it has taken since it left its region of origin and how quickly it has moved.

An air mass is initially classified by temperature. Around western Europe an air mass can be *polar* (from a northern source region) or *tropical* (from a southern source region). It can then be further sub-classified by humidity, depending on whether it formed over the sea (*maritime*) or land (*continental*). Hence there are four principal types of air mass associated with the weather in western Europe.

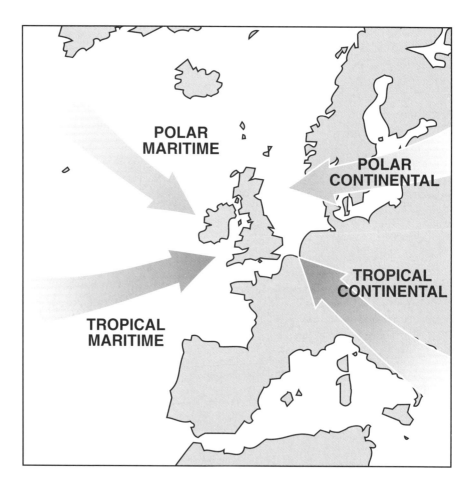

The four principal air masses that affect western Europe

▶ Characteristics of Air Masses

A *tropical maritime* air mass commonly affects the UK and northern Europe in the prevailing south-westerly winds of this region. Tropical maritime air originates in a sub-tropical anticyclone which tends to form and centre over the Azores (for which reason it is sometimes known as the "Azores High"). Such an air mass is predominantly warm and humid, and is usually stable on reaching the UK because it is cooled from below on its northwards journey. In winter, a tropical maritime air mass tends to bring dull weather with low stratus cloud, poor visibility and even advection fog (especially in south-west England and north-west France). During the summer, surface heating effects cause cloud to dissipate inland and visibility to improve, although radiation fog becomes a possibility if the other necessary conditions prevail.

A *tropical continental* air mass comes from the south and south-east, having originated over north Africa and southern Europe. It is hot and dry and, being cooled from below on its northerly path, tends to be stable. This type of air mass brings "heatwave" weather in the summer with clear skies and high temperatures. However, visibility is often poor due to haze and dust.

A *polar continental* air mass usually arrives from Russia or Scandinavia. As one might expect from the name, it is essentially cold and dry and usually brings clear skies and excellent visibility – although visibility can be reduced if the air mass has picked up smoke and dust when crossing some of the heavily industrialised areas of northern Europe. As polar continental air crosses the North Sea during winter, it can pick up enough moisture from the relatively warm sea to trigger off convective clouds and showers on eastern coasts of the UK. In the summer, cooling of polar continental air can result in banks of sea fog (known locally as "*Haar*") over the North Sea. If conditions are right, this fog can move inland overnight.

A *polar maritime* air mass originates over the Atlantic near the Canadian Arctic or Greenland. It begins life relatively humid, cool and initially quite stable. However, on its passage southwards over the Atlantic, this air mass is heated from below by the warmer sea, so the moisture content increases and it tends to become unstable. Arriving at the UK and mainland Europe, polar maritime air brings convective (cumulus-type) clouds which are often well developed and produce showers or even thunderstorms. Outside these showers, visibility tends to be very good.

An unstable 'Polar Maritime' air mass

A 'Polar Maritime Returning' air mass over the UK in summer bringing showers and thunderstorms

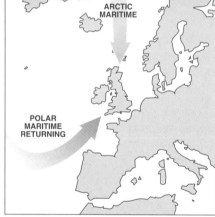

The Arctic Maritime and Polar Maritime Returning air masses

Polar maritime air may also reach Europe by a less direct route. A slow-moving depression to the west of the UK can route the air mass well to the south before it approaches from the south-west. Such an air mass is heated from below on its southerly passage, then cooled from below as it heads northwards again. It follows that the lower layers tend to be stable, although unstable air may persist higher up. This so-called "*returning polar maritime*" air mass often brings low cloud to south-west regions of the UK, but extensive, heavy showers and thunderstorms further inland, especially in the summer.

Occasionally reaching Europe directly from the north is the *arctic maritime* air mass, whose source region is over the Arctic ocean. Such air is cold and fairly dry and will give excellent visibility in the clean, unpolluted air. Any heat and moisture picked up *en route* may give rise to snow showers over north facing coasts. This is a winter air flow, which tends to bring the first snowfall of the year to Scotland and can lead to very low night-time temperatures inland. In Scotland and northern England the lowest night-time winter temperatures usually occur in this air mass.

▶ Revision

43   What is the source region for tropical maritime air?

44   Is tropical maritime air normally stable or unstable?

45   Which air mass brings the lowest night time winter temperatures to Scotland and northern England?

Answers at page MET 182

Low Pressure Systems – Depressions

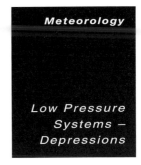

Meteorology

Low Pressure Systems – Depressions

▶ Definition of a Front

▶ The Development and Life-Cycle of a Classic Warm-Sector Depression

▶ The Warm Front

▶ The Cold Front

▶ Occluded Fronts

▶ Stationary Fronts

▶ Secondary Depressions

▶ General Properties of Warm-Sector Depressions

▶ Non-Frontal Lows

▶ Revision

Meteorology

▶ Definition of a Front

Fronts are usually associated with depressions. A depression has already been defined – but what is a front?

The concept of a front was first coined by a Norwegian meteorologist during the First World War. The analogy of the 'battle front' where opposing forces meet in war is not inappropriate.

In meteorological terms, a front is the boundary between two different types of air mass. In the North Atlantic, for example, the front which marks the transitional zone between cold polar maritime air from the north and warm tropical maritime air from the south is known as the *polar front*.

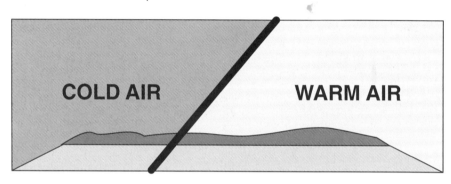

The boundary between two different air masses is called a front

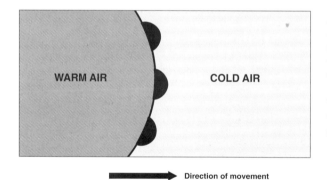

A warm front brings warm air to replace cold air: the 'bobbles' are on the leading edge of the front

Direction of movement

A front is defined according to whether it brings a transition from warm air to cool air or the other way round.

Where a front brings warm air to replace cold air, it is called a *warm front.*

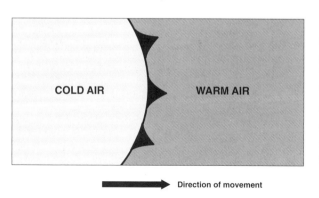

A cold front brings cold air to replace warmer air: the 'spikes' are on the leading edge of the front

Direction of movement

Where a front brings cold air to replace warmer air, it is called a *cold front.*

This basic principle is often misunderstood, so let's restate it in a different way:

Low Pressure Systems – Depressions

■ A front is merely the boundary of two different air masses.
■ A **warm** front brings *warm air* replacing cold air; a **cold** front brings *cold air* replacing warm air.

One consequence is that if a front reverses direction, the type of front will change – even though all the other conditions remain the same.

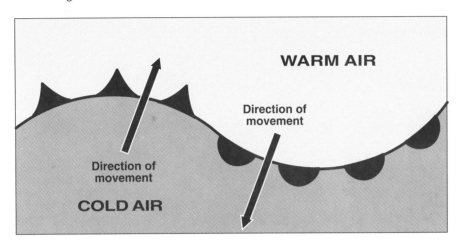

A warm front can change to a cold front (and vice versa) if it reverses direction

Fronts are often regarded as areas of cloud and precipitation, hence their significance to pilots. This is *generally* true of fronts associated with a depression, but is not the absolute invariable it is sometimes believed to be. To understand more, we need to know more about the development and life-cycle of a depression and its associated frontal systems.

▶ The Development and Life-Cycle of a Classic Warm-Sector Depression

This is a good time to reiterate that meteorology is at best an inexact science; indeed, many connected with aviation would regard it as more of a black art. In the mathematical sense, weather systems are chaotic. No two depressions are exactly alike, nor any two fronts. For that matter, neither are any two other meteorological phenomena. The purpose of attempting to describe a 'standard' depression and associated fronts is to provide you with knowledge which you can then use to assess real-life situations. **Don't** take everything that follows literally.

The depressions affecting western Europe are born over the North Atlantic, along the polar front. The position of the polar front is not fixed and changes on a daily basis; in very general terms it lies approximately

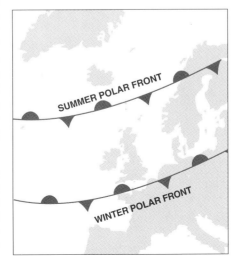

The average position of the North Atlantic polar front in summer and winter

along the 60°N parallel of latitude in the summer (taking depressions to the north of the UK into northern Europe) and along the 50°N parallel in winter (bringing depressions to the southern UK and mid-Europe).

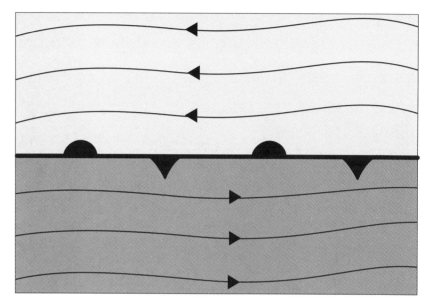

A semi (or quasi)-stationary front with cold air to the north and warm air to the south

Along the polar front, a depression begins as an unstable wave. The fine-scale mechanisms involved in the formation of depressions are complex, and for our purposes it's enough to say that they are associated with the "jetstreams" flowing above the polar front. Jetstreams are fast-moving streams of air at high altitude that tend to form over transition zones such as the polar front. The initial formation and the subsequent movement of the depression are closely linked with the existence of a jetstream.

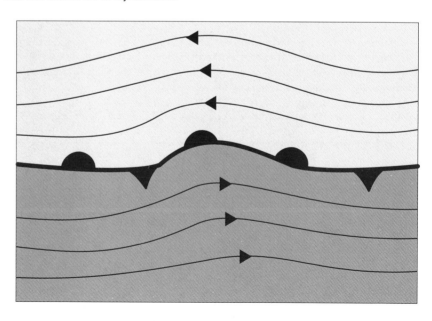

At the surface a 'bulge' of warm air pushes into the cold air, causing a 'kink' in the front

Low Pressure Systems – Depressions

At the surface the first sign of a depression forming is a 'bulge' of warm air into the colder air. Warm air rises at this point and the pressure at the surface begins to fall. As more air flows into this area it acquires a curve in its flow. The combination of curvature and ascent causes the low to begin to 'wind up'. The process is cumulative, and the consequence is an increasing mass of ascending air. As might

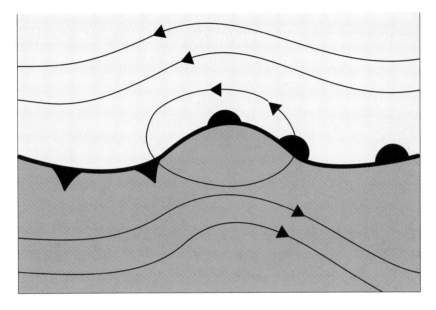

Pressure at the centre of the bulge decreases as air rises. The airflow begins to take on a circular motion

be expected, this cools and condenses to form cloud, and the energy released from this condensation strengthens the depression even more. As the centre of the low deepens (the pressure reduces) the air flow becomes circular. Soon there are well-defined warm and cold fronts marking the boundary between the differing air masses. The area of warmer air between the fronts is called the "warm sector" – which gives its name to this type of depression. By now the depression is moving eastwards, steered by the jetstream and gathering energy as it continues to deepen.

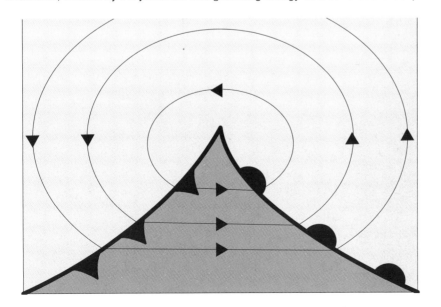

As pressure at the centre continues to deepen the whole depression begins to rotate, with well-defined boundaries (fronts) between the warmer and colder air

▶The Warm Front

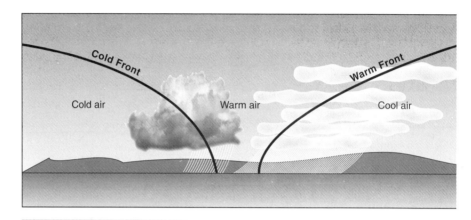

A cross section through a 'classic' warm-sector depression

Late evening, January 6th looking west from Manchester Airport. High-level cirrus cloud thickening and lowering gives the first visual indication of the approaching warm front. Persistent contrails are often also a sign of an approaching front or depression

1020 UTC January 7th The view from the same spot the following morning (16 hours later) as the warm front passes over

In a classic warm-sector depression, the warm front will bring the first signs of its approach. The slope of the warm front is generally quite gentle, the oft-quoted figure is a slope gradient of about 1:150. At the top of the frontal slope, close to the tropopause, are cirrus-type clouds. These can be up to 500nm (925km) ahead of the surface front. As the front approaches, the cloud (usually a stable layer-type) thickens and lowers. Rain or snow first falls from altostratus cloud at around 15,000ft but tends to evaporate before reaching the ground. Slight precipitation first reaches the surface 100-200nm (185-370km) ahead of the surface front. This rain increases to moderate and becomes continuous as the front approaches. All this time the pressure is steadily falling as the front comes closer. The surface front itself is usually marked by the lowest cloud (often nimbostratus) which may come right down to the surface. The transition as the front passes is rarely sharp, even if the frontal zone is narrow (perhaps only 25nm/40km across). The frontal zone of a warm front is often wider than this, up to 90nm/150km, which makes for a gradual transition.

Low Pressure Systems – Depressions

EGCC 071020 071020Z 18008KT 3500 RADZ SCT003
BKN007 OVC010 05/04 1032=

The Manchester METAR at 10:20, the time the photo was taken. The visibility is 3,500m in rain and drizzle, the lowest cloud is at 300ft, with broken cloud at 700ft and overcast cloud at 1000ft

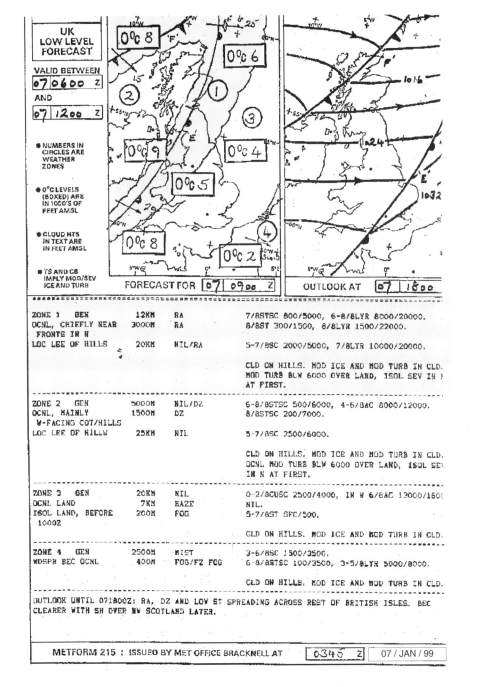

A METFORM 215 forecast for 0600 to 1200 UTC on 7 January. Zone 1 includes the area of the warm front

LEFT> Flying through a warm front. The view taking off from Manchester Airport just ahead of a warm front

RIGHT> The view from above, having climbed through the warm front. Below is the unbroken cloud typical of a 'classic' warm front

BOTTOM> The temperature steadily rises as the warm front passes through. The low cloud and rain gradually clear to allow a spectacular sunset

The first sign of the passage of a warm front may well be a veering of the surface wind, followed by a steadying of the pressure (which usually falls ahead of the front) and an increase in both temperature and dew point. The precipitation should peter out after a while, although low cloud, drizzle and poor visibility often persist behind the front in the warm sector (which in Europe is usually tropical maritime air).

▶ The Cold Front

The slope of the cold front tends to be steeper than that of the warm front, the average cold front having a slope of 1:50. So the zone of cloud and rain tends to be narrower than the warm front and is more likely to include convective cumulus-type cloud, possibly giving rise to outbreaks of heavy precipitation. The actual passage of the surface front may be marked by especially heavy precipitation and 'squally' conditions. An active cold front can be marked by a line of cumulus or cumulonimbus clouds, although these may be hidden to the ground-based observer by lower and more layered clouds persisting in the warm sector.

The passage of a cold front is often marked by a dramatic change in weather. The cloud and rain often clear quickly, leaving drier and much clearer conditions. The temperature and dew point fall but the pressure rises. The surface wind often veers sharply and becomes 'gusty' with the passage of a cold front as a polar maritime air mass is introduced.

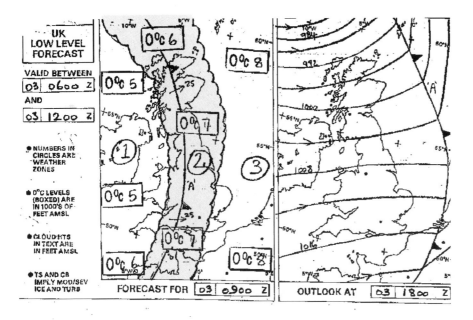

ZONE 1	**GEN**	25KM	NIL	2-5/8CUSC 2000/5000.
	OCNL N, ISOL S	8KM	RA SH	6/8CU 1500/12000.
	ISOL W, AFTER 09Z	4000M	HEAVY RA SH/ TS	7/8CB 1000/18000.

CLD ON HILLS. MOD ICE AND MOD TURB IN CLD.
OCNL MOD TURB BLW 6000 OVER LAND.

ZONE 2	**GEN**	12KM	NIL/RA	4-7/8SC 1500/3000, 5-8/8AC 8000/16000.
	OCNL	6KM	RA	7/8STSC 800/3000, 7/8LYR 5000/16000.
	ISOL, MAINLY AHEAD OF FRONT	3000M	HEAVY RA	5-8/8ST 400/1500, 8/8LYR 1500/20000, + EMBD CU 3000/16000.

CLD ON HILLS. MOD ICE AND MOD TURB IN CLD.
MOD TURB, OCNL SEV, BLW 6000 OVER LAND.

ZONE 3	**GEN**	12KM	NIL	4-7/8STSC 1200/2500, 3/8AC 9000/14000.
	OCNL	3000M	MIST	6-8/8STSC 800/2500, LOC SE NIL.
	ISOL, MAINLY N	1500M	MIST/DZ	6-8/8STSC 500/2500.

CLD ON HILLS. MOD ICE AND MOD TURB IN CLD.
MOD TURB, OCNL SEV IN N, BLW 6000 OVER LAND.

OUTLOOK UNTIL 031800Z: ZONE 1 CONDITIONS SPREADING TO MOST OF THE REGION BEHIND COLD
FRONT. SH MAINLY OVER SEA AND WINDWARD COASTS, AND HEAVIEST AND MOST FREQ IN N.

METFORM 215 : ISSUED BY MET OFFICE BRACKNELL AT | 0350 Z | 03 / DEC / 98

A METFORM 215 forecast for the period 0600 to 1200 UTC on 3 December, showing a cold front crossing the UK. Zone 2 is the frontal zone, Zone 1 the area behind the front. The following photographs were taken at Manchester Airport on this day as the cold front passed through

Meteorology

The view looking north-west across Manchester Airport at 0930 (UTC) as the cold front approaches

EGCC 030920 030920Z
16016G26KT 110V260
8000 RA SCT012 SCT025
11/10 Q1003=

The METAR at Manchester (EGCC) at 0920 UTC. Note the visibility (8000m in rain), the cloud base (scattered at 1200ft), the temperature (+11°C) and the dew point (+10°C). On Manchester's ATIS broadcast, windshear is being reported

As the cold front comes closer, the cloud thickens and lowers and visibility reduces – as seen at 1020

EGCC 031020 031020Z
16016KT 130V210 6000 RA
SCT010 BKN020 11/10
Q1002=

The Manchester METAR at 1020 UTC. Visibility has reduced to 6000m in rain, the cloud has lowered and is more extensive (the lowest cloud base is scattered at 1000ft, with a broken cloud base at 2000ft). The pressure has also fallen

At the moment the cold front passes (1050) there is a burst of heavy rain (probably from embedded cumulonimbus clouds). The large hanger is less than 1000m from the camera

EGCC 031050 031050Z
18014KT 130V220 2500M
+RA SCT010 BKN018
11/11 Q1002=

The METAR at the moment the cold front arrives at Manchester Airport. Visibility falls to 2500m in a downpour of heavy rain; the temperature and dew point are the same at this moment

Within minutes of the passage of the cold front, the clearance is evident, as a 'dry slot' of cold dry air moves in behind the cold front

```
EGCC 031150
031150Z
22012KT 20KM
NILWX SCT015
11/08 Q1004=
```

One hour after the passage of the cold front and conditions have improved markedly. A few hours of good VMC followed

One hour after the passage of the cold front. The wind has veered, the precipitation stopped and the visibility has greatly improved. Almost all the low cloud has cleared, the dew point has fallen significantly (the air is much drier) and the pressure is rising

▶ Occluded Fronts

In a 'classic' warm sector depression, the warm front moves more slowly than the cold front (typically the speed of the warm front is two-thirds that of the cold front). Thus, eventually, the cold front overtakes the warm. When this happens, the most common occurrence is for the warm front to be 'undercut' and the warm air-mass to be lifted clear of the ground. This is known as a *cold occlusion*. Less commonly the cold front rides up over the slope of the warm front, in which case the result is a *warm occlusion*.

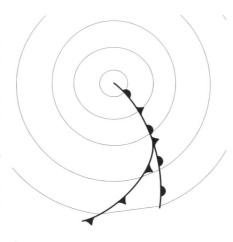

RIGHT> Plan view of a depression beginning to occlude

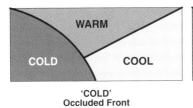

'COLD'
Occluded Front

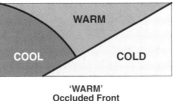

'WARM'
Occluded Front

Cross sections through two types of occluded front

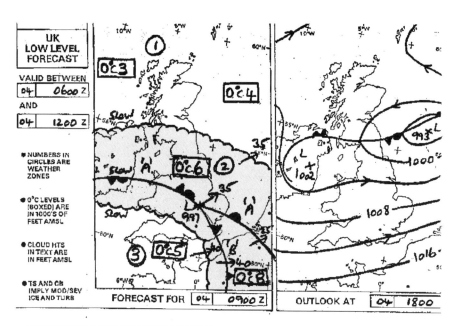

An occluding depression moving across the UK

```
==========================================================================================
ZONE 1    GEN         25KM       NIL            3/8CUSC 2000/6000.
OCNL, MAINLY W SEA SW 12KM       RA SH          6/8CU 1500/10000.
FACING COT & HILLS
ISOL N            ≈ 5000M        RA SH/HAIL/    6/8CB 1000/20000.
                                 TS

ISOL LAND, MAINLY
  56N TO 58N, BEFORE  500M       FOG            NIL.
  1000Z
                                                CLD ON HILLS. MOD ICE AND MOD TURB IN CLD.
                                                MOD TURB BLW 6000 OVER LAND N OF 58N.
--------------------------------------------------------------------------------------------
ZONE 2    GEN         12KM       NIL/RA         4-7/8SC 1700/6000, 4-6/8AC 10000/18000.
OCNL              5000M          RA             7/8STSC 1000/8000, 8/8LYR 10000/20000.
ISOL FRONTS       3000M          HEAVY RA       6/8ST 400/1200, 8/8NS 1500/20000.
ISOL WARM SECTOR  1500M          RA/DZ          7/8STSC 200/6000, 8/8LYR 8000/20000.

                                                CLD ON HILLS. MOD ICE AND MOD TURB IN CLD,
                                                SEV ICE IN NS. MOD, OCNL SEV S & E OF LOW,
                                                TURB BLW 6000 OVER LAND.
--------------------------------------------------------------------------------------------
ZONE 3    GEN         20KM       NIL            3/8CUSC 1800/5000.
OCNL SEA COT, ISOL    10KM       RA SH          6/8CU 1300/12000.
  LAND

                                                CLD ON HILLS. MOD ICE AND MOD TURB IN CLD.
                                                MOD OCNL SEV TURB BLW 6000 OVER LAND.
--------------------------------------------------------------------------------------------

OUTLOOK UNTIL 041800Z:  ZONE 1 CONDITIONS PERSISTING N OF 58N. ZONE 3 CONDITIONS
SPREADING QUICKLY NE ACROSS AREA S OF 53N AND BEC MORE UNSTABLE IN SW.


  METFORM 215 : ISSUED BY MET OFFICE BRACKNELL AT    0330 Z   04/DEC/98
```

Low Pressure Systems – Depressions

```
EGCC 041150 041150Z 24005KT 2000 DZ SCT001 BKN003
07/06 Q1004=
```

A METAR (actual report) from EGCC (Manchester) at 1150 UTC. The visibility is 2000m in drizzle, there is a scattered cloudbase at 100ft and a broken cloudbase at 300ft

In either case, an occlusion has all the cloud and precipitation of the two fronts together – and a slow-moving occluded front can indeed bring persistent low cloud and heavy (and prolonged) precipitation. Often, but not always, there is little change of wind velocity across the occlusion.

The occluding of a depression marks the beginning of the end of its life-cycle. The low gradually fills (the pressure at the centre rises) and it becomes slower moving. The fronts become less active and the winds decrease. Meanwhile, back at the polar front a new depression may well be forming.

Manchester Airport, just ahead of an occluded front

The first sign of the front clearing the airport

The view as the front moves away

▶Stationary Fronts

So far we have largely considered fronts that exist within a 'typical' warm sector depression and are tending to travel across the surface at a speed that might average 20-30 knots. However, a front may move much more slowly than this, or even stop, in which case the front becomes known to the met. office as a 'quasi-stationary' front. Because such a front is going nowhere fast, if it is positioned over you then the conditions it is bringing (e.g. low cloud, poor visibility and precipitation) are obviously going to hang around for some time.

It is not uncommon for a 'quasi-stationary' front to have 'waves' moving long it – you can imagine these as the wave pattern formed on a flag fluttering in a breeze. On a weather chart a 'quasi-stationary' front will be shown with alternating cold and warm front symbols on either side of the front because as waves move along the front one side of the wave is bringing warm air to replace cold air and vice versa.

The 'quasi-stationary' front weather chart symbol

▶Secondary Depressions

Sometimes a slow-moving and fairly inactive depression leaves a long cold front trailing back into the Atlantic. A 'secondary' depression can form within the 'old' primary depression somewhere along this trailing front. Secondary depressions can form and deepen rapidly, bringing bad weather where previously the situation had become quite settled.

At 8 o'clock in the morning it looks like a near-perfect day for flying – light winds, visibility of 50km, some scattered cloud with a base of 2000ft and the bright red higher cloud seen here. But as the saying goes "Red sky in the morning, Shepherd's warning"

```
EGCC 050850 050850Z
140V21006KT 50KM
NILWX SCT020 03/01
Q1010=
```

The Manchester METAR when this photograph was taken. Note the QNH (1010mb/hPa)

Low Pressure Systems — Depressions

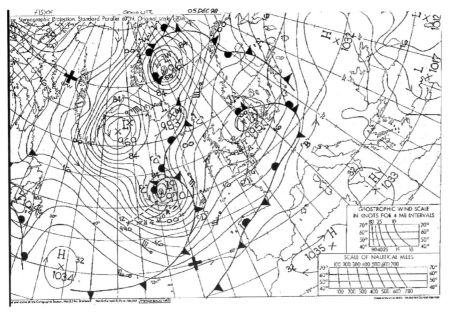

The North Atlantic Surface Synoptic chart reveals a secondary depression (Lc), deepening quickly and approaching Europe

The scene by mid-afternoon. The surface wind is gusting to 26kt, visibility is 5000m in rain and the lowest cloud base is 1200ft, with an overcast layer at 3500ft

```
EGCC 051520 051520Z 130V20013G26KT 5000 RA SCT012
SCT020 OVC035 08/06 Q0999=
```

The Manchester METAR when this photograph was taken. Note the drop in pressure (it is now 999mb/hPa, down from 1010mb/hPa at 0850)

▶ General Properties of Warm-Sector Depressions

In meteorology it is difficult and sometimes dangerous to try to lay down hard and fast rules about the type of conditions a certain atmospheric set-up will cause. A front can bring extensive cloud and rain and a sharp veer in the wind, or it may pass almost unnoticed. In some circles there is an accepted wisdom that *all* warm fronts bring extensive stratus-type cloud and *all* cold fronts bring big cumulus build-ups. **This is simply not true**. A warm front can (rarely) have embedded cumulonimbus clouds associated with it, giving thunderstorms. Equally, a cold front can have extensive layered stratus cloud. The forecasting of the conditions a depression will bring is best left to meteorologists who have the knowledge, experience and data to make informed predictions. That said, there are some generalisations about warm-sector depressions which *tend* to be valid:

■ The track of the depression is largely guided by the jetstream. From surface observations the direction and speed at which the depression is moving is indicated by the isobars in the warm sector.

■ Travelling depressions tend to steer around established anticyclones.

■ Once a depression has occluded and begun to fill up (i.e. the pressure at the centre is rising) the fronts should become less active. A depression that is still deepening (meaning that the pressure at the centre is falling) brings more active fronts and generally worse weather.

■ When a string of depressions is passing through Europe, there is often a ridge of high pressure between each one. This gives a brief period of fine weather; unfortunately this may occur overnight!

■ The weather at the fronts is usually worse near the centre of the depression and better away from the low, or where the fronts cross an area of high pressure.

■ The greater the temperature difference and the steeper the temperature gradient across a front, the more active and sharply defined it will be.

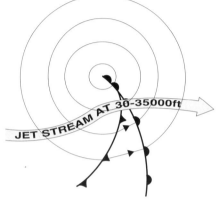

The approximate relationship of a jet stream to a well-developed warm-sector depression

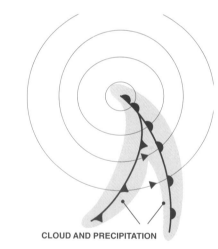

CLOUD AND PRECIPITATION

The approximate areas of low cloud and precipitation in a classic warm-sector depression

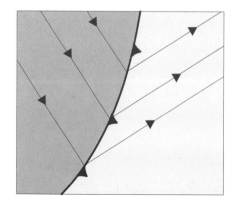

A sharp veering of wind is possible with the passage of a front. The more acute the 'V' in the isobars, the more marked the wind veer is likely to be

Low Pressure Systems – Depressions

■ At the surface, the change of temperature with the passage of a front is not always well-defined. Cloud and rain at the passage of a warm front may actually reduce surface temperature: sunshine in clear skies behind a cold front may increase it. Veering of the wind and change in the dew point are usually more reliable indicators of the passage of a front.

■ The sharper the wind veer associated with a front (as seen by a sharp 'V' in the isobars at the front), the more active the front will be. An acute 'V' in the isobars implies a strong windshear as the wind rapidly veers with the passage of the front. Active cold fronts are particularly good at producing windshear.

■ Fronts may be weak (inactive) or strong (active). In general a strong warm front is followed by a weak cold front and *vice versa*.

■ There is often an area of very cold, clear air just behind a cold front (known by meteorologists as a "dry slot") which may bring clear skies for a few hours until cumulus clouds and showers move in.

■ In addition to fronts, a marked 'trough' (a line of low pressure) may be shown on weather charts. Such a trough often brings weather similar to that associated with a front, without the change in air mass.

■ Finally, a front never seems to clear your airfield as quickly as forecast – especially on the day that you really wanted to go flying....

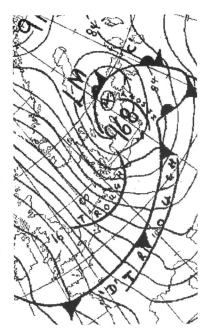

Troughs both in front of and behind a cold front. The trough behind the cold front brought a line of Cumulonimbus clouds

▶ Non-Frontal Lows

We have concentrated on depressions forming over the North Atlantic and bringing fronts to western Europe. Other types of lows – without fronts – also occur, albeit less frequently. Of these, probably the one of most interest to pilots is the *heat low*, which may form over continental Europe in summer. Intense surface heating leads to a widespread ascent of air. The movement of air at low level into this area is curved, and a small 'closed' low may form. These heat lows are often shallow and have little apparent effect on the weather. However, if the air is unstable enough, cumulonimbus clouds and thunderstorms can develop within them.

▶Revision

46 What type of front is shown below?

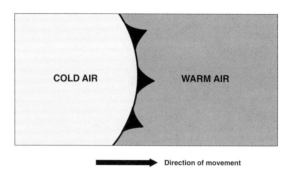

Direction of movement

47 A warm front is approaching your airfield at 20kts, and the radar rainfall picture shows a band of rain 200nm wide. It starts raining at the airfield at 0700. What is the latest time you would expect the passage of the front?

48 What type of front is depicted by the symbol below?

49 What is the typical change in wind direction at the passage of a front?

50 What type of front is likely to have passed between the two METAR reports below?

EGZZ 170920 170920Z 20015KT 2500M RA BKN004 OVC008 08/07 Q1004=

EGZZ 171050 171050Z 27015KT 4000M DZ BKN010 OVC015 11/08 Q1004=

Answers at page MET 182

High Pressure Systems – Anticyclones and Ridges

Meteorology

High
Pressure
Systems –
Anticyclones
and Ridges

▶ Anticyclones

▶ Ridges

▶ Cols

▶ Revision

Exercise

High
Pressure
Systems –
Anticyclones
and Ridges

Meteorology

▶Anticyclones

An anticyclone is an area of high pressure, caused by the widespread descent of air. The air in an anticyclone sinks (or 'subsides') slowly, an average rate being about 2000ft per day. Air descending at this speed (just over one foot per minute) has no noticeable effect on the performance of powered aircraft, although it may have a measurable effect on the sink rate of a modern competition glider. As air subsides, it is compressed and so it warms (which is why a bicycle pump becomes warm after it has been used for a while). If the air is dry, it will be warming at about 3°C per 1000ft (the DALR) in the descent.

The general movement of air within an anticyclone is that it sinks to somewhere near the surface and then diverges (spreads out) from the centre of the high, with the wind flowing in a clockwise direction around it (in the northern hemisphere). Because the pressure gradient within an anticyclone is generally slack, with widely spaced isobars, light winds are a feature of areas of high pressure. Likewise, the general subsidence discourages the formation of cloud – although this does not imply that there will be no cloud within an anticyclone. Local heating of the surface, especially in summer, may cause small cumulus clouds to spring up. Because the atmosphere in an anticyclone is usually stable, these do not normally grow to any great extent; they are often called "fair-weather cumulus", shortened to "cu" in conversation.

A summer anticyclone often brings 'heatwave' weather since its clockwise flow tends to bring tropical continental air from the south, and this can last for long periods since a strong anticyclone will be slow-moving or even stationary. Consequently, the arrival of anticyclonic conditions is initially good news for pilots since they imply light winds, clear skies and generally calm and settled flying conditions. However, there is a price to pay for all this. The subsidence within an anticyclone encourages temperature inversions to form. These were mentioned earlier but, just to recap, a temperature inversion is a layer of the atmosphere through which the temperature *rises* with increasing altitude – in other words the reverse of the normal situation whereby air cools with increasing altitude.

Level	Temperature
6000	+17°C
5000	+20°C
4000	+23°C Top of inversion
3000	+23°C
2000	+22°C
1000	+21°C
Surface	+20°C

The top of the inversion acts very much as a 'lid' on the atmosphere. On a large scale the tropopause can be thought of as an inversion, keeping virtually all water content and weather in the troposphere. On a smaller scale, an inversion acts in a similar way. Any rising thermals from the ground stop on reaching the top of the inversion, and wind flow above and below it can be markedly different – the inversion in effect separating the air above it from the effect of the friction layer. A common result of this effect is often a much stronger wind above the inversion than below. Inversions can have profound effects on VHF radio waves as well – see the Communications section of PPL2.

High Pressure Systems –
Anticyclones and Ridges

As a inversion layer becomes established, so smoke, dust, haze and the like are concentrated in it. There are no strong winds to disperse these pollutants, and little or no precipitation to wash them out of the atmosphere. Over a period of days the visibility within the inversion layer will worsen, and the top of the inversion layer will gradually rise. This situation is likely to persist until either the anticyclone breaks down (often in a burst of thunderstorms and heavy showers) or a depression moves in, leaving much clearer air behind it.

Typical summer anticyclone conditions in the UK. There are light winds and the tropical continental air mass is bringing temperatures of up to 30°C. The downside is increasing haze. Seen from 2500 feet over Essex the top of the haze layer (probably at the top of the inversion level) is clearly visible

In winter an anticyclone brings similar features. At first the clear skies and calm conditions can bring very good (if rather cold) flying conditions – although if temperatures fall below freezing you need to look-out for frosty or icy runways. After a few days the inversion layer appears and the attendant haze reduces visibility. The formation of a persistent layer of turbulence cloud – described in the 'Clouds and Precipitation' chapter – may well make VFR flight below the inversion difficult. A winter anticyclone will probably persist until a strong and fast-moving depression moves in.

```
ZONE 2
GEN   2000M   MIST/DZ          8/8STSC 500/2500
                               3/8AC 9000/14000
OCNL LAND  300M   FOG/DZ        8/8STSC 100/2000
ISOL E&N  6KM  HAZE            4-7/8ST 700/1200
```

It is early December and an anticyclone has been centred over the UK for about 10 days. Zone 2 of the day's METFORM forecast covers just about all of England and Wales. Clearly VFR flight is, to all intents and purposes, not possible. The cloud tops (generally 2500 feet) indicate the level of the inevitable inversion layer

LEFT> The view over southern England on the day of the METFORM forecast. Above the unbroken layer of stratocumulus turbulence cloud the air is clear and smooth. The top of the cloud is at the top of the inversion level at 2500ft

RIGHT> Below the inversion the picture is less pretty. Visibility is less than 1000m and the top of the control tower at London Gatwick airport (137ft AGL) is obscured by cloud

In spring and autumn, the slack winds and (initially) clear skies within an anticyclone can encourage the formation of radiation fog which may persist for days on end. Additionally, cooling of the ground by radiation leaves the air in contact with it much colder than the air above, which naturally encourages the formation of a low-level inversion. The effect of the separation of the wind flow above the inversion from the friction layer below – leading to marked windshear at the top of the inversion – is particularly noticeable in these circumstances.

High Pressure Systems –
Anticyclones and Ridges

▶ Ridges

A *ridge* is an elongated area of high pressure, usually bringing very similar weather to that of an established anticyclone. 'Weak' ridges are a particular feature of winter weather, when they often appear between successive depressions. They will bring a short period of fine weather before the next depression arrives.

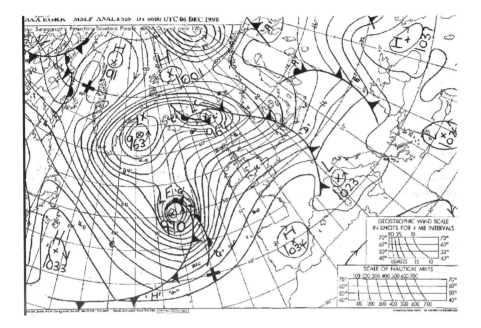

A weak ridge of high pressure building-up over France and the UK from an anticyclone centred over Spain. This ridge brought a brief spell of clear weather before the next depression (Lf) moved in

▶ Cols

A *col* is an area of stagnant air, sandwiched between two highs and two lows. About the only thing you can say with certainty about the weather within a col is that the winds will be light (as witnessed by the lack of isobars). The weather situation within a particular col will often be influenced by the strongest pressure system nearby, but it takes a meteorologist with knowledge of the upper atmosphere to make a half-decent forecast. In spring and autumn the light winds can encourage fog: thunderstorms may break out in summer. But it really is very difficult to make valid generalisations about the weather in and around cols. Treat each one as an individual case and watch the forecasts closely.

▶Revision

51 In the table below, what is the approximate level of the top of the inversion?

Level	Temperature
6000	+10°C
5000	+12°C
4000	+14°C
3000	+16°C
2000	+18°C
1000	+17°C
Surface	+15°C

52 Which of the following weather would you **not** expect to find in an anticyclone?

Thunderstorms, fog, haze, low cloud, fine and clear weather, calm conditions, widespread gales.

53 In the synoptic chart below, which letter marks a ridge?

54 In the synoptic chart above, which letter marks a col?

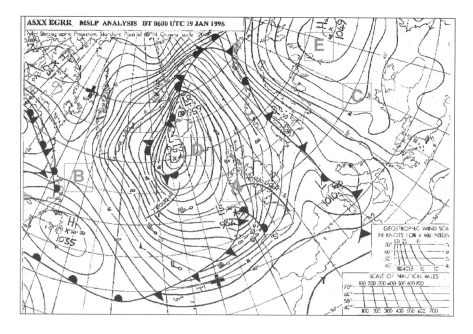

Answers at page MET 182

Icing

Meteorology

Icing

▶ Hazards of Icing

▶ Conditions Conducive to Ice Formation

▶ Hoar Frost

▶ Rain Ice

▶ Piston Engine Icing

▶ Revision

Meteorology

▶Hazards of Icing

Any form of icing is a hazard to an aircraft. Ice on the airframe will markedly increase drag and reduce lift – so much so that *in extremis* take-off becomes impossible, or level flight cannot be maintained even at full power. Likewise an aircraft's flight characteristics can be so drastically affected that the aircraft becomes uncontrollable. Engine icing can cause a marked reduction in power, or even a total failure. Ice can form on the windscreen, block the external pitot and static pressure sources, form inside the lines of the pitot/static system or even freeze the flying controls solid. All in all, ice and light aircraft emphatically do not mix. So at the outset, two particular safety points need to be borne in mind:

■ The basic PPL does not qualify the pilot to fly in cloud, and flight in cloud at temperatures below 0°C is a potential icing situation. Therefore the holder of a PPL without any instrument qualifications should already be avoiding the conditions that commonly lead to airframe icing.

■ The vast majority of light aircraft are not fitted with de-icing equipment. Consequently, the POH/FM for such aeroplanes will state emphatically that the machine is not cleared for flight into known icing conditions. The safety and legal implications of ignoring this advice are obvious.

▶Conditions Conductive to Ice Formation

On the ground, water rarely exists at temperatures below freezing (0°C) because it simply turns into ice. In a cloud, however, water droplets can remain liquid at temperatures well below freezing: as low as -40°C or even colder. Water droplets can remain in this liquid, supercooled state until something comes along onto which they can freeze. An aircraft flying above the freezing level is an ideal candidate. So any aircraft flying in cloud above the freezing level is in potential icing conditions.

When an aircraft meets a small supercooled water droplet, most of the droplet freezes on contact and forms a brittle layer of ice, usually on the leading edges of the wings and tail and also on aerials, struts, etc. This semi-opaque coating is called *rime ice*. A proportion of a larger water droplet may freeze as it flows across the surface of the aircraft. The sheet of clearer ice formed in this way is called – surprisingly enough – *clear ice*.

Brittle 'rime' ice forming on a wing leading edge, with denser and more tenacious 'clear' ice further back along the wing

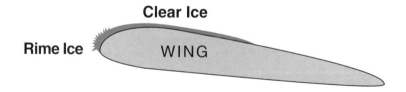

The worst icing is generally considered to occur at air temperatures (OATs) of between 0°C and -12°C. Icing becomes less severe below -20°C and is fairly rare below -40°C because clouds mostly consist of ice crystals at this order of temperature. However, there are times when these rules of thumb do not apply. Within a cumulonimbus cloud, for instance, severe icing can be encountered at any temperature below 0°C.

Ice on an aircraft that had just flown through a warm front (visible below the aircraft. The accumulation of ice was such that the aircraft had been forced to descend, even with full power and at best climb airspeed

Some cloud types give more pronounced icing than others. Cumuliform clouds tend to hold larger water droplets than stratus-type clouds and therefore contain more severe icing conditions. Clouds formed by orographic uplift or mountain-wave conditions can also contain worse icing conditions than elsewhere. Stratocumulus can sometimes give unexpectedly severe icing, particularly when it lies just below an inversion over the sea.

Remember that in addition to the effects of ice on the airframe, icing of the pitot and static tubes will cause the pressure instruments (airspeed indicator, altimeter and vertical speed indicator) to become unreliable. If you are caught out in icing conditions, select the pitot heat immediately.

▶Hoar Frost

Hoar frost can form on an aircraft before it has even left the ground although, less commonly, it can appear on an aircraft in flight as well. Hoar frost forms when the water vapour in the atmosphere changes directly from a gas to a solid (i.e. ice) on to a surface that has a temperature of below freezing.

Almost ideal circumstances for the formation of hoar frost exist when an aircraft is parked in the open on a clear, cold night when the temperature is expected to fall below freezing (0°C). In the morning you may well find the aeroplane covered in a delicate layer of frost. This is very pretty, but extremely dangerous if not removed. Although the frost weighs hardly anything, it will have a dramatic effect on the viability of the aircraft as a flying machine. Even a thin layer of frost will act like any other form of airframe icing; it reduces lift, increases drag, raises the stalling speed and can make the aircraft difficult to control or even unflyable. Performance is also reduced, leading to longer take-off and landing distances, reduced climb rates, cruising speeds and range. The action required is self-evident. Before flight, **all** the frost must be removed from **all** the aircraft surfaces. Likewise, any snow lying on the aircraft must be removed from all surfaces before flight. It is sometimes thought that snow will blow off an aircraft during the take-off but unfortunately this is far from true. Any snow on the aircraft **must** be completely removed before flight. One point to bear in mind here is that if you get caught in a snow shower whilst awaiting take-off and the snow settles on the aircraft (especially over any wing fuel tanks, which tend to be cool) you **must** go back to the apron to remove all the snow from all the aircraft before take-off.

Hoar frost on an aircraft that had been left in the open in sub-zero temperatures over- night

Hoar frost can form on an aircraft in flight if, for instance, you have been flying for a long time in sub-zero air (OAT below 0°C) and descend into an area of warmer and possibly more moist air. Hoar frost can also form on an aircraft if it takes off when the surface temperature is below freezing and then climbs through an inversion into warmer air. However, in this instance the frost normally thaws quickly.

▶ Rain Ice

This is (thankfully) an uncommon form of icing that can occur outside cloud. The classic environment for rain ice is the area just ahead of a warm front in winter. The clouds of the warm front are mostly within the warm sector and so precipitation may fall as rain, through the front, and into the colder air ahead of the front. If this rain meets an object whose surface temperature is below freezing (such as an aircraft) the rain drops may freeze on contact – forming lumps of clear ice which are extremely difficult to remove. Typically, an aircraft may meet rain ice (also known as *freezing rain*) if it is flying in rain ahead of a warm front when the OAT is less than 0°C. Rain ice can also affect aircraft on the ground, on runways and taxiways. In either case the only real solution is avoidance.

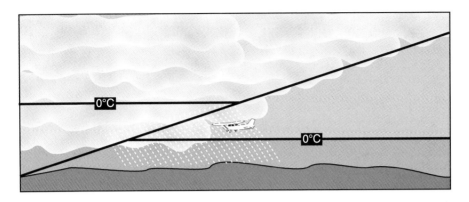

The area just ahead of a warm front in winter is a prime candidate for rain-icing conditions

▶ Piston Engine Icing

The conditions associated with airframe icing can also cause engine icing. Ice may form on the propeller blades of an aircraft (or the rotor blades of a helicopter) and greatly reduce their efficiency. The inevitable mechanical imbalance also results in considerable vibration. Furthermore, flight in freezing precipitation such as sleet or snow can block or restrict the engine intakes. Since flight in known icing conditions is not permitted unless your aircraft has de-icing equipment, avoiding such conditions should rule out the chances of encountering this type of engine icing.

However, by far the most common form of ice-related problem which afflicts a piston engine is *carburettor icing*.

When air enters a carburettor, the combined effect of the fall in pressure within the venturi and the evaporation of the fuel leads to a very large decrease in the temperature; figures of around 25 to 30°C are usually quoted. In these conditions water vapour almost inevitably forms into ice crystals which stick inside the venturi, constricting it and causing a progressive power reduction.

Because of the very marked reduction in temperature inside the venturi, it is not necessary for the air temperature (OAT) to be below 0°C for carburettor icing to occur. In fact, the dominant factor is the moisture content of the air. The more humid the air, the higher the risk of carburettor icing. If you recall that warm air can hold more moisture than cold air, it becomes evident that you are more likely to experience carburettor icing on a warm, humid and cloudy summer day than a cold, dry, clear winter one. The obvious danger signs of carburettor icing conditions are visible moisture such as clouds, fog and precipitation; a moist airflow such as that from over the sea or a large body of water; or localised effects such as wet or water-logged airfields. Carburettor icing is a particular danger at low power settings.

Graphs showing the most likely conditions for the formation of carburettor icing tend to concentrate on the temperature and humidity. At OATs above +30°C even the large temperature reduction in the carburettor should not take the air temperature below freezing. At temperatures below -10°C any moisture is likely to become dry ice crystals which pass through the engine rather than sticking to anything. Attempts have been made by the UK Met. Office to draw up forecast charts showing areas with a high risk of carburettor icing. The problem is that such charts tend to end up as large blocks covering just about the entire country, because carburettor icing can occur over such a wide range of conditions.

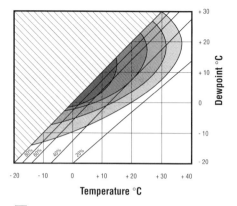

A graph of conditions favourable to carburettor icing

◻ 100% Relative humidity

◼ Serious icing – any power

▨ Moderate icing – cruise power
Serious icing – descent power

▨ Serious icing – descent power

▨ Light icing – cruise or descent power

Although easy enough to deal with, carburettor icing is the chief suspect in a large number of piston-engine failures. All pilots of light aircraft with carburetted piston engines should be particularly knowledgeable about this subject. Carburettor icing and related procedures are covered in more detail in the Flying Training section of the PPL course (Book 1). Further information and advice will also be found in the aircraft's POH/FM, AICs and in other safety information published by the CAA.

▶ Revision

55 Are the majority of light aircraft cleared for flight into known icing conditions?

56 Which of these two situations would you expect to give the worse airframe icing?

A. Summer day, cumulus cloud, OAT -5°C.

B. Winter night, stratus cloud, OAT -20°C.

57 You find your aircraft covered in a thin layer of frost one morning. Assuming that you will be operating well below MTOW and you have more than sufficient runway length available, does this frost have to be removed?

58 Taxying to the runway for take-off, a light snow shower passes over the airfield. Some light snow settles on your aircraft, but you assume that this will blow off during the take-off run. Is this a safe assumption?

59 It is winter, and you are planning a flight with a routing parallel to an approaching warm front. Assuming that you stay clear of cloud, can you guarantee that you will not encounter airframe icing?

60 Which of the two following situation is most likely to produce carburettor icing?

A. OAT +15°C, some early-morning mist patches.

B. OAT -10°C, frost on the ground.

61 Before take-off at a grass airfield, you taxy through and around numerous water patches which are slowly drying out due to the +20°C temperature. Should you take any particular precautions in respect of icing?

Answers at page MET 183

Thunderstorms

▶ Introduction

A well-developed thunderstorm is one of nature's most impressive performances. Seen from a safe place – which from a pilot's point of view is preferably on the ground – it is a truly awesome sight. A thunderstorm contains nearly all the weather hazards an aviator should be most concerned about. Within this maelstrom, containing the energy equivalent of several nuclear bombs, one can find:

■ **Winds** – strong enough to overturn a parked aircraft.
■ **Rain** – heavy enough to flood an area in minutes.
■ **Hail** – capable of denting metal and shattering windscreens.
■ **Lightning** – vastly more powerful than mains electricity.
■ **Turbulence** – severe enough to destroy even a large aircraft in mid-air.
■ **Windshear and downdraughts** – capable of downing an airliner.
■ **Icing** – severe anywhere above the freezing layer (contrary to normal icing theory).
■ And even **tornadoes and waterspouts**.

Not surprisingly, the universal advice from all those who have studied thunderstorms is simple – *keep well away*. And this rule of avoidance is relevant to the pilot of *any* aircraft, whether it is a modern and fully-equipped airliner or a single-seat homebuilt.

▶ **Conditions Required for Thunderstorm Development**

▶ **The Formation and Life-Cycle of Thunderstorms**

▶ **Hazards for Aeroplanes**

▶ **Practical Advice for Thunderstorm Avoidance**

▶ **Revision**

Meteorology

▶ Conditions Required for Thunderstorm Development

Deciding to avoid thunderstorms is certainly the right thing to do, but it helps to know what they look like and how they form.

There are three essential factors for thunderstorm development:

■ An *unstable atmosphere*, with the instability reaching to the upper layers.

■ A supply of *moist air*.

■ Some form of *lifting action* to trigger-off the thunderstorm.

Instability in the atmosphere is the first prerequisite, so a short revision of the principles of stability might be a good idea. Earlier we considered a 'parcel' of air that had been heated so it was warmer than the surrounding air:

Level	'Parcel' Temp.	Environmental Temp.
5000ft	+10°C	+10°C
4000ft	+13°C	+12°C
3000ft	+16°C	+14°C
2000ft	+19°C	+16°C
1000ft	+22°C	+18°C
Surface	+25°C	+20°C

This particular parcel stopped rising at about 5000ft.

Now imagine that the rising air is very moist, so that its dew-point temperature is about +20°C. Condensation will occur at around 2000ft. Once condensation is occurring, the parcel of air is saturated and so it cools at a reduced rate (say 1·5°C per 1000ft – the SALR), whilst the ELR remains constant at about 2°C per 1000ft. Therefore the rising parcel of air remains warmer than the surrounding air as it climbs higher into the atmosphere:

Level	'Parcel' Temp	Environmental Temp	
9000ft	+ 9.5°C	+ 2°C	
8000ft	+ 11°C	+ 4°C	
7000ft	+12.5°C	+ 6°C	
6000ft	+14°C	+ 8°C	
5000ft	+15.5°C	+10°C	
4000ft	+17°C	+12°C	
3000ft	+18.5°C	+14°C	
2000ft	+20°C	+16°C	Condensation occurs
1000ft	+22°C	+18°C	
Surface	+25°C	+20°C	

Thunderstorms

It's quite obvious that this is an unstable situation, and if anything the rising parcel of air is going to accelerate as it climbs because of its increased buoyancy over the surrounding air. Incidentally, this process does not have to start at ground level. Often instability at medium level (say 10,000ft) is the first hint of an atmosphere liable to set off thunderstorms. This may manifest itself in *castellated* (turreted) *altocumulus* clouds. Such clouds can give up to twenty-four hours warning of approaching thunderstorms, although they do not *always* precede thunderstorms.

Altocumulus Castellanus – 'turreted' AC – revealing instability at medium level: one of the conditions favourable for thunderstorm development

Now add to this instability a plentiful supply of moisture. The energy to stoke up a thunderstorm in the first place is supplied by the moisture in the air, by virtue of the process of *condensation*. Warm air can hold more moisture than cold air – so the warmer the air, the more powerful any thunderstorm is likely to be. Indeed, the capacity of air to hold water vapour increases sharply with increased temperature; air at 30°C can hold nearly three times as much water vapour as air at 15°C. Even without the advice of a weather forecaster, you can sometimes feel the humidity in the air that will feed a thunderstorm. On a stiflingly hot day when even the slightest task seems to make you break out in a sweat, the humidity is probably high. If other conditions are favourable (if that is the word), large thunderstorms may be imminent.

Given both instability and high humidity, the final ingredient is a *lifting action*. Lifting at a front can set off thunderstorms. The obvious candidate is a cold front which, classically, tends to form cumulus-type clouds. However, extensive cumulonimbus (the cloud type associated with thunderstorms) can form at warm fronts given the right conditions, albeit rarely. If anything these are more dangerous, because they tend to be embedded in other clouds associated with the front. Likewise, although the lifting action at a cold front might appear to be an obvious trigger of thunderstorms, in summer they are more often set off well ahead of a cold front – sometimes in an organised line called a "squall line". This line of thunderstorms brings all the pyrotechnics and general nastiness you might expect, but when the actual cold front arrives (perhaps many hours later) it is often weak and inactive. In fact, the vast majority of fronts that cross the UK contain no thunderstorms.

Meteorology

Away from fronts, other forms of lifting action can set off a thunderstorm. *Convection* is the obvious one, causing the meteorological violence to begin over 'hot spots' such as cities and industrial areas. Most summer thunderstorms are

A CB being triggered by convection

Convection over a 'hot spot'
– in this case a power station – triggering a thunderstorm

triggered in this way, usually in anticyclonic situations when intense surface heating eventually breaks down the natural stable nature of an anticyclone. An *unstable upper airflow* will also encourage thunderstorms to form, but this is really one for the forecasters to spot. *Orographic lifting*, in which the air is forced to rise by terrain, is also an effective trigger action. This is as good a place as any to make the point that **the combination of mountainous terrain and a thunderstorm is arguably the most lethal which a pilot can encounter.**

A CB being triggered by orographic lifting

Orographic lifting triggering a thunderstorm.

Thunderstorms

Thunderstorms can also be set off by *convergence,* such as that which may occur where a sea breeze moving inland (and carrying warm moist air) meets a general airflow coming the other way.

▶ The Formation and Life-Cycle of Thunderstorms

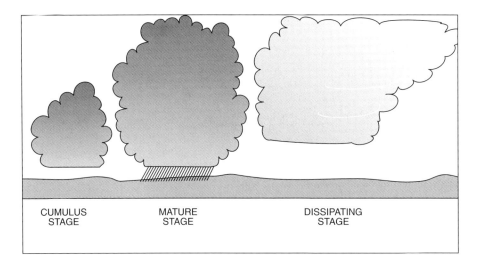

CUMULUS
STAGE

MATURE
STAGE

DISSIPATING
STAGE

The three stages of a thunderstorm's life-cycle

Once lifting has started, the first visible sign of a developing thunderstorm is the formation of cumulus cloud. This is the so-called "cumulus stage". What distinguishes a baby thunderstorm-type cumulonimbus from an ordinary cumulus is vertical growth. It keeps on climbing at an astonishing rate as massive condensation releases energy to keep the cloud rising and the process going. Once a cumulus is taller than it is wide, it can be described as a "towering cumulus", abbreviated in weather reports and forecasts to TCU. Not all towering cumulus develop into a cumulonimbus, but many do. This stage of development commonly sees vertical currents of 3000ft per minute, although currents of up to 6000ft per minute are not unknown. This gives you the first rule of flight around thunderstorms. *Don't* try to out-climb one. Unless the throttle quadrant of the aircraft you are flying has a detent labelled 'reheat', a growing cumulus will simply out-climb the aircraft and you could well

Towering cumulus clouds building up over Germany in the summer

find yourself enveloped. At this stage the cumulus has distinct 'hard' edges and a bright white brilliance; it is not unlike a cauliflower in appearance. Not all cumulus clouds that look like this become thunderstorms, but it is worth giving these "hard-edged cumulus" a wide berth even if thunderstorms are not forecast.

The "mature" stage is marked by precipitation beginning to fall from the cloud. The precipitation is likely to be heavy, and it is at this stage that the vertical currents in

A fast-growing CB with distinctive 'hard' edges and precipitation (the dark area under the cloud). Definitely one to avoid

and around the cumulonimbus are at their most intense. The rain (or snow) can be accompanied by hail and lightning. The cold downdraught from the storm may form a *gust front* pushing out ahead of the storm.

The "dissipating" stage marks the beginning of the end of the storm. As the top of the cloud reaches a marked inversion (probably the tropopause) the ice crystals forming the head of the cloud can spread out laterally in the characteristic anvil shape. The word 'dissipating' is of course relative, the thunderstorm can still be dangerous for some time after the anvil has formed. Although the active stage of a thunderstorm typically lasts less than an hour, the cloud may persist for two or three hours or more.

A well-developed CB with distinctive 'anvil'

This brief description applies to the typical 'single cell' storm. When precipitation begins, it falls through the updraughts within the cloud. The cooling effect damps down the vertical motion and will eventually stop it, thus bringing the storm to an end. However, in certain circumstances – particularly when the winds aloft are much stronger than the winds lower down, causing marked windshear – the whole storm may 'tilt'. This means that the falling precipitation misses the updraughts and the storm can become self-propagating. Sometimes described as "severe local storms" or "supercells", these will be more severe and longer lasting than an 'ordinary' thunderstorm. Although often associated with North America, they are not unknown in western Europe. It should also be borne in mind that the life-cycle described relates to a particular thunderstorm 'cell'. It is quite possible for a cumulonimbus cloud to contain more than one cell, each at a different stage of development. This will naturally prolong the duration of the storm.

Statistically, thunderstorms in Europe are most frequent in the summer months when convection or orographic uplift triggers them. Moving south towards the tropics, thunderstorms become more frequent and more severe. This is chiefly due to the increased temperature and humidity of the air; the higher tropopause in these latitudes also allows the storm greater vertical development.

▶ Hazards for Aeroplanes

As stated at the beginning of this chapter, thunderstorms can contain – in a single package – many of the most destructive weather conditions known to aircrew. From the specific point of view of the aviator, a short summary of these hazards is in order:

Rain and snow Any precipitation is likely to be heavy – a well-documented example is that of the 'Farnborough Storm' of 24 May 1989 when 80mm (over 3in) of rain fell in just one hour. Such an intense downpour of rain may reduce visibility to a couple of kilometres or less, and the high humidity increases the risk of carburettor icing. Snow has an even more dramatic effect on visibility. In very heavy snow, visibility may be as low as 50m.

Hail Precipitation in the form of hail is worthy of a separate mention. Hail forms at first as small ice stones. However, if a falling hailstone meets a strong updraught, it can be carried back up into the storm and so acquire another layer of ice. This may happen several times – if you cut through a hailstone you can count the layers and see how many times it has been 'recycled' in the storm. Hail can cause serious damage to aircraft by battering leading edges, shattering windscreens, destroying aerials and so on. The fall of hail is difficult to predict, and may occur outside the main cloud from the overhanging anvil. Hail can even be thrown out of the side of a thunderstorm – another good reason for giving active CBs a wide berth. Some pilots believe that thunderstorms containing hail have a peculiar greenish tint. There may be some truth in this, although it is a subjective judgement.

Hail damage inflicted on an aircraft by an encounter with an active CB

Turbulence There will inevitably be severe turbulence in and around an active thunderstorm. An aircraft may encounter an updraught of more than 4000ft per minute, followed immediately by a downdraught of a similar magnitude. Such turbulence is in itself strong enough to destroy an aircraft in mid-air, and several instances of this are known. Moreover, particularly in respect of small aircraft, turbulence of much less magnitude is still enough to cause loss of control; the aircraft may then be overstressed in the subsequent

Mammatus cloud, shaped rather like an egg carton, beneath an active CB. Mammatus cloud marks an area of strong downdraughts

recovery manoeuvres. Sometimes you may see 'mamma' clouds (egg-shaped protrusions in the base of the cloud) behind a thunderstorm, which mark an area of downdraughts and turbulence. You should avoid this area, for obvious reasons.

Windshear, Downdraughts and Microbursts Thunderstorms can produce all these phenomena, which are particularly hazardous to aircraft taking-off and landing. Downdraughts often occur under the thunderstorm, where a column of rapidly descending air hits the ground and spreads out. An aircraft flying into such a downdraught may first encounter an increased headwind, followed by the sudden onset of windshear and possibly a tailwind leading to a loss of airspeed. A *microburst* is a very localised and intense downdraught. Whilst downdraughts are usually associated with heavy rain, microbursts are often 'dry'. All in all, the best general advice is **never** to take-off or land into the precipitation from a thunderstorm. Better still, wait until the storm has moved well away. Incidentally, *virga* – rain or snow that evaporates before reaching the ground – may also indicate an area of strong downdraughts.

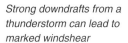

Strong downdrafts from a thunderstorm can lead to marked windshear

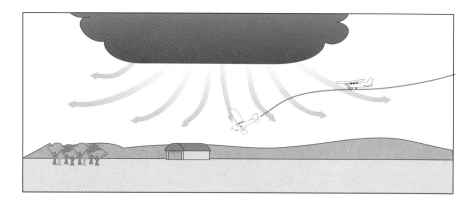

The gust front occurring up to twenty miles ahead of a thunderstorm can cause severe windshear, as the general airflow is replaced by the cold outflow from the storm. The gust front will probably be an area of turbulence which may be marked by 'roll' cloud. However, it does have one redeeming feature. With a sudden change in wind direction and increase in wind speed, and the coldness of the air, the gust front can be a final warning that the arrival of a thunderstorm is imminent. The subject of windshear is covered in more detail later in this chapter.

The cold 'gust front' pushing ahead of a thunderstorm

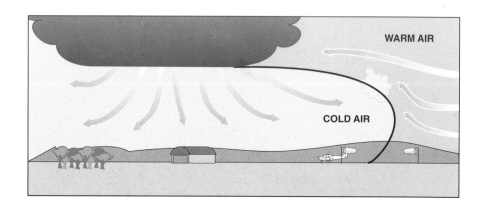

WARM AIR

COLD AIR

Thunderstorms

High winds Even though the general wind flow around a thunderstorm may be light, a thunderstorm itself can produce gale-force winds. The thunderstorm outflow (the cause of the gust front) may have a wind speed of up to 40kts. A downdraught or microburst may give a gust of 60kts or more as it hits the ground.

Tornadoes A tornado is a column of rotating air, bred within a thunderstorm and giving wind speeds of up to 200kts. A tornado may be completely enclosed within the cloud and therefore invisible to the pilot. Alternatively, it can be visible as a 'funnel cloud' underneath the thunderstorm, or even appear as a 'waterspout' where a tornado touches on water. Although tornadoes are often thought of as a North American phenomena, they **do** occur in western Europe – where they are quite capable of taking the roofs off houses, destroying caravans, snapping trees and wreaking other sorts of havoc. Few aircraft are known to have survived an encounter with a tornado.

Lightning Although those on the ground most often regard lightning as the most dangerous aspect of a thunderstorm, to an airborne aircraft it is generally one of the lesser evils. Metal aircraft usually survive a lightning strike (although a few have been destroyed, apparently by the ignition of fuel vapour) with damage to the aircraft often limited to holed or blown-off wing-tips. The damage to the nerves of pilots and passengers is less easy to quantify! After a lightning strike, the radios and other avionics will probably be unusable and the compass will certainly be untrustworthy. Be aware that aircraft constructed from wood, composites or GRP tend not to have such good electrical bonding as their metal counterparts. They and their occupants may consequently not escape a lightning strike so lightly.

Lightning and the general electrical activity in and around a thunderstorm will lead to increased radio 'static' and interference, particularly at the lower frequencies such as those used by the ADF receiver. An ADF needle may well point directly at the nearest active thunderstorm cell, regardless of the location or frequency of the radio beacon to which it is tuned. The VHF portion of the radio spectrum, as used by communication and VOR/ILS radios, is usually less afflicted. It is generally considered that GPS receivers are unaffected by thunderstorm activity, although good airmanship would suggest caution in this respect.

Lightning striking the ground near the Met. office at Bracknell

On the ground, you can establish approximately how far away a storm is by estimating the time interval between a lightning flash and the associated clap of thunder (counting "Thousand and one, thousand and two" etc. works well). Each five-second interval between flash and bang equates to approximately one mile.

Icing Within a thunderstorm, icing is likely to be severe at *any* altitude above the freezing level. Few light aircraft are certified for flight into known icing conditions; be very wary.

▶Practical Advice for Thunderstorm Avoidance

Having read through a lengthy description of the formation, anatomy and hazards of thunderstorms, it might seem tedious to be invited to read another list of no-nos in relation to them. However, the immediate vicinity of a thunderstorm is emphatically *not* the place to be in *any* aeroplane – so anything which is likely to minimise the possibility of an encounter with this particular meteorological phenomenon is worth reiterating. What follows is based on practical experience.

■ The golden rule is *avoidance*. Plan and conduct your flight with this motto in mind.

■ Forecasters will often include thunderstorms in their forecast even if there is only a slight chance of them happening. They may appear as a 'PROB 30' (30% probability) in TAFs, meaning that there is a 30% chance of a thunderstorm at the particular airfield. This is not the same as saying that there is only a 30% chance of thunderstorms in the area. Obtain the most up-to-date area forecasts, as well as current actual reports (METARs) and forecasts for departure, *en route* and destination airfields. Remember that a thunderstorm may go through its entire life-cycle in less than 45 minutes, so a METAR two hours old is of little use to you.

LEFT> An active cold front approaching the UK during a summer 'heatwave'. Note the trough ahead of the cold front

RIGHT> A METFORM 215 forecast for the same day. Note that the thunderstorms are expected to be most frequent in Zone 3 – ahead of the cold front

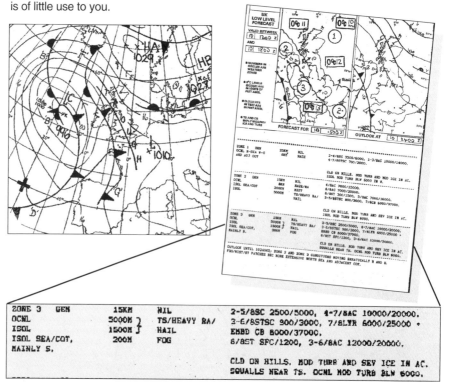

Thunderstorms

```
EGCC 101214Z 101322 15005KT 8000 SCT040 PROB30
TEMPO1422 16015G28KT 3000 TSGR BKN012 BKN035CB=
```

A TAF (forecast) for EGCC (Manchester) for the same day for the period 1300 to 2200 UTC. Visibility generally is forecast to be 8000m, which will allow little time to see and avoid a developed CB at a safe distance.

There is a 30% probability (the lowest allowed in a TAF) that temporarily between 1400 and 2200 UTC the surface wind will gust to 28kts and visibility fall to 3000m in hail from a thunderstorm with a broken cloud base at 1200ft, and broken cumulonimbus with a base of 3500ft.

The significance of the 30% probability is important. A TAF is specific to the immediate vicinity of an airfield, not the general area. Therefore in this TAF the forecaster is not saying that there is only a 30% chance of thunderstorms occurring in general. What he is saying is that there is a 30% chance of a thunderstorm passing overhead Manchester Airport between 1400 and 2200 UTC.

```
EGCC 101520 101520Z 24007KT 1200 TSRA BKN008
BKN015CB 22/20 Q1007=
```

As if to justify the 30% probability, the Manchester METAR at 1520 UTC. The visibility is down to 1200m in heavy rain from a thunderstorm and the cloud base is broken at 800ft with broken cumulonimbus base 1500ft. In fifteen minutes of torrential rain (accompanied by frequent lightning) the runway at Manchester was flooded to a depth of 4mm

■ Bearing in mind what has already been said about air temperature and moisture content, thunderstorms are likely to be particularly severe and violent if the dew point is around +20°C or more.

■ A returning polar maritime air mass gives the greatest risk of thunderstorms, although thunderstorms in tropical continental air tend to be more severe.

■ Be especially wary of thunderstorms forecast to be embedded in other cloud, or those occurring in hazy or misty conditions, because you may not be able to see them coming! Try to fly above any haze layer and stay clear of cloud to improve flight visibility. If you are flying in haze or mist and it suddenly becomes dark, you may have flown into the shadow of a cumulonimbus. Some form of rapid evasive action is advisable.

An organised line of CBs over Essex. There looks to be very little chance of flying VFR through this line – better to land and wait for them to pass

A close view of a line of CBs formed in a trough

■ Thunderstorms triggered by convection tend to be reasonably well separated and hence easier to avoid. Frontal, trough or line-squall thunderstorms are often close together or actually merging; for practical purposes these are impossible to fly around. Frontal, trough and line-squall thunderstorms also tend to be more persistent than the convective variety.

■ Even the smallest thunderstorm cell will be about five miles wide. The biggest can be up to 30 miles across.

■ In flight, use the VOLMET service and ATIS broadcasts to keep updated on the general weather situation. Listen for pilot or ATSU reports of cumulonimbus, or airliners asking to fly headings to avoid "build-ups".

Thunderstorms

LEFT> A CB approaching Ipswich Airport (now closed)

RIGHT> 15 minutes later a close-up view of the same "Cu-nim" – this is the last possible moment to get the aircraft sheltered or tied-down

As the CB crosses the airport it brings sleet and winds gusting to 25kts

■ If you see a developing CB or a full-blown thunderstorm, keep well away from it – at least 10 miles from the edge of the cloud. Avoiding it by 20 miles is even better. *Do not fly over or close to a developing CB.*

■ The more frequent the thunder and lightning from a CB, the more severe the thunderstorm.

■ Remember that many thunderstorm hazards (lightning, hail, windshear etc.) exist outside the associated cloud. Turbulence may be experienced up to 20 miles downwind of the storm.

■ Do not attempt to fly under a thunderstorm, even if there is no precipitation and you can see through to the other side. There may be severe turbulence; precipitation may develop; and updraughts may even 'suck' the aircraft up into the cloud.

■ Do not take-off with a thunderstorm overhead or in the vicinity. If a thunderstorm is over or near your destination airfield, go somewhere else or hold clear until it has moved well away. Do not attempt to land.

■ Report any thunderstorms you see. Pilot reports are invaluable to other pilots and to the Met. service.

■ Remember that thunderstorms are also a hazard to aircraft on the ground. The safest place for your aircraft is inside a hangar.

Finally, remember that much of this advice applies to large growing cumulus clouds which may, or may not, become full-blown thunderstorms.

▶ Revision

62 What are the three principal factors for the formation of thunderstorms?

63 What distinguishes a cumulus cloud growing into a CB from a normal cumulus?

64 In one word, what is the golden rule of flight when thunderstorms are forecast?

65 Approaching your destination airfield, there is a CB over the approach, with light rain, but you can see through the rain and will be able to make a visual approach staying out of cloud. You have ATC clearance to land. Should you continue your approach?

Answers at page MET 183

Flight Over Mountainous Areas and Other Weather Hazards

▶ **Influence of Terrain on Atmospheric Processes**

▶ **Mountain Waves**

▶ **Föhn Effect**

▶ **Strong Winds**

▶ **Turbulence**

▶ **Windshear**

▶ **Revision**

Exercise

*Flight Over
Mountainous
Areas and
Other Weather
Hazards*

▶Influence of Terrain on Atmospheric Processes

Meteorology is often concerned with the large-scale state of the atmosphere, together with influences that gradually alter weather patterns over areas of thousands of square miles. However, weather can also be modified by very localised or even isolated factors. Terrain is one such feature, and mountainous areas are particularly good at altering the weather and causing localised conditions.

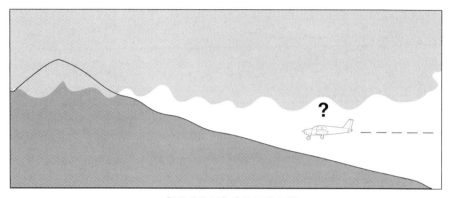

CUMULUS GRANITUS
– the cloud with the hard centre

'Cloud covering hills' as the forecasts say. A bland description of conditions that are potentially deadly to a VFR pilot

Rising ground forces air to rise, even if it had no inclination to do so otherwise. If lifted (and hence cooled) far enough, the air will reach its dew point and cloud will form. The situation in which cloud covers high ground is far more dangerous than many inexperienced pilots realise. It is responsible for a great many weather-related accidents, where pilots fly aircraft into the ground for the simple reason that they never saw it coming.

It is not always appreciated that the process of orographic lifting means that the cloud base around mountains and high ground can actually be lower than elsewhere. Likewise, the cloud base will lower quickly in any precipitation which orographic uplift triggers. Now imagine that you are a VFR pilot trying to stay in visual conditions by flying just below the cloud base; you are employing the technique usually referred to as "scud running". With little forward visibility and possibly lost, you press on irrespective of the fact that you are being forced lower and lower – below the safety altitude – possibly straying in and out of the cloud base. Meantime the ground is rising to meet you. This is the classic set-

The summit of the 'Wrekin' in Shropshire, 1355ft AMSL, hidden by cloud. Continued flight in this direction would be foolhardy

Flight Over Mountainous Areas and Other Weather Hazards

Cloud obscuring the tops of the hills, seen here in the Brecon Beacons of Wales. A pilot attempting to fly VFR up the valley (the floor of which is about 1500ft AMSL) will have a nasty shock as the valley ends in a 2900ft mountain

up for what accident reports refer to as "controlled flight into terrain". If you do not recognise this trap and act to avoid it, you may well be due for an imminent encounter with 'cumulus granitus' – the cloud with a solid centre. For VFR operations, high ground and low cloud simply do not mix. Far too many accident reports and military Boards of Inquiry have come to this painful and expensive conclusion.

As well as inducing cloud formation, mountains and valleys can also influence a general airflow by deflecting its direction, or by funnelling the wind through a narrow valley. Wind through a valley can be veered or backed up to 30° from the general wind direction, and have considerably higher speeds. Possibly the best

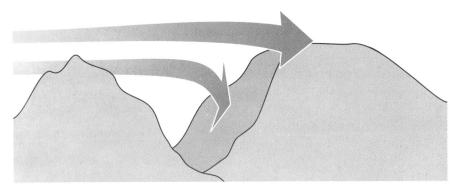

Airflow being 'funnelled' through a valley

known valley wind in Europe is the Mistral, which can easily exceed gale-force as air is funnelled through the Rhône valley. The Tramotane, which affects the French and Spanish Mediterranean coast is another example.

On a more local scale, katabatic winds may flow down a slope or anabatic winds up it. In conditions favourable to radiation fog, the mountain tops often remain clear but fog can linger in the valleys long after it has cleared elsewhere.

Valley winds can exist on a large scale. They are often given local names, such as the Tramotane in southern France

Meteorology

▶ **Mountain Waves**

The wind blowing over a mountain range can also create large-scale disturbances in the atmosphere. These disturbances are usually referred to as *mountain waves* but are also known as "standing waves" or "lee waves", the latter being the usual terminology of glider pilots who make extensive use of them. Mountain waves are so called because the mountains cause the air flow to undulate, like waves in the ocean. Where waves rise up they can give a free ride, and gliders have reached great heights with their assistance. However, where the waves turn down they can force aircraft to descend, even at full power and best climb airspeed. This unfortunate state of affairs can continue right down to ground level.

Downdraughts on the lee (downwind) side of high ground can defeat the best rate-of-climb of a light aircraft

The basic conditions favourable to the formation of an organised mountain-wave pattern are:

■ A wind of 15kts or more at the surface, blowing at right angles to (or within 30° of) the ridge or mountain-range axis, preferably with the wind strength increasing with height but direction remaining little altered.

■ A layer of stable air just above the ridge, bounded by less stable air. This condition is of more interest to meteorologists than pilots, although the latter can look out for an inversion just above the ridge (which is, of course, more likely in an anticyclone).

A mountain wave may not reveal its presence until you notice that the aircraft's rate of climb or descent does not equate to the power setting and attitude. When cloud does form in a mountain wave, it will often be of the so-called "lenticular" variety. This is smooth and elongated (not unlike an almond in appearance) and actually remains

Lenticular clouds forming in mountain waves

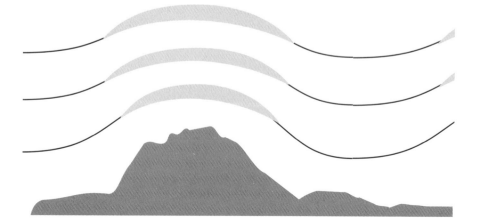

stationary at the 'crest' of the wave, the cloud forming at the leading edge and dissipating at the trailing edge. In favourable conditions there may be lenticular clouds at the crest of each wave, and even several such clouds piled on top of one another.

LEFT> Lenticular cloud formed in a mountain wave over the Lake District. 'Lenticularis' is a type of altostratus cloud

RIGHT> Lenticular clouds forming in wave activity over the Pennines. The two 'streaks' are contrails from high-flying jets

Flight within the wave itself is exceptionally smooth, which may be of little consolation if you are caught in a downdraught. However, severe turbulence will be found in the 'rotor' that can form downwind of the high ground beneath the crest of the waves. The rotor may be given away by a 'roll' cloud, a ragged cumulus that forms in the rotor zone. At first

BOTTOM> The top of this layer of stratus cloud reveals small-scale wave activity

glance a roll cloud may look quite harmless. Look more closely and you will see that it is rolling around its horizontal axis, revealing the violent turbulence in the rotor. Occasionally the roll cloud may form as a long tube just downwind of the ridge. The most extreme turbulence is usually found in the first rotor downwind of the ridge, and the ferocity of it is notorious. Powered-aircraft pilots who have (briefly) encountered a rotor are of the opinion that the turbulence can be strong enough to destroy an aeroplane. It has certainly destroyed gliders which ventured too close to it. All in all, you should appreciate that even in light wind conditions when mountain waves and rotors are not forecast, the area just downwind of and below the level of a ridge or obstruction is a dangerous place to be. It is best avoided as a matter of course.

A turbulent rotor, that may or may not be marked by roll cloud, just downwind of a hill crest

Obviously the first safety feature to have in mind if you are planning to fly over or near high ground in conditions favourable for mountain waves is *height*. The higher you can get above the mountains, the better. The basic rule of thumb is to **double the elevation of the high ground and make that your minimum altitude**. If crossing high ground, think carefully about your route. Although crossing from downwind to upwind holds obvious risks, flight across high ground at an angle, or parallel to and downwind of a ridge, would obviously leave you in wave conditions for much longer. Just as mountains and low cloud don't mix, mountains and strong winds also make a bad combination.

A CB over high ground - to be avoided at all costs

The worst of all worlds is a thunderstorm over high ground. Thunderstorms triggered by orographic uplift seem to have a particular violence all their own, and when the assorted hazards of a thunderstorm are complemented by the dangers of high winds over mountainous terrain, reduced terrain clearance and so on, you have a particularly unpleasant cocktail of flying conditions. No sane pilot would deliberately invite the consequences. Aside from thunderstorms, it is also worth knowing that cloud formed by orographic lifting will almost certainly cause more severe icing than non-orographic cloud.

▶ Föhn Effect

High ground is not all bad news in weather terms. If the air flow is moist enough to give precipitation on the windward side of the mountain range, the downwind side will probably have a higher cloud base, higher temperatures and less precipitation. These are the result of the *Föhn effect*.

Föhn effect is a practical illustration of the difference between saturated and dry adiabatic lapse rates (SALR & DALR). Imagine a moist airflow meeting a mountain range. Forced to rise, the air initially cools at the DALR – say 3°C per 1000ft – until the air reaches its dew point and cloud forms. If it continues to rise, the saturated air will now cool at the SALR, about 1·5°C per 1000ft. As the lifting

Flight Over Mountainous Areas
and Other Weather Hazards

continues, precipitation may fall on the windward side of the mountains. As the air passes the mountain peak, it begins to descend and therefore to warm. Having lost much of its moisture on the windward side of the mountain, the air soon passes its dew point and becomes unsaturated. Thereafter it descends and warms at the DALR121 of 3°C per 1000ft. The net result is that on the leeward (downwind) side of the mountains, conditions tend to be both warmer and dryer than on the windward (upwind) side. Areas on the leeward side of high ground are often said to be in the 'rain shadow' of the mountains. Just such an effect is observed in eastern Scotland, which in the prevailing westerly winds is on the leeward side of the Scottish highlands. It is also seen in the lee of the Welsh hills: the east of the Principality is much drier than the west.

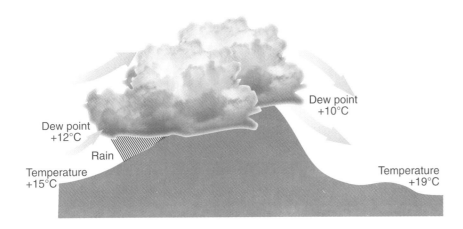

Dew point
+10°C

Dew point
+12°C

Rain

Temperature
+15°C

Temperature
+19°C

'Föhn' effect causing dryer and warmer condition on the leeward side of a range of hills

So high winds and mountain waves permitting, flight on the downwind side of the mountain range can often give better flying conditions (in terms of cloud base and visibility) than flight on the upwind side.

▶ Strong Winds

Widespread strong winds are associated with a steep pressure gradient – the steeper the pressure gradient, the stronger the wind. In theory at any rate, this makes the forecasting of gales and the like reasonably straightforward, and indeed it is comparatively rare for aircraft to be caught out by totally unforecast strong winds.

With the exception of flight over and near high ground, strong winds present the greatest danger to aircraft on and near the ground. The general advice to pilots is not to taxy, let alone take-off or land, if the surface wind speed is more than 50% of the aircraft's stalling speed. It follows that for most light aircraft, surface winds in excess of about 25kts demand extreme caution. Remember that most light aircraft have much lower crosswind limits than this (often 12-15kts) so runway orientation in relation to wind direction is also a consideration.

The strongest gales are usually associated with deep and fast-moving depressions. In this respect, the low to look out for is one which is deepening rapidly. If the pressure at the centre of a low deepens at a rate of more than one mb/hPa per hour for more than twelve hours, the winds are likely to be particularly strong. Of course, at any one place the pressure may fall even more rapidly than this if the low is moving towards that place. However, as far as the pilot is concerned, the point is academic. If the pressure is falling rapidly, the chances are that bad weather and strong winds are on the way. Start checking the forecasts and actuals, and think about getting yourself and your aeroplane under cover. When extreme lows do occur, they usually reach their maximum intensity over the ocean, at least as far as the UK is concerned. But if an extreme low does cross the land while still at its deepest, severe gales are the order of the day.

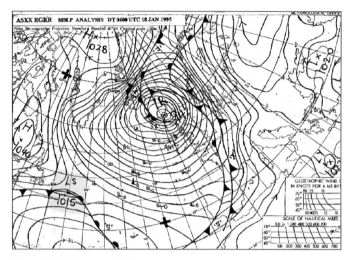

The actual North Atlantic Surface Synoptic chart at 0600 (UTC) on 18 January. At first glance the major weather feature for the next day or two looks to be the depression north of the UK (LR). However, note the small depression (Ls) just beginning to form off Newfoundland

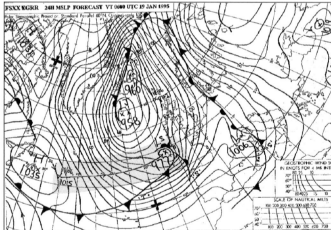

The forecast North Atlantic Surface Synoptic chart, also issued on 18 January, forecasting the situation for 0600 on 19 January. Note how 'Ls' is forecast to deepen by 38mb/hPa in just 24 hours, (from 1015mb to 977mb) and race in towards Europe. There is obviously very bad weather on the way

```
EGKK 181507Z 190018 19007KT 9999 SCT020 BECMG
1013 18017G30KT 6000 –RA BKN012 TEMPO 1215
15022G40KT 4000 RA BKN008=
```

*This 'long range' TAF for London Gatwick (EGKK) was obtained via the METFAX
service during the late afternoon of 18 January. It covers the period from 0000 to
1800 UTC on 19 January. Note the strong winds building up from 1000 to 1300 UTC
(17kts gusting to 30kts) as the depression approaches, and the strongest winds
expected to occur temporarily – e.g. for short periods – between 1200 and 1500 UTC
(22kts gusting to 40kts). If you hadn't taken the hint already, it is obvious from this
forecast that VFR flying on 19 January will not be at all advisable. Aircraft will need to
be hangared or well tied-down in anticipation of the strong winds.*

```
EGKB 191350 191350Z 16045G65KT 3500 +RA SCT003
SCT005 BKN008 05/03 Q0990=
```

*The METAR from Biggin Hill (EGKB) – 15 miles from Gatwick – at 1350 UTC on
19 January. The star feature is obviously the surface wind, 45 knots gusting to 65kts.
This particularly strong wind is in part caused by Biggin Hill's location – it is situated
on a ridge 600ft AMSL. At the same time Gatwick, which is on lower ground, was
reporting a w/v of 15023G40KT. Full marks to the forecaster of the Gatwick 'long
range' TAF for accuracy! Any pilot or aircraft owner caught-out by these strong winds
could really only blame him/herself.*

When high winds are forecast, the best place for an aircraft is in a hangar. If this is
not possible, the aircraft should be tied down in accordance with the instructions in
the POH/FM. Merely parking the aeroplane into wind and putting the control locks
in will *not* guarantee adequate protection during a gale.

A final point about high winds. It is often assumed that the area downwind of high
ground or an obstruction will be sheltered from the worst of the wind. This is not
necessarily true. Downwind of high ground, wave activity can bring fast-moving air
from altitude down to the surface. The result can be that surface winds downwind
of hills are more gusty and less predictable than elsewhere.

▶Turbulence

Turbulence is any disturbance of the air flow causing eddies and variations, and to
some degree it is encountered in the course of most flights. For practical
purposes, turbulence only becomes a problem when it affects the handling of the
aircraft and/or causes discomfort to the aircraft's occupants. Apart from extreme
examples, such as that encountered in and around thunderstorms and rotors,
there are generally two principal causes of low-level turbulence. It may be
convective (thermal) caused by vertical air currents; or frictional (mechanical)
caused by the flow of air over the ground features. As you would expect,
convective turbulence is at its worst in light winds when surface heating is
strongest, and over areas such as cities, towns, or factories generating a lot of
heat. If the air is moist enough, rising convection currents (thermals) may be

topped by cumulus clouds. Avoiding these will steer you clear of some convective turbulence, and also help to avoid gliders that tend to congregate in thermals. Mechanical turbulence is most marked in strong wind conditions involving irregular terrain, particularly downwind of hills or obstructions. In either case, increasing altitude is usually a good way to reach smoother air.

The aircraft's POH/FM will state a recommended turbulence or 'rough air' speed (Va) and you should fly at this airspeed if turbulence warrants it. In turbulence the airspeed may fluctuate, and attempts to 'chase' the speed may make matters worse. It is better to maintain the correct attitude and power setting for the desired performance and accept minor and temporary fluctuations in airspeed.

Turbulence can be a problem during the final approach to land or just after take-off. In both cases the aircraft is subject to the low-level effects of airflow around buildings, trees or local terrain. A slight (5-10kts) increase in approach speed is a worthwhile precaution if approaching to land in turbulent conditions, assuming runway length is not critical. Pilots will often expect turbulence and windshear at their local airfield when the wind blows from a certain direction. Life being what it is, a strong crosswind usually produces the most pronounced turbulence and windshear.

Low-level 'mechanical' turbulence just downwind of buildings and obstructions

▶Windshear

Windshear is the change of wind velocity over a distance. Of course, some element of windshear is always present in the atmosphere. However, it becomes a significant hazard to aircraft when the change in wind velocity is very marked over a small height band.

The real danger of a strong windshear is the dramatic and rapid effect it can have on an aircraft's airspeed. Imagine the wind velocity changing so that an aircraft transitions from experiencing a 20kts headwind component to a 10kts tailwind component in a 100ft height band. As it descends with an airspeed of 90kts, experiencing a 20kts headwind, its groundspeed is 70kts. As the aircraft passes through the windshear zone, the headwind of 20kts becomes a tailwind of 10kts. Due to inertia, the aircraft retains its original groundspeed for a short time, so the airspeed drops suddenly to 60kts. This naturally leads to a marked loss of lift and can even cause a stall. At low level, recovery may be difficult or impossible. The heavier the aircraft and the greater its momentum, the more vulnerable it is to windshear.

Flight Over Mountainous Areas
and Other Weather Hazards

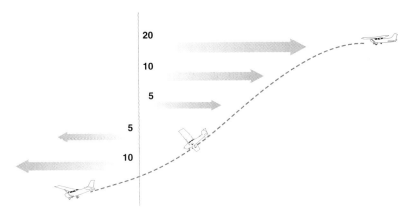

A marked windshear, where a 20kts headwind component turns into a 10kts tailwind component through a narrow height band, causing a potential loss of airspeed of 30kts. The heavier the aircraft, the more vulnerable it is to windshear

The advent of windshear in association with thunderstorms and widespread strong winds has already been discussed. Strong windshear can sometimes also develop when there is a marked temperature inversion near the surface. Such an inversion might exist on a clear night when air in contact with the surface is cooled, whereas the air higher in the atmosphere is warmer because it is not in contact with the surface. The result is to separate the friction layer from the general airflow, possibly leading to very strong winds at low altitude but almost calm conditions at the surface. Clear nights are a particular time to be wary of such low-level windshear. Even if surface winds are calm or nearly so, you should check the upper wind forecasts for the possibility of much stronger winds aloft. If they exist, turbulence and windshear may be marked when passing through the transition zone – which can be as low as a few hundred feet above the surface.

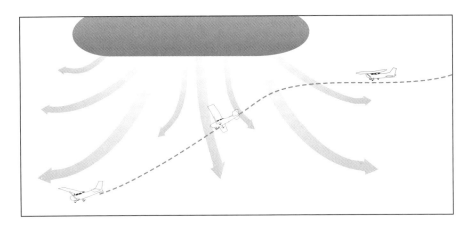

Windshear is often encountered under a thunderstorm

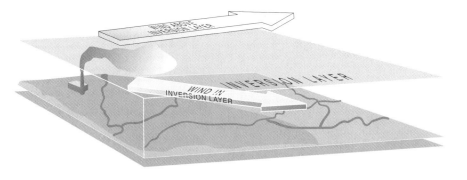

A marked temperature inversion can lead to a strong windshear when passing through the inversion level

In summary, low-level windshear is most often associated with thunderstorms, marked temperature inversions and strong winds – especially where the terrain (such as a valley or ridge on the approach path) encourages its formation. Where windshear is suspected or known to exist, the golden rule is **avoidance:** go somewhere else! If this is not possible, approaching at a slightly higher than normal airspeed will give some element of protection. Be alert to the symptoms of windshear, and be prepared to make an early decision to go-around if you encounter it.

▶Revision

66 What is the rule-of-thumb minimum altitude for crossing a ridge with an elevation of 2000ft, when mountain waves have been forecast?

67 You see a ragged cumulus cloud, apparently stationary and rolling round on itself, just downwind of the top of high ground in strong-wind conditions. Should you fly close to this cloud?

68 Prevailing moist westerly winds blow across a line of hills with a north/south axis. On which side of the high ground would you expect to find a 'rain shadow'?

69 In the cruise you encounter moderate turbulence. At what airspeed should you fly?

70 An airfield is reporting "negative windshear of 20 knots at 200ft on the approach to 24". What does this mean and what is the most likely source for the information?

71 You have been flying in the local area. When you departed, the QNH was 1013. When you return two hours later the QNH is 1009. Should this mean anything to you?

Answers at page MET 183

Climatology

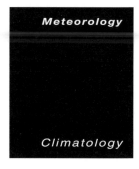

Meteorology

Climatology

▶ Seasonal Atmospheric Circulation Over Europe

▶ Local Seasonal Weather and Winds

Meteorology

▶ Seasonal Atmospheric Circulation Over Europe

Although Europe covers a very wide range of geography and conditions, from the Mediterranean in the south to the arctic circle in the north, from the western seaboard to eastern continental plains, it is possible to make some generalisations about the climate and how it effects the area as a whole. Of course, these generalisations have to be viewed as such; Europe is a part of the world where the weather can, and does, change dramatically from day to day. Snowfall in the summer and spring-like days in the midst of winter are the stuff that weather lore is made of and even if neither lasts for more than a day it can be enough to change your flying plans.

In the winter the predominate climate feature is the low-pressure depressions that form in the North Atlantic and 'deepen' as they sweep in from the west, typically bringing with them cloud and precipitation and occasionally gales. These travelling depressions follow a path largely dictated by the upper wind patterns and in particular the 'jetstream', which tends to lie further to the south in the winter than it does in the summer. The lower the pressure in a depression, the faster it moves and the quicker it deepens (i.e. the faster the pressure falls within the depression), the more active it will be and the worse the weather associated with it. On the continent the Alps can form a barrier to the movement of fronts, with cloud and precipitation persisting along and beyond the western side of their north/south axis. Between the passage of one depression and the arrival of the next there may be a short period of settled weather in a ridge of high pressure. During the winter there is typically a large area of high pressure settled over continental eastern Europe. At times this anticyclone may move over western Europe, 'blocking' the depressions from the Atlantic. This anticyclone will typically bring clear skies initially, but also plummeting temperatures in bitterly cold easterly and north-easterly winds. After a few days low cloud is likely to form within this area and days or even weeks of gloomy weather under unbroken low cloud, possibly with drizzle, can follow.

In the summer the European climate is more likely to be dominated by an area of high pressure pushing up from the mid-Atlantic which is often known as the 'Azores high'. The travelling depressions that do still form in the North Atlantic tend to be less active and track further to the north than in the winter. If high pressure does extend up from the Azores area it generally brings fine and settled weather and, at the height of summer, it can the harbinger of the 'heatwave' so beloved of newspaper headlines. Although visibility is usually good at first, haze and smoke can build up as an anticyclone becomes established. Visibility, particularly under a marked inversion, may well worsen until the high pressure breaks down or moves away.

▶ Local Seasonal Weather and Winds

Localised weather and winds are almost impossible to summarise, they are the sort of phenomena that can take years of experience of a particular location to recognise and be able to predict. This is why sometimes an experienced pilot who knows the local area well can make a more accurate assessment of local weather trends than a remotely-based forecaster. As always, the best advice in this respect is to always err on the side of caution: if locally-based pilots, ATSU personnel or forecasters think that you are pushing your luck with the local weather conditions, you should heed their warnings!

Some well-known localised weather and wind phenomena have already been discussed, such as the 'Mistral' valley wind that brings cold and turbulent northerly winds down the Rhone valley, or the 'Bora' katabatic wind in the Adriatic. Less well-known localised conditions occur throughout Europe, although some general trends are worth knowing. In northern Europe, west and south-facing coasts are particularly vulnerable to low cloud and precipitation sweeping in from the Atlantic on the prevailing westerly winds. South-westerly winds bringing tropical maritime air often mean fog or low cloud, especially in the spring and early summer, which can form almost without warning as the moist airflow hits the landmass. Conversely, land areas to the east of mountains and high ground tend to have drier and brighter conditions, and in general there is less average precipitation as you move eastwards across Europe.

The Mediterranean has almost a 'mini-climate' of its own, often quite different to conditions relatively close by. The winter weather can be surprisingly wet and unsettled, especially along the northerly shores. The summer weather is far more settled, dry and hot. However, it is not all good news as when thunderstorms do occur, they can be of a violence which is impressive even by thunderstorm standards. It is also notable how regularly a dry spell in the northern Mediterranean breaks down, if only temporarily, in around mid-August.

The moral in all this – and no apologies for restating it – is to collect as much information as you can about both what the weather is actually doing and what it is forecast to do, and don't assume that the weather climate and trends you are used to at your home airfield are applicable once you travel further afield. The freedom of flight, and freedom to travel distances in a short space of time, brings with it responsibility as well as enjoyment. So, if one day a local pilot warns you of a 'fools gap' in the weather, or a French forecaster gets all excited in describing to you 'Orages' (thunderstorms): listen up! Their local knowledge could be about to save your neck.

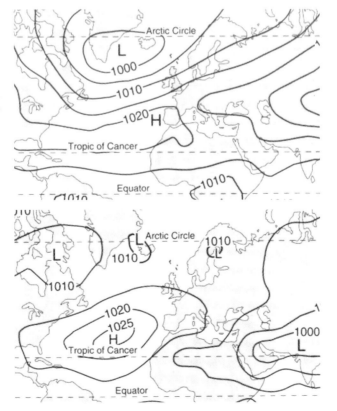

The average pressure distribution over Europe during winter

The average pressure distribution over Europe during summer

Aviation Weather Reports and Forecasts

Meteorology

*Aviation
Weather
Reports
and
Forecasts*

▶ Introduction

In coming to the end of the meteorological section of the PPL course, we come back to the original aim. You are not expected to become a do-it-yourself weather forecaster. Instead, your knowledge of the principles of meteorology, and their applicability to aviation, should enable you to make the best of the information available. It should also help you recognise and avoid potentially hazardous weather situations both before and during flight.

To get the best from any meteorological service, you need to be clear about what you are asking for and receiving.

▶ Introduction

▶ Definitions

▶ Preparation of Aviation Forecasts

▶ Specific Forecast and Actual Formats

▶ Special Forecasts

▶ Obtaining Met. Information Before Flight – Flight Planning

▶ Aviation Weather Products

▶ Obtaining Met. Information In-Flight

▶ A Final Word About Aviation and Weather

▶ Revision

Exercise

Aviation
Weather
Reports
and
Forecasts

Meteorology

▶ Definitions

Met. information is available to pilots in two basic forms:

■ A *weather report*. This is a factual statement of the actual weather conditions at a stated place at a stated time. When a weather report relates to an airfield, and comes from a qualified observer, it is usually in the form of a METAR (often called an "actual").

■ A *weather forecast*. This is a prediction of the expected weather situation during a set period. Various levels of forecast are available: charts covering large sections of the globe (such as synoptic charts); mixed chart/text forecasts for more localised areas (such as AIRMET, METFORM or Significant Weather forecasts); or forecasts for individual airfields (TAFs).

At the risk of over-emphasising the point, you should always be absolutely clear as to whether the piece of weather information you have in your hand is a *report* (i.e. the actual weather) or a *forecast* (i.e. a prediction).

The ever-popular 'Pilot's Weather Forecasting Stone'; this one is at Southend Airport. The legend reads:

Stone is wet ....Rain

Stone is dry ....Not raining

Shadow on ground ....
.............................Sunny

White on top ......Snowing

Can't see stone .....Foggy

Swinging stone ......Windy

Stone jumping up & down
......................Earthquake

Stone Gone........Tornado

Any meteorologist will tell you that this stone is no good for forecasting, but it does give a reasonably accurate actual report!

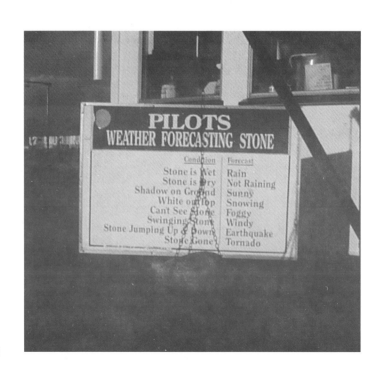

For a forecast to be usable, you must know the place or area it covers and the period to which it refers. For an actual (e.g. a METAR) to be of any value, you *must* know the time and place of the observation. Sometimes, in R/T or telephone conversation, the person on the other end may not be very precise in giving the parameters of a METAR – but you should *never* accept one without knowing "when and where". Otherwise you might assume that you are receiving the most up-to-date weather information, whereas it may in fact be a couple of hours old and no longer reflecting reality. Likewise, when copying weather from an ATIS or VOLMET broadcast, don't forget to note the time of the observation. This is an important point. A meteorologist will *never* accept a weather report without knowing the exact time and place of the observation, and all pilots should follow this example.

▶ Preparation of Aviation Forecasts

It is difficult to forecast anything without having a well-defined situation on which to base some assumptions. As far as weather forecasting is concerned, the job begins with a world-wide network of about 12,000 meteorological reporting stations, each of which measures various aspects of the current weather at its location. Data from these stations is exchanged between National Met. Centres around the world, most of which have very fast and powerful computers. These use the reported data to prepare charts of the actual synoptic situation, together with the forecast synoptic situation at set time-steps into the future.

Charts of the general synoptic situation show highs, lows, fronts and some other information. Based on these, a senior forecaster prepares an *area forecast*. This gives the general conditions likely to affect a specific area over a set time period, and also draws attention to any special features.

The most specific forecast is that for an individual airfield. Taking the general synoptic situation and the area forecast as guidance, and starting with an actual report for the airfield in question, a forecast (usually in the form of a TAF) is produced. It will take into account the forecaster's knowledge of local conditions such as topography which will affect the weather situation. Under the present system in the UK, a single forecaster normally prepares a forecast for all the specified airfields within a particular area. So for example, the forecaster who prepares the London Heathrow TAF will also prepare the London Gatwick TAF.

Even when a forecast has been issued, it will be monitored to see if the actual conditions reflect the forecast. Amended forecasts will be issued if actual conditions are significantly different from those forecast.

▶ Specific Forecast and Actual Formats

SYNOPTIC CHARTS

A synoptic chart will give the general features (pressure distribution, fronts etc.) of the weather situation over a large area, either as an actual observation or as a forecast. The most commonly used chart in Europe is that covering Europe and the North Atlantic, (European weather is most often coming from the North Atlantic). Several daily papers carry synoptic charts, and they are also used by some television weather forecasters – for instance, those on the BBC in the UK. The Met.

Meteorology

Office issue surface synoptic charts for aviation use, usually in the form of a pair of charts showing the actual surface synoptic situation at a specific time and the forecast synoptic situation for 24 hours ahead.

A synoptic chart may be for the surface or for a defined level in the atmosphere, although it is normally the surface chart that is available to pilots. Synoptic charts of high altitudes are of great interest to forecasters, because surface weather is often affected by high-level features not apparent on surface charts.

ASXX EGRR

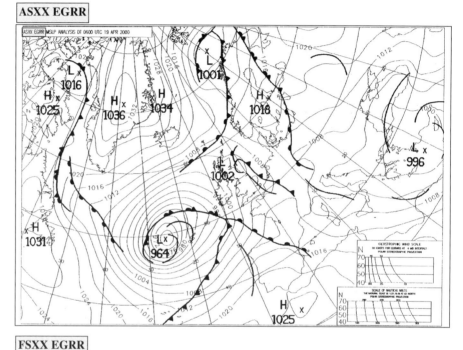

*A synoptic chart of the **actual** North Atlantic sea-level situation at 0600 UTC on the 19th April 2000*

FSXX EGRR

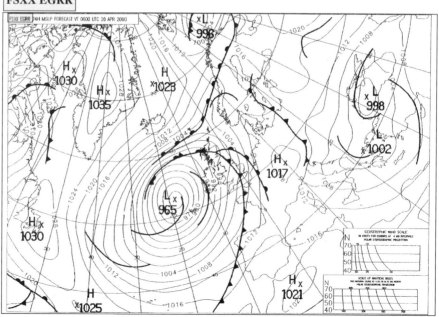

*A synoptic chart of the **forecast** North Atlantic sea-level situation at 0600 UTC on the 20th April 2000*

Although the principal symbols used on synoptic charts have already been covered, it is worth reviewing the main symbols:

ASXX or **FSXX**	Actual or Forecast
MSLP	Mean Sea Level Pressure
▼▼	Cold Front
●●	Warm Front
▲●	Occluded Front
ᴛʀᴏᴜɢʜ	Trough
H **x** 1036	Centre of a High with sea level pressure (+ individual identifying letter)
L **x** 999	Centre of a Low with sea level pressure (+ individual identifying letter)
x——➤x	Forecast movement of centre of high/low pressure
x– – – ➤x	Most recent movement of centre of high/low pressure

SIGNIFICANT WEATHER CHARTS

Meteorological charts for high-altitude flight are based on *pressure levels* rather than *altitudes*. Common pressure levels (and related approximate altitude) are shown below:

850mb	5000ft
700mb	10,000ft
500mb	18,000ft
300mb	30,000ft

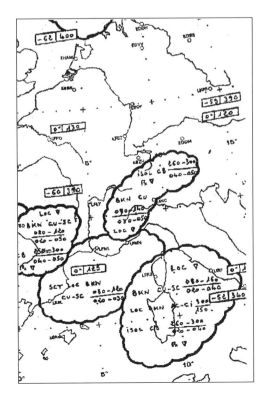

A section from a SIGWX (significant weather) chart

A Significant Weather (SIGWX) chart may cover just one level, or more usually it will be valid between certain levels. It is generally in the form of a forecast. The following symbols and abbreviations are commonly used:

Pressure Systems, Fronts and Convergence Zones

▲▲	Cold front at surface
●●	Warm front at surface
▲●▲	Occluded front at surface
●▲●	Quasi-stationary front at surface
▲▼▲▼	Convergence line
▥	Intertropical convergence zone
Lx 999	Centre of low pressure area (with indication of pressure at centre)
H ○ 1020	Centre of high pressure area (with indication of pressure at centre)
10	Speed of movement
→	Direction of movement
SLW	Slow
STNR	Stationary

Zone Boundaries

∿∿∿	Boudary of area of significant weasther
— — —	Boundary of area of Clear Air Turbulence (CAT)

Significant Weather Symbols

/// /// /// ///	Rain *
,	Drizzle *
★	Snow *
▽	Shower *
▲	Hail *
⏝	Light Icing *
=	Widespread Mist *
≡	Widespread Fog *
⩲	Freezing Fog *
⏜	Widespread Smoke *

∿	Freezing Rain
	Moderate Icing
	Severe Icing
	Freezing Precipitation
∧	Moderate Turbulence
▲	Severe Turbulence
⌇	Severe Sand or Dust Haze
⌇	Widespread Sandstorm or Duststorm
∞	Widespread Haze
CAT	Clear Air Turbulence
	Severe Line Squall
	Thunderstorm
	Marked Mountain Waves
⟨	Tropical Cyclone

* these symbols are not used at high altitude

Temperature and Tropopause

H 400	Tropopause 'High' centre and altitude (FL 400)
340 L	Tropopause 'Low' centre and altitude (FL 340)
0°C | 130	Freezing level (in thousands of feet as a Flight Level)
-62 | 400	Temperature and Flight Level of the tropopause

Cloud Quantities

SKC	Sky Clear
FEW	Few (1 to 2 oktas)
SCT	Scattered (3 to 4 oktas)
BKN	Broken (5 to 7 oktas)
OVC	Overcast (8 oktas)
LYR	Layers
For Cumulonimbus only:	
ISOL	Isolated
OCNL	(occasional) Well Separated
FRQ	(frequent) Hardly or not at all separated
EMBD	Embedded in other cloud

Localisation

COT	Coast
LAN	Land
LOC	Locally
MAR	At Sea (maritime)
MON	Mountains
SFC	Surface
VAL	Valleys

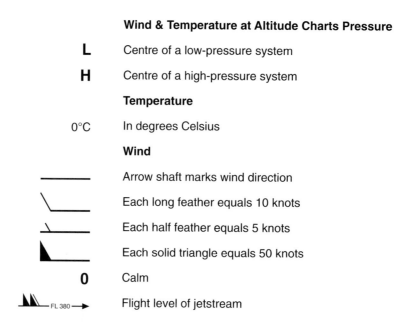

Wind & Temperature at Altitude Charts Pressure

L	Centre of a low-pressure system
H	Centre of a high-pressure system

Temperature

0°C   In degrees Celsius

Wind

Arrow shaft marks wind direction

Each long feather equals 10 knots

Each half feather equals 5 knots

Each solid triangle equals 50 knots

0   Calm

FL 380   Flight level of jetstream

SATELLITE AND RADAR PICTURES

The advent of satellite imagery has revolutionised weather forecasting. Satellite images have been a feature of TV forecasting for several years, and today most – if not all – forecasting offices have direct access to regular satellite pictures. Keen amateurs have also been able to obtain satellite pictures using a specialised radio linked to a home computer, and many communications-based meteorological services such as fax and on-line systems can offer satellite pictures as well. Satellite imagery is now widely available via the Internet. However, access to this wonderful technology is of limited use unless you are reasonably capable of interpreting a satellite picture. What follows is intended as a general guide.

Satellite imagery come in two basic varieties – *visible image* and *infrared* (IR).

A visible image is to all intents and purposes a black-and-white photograph taken from the satellite. Thick cloud tends to show as white, and coastlines and snow-covered ground are also clearly visible where cloud cover permits. Unfortunately, ground covered with snow may be confused with thick cloud, and thin cloud (such as cirrus) may be almost transparent and hence difficult to see. Additionally, a satellite obviously cannot produce a visible image at night. You can often see a black area on a satellite picture taken near sunrise or sunset. Such an area is in darkness.

Aviation Weather Reports and Forecasts

An infrared image is based on temperature differences. As such, it is not affected by the absence of daylight. Cold areas generally show up as white on an IR picture, with darker shades of grey for warmer areas and black for those which are warmest. This type of imagery is useful but has certain limitations. High cloud, being coldest, tends to show as a bright white area. So even a very thin layer of cirrus might totally obscure anything below it. Lower down, very low cloud or fog may have nearly the same temperature as the surface, making the latter very difficult to distinguish.

LEFT> Infrared (IR) satellite image of a deep depression centred north west of the UK. The highest (and therefore coldest) cloud shows brightest

RIGHT> A visible image taken at the same moment. The lower cloud across northern France and the UK is easier to see in this image

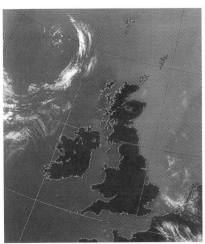 

LEFT> In this Infrared image, the high (and cold) cirrus cloud over northern France can be seen clearly

RIGHT> In the visible image taken at the same time, fog and low cloud in the North Sea and coming ashore along the north-east coast is clearly visible

Satellite images are subjected to a certain amount of processing before they reach the pilot or forecaster. Latitude and longitude grid lines are added, as are coastlines, and the image may be adjusted for the amount of daylight depending on the time of day. Even so, satellite images are generally considered to be of little use on their own, and should only be used in conjunction with other synoptic or Significant Weather information.

Unless your flying machine is decidedly sophisticated, or you visit the cockpit of an airliner, you are unlikely to come across weather radar in an aircraft and its use is outside the scope of this book. However Met Offices and an increasing number of Flight Briefing Units have access to information derived from special radar systems across the country. These are particularly good at detecting areas and intensity of rainfall. They will also have access to a system which pinpoints active thunderstorms, based on their electrical activity. This obviously assists in forecasting but can also provide useful real-time information to a pilot on a day when thunderstorms are forecast. On the other hand, a modern ATC radar is specifically designed to filter out weather 'clutter' from its screen. Do not be surprised if in most circumstances ATC is unable to offer much help from its radar as far as weather avoidance is concerned.

Area Forecasts

Specific area forecasts are arguably one of the most useful developments for general aviation pilots. In the UK, such forecasts are available either as text only (such as AIRMET), or mixed text and chart sheets (such as the METFORM 214/215). The advent of widespread fax, recorded telephone and on-line services has made these products widely available, and there is no reason for not being able to obtain up-to-date weather information even before you leave home or the office – let alone once you arrive at an airfield.

An AIRMET text-only forecast

Aviation Weather Reports and Forecasts

In the UK the METFORM 214/215 is a particularly useful forecast. It is used as the basis on which local forecasters prepare TAFs, and it gives a good overall view of the weather situation – including information on items such as cloud tops, temperatures, icing, turbulence and winds aloft which is not found in TAFs.

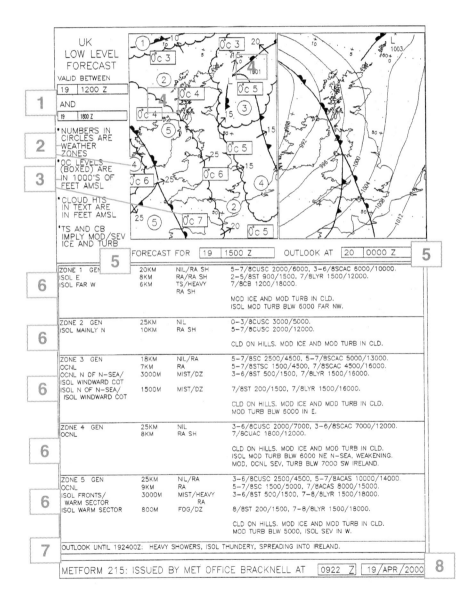

The main features of the METFORM 215 chart:

1. The date of the forecast and the validity times in UTC (in this case, from 1200Z to 1800Z on the 19th).

2. Circled numbers on the chart are weather zones, which are enclosed by 'scalloped' lines. The numbers relate to the zones in the text below.

3. Boxed numbers are the freezing level in thousands of feet AMSL

4. Direction and speed of the surface movement of fronts or significant features. Speed is given in knots. 'Slow' implies a speed of less than 5kts.

5. Specific date and time of the two forecast charts (in UTC).

6. Forecast text, relating to the zones shown in the left-hand chart.

7. Outlook text, relating to the right-hand chart. The outlook chart shows only isobars and major features such as fronts.

8. The time (UTC) and date at which the METFORM was issued.

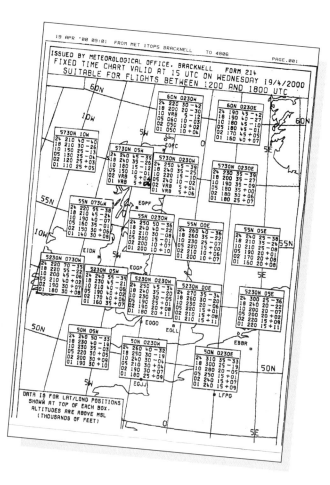

*A METFORM 214.
chart of forecast winds
and temperatures at
altitude*

UK METFORM charts use many of the abbreviations and symbols already listed, including the standard abbreviations for units of visibility, cloud types, cloud amounts and precipitation. Additionally the following abbreviations (which may also be found in Airmet text) are used:

ADJ	Adjacent	**MTW**	Mountain Wave
BEC	Becoming	**NIL**	None
BLW	Below	**SEV**	Severe
CLD	Cloud	**SFC**	Surface
EMBD	Embedded	**TURB**	Turbulence
FRQ	Frequent	**VSP**	Vertical speed
GEN	Generally	**WDSPR**	Widespread
MOD	Moderate	**WKN**	Weakening

Aviation Weather Reports and Forecasts

TAFs & METARs

A METAR is an actual observation of the weather at an airfield, compiled by a trained met. observer. METARs are usually observed at half-hour intervals in the UK (20 minutes and 50 minutes past the hour), although many military and certain civil airfields take one METAR an hour. METARs are usually only available during opening hours of the airfield.

A TAF is a fixed-period forecast of expected weather for a specific airfield. TAFs usually cover a nine-hour period, and are issued every three hours. They are usually available up to an hour in advance of their start time.

9-hour TAF validity times (UTC) in the UK:

Period   01-10, 04-13, 07-16, 10-19, 13-22, 16-01, 19-04, 22-07

Major international airports may also have 18-hour TAFs, which are issued every six hours and available well in advance:

18-hour TAF validity times (UTC) in the UK:

Period 00-18, 06-00, 12-06, 18-12

You will remember the basic premise of a forecast; that to produce one, the forecaster must first know the actual weather conditions and be able to monitor how these actual conditions are changing. For this reason, you may not be able to obtain a TAF for an airfield until some time after it has opened. The forecaster will want to see at least one actual and possibly more before preparing a forecast. Likewise, once an airfield has closed there are unlikely to be any further observations (e.g. METARs) issued. Thus the actual conditions could change markedly from the forecast but no amendment would be issued.

A further subtlety of the forecasting process is the location of the airfield. If an airfield is surrounded by many other weather reporting stations, the forecaster has a lot of information available with which to prepare and monitor forecasts. If an airfield is in a more isolated or remote location, the forecaster may only have one or two other stations in the area to receive information from. Thus there is a greater chance of unexpected weather developments at such airfields. Airfields on the most westerly coasts of the UK and mainland Europe may be the first stations reporting 'incoming' weather from the North Atlantic for hundreds or even thousands of miles. In such areas it pays to treat all weather forecasts with greater caution than normal.

If you obtain a TAF for an airfield, you should also obtain a METAR. Remember that the 'F' in TAF stands for "forecast" and that forecast is a prediction of the *average* conditions expected during the forecast period. It does **not** necessarily represent the existing state of affairs. Even with its great experience and resources, the UK Met. Office manages a (commendable) accuracy rate on TAFs of about 85%. *This means that forecasts are significantly wrong 15% of the time*. By contrast, a METAR is a factual report of actual weather conditions at a specific moment. You should consider TAFs and METARs as inseparable, and never use one without the other.

Meteorology

A knowledge of the codes used in METARs and TAFs is indispensable. Whilst other met. services and methods of presentation (particularly information for general aviation) vary considerably across Europe, the coding of TAFs and METARs is pretty well standardised. Throughout this book, examples of weather reports and forecasts have been used to give examples of the presentation of met. information. The best way to learn to read TAFs and METARs is by practice. The listing of codes and conventions below will give you the detail, but simply reading through the following decode will be a tedious and inefficient way of learning. Obtain a TAF and METAR whenever you can – if possible, each time you fly – and try to read it without referring to a decode. Then check for any mistakes or abbreviations unknown to you. Very soon you should be proficient at reading and understanding TAFs and METARs.

A typical METAR report:

METAR EGCC 301250 301250Z 20015KT 170V250 9999 – RA SCT018CB SCT070 BKN100 16/13 Q1004 RETS NOSIG=

1	EGCC 301250 301250Z	*The location, the date (30th) and time (1250 UTC) at which the observation was made, which is repeated in the second date/time group.*
2	20015KT 170V250	*Surface wind*
3	9999	*Visibility*
4	–RA	*Weather*
5	SCT018CB SCT070 BKN100	*Cloud*
6	16/13	*Temperature and Dew point*
7	Q1004	*QNH*
8	RETS	*Recent weather*
9	NOSIG	*Trend indicator (major airfields only)*
10	=	*Indicates the end of the report*

Aviation Weather Reports and Forecasts

A typical TAF forecast:

```
TAF EGHI    211207Z 211322 17015G28KT 9000 –RA
BKN010 TEMPO 1922 3000 RA BKN005=
```

1	EGHI 211207Z 211322	The location, the date (21st) and time (1207 UTC) at which the forecast was issued and the date (21st) and validity period (1300 to 2200 UTC) of the forecast.
2	17015G28KT	Surface wind.
3	9000	Minimum Visibility.
4	–RA	Significant Weather.
5	BKN010	Cloud.
6	TEMPO 1922 3000 RA BKN005	Significant changes.
7	=	Indicates the end of the forecast.

MET. codes used in METARs (Aviation Routine Weather Reports) and TAFs (Terminal Aerodrome Forecasts):

PREFIX
– METAR To indicate an actual weather report.
– TAF To indicate an aerodrome forcast.

LOCATION INDICATOR

The airfield's ICAO four-letter code.

DATE/TIME

– METAR The date and time of the observation is given as a six figure group, the first two numbers being the date and the four following numbers being the time UTC (Z or Zulu). This number group is repeated.

– TAF The first date and time group represents the date and time at which the forecast was issued, and is in the same format as for a METAR. The second six-figure group gives the date of the start of the forecast period (first two numbers) and the beginning and end of the forecast period in whole hours UTC.

SURFACE WIND

Wind direction is given in degrees true (three digits) rounded to the nearest 10°, followed by wind speed (two digits). Wind speed may be given in knots (KT), kilometres per hour (KMH) or metres per second (MPS).

G	Wind Gust
00000	Wind Calm
VRB	Variable Wind Direction
V	Variation in wind direction of 180° or more provided wind speed is 4 knots or more. If wind speed is 3 knots or less wind direction is reported as 'VRB'

Meteorology

VISIBILITY

Minimum horizontal visibility is given in metres or kilometres.

9999   Visibility 10km or more

0000   Visibility less than 50m

(METAR only). Where there is a marked difference in visibility depending on direction, more than one visibility may be reported, followed by the direction in which that visibility exists e.g. S is south, NE is north-east etc.

RUNWAY VISUAL RANGE – METAR Only

R   RVR, followed by runway designator and the touchdown-zone visibility in metres. If visibility is greater than the maximum RVR that can be assessed, or more than 1500m, it will be preceded by a P. The letter M implies an RVR below the minimum that can be assessed.

At non-UK aerodromes an additional designator may be added after the RVR indicating how it has changed: U - Up; D - Down; N - No change. If there is a significant variation in RVR the letter V will be used in between the minimum and maximum RVRs.

WEATHER

Weather Phenomena

Description	Precipitation	Visibility Factor	Other
MI Shallow	DZ Drizzle	BR Mist	PO Well developed dust/sand whirls
BC Patches	RA Rain	FG Fog PR FG Partial Fog (Fog banks)	
DR Drifting	SN Snow	FU Smoke	SQ Squalls
BL Blowing	SG Snow Grains	VA Volcanic Ash	FC Funnel Cloud(s) (tornado or water-spout)
SH Shower(s)	IC Diamond Dust	DU Widespread Dust	SS Sandstorm
TS Thunderstorm VCTS Thunderstorm in the vicinity	PE Ice-Pellets	SA Sand	DS Dust-storm
FZ Super-Cooled	GR Hail GS Small Hail	HZ Haze	

Intensity or Proximity of precipitation

-    Light   e.g. -SH, a light shower

     Moderate (no qualifier)   e.g. SH, a moderate shower

+   Heavy   e.g. +SH, a heavy shower

Aviation Weather Reports and Forecasts

VC In the vicinity (within 8km of the airfield boundary)

NSW (TAF only) - No Significant Weather

CLOUD

Cloud amount may be described as:

FEW (Few)   1-2 oktas

SCT (Scattered)   3-4 oktas

BKN (Broken)   5-7 oktas

OVC (Overcast)   8 oktas

Note: 1 okta is 1/8 cloud cover

Cloud base is given in hundreds of feet above aerodrome level (AAL).

Cloud type is not identified, except:

CB   Cumulonimbus

TCU   Towering Cumulus

SKC   Sky Clear

NSC   No Significant Cloud (TAF only)

If the sky is obscured, the letters VV are inserted followed by the vertical visibility in hundreds of feet.

VV///   Sky obscured, vertical visibility cannot be assessed.

CAVOK

Ceiling And Visibility OK – pronounced "Kav-o-kay". Used to replace the visibility, RVR, weather and cloud groups if the following conditions apply:

a   Visibility: 10km or more.

b   Cloud: no cloud below 5000ft or below highest Minimum Sector Altitude, whichever is greater, and no CB at any height.

c   No significant weather phenomen at, or in the vicinity of, the aerodrome.

AIR TEMPERATURE/DEW POINT - METAR Only

These are given in whole degrees Celsius

M   Minus

QNH - METAR Only

Rounded down to the next whole millibar and given as a four-figure group in millibars/hectopascals, preceded by Q. If the value is less than 1000, the first number is 0.

SUPPLEMENTARY INFORMATION

METARs:

/////   information not available

RE   Recent weather

WS   Windshear

DENEB Fog dispersal operations in progress.

TREND A METAR from certain major airfields may include a trend indicator – a forecast change in conditions during the two hours after the observation time.

BECMG*   Becoming.

TEMPO* Temporary; may be followed by time (in hours and minutes UTC) preceded by FM (from), TL (until) or AT (at).

NOSIG No significant changes forecast during the trend period.

* BECMG is an expected permanent change in conditions, occuring sometime during the period indicated.

* TEMPO is a temporary fluctuation in conditions expected to last less than one hour at a time and not occur in total during more than half the period indicated.

Aviation Weather Reports and Forecasts

TAFs:

The terms FM, TEMPO and BECMG are also used in TAFs.

Probability:

PROB 30   30% probability

PROB 40   40% probability

The abbreviations TEMPO and BECMG are followed by a four figure time group, which marks the beginning and end of the period (in hours UTC) during which the change may ocur.

The abreviation FM is followed by a four figure time group (hours and minutes UTC) when the change is expected to begin.

'=' is used to mark the end of the METAR or TAF

AMENDMENTS

AMD is inserted after TAF and before the ICAO four-letter code. AMD is used when the original TAF is withdrawn and replaced for some reason.

RETARD

(R) used when the TAF is received late. Most often seen on METFAX

TAF ACCURACY

Once a TAF has been issued, it will be monitored against the actual weather conditions until it is superseded by the next TAF. A significant change in conditions outside the forecast parameters may trigger an amended TAF. The exact criteria for issuing an amended TAF are of more interest to forecasters than to aviators. However, from a VFR pilot's point of view it is worth noting that there can be a significant deterioration below the TAF parameters before an amendment **must** be issued. For example, imagine that an airfield is forecast to be CAVOK – meaning in essence visibility of 10km or more, no precipitation, and no cloud below 5000ft. During the forecast period the actual situation could deteriorate to 10km visibility in light rain and a *cloud ceiling* (i.e. more than 4 oktas of cloud) at 1600ft, or less than 4 oktas of cloud below 1500ft, without the forecast having to be amended. That said, in reality the forecast probably would be amended – weather forecasters do say that they try hard **not** to kill-off their clients!

Once again the moral is obvious – *always* use a TAF (or any other forecast) with an *actual* report of weather conditions.

▶Special Forecasts

If you are planning a flight for which normal weather briefing information is not available for some reason, you can request a *special forecast* from a forecast office. You must give plenty of notice to receive a special forecast, with an absolute minimum of two hours for flights of up to 500nm and four hours for longer flights.

Meteorological offices can often also provide specialised forecasts by arrangement for certain activities such as gliding, ballooning etc.

▶Obtaining Met. Information Before Flight – Flight Planning

You should plan to obtain met. information very early in the flight planning process. The reason is obvious: the weather can have a profound effect on your planned flight and influence routings, timings etc. In looking at weather, why not follow the lead of a forecaster? Start by looking at the general synoptic situation; then check area forecasts or Significant Weather charts; finally, narrow down your checking to the forecasts and actuals (where available) for the departure, destination and alternate airfields.

General synoptic situation There is no need to seek out a specifically aviation-oriented product for this information. Several newspapers print synoptic charts, and the BBC weather forecasts on the day(s) before your planned flight – with their synoptic charts and satellite sequences – will give you a general feel for the

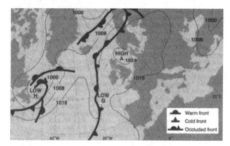

A synoptic chart as published daily in the 'Times' newspaper

weather and how it is developing. It can be useful to use a VCR to record a TV weather forecast with its satellite and radar picture sequences so that you can play it back later. By keeping a "weather eye" open in this way you can often save yourself much wasted time in the actual flight planning process, because you will already have a good idea of the weather situation.

Area forecasts or Significant Weather charts These may well be available at the departure airfield but can also be obtained in other ways, which are listed in the following pages. As already mentioned, the METFORM 214/215 is particularly useful in the UK and the AIRMET text is handy if you have to obtain information by telephone. Check the validity times of the forecast, and when the next one will be available.

Airfield forecasts and actuals You should now be in a position to relate the general weather conditions and predicted changes to the weather at specific airfields. Again, check the times of the forecasts and actuals. In some weather situations (e.g. forecast thunderstorms, fog, or an approaching front) you should update the TAFs and METARs immediately before departure. One difficulty here is that a smaller airfield may have neither a TAF nor a METAR available, and a private strip certainly will not. In these cases, obtaining TAFs and METARs for nearby airfields is a wise move – but you will still want some idea of what is happening at the destination itself. Most smaller airfields are PPR (Prior Permission Required) so the phone call to obtain the permission is also a good opportunity to check the weather. However, treat any such information with a degree of caution. You may be talking to an experienced controller or pilot, who can give an accurate assessment of conditions based on years of local knowledge. Alternatively, the person on the other end of the telephone could be someone who just happened to be passing it at the time, and who may well be completely ignorant of the finer points of aviation meteorology. Ask some pertinent questions about surface wind, visibility, weather and cloud cover and you should soon get an idea of how reliable the information is. There is a celebrated story of a pilot who phoned a smaller airfield and was told "The weather's fine, no wind, the sun is shining". On arrival over the airfield he discovered that the sun was indeed shining – through a layer of thick fog…

▶ Aviation Weather Products

Obtaining weather information used to be a relatively simple matter. Most larger airfields had their own Met. Office and a resident forecaster, and a weather briefing could as often as not be obtained on a face-to-face basis. Even at a smaller airfield one could usually telephone the local "met. man" and discuss the weather situation and the proposed flight in detail.

Needless to say, these times are now long gone and the emphasis today is on what the aviation authorities like to call "self-briefing". Personal contact with a real live forecaster is virtually unheard-of in civilian flying, and most present-day general aviation pilots never see the inside of a Met. Office. This is a shame, because there is a danger that those who provide weather information and those who use it may become increasingly isolated from each other. On the other hand, advances in communications and information technology have greatly improved the accessibility and range of meteorological information available to pilots, especially those who fly from smaller airfields.

Weather information can be obtained in a number of ways:

Flight Briefing Units

Most airfields with a number of resident aircraft will have some form of *Flight Briefing Unit* (FBU). In weather terms, these usually have available an area forecast (most often in the form of an AIRMET or METFORM), any aerodrome warnings and possibly TAFs and METARs also. Even where there is no FBU, a resident flying school may well have a flight briefing board with similar information, and an ATSU should likewise be able to offer some material. Take care, however, not to assume that any information you find is automatically valid. Check *all* dates and times carefully, remembering that this should be the first thing you do whenever you receive *any* weather information. If the information is not being regularly updated, it must be treated with some caution. An area forecast, valid for the early part of the day and probably prepared at around 0330 in the morning, will be of limited use to you if you are about to go night-flying at 1900 the same day. An out-of-date forecast or actual should be disregarded altogether.

By Phone

If you can get to a telephone, you can get up-to-date weather information – it's as simple as that. In the UK there are two principal services. The AIRMET service provides several area forecasts, updated throughout the day, and the AIRMET text is also available by fax. In the UK you can also obtain METARs and TAFs for a wide range of airfields on an automated service. Be aware, however, that both these services are on premium-rated lines (up to 49p a minute at the time of writing). If you are going to use public telephones a lot, a credit card, a telephone charge card or a bag full of coins is a must! A mobile telephone makes life easier, of course, but remember *never* to use it in an aircraft. You should also be circumspect about using it in the vicinity of fuel bowsers, fuel pumps, petrol tanks and the like.

It is also possible to contact a forecast office direct, on normal non-premium lines; the telephone numbers are widely available in flight guides and so on. Forecast offices should be able to give you some TAFs and METARs if you are unable to obtain them elsewhere. At most forecast offices you can also ask to speak directly to a forecaster. Under the rules by which this service operates, the forecaster should first be satisfied that you have already obtained some weather information and that you wish to obtain clarification of the forecast. If you get through to a forecaster and then ask "What's the weather like?", you are unlikely to get very far. On the other hand, a more professional approach, along the lines of "I am planning a VFR flight from Biggin Hill to Valley, departing at 1100Z. I see in the METFORM and TAFs a probability of thunderstorms, but none yet reported in the METARs. Are they developing anywhere along the route?" is more likely to elicit a helpful response. Most forecasters are fairly accommodating, provided that you have already done the basic homework.

Details of the Met. Office 'METFAX' service as published in the UK VFR Flight Guide

By Fax

If you have a fax machine with a polling facility, you can obtain a large range of weather information. A report in 1995 suggested that something like 85% of private pilots in the UK have access to the METFAX service. AIRMET forecasts, TAFs and METARs, synoptic charts, outlook forecasts and even satellite images are all available by fax, together with probably the most useful general forecast – METFORM 214/215.

Aviation Weather Reports and Forecasts

On-line

This area of weather information dissemination is advancing more rapidly than any other, and arguably it is on-line services of one sort or another which will provide the majority of weather information in future. Several are now available, including the Met Office's MIST service; additionally satellite images, TAFs and METARs are widely available via the Internet.

The availability of weather information – whether on-line, by phone or by fax – is improving all the time, and it pays to keep up with new developments. These are usually well publicised in the aviation press and AICs.

TAF forecasts and METAR actual reports for Newcastle (EGNT) obtained via the internet

▶ Obtaining Met. Information In-Flight

Having decided that the weather is suitable for you to commence your flight, once in the aircraft you can start to assess the actual weather against that forecast and reported.

The best instrument for checking weather in-flight is the Mk 1 eyeball, preferably connected to an enquiring mind. No weather forecast or report is more accurate than the view from the cockpit. Simple observation should tell you whether the weather, cloud and visibility are as advertised. Furthermore, a comparison of heading against track, and actual groundspeed against that planned, will tell you whether the winds are close to those forecast. The altimeter setting will alert you to a pressure significantly different from what was anticipated, and the OAT gauge will tell you whether the air temperature at your altitude is close to that forecast. A wind much stronger than expected, a lower pressure than predicted, or a higher temperature than forecast could be a sign that the weather is not shaping as per the forecast.

Added to basic observation, a pilot in a radio-equipped aircraft can also make use of a number of broadcasts to check METARs at larger airfields.

Meteorology

The VOLMET service is a recorded broadcast giving the METARs for around ten airfields. VOLMET broadcasts are available throughout Europe; those in the UK are:

London VOLMET Main	London VOLMET South	London VOLMET North	Scottish VOLMET
135.375	128.60	126.60	125.725
Amsterdam	Birmingham	Blackpool	Aberdeen
Brussels	Bournemouth	East Midlands	Belfast (Aldergrove)
Dublin	Bristol	Leeds/Bradford	Edinburgh
Glasgow	Cardiff	Liverpool	Glasgow
London-Gatwick	Jersey	London-Gatwick	Inverness
London-Heathrow	Luton	Manchester	London-Heathrow
London-Stansted	Norwich	Newcastle	Prestwick
Manchester	Southampton	Isle of Man	Stornoway
Paris (CDG)	Southend	Teesside	Sumburgh

As might be expected from a VHF radio service, reception of VOLMET depends very much on your location and altitude – you will not receive Scottish VOLMET at 2000ft over the home counties, for example. Conversely, in some locations you can receive VOLMET even on the ground. This is useful, particularly if you have a small portable VHF receiver available. In a VOLMET broadcast METARs are given in alphabetical order, as shown above. VOLMET reports may include a 'TREND' which is any expected change in conditions during the two-hour period following the time of the METAR.

For completeness, it should be added that there is an RAF VOLMET broadcast available on HF (4715 and 11,193kHz) which covers UK and a few European military airfields. This could be useful in certain circumstances, and one or other frequency should always be audible anywhere in the UK. However, very few civilian light aircraft have an HF capability, and this service may consequently only be available to those who possess the appropriate receiver and a suitable antenna at home.

Many individual airfields also transmit arrival and departure information (the current METAR together with any other relevant information) in the form of an

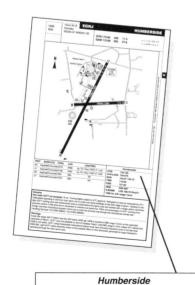

The ATIS frequency for Humberside, published here in the UK VFR Flight Guide

Humberside	
ATIS	124.125
APP/LARS	124.675

Aviation Weather Reports and Forecasts

ATIS – Automatic Terminal Information Service – broadcast. The ATIS broadcast may be on a dedicated frequency or on that of a nearby VOR navigational beacon. ATIS broadcasts are useful for *en route* or alternate airfields, and the ATIS should be checked where it exists at your destination or departure airfield.

If your destination is not on VOLMET or does not have ATIS, weather information can probably be obtained from the ATSU when you are within radio range. Exceptionally, if you need weather information whilst still out of radio range of an airfield, the ATSU at a local airfield or even the FIS controller for the FIR you are within *may* be able to help. However, you should use your discretion before making such a request. Most ATSUs or FIS controllers would be swamped if everybody started calling them for weather information all the time. Nevertheless, controllers will always try to help, especially if the weather is worsening.

SIGMET

A SIGMET message is a warning of reported or forecast hazardous in-flight conditions. A SIGMET message can be passed to aircraft in flight, and will also appear on meteorological broadcasts and messages. The following hazards (shown below with their respective abbreviations) can trigger a SIGMET:

OBSC TS	**OBSC**ured (by smoke, haze or darkness) **T**hunder**S**torms or Cumulonimbus
EMBD TS	**EMB**edde**D** (in other cloud) **T**hunder**S**torms or Cumulonimbus clouds
FRQ TS	**FR**e**Q**uent - an area of **T**hunder**S**torms with little or no separation between storms
LSQ TS	(**L**ine **SQ**uall) A line of **T**hunder**S**torms with little or no separation between storms
HVYGR	**H**ea**VY** hail (**GR**) accompanying the above categories
TC	**T**ropical **C**yclone (with name)
SEV TURB	**SEV**ere **TURB**ulence - other than that in CBs or a tropical cyclone
SEV ICE	**SEV**ere **IC**ing - other than that in CBs or a tropical cyclone
FZRA	**F**ree**Z**ing **RA**in causing severe icing conditions
SEV MTW	marked **M**oun**T**ain **W**aves
HVY DS	widespread **D**ust**S**torm
HVY SS	widespread **S**and**S**torm
VA	**V**olcanic **A**sh (volcano name added)

There are also additional SIGMETs for SST (supersonic) flights. However, these are unlikely to concern most of us!

A SIGMET can refer to an actual or forecast hazard :

OBS   **OBS**erved

FCST   Fore**C**a**ST**

The movement of the hazard can also be included:

MOV   **MOV**ing (usually with direction and speed of movement)

STNR   **ST**atio**N**a**R**y

and a change of intensity:

INTSF   **INT**en**S**i**F**ying

WKN   **W**ea**K**e**N**ing

NC   **N**o **C**hange

▶ A Final Word about Aviation and Weather

Isolated showers such as this one should be easy for a VFR pilot to see and avoid

Aviation Weather Reports and Forecasts

All the meteorological knowledge and aviation wisdom in the world is of no use to you if you are not prepared to apply it. Every year, a large percentage of serious accidents to general-aviation aircraft are blamed on weather factors. Therefore, if at some stage a real doubt creeps into your mind about the chances of safely completing a flight, *right there and then is a good time to start reviewing your alternatives whilst they are still open to you.* Sometimes simply deciding not to commence a flight because the weather conditions are poor is the best decision a pilot can make. If in-flight conditions become markedly worse than forecast – and you are stretching the limits of your licence, abilities and the definition of VFR to carry on – *now* is the time to turn back or divert. All experienced VFR pilots occasionally have to cancel or abort a flight. Deciding to do so is a sign of good airmanship and sound judgement. The age-old pilot diseases of 'press-on-itis' and 'get-home-itis' have been responsible for the wrecking of more perfectly serviceable aircraft (and their occupants) than anyone can count. There is always a degree of pressure to get to your home airfield, or to complete the planned flight against the odds. Be aware that this pressure can very easily cloud your judgement and decision-making ability.

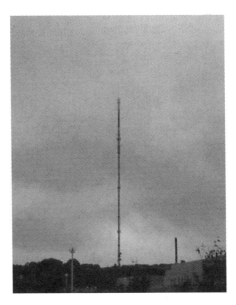

This TV transmitter mast near Cardiff rises to 1212ft AMSL (787ft AGL) and the top of the mast is just covered by stratocumulus. A pilot 'scud-running' just under the cloud base could have a nasty shock here!

Many airfields seem to have a self-appointed 'hero' pilot, who always completes his flight and always gets home no matter what the weather. Human nature is such that a more experienced pilot than you – or one of these local heroes – can exert strong peer pressure, whether consciously or not. The result can be that you either commence a flight against your better judgement, or you continue into conditions you are not happy with. However, as pilot in command *you must always judge for yourself the safest course of action.* It is worth remembering that many 'ace-of-the-base' types gain their ultimate fame by featuring in an accident report.

Unforecast low stratus covering the higher ground of the Scottish island of Islay. The cloud base as seen here is about 400ft; the ground hidden behind this cloud rises to over 1600ft. Clearly further VFR flight in this direction is impossible

More often than not, weather-related accidents are shown to be totally avoidable. Flying is not cheap, and there seems little point in paying good money to frighten yourself and your passengers. If you use your meteorological knowledge to make good decisions and build sound pilot judgement, you can relax and **enjoy** your flying.

▶Revision

72 Based on the METFORM 215 chart below, is the following 18-hourTAF most likely to be for airfield A, B or C?

1305582 131206 16007KT 7000 SKC BECMG 1720 3000 BR BKN005 PROB 30 TEMPO 1206 0400 FG BKN001=

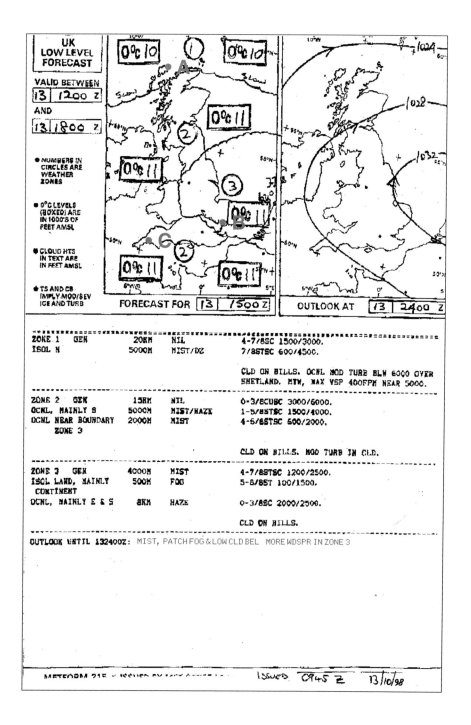

73 Based on the METFORM 215 chart below, is the following METAR most likely to be for airfield A, B or C?

071020 071020Z 18008KT 3500 RADZ SCT003 BKN007 OVC010 5/4 Q1032=

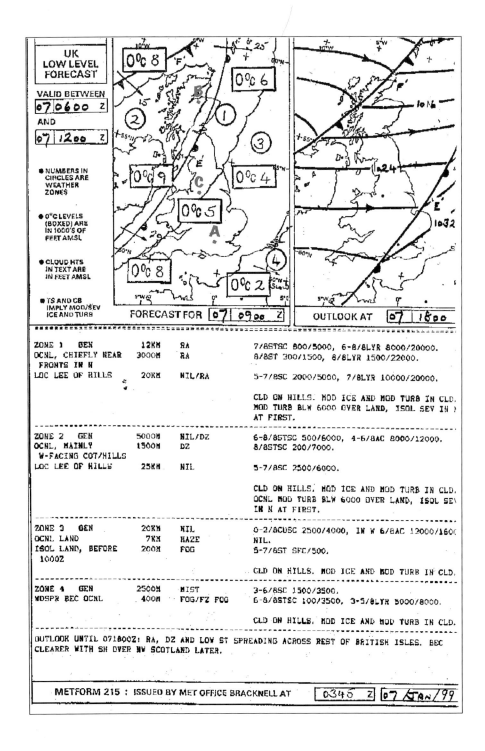

74 Based on the METFORM 214 chart below, estimate the 5000ft w/v and temperature at the marked point.

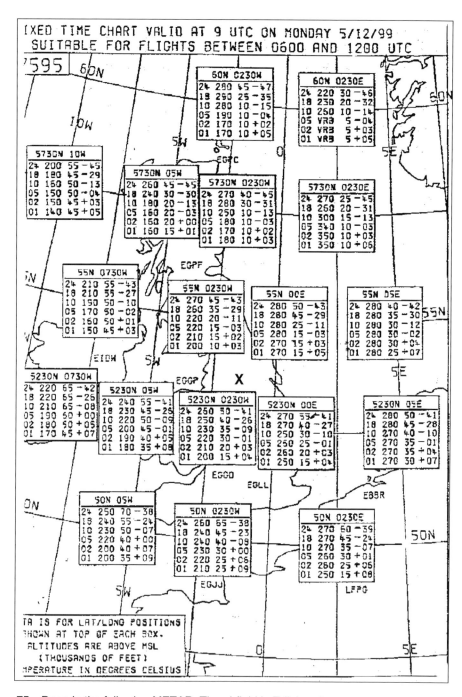

75 Decode the following METAR. The airfield is Edinburgh.

EGPH 050620 050620Z 26005KT 6000N VCFG MIFG SCT003 04/03 Q1032
TEMPO 0400 BCFG=

76 Decode the following TAF. The airfield is Bristol.

EGGD 131719Z 140624 06015KT 3000 BR BKN004 PROB30 TEMPO 0608
TSRA BECMG 0709 6000 HZ NSC TEMPO 1124 4500 RA PROB40 TEMPO
1224 2000 +TSRA BKN050CB BECMG 1316 14005KT BECMG 1922 3500
BR SCT003=

77 Decode the following SIGMET message.

Marseille FIR: FRQ TS OBS AXIS ST FLOUR – VALENCE-GRENOBLE. TOP
FL 350. STNR=

78 Describe the weather and cloud forecast in the shaded area on the SIGWX
chart below (and as seen in the photograph below).

*A view of the area marked
(over the Maritime Alps
south of Lyon, France)*

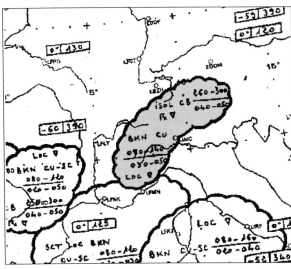

79 You are planning a two-hour local flight from Newcastle airport (in North East England), departing at 1500 local time. Based on the AIRMET forecast below, and before you can obtain the latest AIRMET forecast, what is the most significant weather problem you can expect?

```
AIRMET AREA FORECAST, NORTHERN REGION.
VALID JUL 11/0500Z TO 1300Z.

MET-SITUATION: A VERY MOIST, WARM, HUMID AND UNSTABLE AIRMASS, WILL
               AFFECT MOST PARTS, BUT A WEAK RIDGE OF HIGH PRESSURE
               WILL JUST ABOUT HANG ON TO NE ENGLAND.

               STRONG WIND WARNING: SFC WINDS, MAY GUST TO 30KT, IN
               TS.

WINDS:
  1000FT: 100/20KT PS20.
  3000FT: 120/28KT PS17.
  6000FT: 120/20KT PS12.
FREEZING LEVEL: 11000FT.

   ZONE 1: NE ENGLAND.

          15KM WITH 0-3/8STSC 1000FT/2000, AND 0-4/8AC
          7000FT/11000.
          OCNL 3000M IN MIST, WITH 5-8/8STSC 500FT/2000, MOSTLY
          CLEARING BY 1000Z.
          ISOL BEFORE 0800Z, 500M IN FOG, WITH 8/8ST SFC/800.
     WRNG: CLD WILL COVER HILLS.
          MOD TURB AND MOD ICE IN CLD.
          LOC MOD TURB BLW 6000FT.

   ZONE 2: REST OF REGION.

          12KM WITH 2-5/8AC 8000FT/15000.
          WDSPR 6KM IN HAZE, WITH 3/8AC 8000FT/15000.
          OCNL 6KM IN RA, WITH 6/8AC 7000FT/20000.
          ISOL 3000M IN HEAVY RA, OR TS WITH HAIL, WITH 3-5/8STSC
          800FT/3000, AND 7/8CB 5000FT/37000.
          OCNL 3000M IN MIST, WITH 4-7/8ST 500FT/1000, CLEARING BY
          0500Z.
          ISOL 200M IN FOG, WITH 8/8ST SFC/1000, CLEARING BY
          0800Z.
     WRNG: CLD WILL COVER HILLS AT TIMES.
          MOD TURB, AND MOD ICE IN CLD, BUT SEV ICE AND SEV TURB
          NEAR CB.
          LOC SEV TURB BLW 6000FT IN AND NEAR TS.

OUTLOOK: UNTIL JUL 11/1900Z:

          THUNDERSTORMS WILL BEC MORE FRQ AND SPREAD INTO NE
          ENGLAND.
```

80 It is 6 July and you are planning a VFR flight from A to B (marked on the chart). The planned departure time is 0900Z, with an en-route time of two hours. You find the following METFORM 215 on the briefing board. Given a planned cruising altitude of 2000ft, and minimum acceptable in-flight visibility of 6km, do you expect to be able to complete the flight safely and legally? You are a PPL without instrument qualifications.

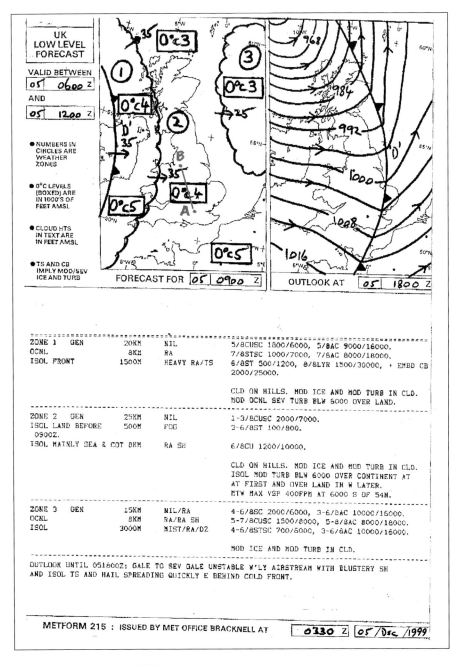

Appendix 1
Aerodrome Warnings

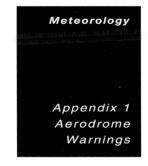

In addition to the normal forecasts and reports available to pilots, several specific warnings can be passed to an airfield and its operators if bad weather is expected or imminent. The exact criteria for triggering these warnings can be agreed between the airfield and the forecast office, but the following are common.

Gale warning: normally issued if the surface wind speed is expected to exceed a mean of 33kts, or gusts are expected to exceed 42kts. However, airfields with many resident light aircraft often receive a gale or strong-wind warning for lesser wind speeds.

Squalls, hail or thunderstorm warning.

Snow warning: the warning will include the expected duration and accumulation of the snowfall.

Frost warning.

Fog warning: normally issued if visibility is expected to fall below 600m.

Rising dust or sand, dust or sand-storm warning.

Appendix 2
Pilot Reports

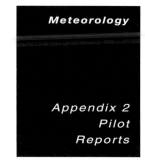
Pilots are legally and morally obliged to report any hazardous conditions they see or encounter. Obvious examples are thunderstorms, turbulence and icing. Reports of turbulence outside cumuliform clouds (often called Clear Air Turbulence, even if it occurs inside cloud); icing; and windshear should be made in the following standardised formats to be of the most use to other pilots.

Turbulence

Turbulence reports are considered to be particularly important to aircraft flying above FL150. The 'aircraft reaction' is based around the effect on a transport sized aircraft.

The rate of occurrence of turbulence can be reported as:

Occasional – less than 1/3 of the time;

Intermittent – 1/3-2/3 of the time;

Continuous – more than 2/3 of the time.

The intensity of turbulence is reported based on the criteria below:

Intensity	Transport sized aircraft reaction	Response inside aircraft
LIGHT	Slight changes in altitude & attitude. IAS fluctuates 5-15kts. Reported as 'light turbulence'.	Slight strain felt on seat belts/harnesses, unsecured objects move slightly.
	Slight, rapid and rhythmic bumpiness, but no real change in altitude or attitude. Reported as 'light chop'.	
MODERATE	Greater changes in altitude or attitude, but aircraft remains in control at all times. IAS fluctuates 15-25kts. Reported as 'moderate turbulence'.	Definite strain felt against seat belts/harnesses. Unsecured objects dislodged.
	Rapid bumps or jolts causing no appreciable change in altitude or attitude. IAS may fluctuate slightly. Reported as 'moderate chop'.	
SEVERE	Large and abrupt changes in altitude and attitude. Aircraft may momentarily be out of control. IAS fluctuates by more than 25kts. Reported as 'severe turbulence'.	Occupants are forced violently against seat belts/harnesses. Unsecured objects are thrown about.

If reporting turbulence, don't forget the met. report essentials of 'when and where', not forgetting altitude/flight level.

Meteorology

Icing

The following definitions are those used for *pilots reporting* the intensity of icing; they are **not** the same as the criteria used to forecast icing. Neither are they the same as the icing definitions in the aircraft's flight manual or de-icing equipment handbook:

Intensity	Ice accumulation
TRACE	Icing is just perceptible, and not hazardous even if de-icing or anti-icing equipment is not used unless encountered for more than one hour.
LIGHT	Rate of accumulation might be a problem if conditions persist for more than one hour. Occasional use of de-icing or anti-icing equipment removes ice.
MODERATE	Even short times in these conditions are potentially hazardous. Use of de-icing or anti-icing equipment, or a diversion, is necessary.
SEVERE	Use of de-icing or anti-icing equipment fails to reduce or control icing accumulation. Immediate diversion necessary.

Again, when reporting icing remember to include the 'when and where'.

Windshear

Windshear is most commonly reported when it occurs after departure or during an approach to land. In reporting windshear pilots should give the effect on the aircraft (usually in terms of airspeed change) and the position (including altitude), for example:k knots".

"Abrupt windshear at 200ft on approach to 24, airspeed loss of 20kts".

It is worth making a report even if the hazard has previously been forecast or reported. Human nature being what it is, if a pilot hears just one report, then nothing further, he may assume that the hazard no longer exists.

Appendix 3
Conversions

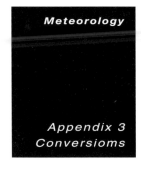
Metric/Imperial Measurement

Metres	Feet		Feet	Metres
1	3.28		1	0.30
2	6.56		2	0.61
3	9.84		3	0.91
4	13.12		4	1.22
5	16.40		5	1.52
6	19.69		6	1.83
7	22.97		7	2.13
8	26.25		8	2.44
9	29.53		9	2.74
10	32.81		10	3.05
20	65.62		20	6.10
30	98.43		30	9.14
40	131.23		40	12.19
50	164.04		50	15.24
60	196.85		60	18.29
70	229.66		70	21.34
80	262.47		80	24.38
90	295.28		90	27.43
100	328.08		100	30.48
200	656.16		200	60.96
300	984.25		300	91.44
400	1,312.34		400	121.92
500	1,640.42		500	152.40
600	1,968.50		600	182.88
700	2,296.59		700	213.36
800	2,624.67		800	243.84
900	2,952.76		900	274.32
1000	3,280.84		1000	304.80
2000	6,561.70		2000	609.60
3000	9,842.50		3000	914.40
4000	13.123.40		4000	1,219.20
5000	16,404.20		5000	1,524.00
6000	19,685.00		6000	1,828.80
7000	22,965.90		7000	2,133.60
8000	26,246.70		8000	2,438.40
9000	29,527.60		9000	2,743.20
10000	32,808.40		10000	3,048.00

Conversion Factors:

Centimetres to Inches x .3937

Metres to Feet x 3.28084

Inches to Centimetres x 2.54

Feet to Metres x 0.3048

Km/Nautical Miles/Statute Miles

NM	Km	St		Km	NM	St		ST	NM	Km
1	1.85	1.15		1	.54	.62		1	.87	1.61
2	3.70	2.30		2	1.08	1.24		2	1.74	3.22
3	5.56	3.45		3	1.62	1.86		3	2.61	4.83
4	7.41	4.60		4	2.16	2.49		4	3.48	6.44
5	9.26	5.75		5	2.70	3.11		5	4.34	8.05
6	11.11	6.90		6	3.24	3.73		6	5.21	9.66
7	12.96	8.06		7	3.78	4.35		7	6.08	11.27
8	14.82	9.21		8	4.32	4.97		8	6.95	12.87
9	16.67	10.36		9	4.86	5.59		9	7.82	14.48
10	18.52	11.51		10	5.40	6.21		10	8.69	16.09
20	37.04	23.02		20	10.80	12.43		20	17.38	32.19
30	55.56	34.52		30	16.20	18.64		30	26.07	48.28
40	74.08	46.03		40	21.60	24.86		40	34.76	64.37
50	92.60	57.54		50	27.00	31.07		50	43.45	80.47
60	111.12	69.05		60	32.40	37.28		60	52.14	96.56
70	129.64	80.55		70	37.80	43.50		70	60.83	112.65
80	148.16	92.06		80	43.20	49.71		80	69.52	128.75
90	166.68	103.57		90	48.60	55.92		90	78.21	144.84
100	185.2	115.1		100	54.0	62.1		100	86.9	161.0
200	370.4	230.2		200	108.0	124.3		200	173.8	321.9
300	555.6	345.2		300	162.0	186.4		300	260.7	482.8
400	740.8	460.3		400	216.0	248.6		400	347.6	643.7
500	926.0	575.4		500	270.0	310.7		500	434.5	804.7
600	1111.2	690.5		600	324.0	372.8		600	521.4	965.6
700	1296.4	805.6		700	378.0	435.0		700	608.3	1126.5
800	1481.6	920.6		800	432.0	497.1		800	695.2	1287.5
900	1666.8	1035.7		900	486.0	559.2		900	782.1	1448.4

Conversion Factors:

Statute Miles to Nautical Miles
x 0.868976

Statute Miles to Kilometres
x 1.60934

Kilometres to Statute Miles
x 0.62137

Kilometres to Nautical Miles
x 0.539957

Nautical Miles to Statute Miles
x 1.15078

Nautical Miles to Kilometres
x 1.852

Meteorology

Millibars/Inches of Mercury

Mbs	ins	Mbs	ins	Mbs	ins	Mbs	ins	Mbs	ins
950	28.054	970	28.644	990	29.235	1010	29.825	1030	30.416
951	28.083	971	28 674	991	29.264	1011	29.855	1031	30.445
952	28.113	972	28.703	992	29.294	1012	29.884	1032	30.475
953	28.142	973	28.733	993	29.323	1013	29.914	1033	30.504
954	28.172	974	28.762	994	29.353	1014	29.943	1034	30.534
955	28.201	975	28.792	995	29.382	1015	29.973	1035	30.564
956	28.231	975	28.821	996	29.412	1016	30.002	1036	30.593
957	28.260	977	28.851	997	29.441	1017	30.032	1037	30.623
958	28.290	977	28.880	998	29.471	1018	30.062	1038	30.652
959	28.319	979	28.910	999	29.500	1019	30.091	1039	30.682
960	28.349	980	28.939	1000	29.530	1020	30.121	1040	30.711
961	28.378	981	28.969	1001	29.560	1021	30.150	1041	30.741
962	28.408	982	28.998	1002	29.589	1022	30.180	1042	30.770
963	28.437	983	29.028	1003	29.619	1023	30.209	1043	30.800
964	28.467	984	29.058	1004	29.648	1024	30.239	1044	30.829
965	28.496	985	29.087	1005	29.678	1025	30.268	1045	30.859
966	28.526	986	29.117	1006	29.707	1026	30.298	1046	30.888
967	28.556	987	29.146	1007	29.737	1027	30.327	1047	30.918
968	28.585	988	29.176	1008	29.766	1028	30.357	1048	30.947
969	28.615	989	29.205	1009	29.796	1029	30.386	1049	30.977
								1050	31.007

To convert Inches into millibars
multiply by 33.86
To convert millibars into Inches
multiply by 0.0295

Appendix 4
Abbreviations

The following is a list of abbreviations used in aviation meteorology. Although most are explained in full in the relevant part of the main text, they are listed here alphabetically to make an easy 'quick' reference.

AC	Altocumulus		FG	Fog
ADJ	Adjacent		FL	Flight Level (i.e. altimeter reading with 1013 mb/hPa set on the altimeter sub-scale
AMD	AMENDMENT			
AMSL	Above Mean Sea Level			
AS	Altostratus		FM	From
AT	At		FRQ	Frequent
ATIS	Automatic Terminal Information Service		FU	Smoke
			FZ	Freezing (Super-Cooled)
BC	Patches		G	Wind Gust
BEC	Becoming		GEN	Generally
BECMG	Becoming.		gm	gram
BL	Blowing		GR	Hail
BLW	Below		GS	Small Hail
BR	Mist		hPa	hectopascal
CAT	Clear Air Turbulence		HVY DS	Widespread Duststorm
CAVOK	Ceiling And Visibility OK		HVY SS	Widespread Sandstorm
CB	Cumulonimbus		HVYGR	Heavy Hail
CC	Cirrocumulus		HZ	Haze
CI	Cirrus		IC	Diamond Dust
CLD	Cloud		INCR	Increase
COT	Coast		INTSF	Intensifying
CS	Cirrostratus		IRVR	Instrumented RVR system
CU	Cumulus		ISA	International Standard Atmosphere
DALR	Dry Adiabatic Lapse Rate			
DECR	Decreasing		ISOL	Isolated
DR	Drifting		Kg	Kilogram
DS	Duststorm		KMH	Kilometres Per Hour
DTRT	Deteriorate		KT	Knot(s)
DU	Dust		LAN	Land
DZ	Drizzle		LOC	Locally
ELR	Environmental Lapse Rate		LSQ TS	Line Squall Thunderstorms
EMBD	Embedded (in cloud)		LYR	Layers
FBU	Flight Briefing Unit		m	metres
FC	Funnel Cloud(s)		M	Minus (temperature)
FCST	Forecast		MAR	Maritime
FEW	Few (1 to 2 oktas of cloud cover)		mb	millibar
			Met	Meteorological or Meteorology

METAR	Met. Airfield Report
MI	Shallow
MOD	Moderate
MON	Mountains
MOV	Moving
MPS	Metres Per Second
MTW	Mountain Wave
NC	No Change
NIL	None
NOSIG	No Significant changes forecast
NS	Nimbostratus
NSC	No Significant Cloud
NSW	No Significant Weather
OAT	Outside Air Temperature
OBS	Observed
OBSC TS	Obscured Thunderstorms (or Cumulonimbus)
OCNL	Occasional
PE	Ice Pellets
PO	Well developed (sand/dust swirls)
PRFG	Partial Fog (fog banks)
PROB	Probability
QFE	Atmospheric pressure at an aerodrome
QNH	Altimeter sub-scale setting to obtain *altitude*
R	Retard (used when a TAF is received late)
RA	Rain
RE	Recent weather
RH	Relative Humidity
RVR	Runway Visual Range
SA	Sand
SALR	Saturated Adiabatic Lapse Rate
SC	Stratocumulus
SCT	Scattered (3 to 4 oktas of cloud cover)
BKN	Broken (5 to 7 oktas of cloud cover)
OVC	Overcast (8 oktas of cloud cover)

SEV	Severe
SFC	Surface
SG	Snow Grains
SH	Shower(s)
SIGMET	Significant Met. (warning of reported or forecast hazardous in-flight conditions)
SIGWX	Significant Weather
SKC	Sky Clear
SLW	Slow
SN	Snow
SNOCLO	Closed due to snow
SQ	Squalls
SS	Sandstorm
ST	Stratus
STNR	Stationary
TAF	Terminal Airfield Forecast
TC	Tropical Cyclone
TCU	Towering Cumulus
TEMPO	Temporary
TL	Until
TREND	Trend – forecast changes in conditions in the next two hours
TS	Thunderstorm
TURB	Turbulence
V	Variation (in wind direction)
VA	Volcanic Ash
VAL	Valleys
VC	In the Vicinity
VOLMET	Voice Met. Broadcast
VRB	Variable Wind Direction
VSP	Vertical speed
VV	Vertical Visibility
WDSPR	Widespread
WKN	Weakening
WS	Windshear
Z	Zulu (UTC)

Revision Answers

▶ Properties of the Atmosphere

1 – 21%

2 – The tropopause.

3 – With increasing temperature, density reduces; with decreasing temperature, density increases (if all other factors remain unchanged).

4 – 27ft

5 – 10 hPa.

6 – 3°C per 1000ft.

7 – -3°C

▶ Motion of the Atmosphere

8 – A line joining places of equal sea-level pressure.

9 – A

10 – In degrees True.

11 – Magnetic.

12 – Veering.

13 – 060/15

14 – 120° (remembering to allow for the veering of the wind by Coriolis force).

15 – The wind will probably veer, increase in strength and become more gusty.

16 – A

▶ Pressure and Altimetry

17 – Mean Sea Level.

18 – QFE

19 – 1003 (1015-12mb).

20 – The altimeter will start to over-read because the aircraft is flying towards an area of low pressure. The aircraft is lower than indicated on the altimeter.

▶ Humidity and Stability

21 – The temperature at which air will become saturated.

22 – The parcel of air with 90% humidity because it is nearer saturation.

23 – The warmer parcel of air (+25°C) has the greater moisture content.

24 – A change of state directly from solid to gas will absorb heat energy.

▶ The International Standard Atmosphere

25 – -15°C.

26 – 5000ft, 846mb/hPa.

27 – - 11°C.

28 – 1013.25 hPa.

▶ Clouds and Precipitation

29 – Cumulus cloud.

30 – Cirrus.

31 – Stratocumulus (ST) lowest, Cumulus (CU) and Cirrus (CI) highest – of which 2 oktas.

32 – Cumulonimbus (CB), a thunderstorm.

33 – Overcast (OVC).

34 – + SN

35 – Scattered (3 to 4 oktas) cumulonimbus cloud, heavy rain.

▶ Visibility

36 – Forecast visibility of 10km or more.

37 – An anticyclone.

38 – A

39 – Advection fog.

40 – Light winds; a cloudless night; high relative humidity.

41 – 700 metres in fog.

42 – Heavy snow.

▶ Air Masses

43 – The Azores area of the Atlantic.

44 – Stable.

45 – The arctic maritime air mass.

▶ Low Pressure System – Depressions

46 – A cold front.

47 – About 1700. Alternatively, ten minutes before the airfield closes for the day.

48 – An occluded front.

49 – The wind veers.

50 – A warm front

▶ High Pressure Systems —Anticyclones and Ridges

51 – 2000ft.

52 – Gales.

53 – C

54 – B

Revision Answers

▶ Icing

55 – No. You will find the definitive answer in the aircraft's POH/FM.

56 – A

57 – Most certainly. Frost reduces the aircraft's controllability as well as reducing performance. Always remove **all** ice, frost and snow from an aircraft before flight.

58 – No. You should shut down the aircraft and clear the snow from **all** surfaces.

59 – No. There is a risk of rain ice in this situation. By flying parallel to the front (and thereby staying in the risk area for longer) the risk is increased.

60 – A

61 – Yes. Carburettor icing is a possibility even on the ground, especially with so much visible moisture around. A thorough power check, and an extra carburettor heat check immediately before take-off, is recommended.

▶ Thunderstorms

62 – An unstable atmosphere, high relative humidity, some form of lifting action.

63 – The much greater rate of vertical development.

64 – Avoidance.

65 – Absolutely not. Flight near or under a CB is asking for trouble, especially at low level. The ATC clearance is irrelevant to this decision. As pilot, **you** are responsible for the safety of the aircraft.

▶ Flight Over Mountainous Areas and Other Weather Hazards

66 – 4000ft (i.e. double the elevation of the high ground).

67 – No. It may well be a rotor cloud, marking an area of severe turbulence.

68 – On the leeward side, in this case the eastern side.

69 – At the Va airspeed (sometimes also known as the 'rough air' airspeed).

70 – This report is most likely to have come from a pilot, who has experienced an airspeed loss of 20kts due to windshear at a height of 200ft on the approach to runway 24.

71 – Yes. Such a marked fall in pressure in the space of two hours almost certainly means that a deepening depression is approaching rapidly. On the ground you should be checking forecasts and any strong-wind warnings, and thinking of getting the aircraft in a hangar or securely tied down.

▶Aviation Weather Reports and Forecasts

72 – B

73 – C

74 – 240/20, -2°C.

75 – Edinburgh airport actual weather report at 0620 UTC on the 5th. Surface wind 260° true at 5 knots. Visibility looking north is 6000 metres, there is fog in the vicinity (within 8km) of the airport perimeter. At the airport the weather is shallow fog. There are 3-4 oktas of cloud with a base of 300 feet above aerodrome level. The temperature is +4°C, the dew point is +3°C. Temporarily within the next two hours the visibility will fall to 400 metres in fog patches.

76 – Bristol airfield, forecast for period 0600 to 2400 UTC on the 14th. Surface wind 060° true at 15 knots. Visibility 3000 metres in mist, broken (5-7 oktas) cloud, base 400 feet aal. 30% probability that temporarily between 0600 and 0800 UTC there will be thunderstorms with rain. Weather becoming 0700 to 0900 UTC visibility 6000 metres in haze, no significant cloud. Temporarily between 1100 and 2400 UTC visibility 4500 metres in moderate rain. 40% probability that temporarily between 1200 and 2400 UTC visibility will be 2000 metres in heavy thunderstorms and rain, with 5-7 oktas of cumulonimbus base 5000 feet aal. Weather becoming 1300 to 1600 UTC surface wind 140° true at 5 knots. Weather becoming 1900 to 2200 UTC 3500 metres visibility in mist, 3-4 oktas of cloud, base 300 feet aal.

77 – In the Marseille Flight Information Region frequent thunderstorms observed along an axis between St Flour and Valence-Grenoble. Top of the thunderstorms is Flight Level 350. They are stationary.

78 – Local showers. Broken cumulus and stratocumulus base between Flight Level (FL) 20 and FL 50, tops between FL 80 and FL 120. Isolated cumulonimbus, base FL 40 to FL 50, tops FL 250 to FL 300, thunderstorms and showers.

79 – Thunderstorms spreading into the area (see "Outlook" at the bottom of the sheet).

80 – It is impossible to say. You are looking at yesterday's METFORM (see date, top left and bottom right).

Navigation introduction

Flying aeroplanes is, for most pilots, a fun thing to do. At the beginning of the PPL course there is nothing to compare with the feeling of mastering the manoeuvring of an aircraft, making it do what you want. Before long you're flying around the circuit and, with practice, you will find yourself reuniting the aircraft with the runway with increasing control and grace. Then, after the momentous first solo, there are different types of circuits, and more solo flying.

Yet the chances are that at times you will look longingly beyond the circuit. You may go out into the local area occasionally, to see if there is life more than two miles from the airfield. Maybe you will look to the horizon, and imagine flying over and beyond it, leaving the home airfield far behind, out of sight.

But to do this you will need more than just the basic aircraft handling skills. You need to be able to navigate visually, following a chosen route and fixing your exact position by reference to the map. In these days of radio navigation aids, global communications and (best of all) GPS, it is only human to wonder whether learning basic visual navigation – map reading, mentally calculating ETAs and heading corrections etc. – is *really* necessary. Being able to navigate with just a map, a compass and a stopwatch is a nice trick; but is it relevant? The answer is an unequivocal **YES**. To make the best use of any navigational aid, you must understand the basic navigation principles. What good is the advanced technology of a moving-map display if you don't understand the map symbols? What use knowing your off-track error to within a hundred metres, if you can't alter heading to reach the destination? What about finding an airfield that isn't in a GPS database? (and there are plenty of them). And if your favourite navigational gizmo goes on strike, what are you left with other than the tried and trusted principles of navigation, proved hundreds of years before the first aircraft flew?

However you plan to navigate, you also need to consider the business of flight planning. Will the airfield be open, how long are the runways, which are long enough for landing *and* take-off? How much fuel is needed for the flight? What are the ATC frequencies and services, are any unavailable at the moment? Is there anything en-route to note – air displays, military exercises, parachuting competitions etc? If you need to divert, where will you go?

None of this need be a chore. The unique perspective of our planet as seen from a few thousand feet is one of the pleasures of VFR flying. Even your home area will yield new secrets when seen from the air – if you have the wit to look for them. And proper flight planning will remove the nasty surprises that can sabotage an otherwise delightful flight. The majority of general aviation 'en-route' accidents have their root cause in a lack of proper flight planning. In essence the accident was waiting to happen once the decision had been made to take off, after which the pilot was merely taking the aircraft to the scene of the accident.

But, of course, flying should be fun. Take the time to learn how to visually navigate properly, take care with the flight planning, and the 'freedom of the skies' really will be yours, without worries or crossed fingers!

Now the standard disclaimer. Throughout, the pilot is referred to as 'he'. This has been done purely to avoid the repetitive use of "he or she" and I ask for the reader's understanding.

Finally, a point of navigation etiquette. I have not made any distinction between 'maps' and 'charts'. The differences, and dictionary definitions, can no doubt keep those with a precise turn of mind occupied for many an hour. However, for practical purposes 'maps' and 'charts' are taken to be one and the same, and I have freely mixed the usage of these terms.

The Earth

▶ Form of the Earth, Latitude and Longitude

▶ Lines on the Surface of the Earth

▶ Axis and Poles, Hemispheres

▶ Direction

▶ Distance

▶ Revision

Navigation

▶ Form of the Earth, Latitude and Longitude

Since virtually all navigation takes place in relation to the earth's surface, it makes sense to begin by looking at the shape and characteristics of our planet.

To all intents and purposes the earth is spherical. To be precise, it is slightly flattened at the poles so that the diameter pole-to-pole is 23 nautical miles less than the diameter across the equator. Given that the diameter across the equator is 6,883 nautical miles, this is not a major discrepancy and navigators don't bother about it. No-one ever got lost by treating the earth as a sphere.

Clearly we need some way of defining where we are on the sphere, so we divide it into angles measured out from the centre of the earth. Degrees of *latitude* are measured north and south of the **equator** (which is a line around the earth exactly halfway between the poles) from 0° at the equator to 90° at the poles. Each degree is divided into 60 minutes, and each minute is further divided into either seconds (60ths) or decimals (100ths). Lines of latitude are often called *parallels* because they run parallel to each other.

Lines of latitude are measured as angles north and south from the centre of the earth

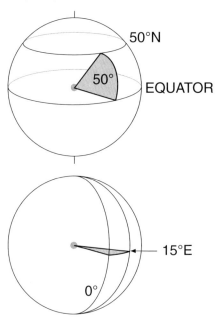

Lines of longitude are measured as angles east and west from the centre of the earth

Degrees of *longitude* are measured east or west from 0° longitude. Unfortunately there is no arbitrary physical reference from which to measure longitude, so one had to be invented. In the last century, the line (more formally known as a *meridian*) of 0° longitude was designated as passing through Greenwich in London, and to this day the 0° meridian of longitude is sometimes known as the 'Greenwich' or 'Prime' Meridian. Meridians of longitude extend to 180° East and 180° West, making a total of 360° around the earth. As with latitude, each degree is divided into 60 minutes and each minute is further divided into either 60 seconds or 100 decimals.

With this system, any point on the earth can be precisely defined by measuring its latitude north or south of the equator and its longitude east or west of the Prime Meridian. A 'lat and long' position is always given first in latitude, then longitude. A latitude is preceded with 'N' if it is north of the equator and 'S' if south of it. A longitude is preceded with 'W' if it is west of the prime meridian and E if it is to the east.

A latitude or longitude figure is given as three groups of numbers, which are degrees, minutes and seconds or decimals. For example, Woodford airfield is at latitude N 53 (degrees) 20 (minutes) 17 (seconds) and longitude W 002 (degrees) 08 (minutes) 56 (seconds). Note that degrees of latitude are given as a two-figure number because they run from 0 to 90, but degrees of longitude are given as a three-figure group because they run from 0 to 180.

The Earth

Latitude and longitude figures are often written without spaces, so the position of Woodford would appear as:

N5320·17 W00208·56

Unfortunately, there is no clear convention to differentiate the units of the last two digits, so that they may be either seconds (60ths) or decimals (100ths). However, a publication listing latitude and longitude should state (somewhere) which units are being used.

In visual navigation the consequences of mixing seconds and decimals are not critical, given that in latitude one second is equivalent to about 101ft, and a decimal about 61ft. Thus a position given as ·56 seconds is about 2240ft (683m) distant to a position given as ·56 decimals. This might seem a long way, but on a standard 1:500,000 scale map it is a distance of about 1.3mm

Just as nobody ever got lost by treating the earth as a sphere, nobody ever missed a point on a map because it was displaced by 1.3mm.

▶ Lines on the Surface of the Earth

A line drawn between two points on the earth's surface can be defined in one of three ways:

Small Circle

A small circle is a line across the surface of the earth whose plane does *not* pass through the centre of the earth. All parallels of latitude (except the equator) are small circles.

*The plane of a small circle **does not** pass through the centre of the earth*

Rhumb Line

A rhumb line crosses all meridians of longitude at the same angle. Parallels of latitude are rhumb lines.

A rhumb line crosses all meridians at a constant angle

Great Circle

A great circle is a line across the surface of the earth whose plane passes through the centre of the earth. A line drawn as a great circle is always the shortest distance between two points on the earth's surface.

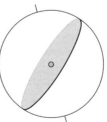

*The plane of a great circle **does** pass through the centre of the earth*

▶ Axis and Poles, Hemispheres

The earth has two poles, and in technical terms these are the points at which the meridians of longitude converge. The one at the northern end of the planet (the 'top' of the planet as it is usually depicted) is the north pole in the Arctic, that at the 'bottom' southern end of the earth is the south pole in the Antarctic. These are the spots where polar explorers plant their flags.

The poles are joined by an imaginary straight line running through the earth which is the earth's axis. The earth rotates around this axis. Viewed from above the north pole the earth rotates anticlockwise and the poles can also be described as being at either end of the earth's axis.

As we have already seen, the line around the earth exactly halfway between the poles is the equator, which is perpendicular (at a right angle or 90° to) the earth's axis. The equator divides the earth into two halves or hemispheres: a northern hemisphere and a southern hemisphere. Several important concepts concerning meteorology and navigation act differently depending on whether you are in the northern or southern hemisphere but unless specifically stated otherwise, this book will concentrate on the northern hemisphere.

The earth's poles, axis and hemispheres

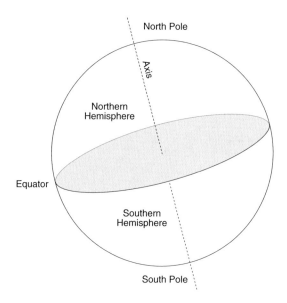

▶ Direction

Once we can precisely define two positions on the earth and draw a line between them, we can measure the *direction* of the line. Direction is an angle, measured clockwise from north and always expressed as a three-digit number between 000° and 359°. That's the easy bit. Unfortunately, the concept of 'north' is a little slippery and there is more than one 'north'.

True north is the direction to the *actual north pole*. True direction is easy to find on a map because direction can easily be measured with reference to a meridian – all you need is a protractor. However, true direction is difficult to measure in an aircraft because at present there is no widely used aircraft instrument that points directly to true north.

The Earth

Magnetic north is the direction to the *magnetic north pole*, which is **not** at the same point as the actual north pole. At present, the magnetic north pole is underneath Northern Canada although it slowly moves around. The advantage of measuring a magnetic direction is that it is easy to find magnetic north using a freely suspended magnetic needle (such as that in a *compass*) which points to the magnetic north pole.

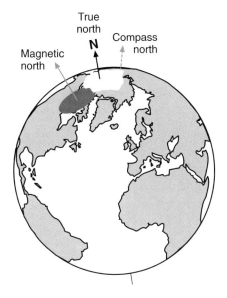

The True north pole, the Magnetic north pole, and a theoretical Compass north pole

Compass north is the direction of north as measured by a compass. This simple device is found in the cockpit of all aircraft, even the latest airliner with every modern aid to navigation. When all else fails, the earth's magnetic field won't – so the compass is a great comfort. But to be of any use, you need the compass in the aircraft with you. This means that the compass is influenced not just by the earth's magnetic field, but also by the magnetic field of the aircraft itself. The compass can be adjusted by an aircraft engineer to minimise this effect, but there will inevitably be a small residual error. So the compass in an aircraft points towards its own imaginary 'compass north' rather than directly to magnetic north.

To avoid confusion, a direction should always be qualified with one of the following:

– True (abbreviated T);

– Magnetic (abbreviated M);

– Compass (abbreviated C).

So a direction of 087°M is 87 degrees measured clockwise from magnetic north. A direction of 296°T is 296 degrees measured clockwise from true north.

We will look at the measurement and calculation of direction in more detail in the next chapter (Aeronautical Maps).

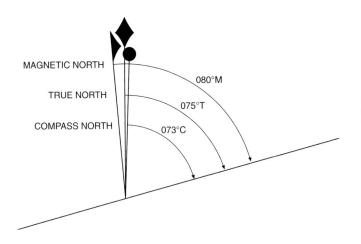

A direction can be measured in relation to True north, Magnetic north or Compass north

Navigation

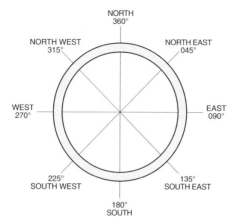

The cardinal points of the compass

▶ Distance

For aviation navigation, distance is commonly measured in *nautical miles*. The obvious question is why aviation should have borrowed these non-standard units from marine navigators. Nautical miles are not the same as the miles on a car speedometer, and obviously not the same as kilometres. And why should we use units of speed called *knots*, which are nautical miles per hour?

The reason for using nautical miles takes us back to the measurement of position using latitude and longitude. Measured from the centre of the earth, an angle of one minute of latitude amounts to a distance of one nautical mile at the earth's surface. So the distance between the 51° 43'N and 51° 44'N parallels of latitude (i.e. one minute of latitude) is one nautical mile. The distance between the 51°N and 52°N parallels of latitude (i.e. one degree or 60 minutes of latitude) is 60nm. This convenient relationship, and the fact that it made life easier for the early ocean-going navigators, is the reason why the nautical mile became the unit of distance used in marine navigation. Since the basic navigational principles are common to both disciplines, nautical miles became and remain the most commonly used unit of distance in both aviation and maritime circles.

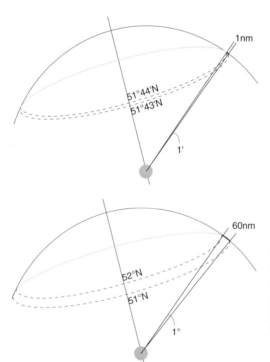

1' of latitude represents a distance of 1nm at the earth's surface

1° of latitude represents a distance of 60nm at the earth's surface

The Earth

However, that is not to say that no other distance units are used in aviation. In addition to nautical miles, *statute* miles and *kilometres* can be used to measure distance.

The statute mile is an arbitrary unit, used in many countries to measure distances on land. It is usually used for road distances, car speeds and so on. A nautical mile is slightly larger than a statute mile – one nautical mile (nm) is equal to 1·15 statute miles (sm).

The kilometre is used in countries which do not use the statute mile. A nautical mile is almost twice the distance of a kilometre – one nautical mile is equal to 1·85 kilometres (km).

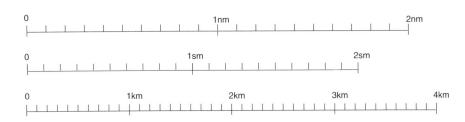

The relationship between nautical miles (nm), statute miles (sm) and kilometres (km)

1 nautical mile = 1·15 statute miles = 1·85 kilometres

▶Revision

Revision questions are printed at the end of each chapter in this book. The aim of the revision questions is to enable you to test your knowledge of the chapter subject, and to help you retain the principal elements of each subject.

Attempt the revision questions once you are satisfied that you have understood and learnt the main points of each chapter. You should aim for a 'success' rate of around 80%.

1   Give the approximate latitude (in degrees and minutes only) of the position marked below.

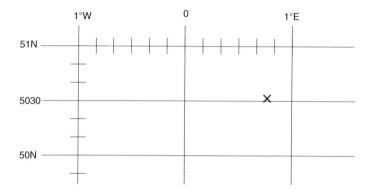

2   What type of line will always be the shortest distance between two points on the earth?

3   To which 'north' does an aircraft's compass point?

4   Describe the direction shown below.

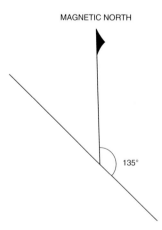

5   Without using a map, estimate the distance (in nautical miles) between Aberporth airfield (N5207 W00433) and RAF Valley (N5315 W00432).

Answers at page NAV 203

Aeronautical Maps

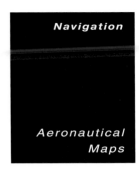
▶ Introduction

The bad news about maps is that it is a complex and time-consuming business to represent the curved surface of the earth on a flat piece of paper. To see why, try cutting an orange in half and flattening it out without distorting the skin. Even when the map-maker has made a reasonable portrayal of the earth's surface on paper, all the necessary aeronautical information must be added. As you will know by now, this information has an annoying habit of changing regularly.

The good news is that all this is a problem for the cartographers who draw maps. As a pilot, you only have to worry about having an up-to-date map and knowing how to use it.

Reference is made in this book to *topographical* maps. A topographical map is one showing a significant number of ground features (hills and mountains, rivers, lakes, towns and cities, roads and railway lines etc.) and can therefore be used for map-reading navigation. Topographical maps thus portray the ground in much greater detail than those which are primarily for IFR flying and generally show only coastlines and airfields in addition to aeronautical information.

▶ **Introduction**

▶ **Map Projection**

▶ **Conformity and Equivilance**

▶ **Locating a Point on an Aeronautical Map**

▶ **Measurement of Direction**

▶ **Scale and Distance**

▶ **Converting Units of Distance**

▶ **Depiction of Relief**

▶ **Depiction of Cultural Features**

▶ **Depiction of Airfields**

▶ **Depiction of Aeronautical Information**

▶ **The Map Checklist**

▶ **Revision**

Navigation

▶Map Projection

To portray the curved surface of the earth on a flat sheet of paper, a technique known as *projection* is used. Many different types of projection are available to cartographers, and each has its own properties, advantages and disadvantages. The geometry and mathematics of map projection are formidably complicated, but happily they can be left to the cartographer.

The most commonly used projection for aeronautical maps is the '*Lambert Conformal Conic*'. To make this projection, a light is placed at the centre of a transparent earth and the map is drawn where an imaginary cone slices through the earth. A straight line drawn on a "Lambert" map is for practical purposes a great circle. Hence it is the shortest distance between two points. However, a great-circle direction is not easy to measure over long distances because it crosses each meridian of longitude at a different angle. Similarly, it is not simple to fly a great-circle route because it is a curved track with a constantly changing direction.

*A Lambert Conformal
Conic map projection*

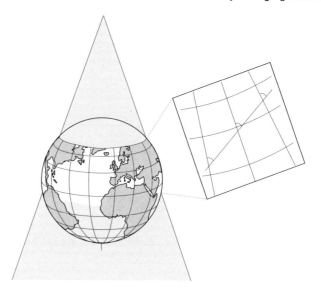

*The legend of this CAA
1:500 000 chart states
that it is drawn using the
Lambert Conformal Conic
projection*

Lambert Conformal Conic Projection
50   60
30

A different type of projection – a '*Transverse Mercator*' projection – is sometimes used for a map covering a small area. The map is drawn on the surface of an imaginary cylinder traversing the earth. An advantage of this projection is that a straight line drawn on such a map is a rhumb line. A rhumb line is easy to measure and easy to fly because it crosses all meridians of longitude at the same angle. Hence it has a constant direction.

Aeronautical Maps

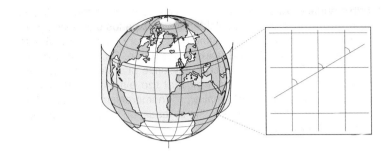

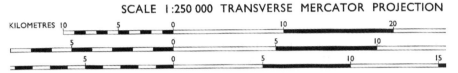

SCALE 1:250 000 TRANSVERSE MERCATOR PROJECTION

The difference in distances between rhumb lines and great circles only really becomes a factor when flying directly between points more than 500 miles apart. For example, if you draw a straight line between RAF Mona and Wickenby airfield on a Transverse Mercator-projection map, the distance (rhumb line) is 144nm. Draw a straight line between the same airfields on a Lambert Conformal Conic-projection map, and the distance (great circle) is 143nm.

▶ Conformality and Equivilance

We have already touched on the problems of portraying the sphere of the earth onto a flat piece of paper. There is no perfect representation (if there was, all maps would use it), and so the chart producer has to compromise between the major qualities required of an aeronautical chart.

Arguably the primary requirement is that the chart should be *conformal*. Conformaltity (also known as *orthomorphism*) means in essence that directions (bearings) measured on a map are represented correctly. To do this the parallels of latitude must cross the meridians of longitude at right angles (90°). If you look again at the parallels and meridians on the Lambert and Mercator projections you will see that on both the lines of latitude and longitude do indeed cross at right angles. If the bearings on a map are correct, it follows that the shape of the features depicted on the map should accurately represent the actual shapes of the feature on the earth's surface.

Of course, the shape of a feature is only one of its properties, its size must also be accurately represented. As an aeronautical chart is a reduced depiction of the earth's surface, the scale of the map (the ratio of reduction from full size to map size) is important so that a line or area measured on a map is the equivalent to that on the real earth. As far as possible a cartographer will attempt to have a constant scale across a map, nevertheless the fact is that it is impossible to do this whilst also making a chart truly conformal, and so the practical aim is to make any scale error constant across the map. The mechanics of this need not detain us – the map makers do their job well enough that scale errors are too small to have any appreciable effect on practical navigation using an aeronautical chart. However, if you are curious enough to explore the legend sheet of a Lambert Conformal Conic projection chart such as the CAA 1:500,000 series, you will find listed two standard parallels. These are the parallels at which the cone of the projection cuts through the imaginary earth's surface. At the standard parallels scale is correct; between the standard parallels scale contracts and outside them it expands but, once again, it must be emphasised that this error is not something you are going to be able to measure on a standard aeronautical chart using a scale rule. So, if you need an excuse for missing your ETAs, a discourse on equivilance and standard parallels will not get you very far! However, in the way that the aviation world works sometimes, knowing terms such as 'conformality', 'orthomorphism' and 'standard parallels' not only allows you to tick off a box in the syllabus, but might also win you points at a flying club quiz some day!

The standard parallels on the CAA 1:500,000 Southern England chart (Lambert Conformal Conic projection)

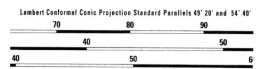

▶ Locating a Point on an Aeronautical Map

Aeronautical maps are overlaid with lines of latitude and longitude. As we have seen, these are used to define a precise position on a map.

A more general location can be given using a range and bearing from a known point. For example, a radar controller might tell a pilot "You are identified 10 miles south of Manchester Airport". This means that the aircraft is at a distance of 10 miles from the airfield on a bearing of 180°. Bearings are usually given in degrees magnetic and distances in nautical miles. The position of an airfield or ground feature can also be described in terms of a range and bearing. So White Waltham airfield can be described as being located "2nm SW (south-west) of Maidenhead".

The location of White Waltham airport as given in the UK VFR Flight Guide. The right-hand box gives range and bearings from nearby VOR/DME radionavigation beacons

ELEVATION	LOCATION	EGLM			WHITE WALTHAM	
130ft 5mb	2nm SW of Maidenhead N5130.05 W00046.42	LON 113.60	278	11.8	•–••/–––/–•	
PPR	Diversion AD	BNN 113.75	216	16.0	–•••/–•/–•	
		CPT 114.35	094	16.7	–•–•/•––•/–	

Another method for fixing position in the UK is the *National Grid*, which in this case has nothing to do with the electricity supply system. The cartographer's national grid consists of a series of squares overlaying topographical maps. The UK is covered by six squares lettered H, J, N, O, S and T. Each square is further divided into 25 two-letter squares (e.g. NA, NB, NC etc.). A location is then given within a square as a distance in kilometres (and possibly metres) east and north of the square's south-west corner. To give a position accurate to within one kilometre, four figures are used after the square identifier. The first two figures are eastings – kilometres **east** of the south-west corner of the designated square. The second two

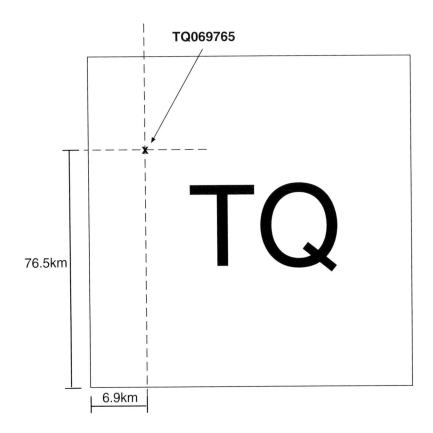

Locating the point
TQ069765 (London-
Heathrow airport)

figures are northings – kilometres **north** of the south-west corner of the designated square. Therefore a reference of 'TQ0676' describes a point within the TQ square that is 6km **east** of the square's south-west corner and 76km **north** of it. Extra figures can be added to give a more accurate location, representing hundreds or even individual metres. Thus a reference of 'TQ069765' is a position 6.9 kilometres east of the south-west corner of the TQ square and 76.5 kilometres north of it. 'TQ0694376597' gives a position to within one metre.

National grid positions are used by the search and rescue services and are also often used to describe the location of helipads, glider sites, microlight airfields, hang gliding and FLPM sites. The national grid is overlaid on Ordnance Survey 1:50,000 (Landranger) maps. These are particularly popular with helicopter pilots who may give a national grid position using the Landranger map number first, followed by figures representing the eastings and northings printed on the map's border, e.g. "OS Sheet 163/312237".

▶ Measurement of Direction

A line drawn on a map is usually measured in degrees True (T) by reference to lines of longitude.

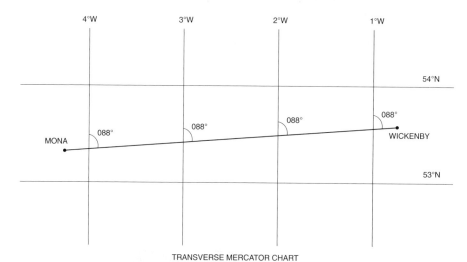

The track Mona – Wickenby on a Transverse Mercator chart

TRANSVERSE MERCATOR CHART

A straight line on a Transverse Mercator map is a rhumb line, which has a constant direction. So in principle, the direction can be measured anywhere along track; direction should be constant at all points along the line. By contrast, a straight line on a Lambert conformal conic map is a great circle, which does not have a constant direction – it crosses each meridian of longitude at a different angle. Let's return to the line from Mona to Wickenby. On a Transverse Mercator map the direction (true) measured anywhere along track is 088°(T). On a Lambert Conformal Conic map, direction is 087°(T) measured at Mona but 089°(T) measured at Wickenby. Half-way between the two airfields, the track direction is 088°(T).

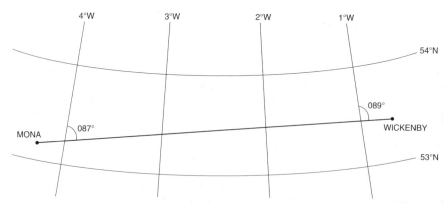

The track Mona – Wickenby on a Lambert Conformal Conic chart

LAMBERT CONFORMAL CONIC CHART

Aeronautical Maps

So, the best way to measure direction on any map is to place the centre of a protractor about halfway along the line to be measured, aligning the north arrow of the protractor with true north (i.e. by reference to the meridians of longitude). True direction is then read off where the track line crosses the edge of the protractor in the direction of flight. By measuring the line at its mid-point you should obtain the same result regardless of the type of map projection.

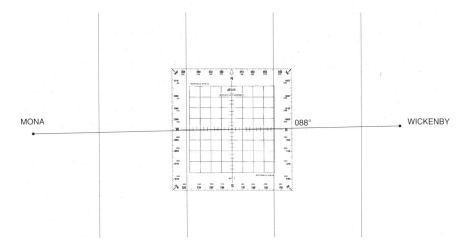

Measuring a track direction using a square protractor

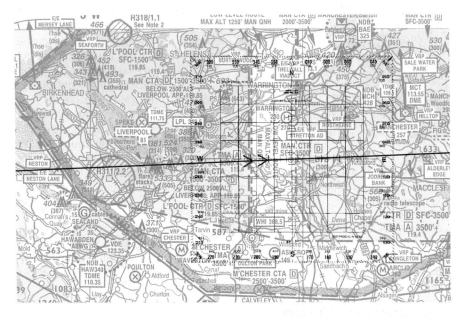

Using a square protractor to measure the track from Mona to Wickenby – 088°

FROM/TO	MSA	PL/ALT	TAS	TR(T)	W/V	HDG(T)	HDG(M)	G/S	DIST	TIME	ETA	ATA
MONA _____ **WICKENBY**				**088**	/							
_____					/							

The true track Mona – Wickenby entered onto a flight log

You will remember that the true north pole and the magnetic north pole are not at the same spot. So having measured true direction, we must now make allowance for the difference between true north and magnetic north. The difference in direction between them depends on your position relative to the geographical north pole and the magnetic north pole. For example, magnetic north and true north are quite closely aligned when viewed from Europe, so the difference in degrees between magnetic north and true north is fairly small. This is not true of a location such as Northern Canada, where it can be very marked indeed.

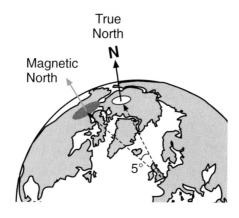

A variation of 5°W between true north and magnetic north

The difference, measured in degrees, between true north and magnetic north is known as *variation*. On aeronautical maps, variation is given in figures and also marked by lines called *isogonals*. An isogonal is a line joining places of equal magnetic variation and often takes the form of a dashed line across the map. So from the map you can determine the average magnetic variation over the route you will be flying. A single average variation figure is usually sufficient for a flight of less than 500nm. In the case of our hypothetical route from Mona to Wickenby, we see from a map that the variation at Mona is about 5·5°W whereas at Wickenby it is about 3·5°W. Mid-way between the two you might intuitively expect a variation of 4·5°W, and the 4·5°W isogonal does indeed pass through the centre of the route. So the average variation we would use in planning this flight is 4·5°W.

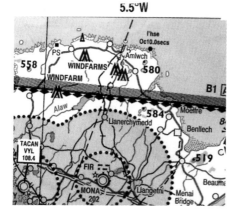

An isogonal on a UK aeronautical chart – in this case variation along the isogonal is 5·5° west

Variation will be either W (west) or E (east). To convert a true direction to a magnetic direction – which of course is one we can in principle fly by following the compass – **westerly** variation is **added** to true to give magnetic and **easterly** variation is **subtracted** from true. This is easily remembered in terms of the old (and nowadays politically incorrect) saying:

West is Best and East is Least.

The true track Mona to Wickenby is 088° (T). The average variation is 4·5°W. So the magnetic track is (088 + 4·5) = 092·5° (M).

Variation is not fixed, because the magnetic north pole moves around slowly under the earth's crust. Some aeronautical maps show the annual rate of change of variation (which is usually very small) but you can be quite sure that any aviation-related map will go out of date for other reasons long before the isogonals move significantly. As a matter of interest, the slow change in variation is the reason why runway headings are revised every now and then.

TO				SUNSET			VAR. **4.5°W**	
DISTANCE		FLIGHT TIME		2000' w/v			TEMP.	
F FUEL		**FUEL CONSUMPTION**		5000' w/v				
R RADIO		TOTAL REQUIRED		DEPARTURE INFO.				
E ENGINE		FUEL ON BOARD						
D DIRECTION		RESERVE						
A ALTIMETER		TOTAL ENDURANCE						
BRAKES OFF		TAKE OFF		LANDING			BRAKES ON	

FROM/TO	MSA	PL/ALT	TAS	TR(T)	W/V	HDG(T)	HDG(M)	G/S	DIST	TIME	ETA	ATA
MONA WICKENBY				088								

The average variation for the route of 4·5°W entered onto a flight log

Having calculated magnetic direction, a further calculation can be made to correct for *deviation.* This is the effect of the aircraft's own magnetic field on the compass reading. Deviation is the difference between **magnetic north** and **compass north.**

Every aircraft should have an individual *deviation card*, which is usually fixed near the compass. This contains figures to convert a magnetic direction into a compass direction. Deviation may be given as east and west, in which case it can be applied to the magnetic direction in the same way as easterly or westerly variation ("West is Best..."). More commonly, the deviation card shows what compass heading should be flown to achieve a specified magnetic heading.

For	N	30	60	E	120	150
Steer	359	032	061	090	119	151
For	S	210	240	W	300	330
Steer	184	213	241	269	229	332
DATE						**AIRPATH**

A typical compass deviation card

For instance, assume you want to convert a magnetic direction of 135° into a compass direction. The deviation card for the aircraft states:

For (magnetic)	090	180
Steer (compass)	090	184

135° is half-way between 090° and 180°. We see from the card that for 090° the deviation is zero (magnetic and compass headings are the same). We also see that for 180° the deviation is +4° (i.e. 4° west). For a magnetic heading of 135°, therefore, the deviation will be about +2°, that is 2° west. Remembering that 'West is Best', we can work out that (135 + 2) = 137° (C).

In summary:

True direction corrected for *variation* gives **magnetic direction.** Correcting this for *deviation* gives **compass direction.**

or

True ± **V**ariation = **M**agnetic ± **D**eviation = **C**ompass
T   V   **M**   D   **C**

Or in reverse, '**C**adbury's **D**airy **M**ilk **V**ery **T**asty'. There are several other mnemonics for remembering this formula, none of which are printable.

It should be mentioned here that deviation is usually small, less than 3° on average. Because of this, pilots flying real-life routes in aircraft with which they are familiar often choose not to calculate a compass heading but simply to fly magnetic headings instead. Check with your instructor for his/her preference in this respect.

▶Scale and Distance

An aeronautical map is a depiction of the earth's surface, reduced by a certain amount. A navigator needs to know the exact reduction in order to measure distance, and for this reason all maps have their scale clearly marked. On aeronautical maps, scale is shown as a *representative fraction*: for example '1:500 000'. This means that 1 unit on the map equals 500,000 units on the earth. If you bend your thumb and place the top half on a 1:500 000 scale map, the distance it covers represents 500,000 times the length of the top half of your thumb across the earth.

Of course this knowledge in itself is of limited practical value to the pilot, so let's introduce a useful "rule of thumb". Bend your thumb at its joint and place the top half on a 1:500 000 map. If your thumb is anything like that of the average adult, the top half will now be covering a distance of about 10nm. Do the same on a 1:250 000-scale map and the top half of your thumb will cover 5nm. On a 1:1000 000-scale map it will cover 20nm.

These three scales are commonly used for aeronautical topographical maps, so it is worth knowing that they are colloquially referred to as follows:

A 'rule of thumb' for measuring distances on a map

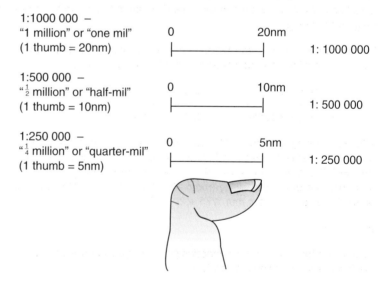

1:1000 000 –
"1 million" or "one mil"
(1 thumb = 20nm)

1:500 000 –
"$\frac{1}{2}$ million" or "half-mil"
(1 thumb = 10nm)

1:250 000 –
"$\frac{1}{4}$ million" or "quarter-mil"
(1 thumb = 5nm)

Measuring distance using your thumb is fine for rough and ready calculations, but it rather lacks the high-tech, high-precision image that most pilots feel modern aviation navigation should have. Leaving aside your thumb, as it were, there are three practical ways of measuring distance accurately on an aeronautical map.

1 Measure the track distance with a pair of dividers. Failing that, and in the best Star Trek tradition, use a piece of string, a length of wood or anything else with a straight edge that can be marked. Compare this distance against the latitude markings on the map, remembering that 1 minute of latitude equals 1nm – the scale of the map makes no difference. However, you *cannot* check distance in this way in longitude.

2 Measure the track distance as above and then compare it against the scale markings in the map key (also known as the map legend). Do this for your thumb to see whether it is of average size.

Measuring a track distance along a latitude scale

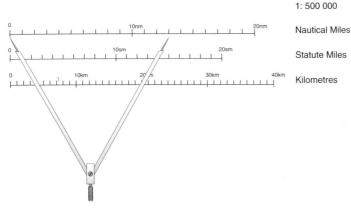

1: 500 000

0   10nm   20nm   Nautical Miles

0   10sm   20sm   Statute Miles

0   10km   20km   30km   40km   Kilometres

Measuring a track distance along a map distance scale

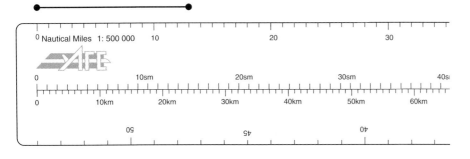

Measuring a track distance using a scale rule

3 Use a scale rule. This is obviously the most practical and accurate method, provided you take care to use the correct scale and distance units on the scale rule. More than one pilot has measured distance on a 1:500 000 map using the 1:250 000 side of a scale rule, resulting in some rather unlikely distances and ETAs. The solution is simple:

CHECK to be **SURE**

▶ Converting Units of Distance

We have already seen that distances can be expressed in nautical miles, statute miles or kilometres. Unfortunately this variability of units is not rare in aviation, so the ability to convert between units quickly and accurately is essential. For this reason we need to spend some time considering the basics of conversions.

One method of conversion is simply to refer to the scale and conversion markings which might be given in the map key. For a more accurate calculation, or if there are no conversions on the key, we need a *flight computer*.

Belying its name, the flight computer (also known as a "whiz wheel" or 'Dalton', after the man who invented the thing) is an instrument of anachronistic appearance, with no keyboard, screen or electrical components. As a matter of fact, the basic design has been around since well before the first electronic computers came into use. At first glance it may appear a fiendishly complex device, but in fact it is surprisingly simple to use. Conversions are done on the 'conversion' side of the computer, which is essentially a circular slide rule with aviation-type markings. Incidentally, don't worry if the words "slide rule" induce a sharp stab of pain in the brain (or a total blank in the memory) – it's all very straightforward.

The conversion side of the flight computer consists of two rings of numbers – an outer scale printed on to the body of the flight computer, and an inner scale printed on a rotating disk. Remember that a number printed on the flight computer as "50" can be interpreted as 0·5, or 5, or 50, or 500, etc. It is up to you to apply a little thought about the actual numbers you are calculating. Also there is a moveable 'cursor line' to help with lining up numbers precisely. There are other markings and windows, but don't bother about those for now.

The 'conversions' side of the ARC-1 Flight Computer

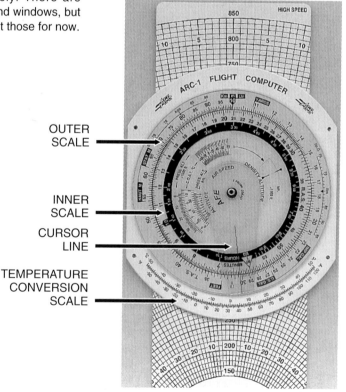

OUTER SCALE →

INNER SCALE →

CURSOR LINE →

TEMPERATURE CONVERSION SCALE →

Aeronautical Maps

To get the idea of how to use the flight computer, let's start with a simple multiplication – say 5 x 4. Set 1 on the inner scale under 5 on the outer scale. Without moving the scales, look around to 4 on the inner scale. Above it is 20 – which is the answer.

The basic flight computer set-up for multiplication

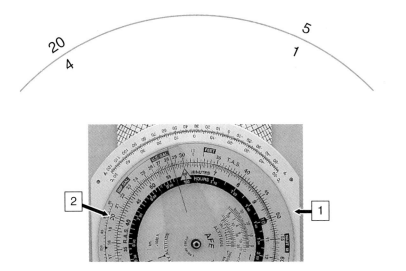

Multiplying 5 x 4 on the flight computer

A little thought suggests that to multiply 50 x 40, or 500 x 400, the flight computer would be set up in exactly the same way. The answers would be 2000 and 200,000 respectively. And herein lies a slight snag. Obviously the user must have a rough idea of the sort of answer expected and apply the decimal point correctly – both in setting up the flight computer and in interpreting the answer. Mind you, the converse argument says that this is one of the prime advantages of a flight computer. By keeping you "in the loop" of the conversion, the chances of a gross error (e.g. calculating 5 x 4 as 200) are reduced.

Now for a quick division, say 18 ÷ 4 (think of it as $\frac{18}{4}$). Set 4 on the inner scale under 18 on the outer scale. Above 1 on the inner scale, read off the answer of 4·5 on the outer scale. Easy.

The basic flight computer set-up for division

18 divided by 4 on the flight computer

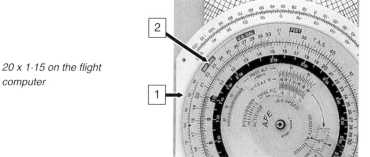

20 x 1·15 on the flight computer

So much for multiplication and division. Let's look at a more practical application, such as converting between units of distance. Assume that we need to convert 20 nautical miles into statute miles. If you happen to know that the conversion factor is 1·15078, you will realise that the calculation is simply 20 x 1·15078. This can be set up on the flight computer with 1 on the inner scale against 20 on the outer scale. Reading off the answer above 1·15078 (1·15 for practical purposes) we should find 23. So the answer is 23 statute miles.

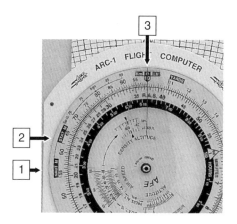

A more practical way to convert units on the flight computer. 20 nautical miles converts to 23 statute miles and 37·1 kilometres

However, there is an easier way to convert which does not involve memorising conversion factors. Start off with a mental check. Given 20 nautical miles and a conversion factor to statute miles of 1·15, an answer of "about 23" can be expected. On the flight computer, look around the outside of the outer scale for a blue box marked "Naut M" – i.e. nautical miles – with a marker line. Set 20 on the inner scale under this line. Use the cursor line if necessary to get an accurate line-up. Under the "Stat M" line, read off (on the inner scale) 23.

No problem, was it?

There are further markings to enable you to make more conversions. For the necessary mental checks, it's worth committing to memory the following:

1nm = 1·15sm = 1·85km.

1nm = 6080ft.

1km = 1000m.

1m = 3·28ft.

So, with 20 set under the "Naut M" line you can further convert to kilometres (37·1) and even feet (121,600). Given a little basic knowledge of the relationship between the figures you are converting, it really is as quick and simple as that.

For shorter distances, such as converting feet to metres and *vice versa*, the technique is exactly the same.

Example: convert 1200m into feet

A mental check (based on 1 metre = 3·28 feet) suggests an answer somewhere over 3600ft. On the flight computer place 1200 under the "Km m Ltr" line (m = metres). Under the "feet" line read-off the answer on the inner scale – 3940ft.

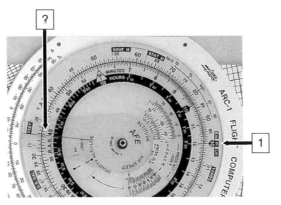

Converting 1200 metres to 3940 feet

The handbook supplied with your flight computer will give further instructions and examples, and it pays to start using the device as soon as possible. If you can use a flight computer quickly and accurately, you will save a lot of time during flight planning and the written exams. But don't forget the importance of establishing some idea of what the answer will be before you spin the wheels. There are various calculator-like electronic versions of the flight computer, and you might well be tempted to acquire one. However, most countries still require that the mechanical flight computer is used in the navigation exams. Furthermore, acquiring a degree of fluency with the old-fashioned mechanical item will give you far more insight into what you're trying to achieve and why, even if you eventually buy an electronic flight computer. It'll also stand you in good stead for the day the electrons decide not to co-operate. Electronic navaids of all kinds can be extremely useful; however, experience has shown that they will inevitably fail or become mysteriously unavailable one day, almost always at the worst possible time.

▶ Depiction of Relief

Returning to the aeronautical map, one of the first things to establish is how terrain is portrayed.

The first and most important step is to establish whether *elevations* (distances above mean sea level – AMSL) are shown in feet or metres. Given that 1 metre equals 3·28 feet, there is clearly a big difference between a hill 1000ft high and one 1000m high. The map key will clearly state which units are used, but for safety's sake **make sure you know what they are**. Something so fundamental is not worth leaving to chance:

ELEVATIONS IN FEET

ALWAYS check a new chart to see whether elevations are in feet or metres

CHECK to be *SURE*.

Having established the units in use, you can look more closely at how terrain is shown.

Contour lines are used to depict the shape and elevation of high ground on the majority of maps. A contour line joins places of equal elevation. So the elevation of any place on a contour line can be seen, and the shape and spacing of the contour lines gives the general shape of the ground. The closer together the contours, the steeper the slope. The vertical interval between the contours will be stated in the

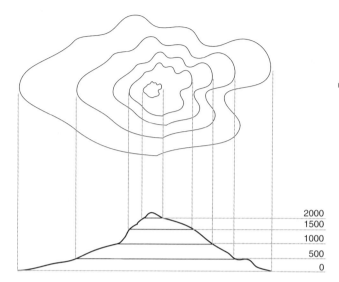

A section from the map legend of a UK 1:500 000 chart defining contour spacing

CONTOURS ARE SHOWN AT
INTERVALS OF 500 FEET AMSL

CAUTION
CONTOURS AND ELEVATION TINTS
BELOW 500 FEET AMSL ARE NOT
SHOWN ON THIS CHART.

Use of contour lines to depict a mountain

map key. It is not the same on all maps, so here again:

CHECK to be **SURE**.

Layer tinting is commonly used in conjunction with contour lines. Brown is often used, the shade becoming darker for higher ground. Yet again, check the map key for the shades and colours used and the elevation of each shade.

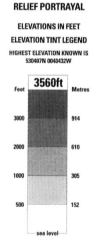

RELIEF PORTRAYAL

ELEVATIONS IN FEET

ELEVATION TINT LEGEND

HIGHEST ELEVATION KNOWN IS
530407N 0040432W

LEFT> Tint layers as used on UK 1:500 000 charts

RIGHT> Use of layer tinting to depict a mountain

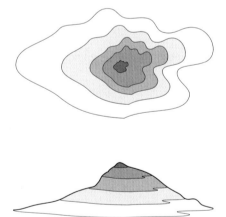

SPOT ELEVATION (AMSL).... • 2270

Spot heights indicate exact elevations, usually of summits or particular peaks. A spot height in a box indicates the highest elevation on the map.

A boxed elevation is the highest on the chart

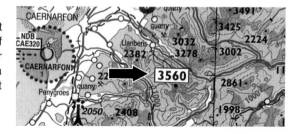

Aeronautical Maps

Hill shading is intended to depict the appearance of high ground, assuming that the sun is shining across it from the north-west corner of the map. The shading shows the shadow cast by the high ground under these conditions. This can give a useful 3 D effect, but unfortunately detail in the shadow can be lost.

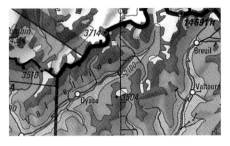

Hill shading on an aeronautical chart

Hachures are not commonly used on aeronautical maps, although they can be useful around a spot elevation to emphasise the shape and location of high ground.

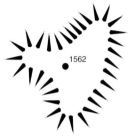

Hachures used to depict terrain

▶ Depiction of Cultural Features

The depiction of cultural features – map reading landmarks such as roads, rivers, railway lines, towns, woods, water features etc. is now becoming more and more standardised on aeronautical charts produced by ICAO states although, unfortunately, significant variations still exist. Within the process of standardisation it is also not unknown for the method of depiction – in particular the colours used for certain features – to change from time to time.

The only way to be absolutely sure that you do understand how cultural features are being portrayed is the look at the map key for the actual map you are using – especially if the map is new to you.

CULTURE

ROADS

Motorway, with Service Area
Dual Carriageway, with Service Area
Multi-level Intersection
Primary
Secondary and selected Minor
Under Construction
Bridge or Viaduct, Tunnel

RAILWAYS

Multiple Track
Single Track
Narrow gauge Track
Former railway, track removed (selected)
Bridge or Viaduct, Tunnel

BUILT-UP AREAS

City or large Town .... over 2 Sq km
Town .... 1 to 2 Sq km
Small Town, Village or Hamlet .... under 1 Sq km
Large Industrial Area

GENERAL FEATURES

Reservoir under construction
Power Station .... PS ■
Mine (selected) .... ✕
Racecourse or Racetrack
Landmark, annotated .... ■
Hill Figure
Monument (selected) .... ▲

Cultural features as portrayed on the CAA 1:500 000 aeronautical chart

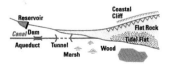

▶ Depiction of Airfields

AERODROME - Civil .... ○

AERODROME - Civil, limited or no facilities .... ○

HELIPORT - Civil .... Ⓗ

AERODROME - Government, available for Civil use. See UK AIP AD 1.1.1 .... ◎

AERODROME - Government .... ◎

HELIPORT - Government .... Ⓗ

MICROLIGHT FLYING SITES - Intense Activity also takes place at certain
Licensed and Unlicensed Aerodromes. See UK AIP ENR 1.1 .... Ⓜ

DISUSED or ABANDONED Aerodrome. Shown for navigational
landmark purposes only. See AIC 17/97 (Pink 135) .... ⊗

ELEVATIONS of Active Aeronautical Sites are shown adjacent to the symbol.
Shown in feet above Mean Sea Level 250 250

CUSTOMS AERODROMES are distinguished by a pecked line around
the name of the aerodrome and elevation .... ⌐MANCHESTER⌐
                                                       └ 256 ┘

AERODROME LIGHT BEACON .... ☆ FIG ⋮▪⋮▪ ☆ FIR ⋮▪⋮▪

FOR CURRENT STATUS, AVAILABILITY, RESTRICTIONS AND WARNINGS APPLICABLE TO
AERODROMES SHOWN ON THIS CHART CONSULT AIR INFORMATION PUBLICATIONS AND
AERODROME OPERATORS OR OWNERS. PORTRAYAL DOES NOT IMPLY ANY RIGHT TO USE
AN UNLICENSED AERODROME WITHOUT PERMISSION.

GLIDER LAUNCHING SITES. UK AIP ENR 1.1.

a. Primary activity at locations showing Maximum Altitude of winch launch. AMSL...... Ⓖ/2.5

b. Additional activity at locations showing Maximum Altitude of
winch launch. AMSL .... ○ᴳ/2.5

c. Additional activity without cables .... ○ᴳ

HANG/PARA GLIDING - Winch Launch Sites showing Maximum Altitude of
winch launch. AMSL. See UK AIP ENR 1.1 .... ⌣/2.5

WINCH LAUNCHED ACTIVITIES. Maximum Altitude of cables is represented in thousands and
hundreds of feet above mean sea level calculated using a minimum cable height of 2000ft AGL
plus site elevation. At some sites the cable may extend above 2000ft AGL. Due to the

The portrayal of airfields and aeronautical sites on UK 1:500 000 charts

Airfields, unsurprisingly, are important features of aeronautical maps.

The map key will show how different types of airfields are illustrated. It is common to mark civilian airfields in a different colour to military ones but – despite the best efforts of ICAO – the colours are not fully internationally standardised. There is no point trying to memorise which state uses which colour, the only solution is to look at the map key:

CHECK to be **SURE**.

The airfield name and the *airfield elevation* should be shown and the runway layout may also be depicted, which can be useful. The airfield elevation is the vertical distance above mean sea level (AMSL) of the highest part of the landing area. This is an important figure for *en route* aircraft as well as those using the airfield, since UK Aerodrome Traffic Zones (ATZs) extend to 2000ft above airfield elevation.

London Gatwick as depicted on a 1:500 000 scale map, note the airfield elevation (196ft)

▶ Depiction of Aeronautical Information

The aeronautical information on the map is obviously of prime interest to pilots. Once again the map key will tell you everything you need to know about the symbols and representations used. For an overview of the main airspace markings now is a good time to revise the subjects of airspace and airspace restrictions in the air law section (Book 2).

Right. Airspace as depicted on UK 1:500 000 charts

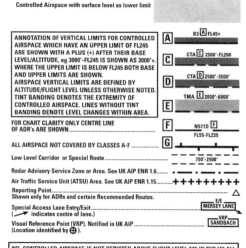

Controlled Airspace with surface level as lower limit

ANNOTATION OF VERTICAL LIMITS FOR CONTROLLED AIRSPACE WHICH HAVE AN UPPER LIMIT OF FL245 ARE SHOWN WITH A PLUS (+) AFTER THEIR BASE LEVEL/ALTITUDE, eg 3000'-FL245 IS SHOWN AS 3000'+. WHERE THE UPPER LIMIT IS BELOW FL245 BOTH BASE AND UPPER LIMITS ARE SHOWN. AIRSPACE VERTICAL LIMITS ARE DEFINED BY ALTITUDE/FLIGHT LEVEL UNLESS OTHERWISE NOTED. TINT BANDING DENOTES THE EXTREMITY OF CONTROLLED AIRSPACE. LINES WITHOUT TINT BANDING DENOTE LEVEL CHANGES WITHIN AREA.	Ⓐ B3 Ⓐ FL45+
	Ⓒ CTA Ⓒ 2500'-FL200
	Ⓓ CTA Ⓓ 2500'-3500'
	Ⓔ TMA Ⓔ 2000'-6000'
FOR CHART CLARITY ONLY CENTRE LINE OF ADR's ARE SHOWN	Ⓕ N571D Ⓕ / FL55-FL235
ALL AIRSPACE NOT COVERED BY CLASSES A-F	Ⓖ
Low Level Corridor or Special Route	750'-2500'
Radar Advisory Service Zone or Area. See UK AIP ENR 1.6	▪—▪—▪
Air Traffic Service Unit (ATSU) Area. See UK AIP ENR 1.15	+++++++++
Reporting Point. Shown only for ADRs and certain Recommended Routes.	△
Special Access Lane Entry/Exit (⟶ indicates centre of lane.)	E/E ⌐MERSEY LANE⌐
Visual Reference Point (VRP). Notified in UK AIP (Location identified by ⊕).	VRP ⌐SANDBACH⌐

NB. CONTROLLED AIRSPACE IS NOT DEPICTED ABOVE FLIGHT LEVEL 245 IN THE UK ALL
CLASS Ⓑ AIRSPACE IS ABOVE FL245. NO AIRSPACE IS DESIGNATED CLASS Ⓒ IN THE UK.

▶The Map Checklist

From the foregoing, you will appreciate that a few minutes spent looking over a map before using it can save a lot of trouble. Here are a few basic things to look for whenever you pick up an aeronautical map:

Date Is the map current, or is a new edition due?

Coverage Does the map cover the area you intend to fly over, including a possible diversion? What are the vertical limits of the map? A map with a vertical limit of 5000ft is not very useful if you are planning to cruise at FL70.

Depiction of terrain & airfields Are elevations in feet or metres? How is terrain shown (contours, layer tinting, hill shading etc.)? What is the lowest elevation shown, and the contour spacing? How are airfields marked?

▶Revision

6   Using a 1:500 000 Southern England or Northern England aeronautical chart, measure the track direction (True and Magnetic) and the distance (nautical miles) of a straight line between the following points:

A: The airfield 5nm NNW of Nottingham to the airfield at N5318·00 E00010·00

B: The airfield at N5310.41 W00258.40 to the airfield at N5328.17 W00223.21

C: The airfield 5nm SE of Holyhead (on Anglesey) to the airfield at N5319.01 W00111.46

D: The disused airfield at N5328.47 W00100.18 to the civilian airfield at N5306.07 W00420.14

7   What type of line is a straight line drawn on a Lambert Conformal Conic-projection map, and what is its significance?

8   Complete this table of directions:

True	Variation	Magnetic	Deviation	Compass
184	5W	–	2E	–
–	3W	303	–	305
–	5E	359	2W	–
–	10W	–	3E	002

9 What is the distance between A and B on the chart below (scale is unknown)?

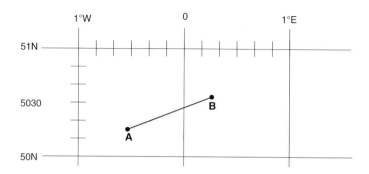

10 Complete the following table of distances:

Nautical Miles	Statute Miles	Kilometres
17	–	–
–	259	–
–	–	702
–	150	–
95	–	–
–	–	73

11 An aircraft has a calculated take-off distance required of 1635ft. The runway has a take-off distance available of 550m. Is this sufficient?

12 Using an aeronautical chart, what is the elevation of the airfield at N5320.17 W00208.56?

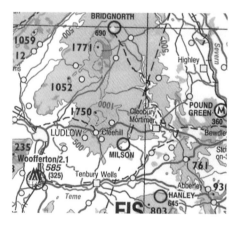

13 Estimate the approximate elevation of Milson airfield on the chart section reproduced below (elevations are given in feet).

14 On an Ordnance Survey 1:50 000 Landranger map, a 320m contour passes through a landing site. What is the approximate elevation in feet of the site?

Answers at page NAV 203

Navigation Principles:
The Triangle of Velocities

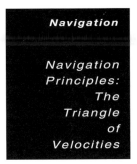

Navigation

*Navigation
Principles:
The
Triangle
of
Velocities*

▶ **The Triangle of Velocities**

▶ **Triangle of Velocities Calculations
on the Flight Computer**

▶ **Revision**

Exercise

*Navigation
Principles:
The
Triangle
of
Velocities*

▶The Triangle of Velocities

At first glance, the business of planning and flying in a set direction looks elementary. You can just measure the track direction on a map; allow for magnetic variation and possibly compass deviation; then jump into the aeroplane and fly the calculated heading. In real life, things are not quite so simple because of a phenomenon present virtually every time you fly – the **wind**.

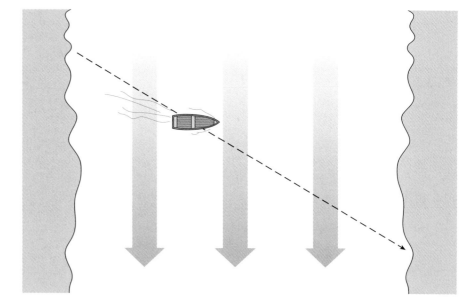

A boat crossing a fast-flowing river without making allowance for the current

Imagine a boat crossing a wide and fast-flowing river. The person sailing the boat is aiming at a point on the bank directly opposite the starting point. However, the flow of the current quickly takes the hapless sailor some way downstream. An aircraft moves through the air just as a boat moves through water, so the effect of the wind across the path of the aircraft (a *crosswind*) is much the same. Consider an aircraft flying at an airspeed of 100kts with an intended track direction of 090° between two points 120nm apart. If there is a 30-knot wind blowing from 360° (i.e. directly across track) and if our pilot makes no allowance for the effect of wind, he will end up around 35 nautical miles south (i.e. downwind) of the intended destination. Neither instructors nor passengers are likely to be impressed by this sort of thing.

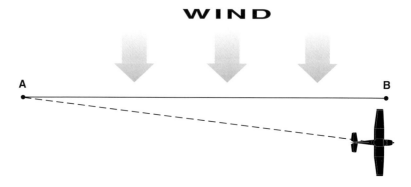

An aircraft's track if it does not make allowance for a strong crosswind

Navigation Principles: The Triangle of Velocities

So, back to the boat. To reach the desired point on the opposite bank, our sailor only has to head the boat slightly into the current to allow for the downstream 'drift' caused by the flow of the river. The pilot of an aircraft can achieve exactly the same effect, by heading the aircraft slightly into the wind to allow for the drift caused by the wind. This is not a hit-and-miss procedure – there is a simple and accurate way to work out the necessary correction for wind-induced drift. This is where the *triangle of velocities* comes in.

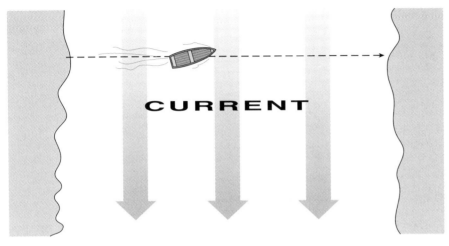

*Just as a boat can head into the current to maintain the desired track, so an aircraft can head into wind. The angle between the aircraft's heading and track is **drift***

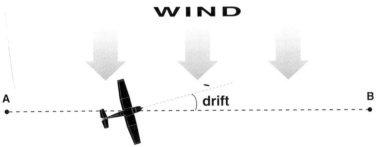

If you take the wind, airspeed and track figures from the above example, they can be drawn to scale on a piece of graph paper or something similar.

First the required track direction (090°) and distance (120nm):

Then the wind direction and speed vector – i.e. the wind velocity – (360°/30 knots):

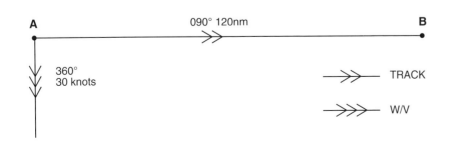

Wind velocity 360° 30 knots, desired track 090°, distance 120nm

Now open out a pair of compasses to represent the airspeed (100kts). Put one end of the compass at the end of the wind vector, and make a mark where the other end crosses the track line. Draw a line between the end of the wind vector and the cross on the track line.

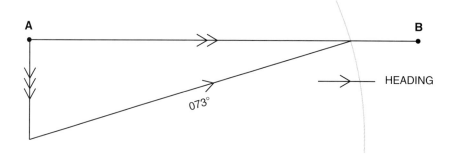

Heading required (to maintain a track of 090°) = 073°

The direction of the line just drawn is the heading necessary to maintain a track of 090° over the ground. In this case, you should find that the heading required is 073°. Easy

Before going further let's just establish a couple of important definitions:

The **track** is the actual or desired path of the aircraft over the ground.

The **heading** is the direction the aircraft is pointed (heading) in.

Drift is the difference between the aircraft's heading and the aircraft's track (also sometimes referred to as the *wind correction angle* or *WCA*).

Wind velocity is the direction *and* speed of the wind.

▶Triangle of Velocity Calculations on the Flight Computer

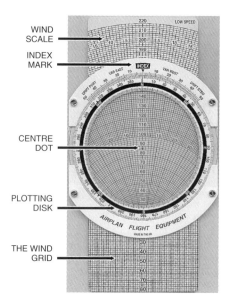

The 'wind-scale' side of the ARC-1 Flight Computer

Of course, messing about before flight with compasses and reams of graph paper would be both wasteful and time-consuming. Fortunately, there is an easy solution found on the wind-scale side of the flight computer. The wind scale has a circular 'plotting disk' which rotates inside the body of the flight computer, and a 'wind slide' which slides under the plotting disk. To see how to use this, let's start with the figures from the previous example.

We were given a track direction of 090°, an airspeed of 100kts and a wind velocity of 360/30. We want to find the heading necessary to maintain the desired track. A mental check (remember the importance of this every time you use the computer) confirms that heading should be 'into' the wind. This means that the heading will be *left* of track, therefore the heading should be *less* than 090°.

WIND
DIRECTION
360°

WINDSPEED
30kts

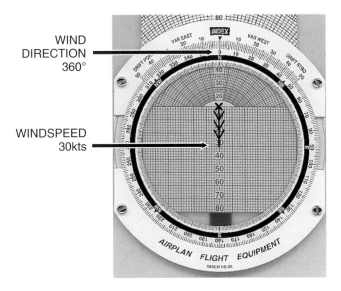

The W/V (360°/30kts) set on the flight computer

Here we go. On the flight computer, place the centre dot of the plotting disk over the '30' mark on the wind grid. This sets the wind speed. Now rotate the disk to set N (representing the wind direction) against the index mark and mark a cross on the plotting disk over the top line of the wind grid on the centre line. This cross represents the wind velocity. If you want to emphasise it, you can draw a line between 30 and the top of the wind grid. Now rotate the plotting disk so that the desired track of 090° is placed under the index mark and move the wind slide until the wind cross is on the arc representing the 'true airspeed' of 100kts (don't worry about the term 'true' airspeed for now, we'll come to that later). The wind line is 17° to the left of the centreline. If this drift angle of 17° is applied on the inner scale – left of the index mark – it gives a heading of 073°. Brilliant.

17° LEFT,
Heading = 073°

TRACK
090°

True airspeed
100kts

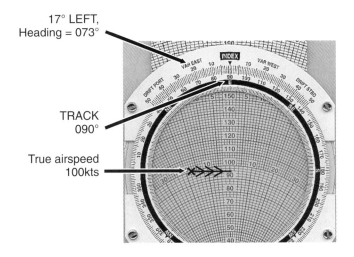

The track of 090° and true airspeed of 100kts set on the flight computer. The end of the wind arrow is 17° to the left. Apply this from the 'INDEX' line and you have the required heading – 073°

Now go back and re-read the above description. Then try it on the computer again until you feel quite happy that you can see what we're trying to achieve. The principle of the triangle of velocities is not always that easy to grasp straight away, especially for those of us who took our last maths examination some years ago. However, if you sit and think about it and work through some examples, the penny will drop.

The method just described is known as the "wind up" technique (because the wind cross is marked above the centre dot on the plotting disk). Predictably, there is an alternative way of doing the same calculation – the "wind down" approach, in which (surprise, surprise) the wind cross is marked below the centre dot.

To do the same calculation using the wind down method, first make the rough check as before. On the flight computer, set the centre dot of the plotting disc over the top of the wind grid. Rotate the plotting disc to set the wind direction (N) under the index, and make a cross on the disk over the '30' line (i.e. 30kts) on the wind grid. To help visualise the triangle of velocities, you might like to draw in a line down from the top of the wind grid to the cross at 30 to represent the wind velocity.

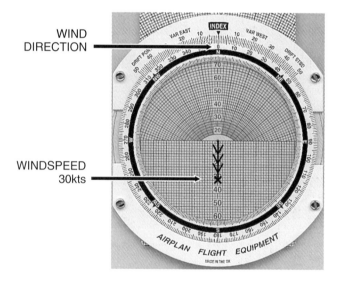

WIND
DIRECTION

WINDSPEED
30kts

A W/V of 360°/30kts set 'wind down' on the flight computer

Now move the wind slide so that the centre dot is over the '100' arc. This represents the aircraft's true airspeed – don't worry, we're coming to 'true airspeed' – and rotate the disc to set the desired track of 090° under the index.

TRACK
090°

16° of drift

True airspeed
100kts

When the true airspeed of 100kts and the track of 090° is set, the end of the wind arrow is showing 16° of drift

Navigation Principles: The Triangle of Velocities

Now you can see that the cross is about 16° to the right of the centreline. As an initial estimate, rotate the plotting disc clockwise by 16°, which will move the wind cross down. There is now a figure of 074° at the index, indicating 16° of drift, but the wind velocity line is 17° out from the centreline – indicating 17° of drift. There must be the same drift angle on the plotting disc as at the index. So move the disc a further one degree so that 073° is showing at the index.

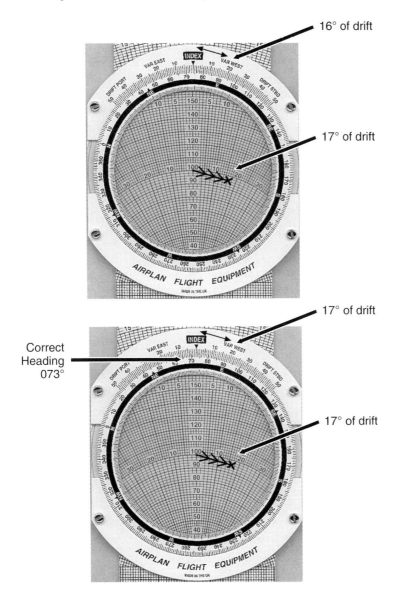

16° of drift

17° of drift

The wind is moved 'down' until 16° of drift is shown at the 'INDEX'. However there is now 17° of drift at the end of the wind arrow

17° of drift

Correct Heading 073°

17° of drift

With 17° of drift set at the 'INDEX', and 17° of drift at the end of the wind arrow, the correct heading is under the 'INDEX' – 073°

The wind arrow on the plotting disc still shows 17° of drift. The figure at the index – 073° – also indicates 17° of drift (90 minus 73). Therefore you have found the correct heading of 073° to maintain the desired track of 090°.

Obviously drift can be either left or right of the track. Left can also be referred to as 'Port' and right as 'Starboard'. To help remember these, they are marked on the flight computer.

Navigation

As you can see, both methods arrive at the same answer. Which one you use is a matter of personal choice – most often it will be the one your instructor prefers! From here on, both methods will be illustrated in the example calculations. You should concentrate on following your chosen method to avoid confusion. By the way, don't rub out the wind cross just yet – we're coming back to it.

Returning to the boat crossing the river, *direction* is only half the story. We also need to consider *speed*.

Imagine a boat sailing at a speed of 5kts. This speed is measured (and indicated on the vessel's speedometer) as the speed of the boat *through the water*. However, if the craft is heading into a current flowing at 5kts it will be stationary as far as the river bank is concerned. Conversely if the boat turns around and sails with the current, it will make a speed in relation to dry land of 10kts even though it is still only moving at 5kts relative to the water.

A boat sailing at 5kts into a current of 5kts is stationary relative to terra firma. A boat sailing at 5kts with a current of 5kts is travelling at 10kts relative to terra firma

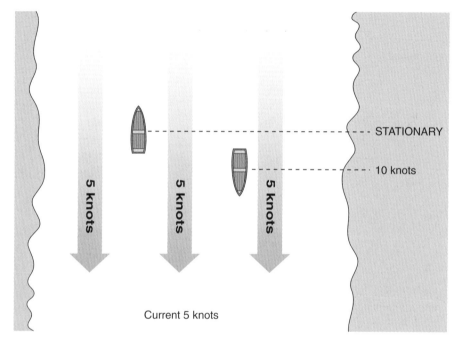

An aircraft is affected in much the same way. An aircraft flying at a speed through the air (referred to as *airspeed*) of 90kts and heading directly into a wind of 30kts will have a speed over the ground (referred to as *groundspeed*) of just 60kts (90 minus 30kts). If it turns around so that it is flying with the wind directly behind it, the

The effect on an aircraft's groundspeed of a headwind or tailwind component

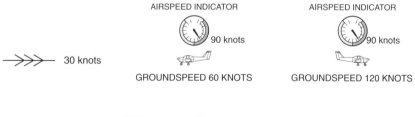

groundspeed will now be 120kts (90kts plus 30kts). Its speed through the air has not changed, only its speed over the ground. Airspeed and groundspeed are both very important concepts in navigation, and it's important to be clear about the difference.

Airspeed – speed relative to the air mass in which the aircraft is flying.

Groundspeed – speed relative to the ground over which the aircraft is flying.

The triangle of velocities also allows groundspeed to be calculated. Returning to our original example drawn to scale on graph paper, the length of the track line up to where the heading line crosses it is the groundspeed – in this case 96kts.

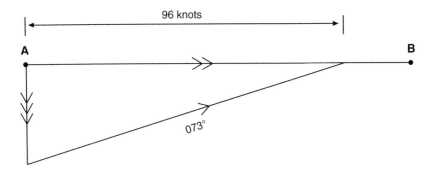

Groundspeed can also be found when heading required is calculated on the flight computer. Let's return to our original example. Given a track direction of 090°, a true airspeed of 100kts and a wind velocity of 360°/30kts find the groundspeed when the necessary heading is being flown to maintain track.

A mental check indicates that because we are heading slightly into wind, groundspeed will be less than airspeed.

On the flight computer, repeat the steps from the previous example using your chosen method (wind up or wind down).

Using the wind up method – when the aircraft heading has been calculated, the centre dot should be over the '96' arc. This represents the groundspeed.

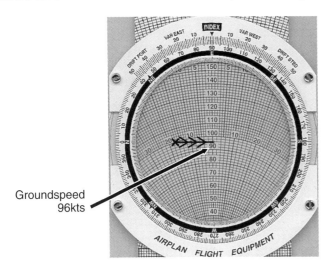

Groundspeed 96kts

The centre dot is on the arc of the groundspeed – 96kts

Using the wind down method – when you have calculated the required heading, the end of the wind arrow (or the wind cross) should be on the '96' arc. This represents the groundspeed.

With the correct heading at the index mark, the end of the wind arrow (or wind cross) is on the groundspeed arc – in this case 96kts

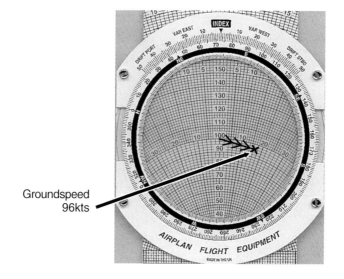

Groundspeed
96kts

It is as simple as that. Given a track, a true airspeed and a wind velocity (W/V) you can now calculate the required heading and the resulting groundspeed. If you're not entirely convinced, go over this again from the beginning until the whole thing falls into place. When you're happy with the general idea, consider these additional points:

– Track direction is first measured on the map in degrees true. The wind direction given in weather reports and forecasts is also given in degrees true. Therefore it is customary to calculate the heading in degrees true, and then to apply magnetic variation and compass deviation as appropriate.

– The proportion of wind speed blowing across the aircraft's track is called the *crosswind component*, more of which later.

– An aircraft flying into the wind is experiencing a *headwind*. An aircraft flying with the wind behind it is experiencing a *tailwind*. The difference between the aircraft's airspeed and groundspeed can be described as the *headwind component* or the *tailwind component*. So with a true airspeed of 100kts, and a groundspeed of 96kts, the aircraft is experiencing a headwind component of 4kts (100kts minus 96kts).

While looking at the wind-scale side of the computer, another less common calculation can be made. This is finding the wind velocity. Given a heading and airspeed, an actual ground track (or *track made good* – TMG) and groundspeed, it is possible to calculate the actual W/V. As we know from the Meteorology section of this book, it is rarely the same as the forecast wind velocity. In the air, this is the sort of calculation you are only likely to do if there is an autopilot (or preferably another pilot, who can keep a good lookout) flying the aeroplane and you have the time to spare. However, as a theoretical exercise it does help to reinforce the principle of the triangle of velocities.

Navigation Principles: The Triangle of Velocities

Example: given a true airspeed of 110kts, a groundspeed of 135kts, a heading of 230°(T) and track of 240°(T); find the W/V.

Mental check – groundspeed is more than true airspeed, so the aircraft is experiencing a tailwind component. As the aircraft heading is left of track, the wind direction is from the left.

TRACK 240°

Groundspeed 135kts

'Wind Mark' on arc of true airspeed (110kts) and 10° left (representing the heading of 230°)

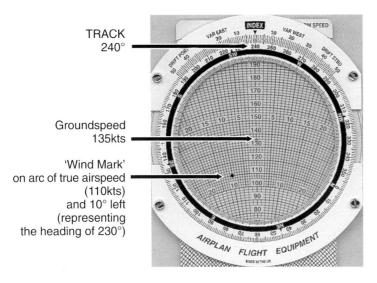

Finding W/V, the wind up method. The track and groundspeed are set on the flight computer, and a 'wind mark' is made representing the heading and true airspeed

Wind up method. Place the centre dot over the groundspeed (135) and set the track (240) at the index. On the plotting disc, make a mark 10° to the left of the centreline on the true airspeed arc (110). Rotate the plotting disc until the wind mark is directly over the centre dot, and move the wind slide until the wind mark rests at the top of the wind grid. Read-off 095°(T) at the index and 33kts at the centre dot on the wind grid. Hence W/V is 095/33.

Wind direction

Wind mark

Windspeed

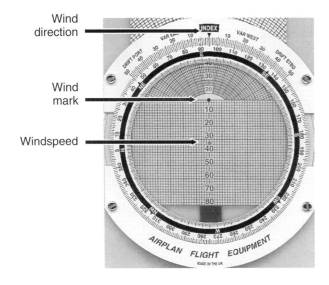

The plotting disk is rotated to put the wind mark over the centre dot, and the wind mark taken down to the top of the wind grid. Read off wind direction at the 'INDEX' (095°) and windspeed at the centre dot (33kts)

Navigation

Wind down method. Place the centre dot over the true airspeed and set the heading under the index. At 10° to the right of the centreline and on the '135' arc, make a mark on the plotting disc. Move the windslide to bring the centre dot down to the top of the wind grid. Rotate the plotting disc so that the wind mark is directly under the centre dot. Read off a direction of 095° at the index and a speed of 33kts on the wind grid at the wind cross. Hence W/V is 095/33.

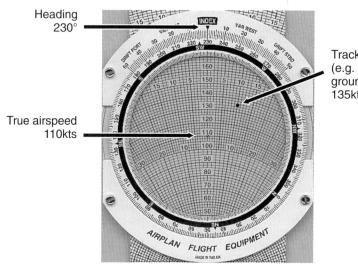

Heading 230°

Track 240° (e.g. 10° drift) groundspeed 135kts

True airspeed 110kts

Finding W/V, the wind down method. The heading and true airspeed are set on the flight computer, and a 'wind mark' is made representing the track and groundspeed

Wind direction (095°)

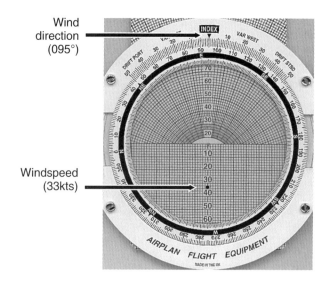

Windspeed (33kts)

The plotting disk is rotated to put the wind mark below the centre dot, and the centre dot is taken down to the top of the wind grid. Read off wind direction at the 'INDEX' (095°) and windspeed at the wind mark (33kts)

With a little practice, these operations should come quite naturally and quickly. Soon you will also be able to make educated guesstimates, thinking about the sort of answer you expect and cross-checking this against the answer calculated on the flight computer. It is possible to work out other useful things in the same general way (e.g. track made good and groundspeed given W/V, heading and true airspeed). Instructions on this type of calculation, together with further worked examples and sample questions can be found in the handbook which comes with the flight computer. And by the way, true airspeed is dealt with in detail in the next chapter...

▶Revision

15 Complete the "HDG (T)", "HDG (M)" and "G/S" columns of this flight log. Variation is 5°W (TAS = true airspeed).

D DIRECTION	RESERVE											
A ALTIMETER	TOTAL ENDURANCE											
BRAKES OFF	TAKE OFF				LANDING			BRAKES ON				
FROM/TO	MSA	PL/ALT	TAS	TR(T)	W/V	HDG(T)	HDG(M)	G/S	DIST	TIME	ETA	ATA
————			80	167	280/20							
————			97	242	280/20							
————			101	330	300/30							
————			110	010	090/15							
————					/							

16 A aircraft has a true airspeed of 89 statute miles per hour (mph) and a groundspeed of 97 nautical miles per hour (knots). What is the headwind/tailwind component (in knots)?

17 Find the W/V in the following table (variation is 4°W):

TAS	TR(T)	W/V	HDG(T)	HDG(M)	G/S
95	107		115	119	87
104	325			319	115
86	178			190	98
120	004			354	107

Answers at page NAV 204

Navigation Principles: Airspeed, Groundspeed, Time and Distance

Navigation

Navigation
Principles:
Airspeed,
Groundspeed,
Time and
Distance

▶ Airspeed

▶ Time, Speed and Distance

▶ Revision

Exercise

*Navigation
Principles:
Airspeed,
Groundspeed,
Time and
Distance*

Navigation

▶ Airspeed

Several tantalising references were made in the previous chapter to *true airspeed* (TAS). As you might imagine, TAS is the true (in the sense of real or actual) speed of the aircraft through the air. Less predictably perhaps, *indicated airspeed* (IAS) as shown on the airspeed indicator is rarely – if ever – the same as TAS. Indeed, in the case of an aircraft flying high and fast, the difference could be as much as a few hundred knots. Obviously there are significant factors at work, which we need to investigate.

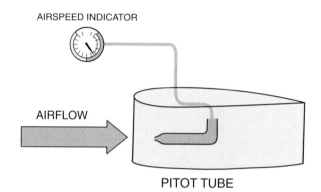

The measurement of airspeed by the pitot tube

The speed of the airflow around the aircraft is sensed at the *pitot tube*. This is a tube attached to the aircraft so that it is aligned with the airflow at normal cruising airspeeds. The pressure of the airflow is measured and displayed on the airspeed indicator. Inevitably, small discrepancies occur between the sensing of airspeed at the pitot head and the position of the airspeed needle on the airspeed indicator. These are collectively known as *instrument error*. Manufacturers do their best to minimise this error and it is rarely significant.

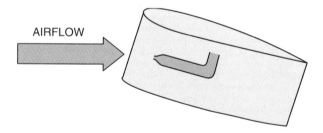

At high angles of attack, errors in airspeed reading may occur

Indicated airspeed is more significantly affected by *position error*. Position error is caused if the airflow into the pitot tube is disturbed, or if the airflow is not directly entering the tube. Position error is usually most significant during flight at high angles of attack (often associated with slow flight) or when manoeuvring, side-slipping or using flaps and slats. In some older aircraft, flying with any significant yaw causes marked position error.

When IAS is corrected for instrument error and position error the result is *calibrated airspeed* (CAS) – also known as *rectified airspeed* (RAS). There may be a position-error table in the aircraft's POH/FM comparing IAS with CAS over a range of airspeeds. At normal cruising airspeed the difference between the IAS and CAS is usually small, perhaps a knot or two. However, at low airspeeds a position error of up to 10kts is not unknown.

Having found CAS, this figure can be further corrected for *density error*. From the Meteorology section of this book, you may recall that air density is principally affected by temperature and pressure. In International Standard Atmosphere (ISA) conditions at sea level the air density is 1225 grams per m^3. Flying at sea level on an ISA day, CAS should equal TAS because the density is 'standard'. In anything other than ISA sea-level conditions, the density is different and a density error is introduced. When CAS has been adjusted for density error, the result is *true airspeed* (TAS). As a general rule, the higher and faster the aircraft flies, the greater the difference between indicated airspeed and true airspeed. It is almost always true that TAS is higher than IAS and CAS. As an approximate rule of thumb, in a 'standard' atmosphere TAS is 2% more than CAS for every 1000ft above sea level. This rule of thumb works up to about 10,000 feet.

The actual formula for calculating density error is relatively complex, but again the flight computer has the answer. On the circular slide rule side of the computer you will find a window marked 'airspeed'. The use of this is best described by example.

Example: at a cruising altitude of 7000ft, an outside air temperature of 0°C and a CAS of 120kts, what will the true airspeed (TAS) be?

A mental check says that TAS will be greater than CAS. On the conversions side of the flight computer, find the airspeed window. In this window, set the temperature (0°) against the altitude (7000). Use the cursor line to line up the numbers exactly. Without further movement of the scales find the CAS (or RAS) of 120kts on the inner scale and read-off TAS above it on the outer scale. The answer is 133kts.

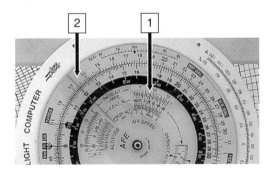

To calculate TAS, air temperature (0°C) is set under altitude (7000ft) in the "Air Speed" window. Above the CAS of 120kts the TAS is read off as 133kts

There are three points to note about CAS and TAS.

1 Strictly speaking, the altitude used should be the *pressure altitude* i.e. the altitude with 1013mb/hPa set on the altimeter sub-scale. However, the difference between actual altitude and pressure altitude is rarely enough to affect the TAS calculation significantly. Moreover, most flying above 3000ft tends to be done at Flight Levels (i.e. pressure altitudes) in any case.

2 You may see the abbreviation COAT, which stands for 'Corrected Outside Air Temperature'. COAT is the air temperature read from the OAT gauge and corrected for any temperature rise caused by friction between the aircraft and the air. However, temperature rise caused by friction does not become significant until the aircraft has a TAS of over 250kts – which rules out the majority of general-aviation aeroplanes.

3 Airspeed can be further corrected for *compressibility error*. Compressibility concerns high-speed aircraft flying at high altitude, and is not really significant at TASs of less than 300kts.

▶ Time, Speed and Distance

Knowing the distance between two points, and the aircraft's groundspeed, you can work out another important piece of information – how long it will take to fly between them.

Time is often the forgotten factor in navigation. All too often, a pilot will carefully calculate the heading to fly and then do his best to fly that heading accurately. However he totally forgets to check the time. He then ploughs on, holding the heading religiously and assuming that the destination will somehow miraculously appear if he sticks to it long enough. As soon as our man sees something vaguely resembling where he wants to go, he will probably go for it – regardless of the fact that a simple check of the time and the Estimated Time of Arrival (ETA), if he remembered to calculate it, would tell him that he is highly unlikely to have reached his destination yet.

Time is an important feature of navigation, which is the cue for another rule of thumb. Assuming that the airspeed indicator reads in knots (nautical miles per hour) and you have measured distances in nautical miles, it helps to know that:

At 60kts groundspeed an aircraft covers 1 nautical mile per minute.
At 90kts groundspeed an aircraft covers 1½ nautical miles per minute.
At 120kts groundspeed an aircraft covers 2 nautical miles per minute.

You might be intereted to know that military fast-jet pilots usually plan for a speed of 420kts at low level. This may sound like a curious choice but it equates to a figure of seven nautical miles a minute ($\frac{420}{60}$), making navigation more straightforward.

When dealing in simple numbers, these rules of thumb give fairly accurate times and ETAs. For example, if groundspeed is 90kts, a distance of 30nm will be covered in 20min. This rule of thumb can be used to make a mental check, against which the flight computer calculation is verified.

The basic set-up of a flight computer for time/speed/distance calculations

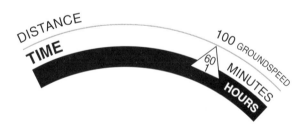

The circular slide rule side of the flight computer is used for time/speed/distance calculations. The key is to remember that on the flight computer the inner scale represents *time*, and the outer scale represents *distance*. On the inner scale there is a 'time index'. This mark represents 60 minutes (i.e. one hour) so a speed of 100kts is represented by setting the time index on the inner scale under the distance covered (100) on the outer scale.

Navigation Principles:
Airspeed, Groundspeed, Time and Distance

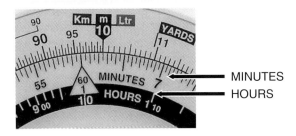

MINUTES

HOURS

The time index represents 60 minutes (i.e. one hour). The edge of the inner scale represents minutes, the coloured band represents hours

Example: how long will it take for an aircraft to fly 34nm at a groundspeed of 97kts?

A mental check based on about $1\frac{1}{2}$ nautical miles per minute gives a figure of around 20min. On the flight computer, set the time index under 97. In effect, doing so 'tells' the computer that the aircraft travels 97nm in one hour. Without moving the scales, under the distance (34) on the outer scale, read off time on the inner scale – 21min.

Distance 34nm
Time 21min

Groundspeed 97kts

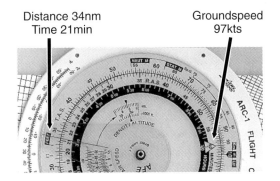

With the time index set to the groundspeed, time can be read under distance

This is all simple stuff. Once you understand the principle of this calculation, you will realise that you can just as easily calculate groundspeed if you know the time taken to cover a set distance. Remember that time is on the inner scale, distance on the outer.

Example: it takes 25min to cover a distance of 45nm; what is the groundspeed (G/S)?

Groundspeed 108kts

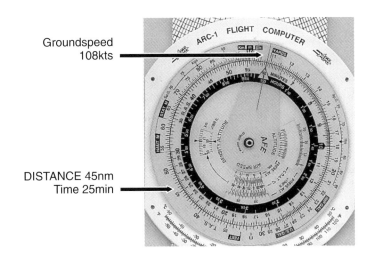

DISTANCE 45nm
Time 25min

With distance set over time, groundspeed can be read at the time index

A mental check suggests that the answer must be around 100kts, on the basis that in 50min (nearly an hour) the distance would be 90nm. On the flight computer, place time on the inner scale (25) under distance on the outer scale (45). Above the time index, which represents 60 minutes/one hour, read off groundspeed (G/S) – 108kts.

As an extension to this example, you can use the actual time between two points to calculate actual groundspeed and so calculate or revise an ETA.

Example: You were overhead point A at 1314, and set course for point B which is 47nm away. At 1329 you fix your position as being 26nm from point A. What is your ETA at point B?

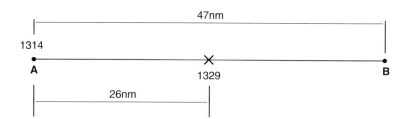

The time elapsed since passing point A is 15min. Therefore on the flight computer set time (15min) under distance travelled (26nm). At the time index you can read off the groundspeed - 104kts. Without moving the scales (in other words leaving this groundspeed set) look around to the total distance for the leg (47) and read off time under it (27mins). Add 27mins to the time overhead point A (also known as the Actual Time of Arrival, ATA) – which was 1314 – and you have the ETA for point B: 1341.

Given a distance travelled of 26nm, in a time of 15min, the flight computer can be used to calculate a groundspeed of 104kts

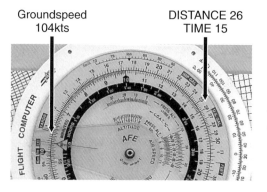

Groundspeed
104kts

DISTANCE 26
TIME 15

Now the groundspeed is known, it can be used to calculate the time over the total distance

Groundspeed
104 knots

Distance 47nm
Time 27min

►Revision

18 In the table below, at what IAS is there the greatest position error?

IAS	40	50	60	70	80	90
CAS	48	55	63	71	81	89

19 Complete the following CAS/TAS table:

CAS (Knots)	Pressure Altitude (feet)	OAT	TAS	
89	3000	+20°C	–	kts
120	9000	+10°C	–	mph (Statute mph)
75	5000	-10°C	–	km/hr
102	7500	0°F	–	kts

20 Complete the Time section of flight log:

MSA	PL/ALT	TAS	TR(T)	W/V	HDG(T)	HDG(M)	G/S	DIST	TIME	ETA	ATA
–				/			95	49			
–				/			79	89			
–				/			113	9			
–				/			89	124			

21 Complete the G/S, DIST AND TIME columns of the following table:

	TAKE OFF			LANDING			BRAKES ON				
MSA	PL/ALT	TAS	TR(T)	W/V	HDG(T)	HDG(M)	G/S	DIST	TIME	ETA	ATA
——				/				139	49		
——				/			99		1:14		
——				/			56.5	34			

22 An aircraft covers a distance of 176nm in 107min; what is the G/S (in knots)?

23 An aircraft passes point A at 0932, with an ETA at point B of 1007. The leg distance is 64nm. After some manoeuvring, at 0955 the aircraft position is fixed as being 33nm from point B. Based on the **original** groundspeed calculation what is the revised ETA for point B?

24 An aircraft covers a distance of 120sm in 1hr 20min. What is the G/S (in km/hr)?

Answers at page NAV 204

Vertical Navigation

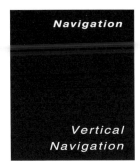

▶Introduction

So far we have only considered navigation in two dimensions, whereas aircraft travel in a third dimension – the vertical. The primary consideration in vertical navigation is **safety**, which in this case primarily means obstacle clearance. To put it in even simpler terms, flying from A to B whilst not hitting anything in between.

▶ **Introduction**

▶ **Obstructions**

▶ **Calculation of Minimum Safety Altitude**

▶ **Altimeter Settings**

▶ **Checking the Altimeter**

▶ **Vertical Navigation Calculations**

▶ **Revision**

Navigation

▶ Obstructions

The presentation of obstructions on aeronautical maps is becoming fairly standardised – but to be sure, you must check the map key. Are obstruction heights marked in feet or metres? What is the **minimum** height for an obstruction to be marked? How are different types of obstructions depicted? Here is another good reason for only using a current map. Whilst mountains and hills tend not to grow or move around very much, new obstructions often appear on updated map editions. Having a close encounter with an obstruction which wasn't there last year (and so

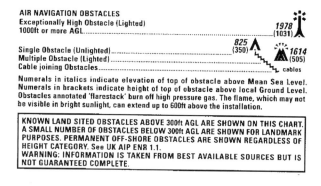

The depiction of obstructions on UK 1:500 000 charts

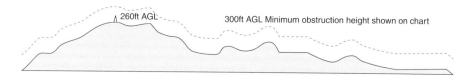

On a chart which does not depict terrain below 500ft, there can be unmarked terrain up to 499ft AMSL

wasn't there on last year's map, which you haven't yet got round to replacing) is just the sort of event to cast a shadow over an otherwise pleasant flight. As always:

CHECK to be **SURE**.

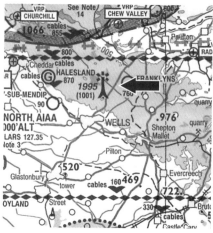

This obstruction on the Mendips (south of Bristol) has an elevation of 1995ft AMSL. The mast itself has a height of 1001ft AGL. From this you can calculate that the mast is standing on ground 994ft AMSL

As a **general** rule, obstructions are marked on aeronautical maps once they exceed 300ft AGL. Next to the obstruction, the bold figure is the elevation (AMSL) of the top of the obstruction. The smaller figure (often in brackets) is the height of the obstruction above local ground level. Cables between masts or lighted obstructions may also be depicted. Very tall obstructions are often supported by cables spreading out a considerable distance from the mast, which can be almost impossible to see from the air. You *must* give these a wide berth.

Vertical Navigation

Obstructions around airfields, even those which are too low to be shown on an aeronautical map, can present hazards to aircraft just after take-off or during the approach to land. If the airfield is listed in the Aeronautical Information Publication (AIP), any significant terrain and obstructions are noted within the airfield's entry in the AD (Aerodromes) section. This type of information may also be found in commercial flight guides. Remember that an unlicensed airfield may have obstructions on and around it which would not be acceptable at a licensed airfield. If you fly regularly to unlicensed airfields, private strips, helipads or microlight sites (which tend not to be in the AIP) it may be worth using large-scale maps such as the UK 1:250 000 series which show terrain at low elevations, as well as low-level obstructions such as power lines.

▶ Calculation of Minimum Safety Altitude

Once you have drawn a route on a map, your first priority is the calculation of the safety altitude (or minimum safe altitude – MSA). The usual recommendation is that the area 5nm either side of track and within 5nm radius around the departure, destination and turning points is checked. In this area, look carefully for the highest point – be it an obstacle or terrain.

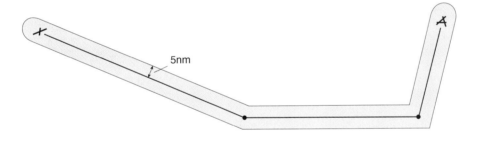

A corridor 5nm each side of track for MSA calculations

The highest en-route point – in this case an obstruction 822ft AMSL

BRAKES OFF		TAKE OFF	
FROM/TO	MSA	PL/ALT	TAS
MUCH MICKLE ――――― SOMEWARE	1900		
―――――			

The Minimum Safety Altitude for the sector Much Mickle – Someware entered onto a flight log

If the highest point is an obstacle, round up the elevation to the next 100ft. Then add a further 1000ft (the safety margin) to arrive at the MSA. For example, if the highest point *en route* is a mast with an elevation of 882ft, round this to 900ft and add a safety margin of 1000ft to arrive at the MSA of 1900ft.

If the highest point is a terrain peak, an allowance must be made for any obstruction which may be sited on the peak, but is too low to be shown on the map. Television and radio transmitter masts often fall into this category. If the minimum obstruction height for the chart is 300ft, there could in principle be an obstruction 299ft high just on top of the highest ground – which would not be shown on the map. To make allowance for this type of possibility, add 300ft to the rounded-up terrain elevation before adding the 1000ft safety margin.

On a chart which does not depict obstructions below 300ft AGL, there can be unmarked obstructions up to 299ft AGL

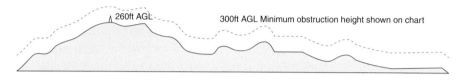

Example: the highest point found *en route* is terrain with a spot height of 830ft. What is the MSA?

Round the spot height up to the next 100ft (making 900ft), add 300ft for a possible unmarked obstruction (making 1200ft) and finally add a safety margin of 1000ft. This gives an MSA of 2200ft.

The highest en-route point – in this case terrain at 830ft AMSL

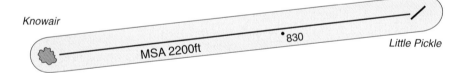

MSA Little Pickle – Knowair entered onto a flight log

FROM/TO	MSA	PL/ALT	TAS
LITTLE PICKLE / KNOWAIR	2200		

The calculation of MSA is also affected by how terrain is depicted on the map. Most maps will have a minimum elevation below which terrain is not shown. The minimum elevation shown on the UK CAA 1:500 000 aeronautical chart is 500ft (although some significant spot heights below 500ft *are* marked). The minimum elevation shown varies from map to map. Review the map key;

CHECK to be **SURE**.

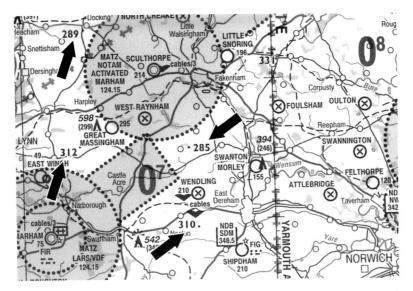

Although the lowest terrain shaded on a UK 1:500,000 chart is 500ft AMSL, spot heights below this are sometimes depicted where they are significantly above local terrain

If the lowest depicted terrain is 500ft, it is theoretically possible to have terrain at 499ft not shown on the chart. On this basis, even over the flattest and most obstacle-free areas depicted on a UK 1:500 000 map, MSA will never be less than 1800ft. Why should this be?

A quick MSA calculation shows the reason. A section of map with no terrain marked has a theoretical maximum terrain elevation of 499ft. This rounds up to 500ft. With no obstructions marked, the maximum theoretical obstacle height is 299ft. This rounds up to 300ft. Adding them up, (500 + 300) = 800ft. If you add a 1000ft safety margin, that gives an MSA of 1800ft.

Maps may be marked with safety altitudes or *Maximum Elevation Figures* (MEFs). Check the map key to see how these figures are calculated and what they represent. On the UK CAA 1:500 000 aeronautical charts, the MEF represents the maximum possible elevation of an obstruction within each box bounded by half a degree of latitude and longitude. It is **NOT** a safety altitude. A safety margin of at least 1000ft **must** be added to the MEF to find MSA or safety altitude.

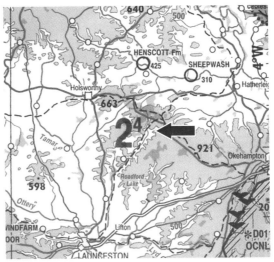

A Maximum Elevation Figure – MEF – on a UK 1:500 000 chart

The purpose of an MSA or safety altitude is to give the minimum altitude to keep you clear of the ground and obstructions, if for any reason you do not have clear sight of the surface.

MAXIMUM ELEVATION FIGURES (MEF)

3 2 Maximum Elevation Figures are shown in quadrangles bounded by graticule lines for every half degree of latitude and longitude. MEFs are represented in thousands and hundreds of feet above mean sea level. Each MEF is based on information available concerning the highest known feature in each quadrangle, including terrain and obstacles and allowing for unknown features.
<u>NB</u> THIS IS NOT A SAFETY ALTITUDE.

Explanatory chart note regarding MEFs

Don't get all this out of perspective; hundreds of safe VFR flights take place every day at altitudes well below MSA when pilots have good sight of the ground. However, especially over hills or inhospitable terrain, the MSA is a good guide to the minimum altitude you should plan to fly at. If you find yourself being forced below MSA by low cloud or bad weather, and you do not have clear sight of the terrain ahead, this is the time to think seriously about diverting or turning back.

▶ Altimeter Settings

Having carefully established the MSA, you need to give some thought about how to monitor it during the flight. So before going further, please revise the 'Altimeter Setting Procedures' chapter of PPL 2.

By this stage of the PPL course, you will appreciate that the altimeter is *not* a magic instrument that faithfully measures the aircraft's exact distance above the surface. It is in essence a barometer. Static pressure is measured and displayed as a distance, usually in feet (although some countries use metres) above a specific datum. The altimeter has a sub-scale that allows the pilot to select a specific pressure setting.

Just to refresh your memory, there are three main altimeter pressure settings:

QNH – when the QNH pressure is set on the altimeter sub-scale, **altitude above mean sea level** is indicated.

QFE – when QFE is set on the altimeter sub-scale, **height above a set datum (usually an airfield)** is indicated.

Flight Level – when the standard pressure setting (1013mb/hPa or 29·92 inches of mercury) is set on the altimeter sub-scale, **flight level above the 1013 pressure level** is indicated.

The Aeronautical Information Publication (AIP) contains recommended altimeter setting procedures which are summarised below:

Take-off and climb.

On departure from an airfield outside controlled airspace, any desired setting can be used. However, when flying IFR, vertical distance must be expressed as a flight level once the aircraft has climbed through the transition altitude. When taking-off beneath a TMA or CTA, aerodrome QNH should be used when flying below the transition altitude – although aerodrome QFE may be used when flying in the circuit. On departure from an airfield inside controlled airspace, at least one altimeter must be set to aerodrome QNH until cleared to climb to a Flight Level.

En route.

Outside controlled airspace at or below the transition altitude, you may use any desired pressure setting. Regional QNH is the usual setting except within a MATZ, where QFE is normally used. When flying under a TMA or CTA, the QNH of an airfield beneath that airspace should be used. Flying at or below transition altitude on an advisory route, regional QNH must be used. If flying IFR above the transition altitude, the standard altimeter setting (1013mb/hPa) *must* be set on an altimeter, and a flight level selected according to the quadrantal/semi-circular rule. Flying VFR above the transition altitude, it is advisable to do the same wherever possible.

Remember that the *Regional Pressure Setting* (i.e. the regional QNH) can be used to check terrain clearance.

Inside controlled airspace at and above the transition altitude, the standard altimeter setting (1013mb/hPa) should be set on an altimeter and vertical distance reported as a flight level. Regional QNH is used for terrain clearance. Below the transition altitude, the appropriate QNH should be used.

Approach and landing.

When descending from a flight level to an altitude, aerodrome QNH is used once the aircraft has vacated the last flight level unless further flight-level reports are requested by ATC. After the last flight-level report, QNH is used until established on final approach, when QFE (or any other desired setting) can be used. If landing at an airfield under a TMA or CTA, aerodrome QNH is used when flying below the transition altitude. Aerodrome QFE can be used in the circuit.

Missed approach.

During a missed approach (go-around) the pilot can continue to use the altimeter setting used on final approach, although ATC will usually expect vertical position to be referred to as altitude based on the aerodrome QNH.

So when flying *en route* below 3000ft, QNH is the usual altimeter pressure setting. Even if flying at a Flight Level, you can use regional QNH is used to check terrain clearance – preferably on the second altimeter if there is one.

From the Meteorology section you will remember that barometric pressure can vary significantly, even over a relatively short distance. We saw with the aid of an example that not keeping the altimeter setting updated can lead to unfortunate consequences. To help avoid such an accident, the country is divided into *altimeter setting regions* – ASRs. Within each ASR a *regional pressure setting* (RPS) is calculated. This is the lowest QNH expected to occur anywhere within the ASR during the next hour. RPS is also known as the "regional QNH". Any ATSU should be able to give you the current regional QNH in their ASR. Additionally a forecast office should be able to provide the regional QNH for any ASR, and the forecast regional QNH for one and two hours ahead (any change in RPS will always take place on the hour). This service is particularly useful during flight planning if flying a non-radio aircraft.

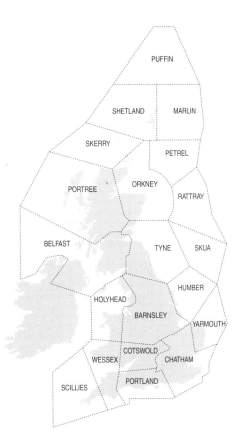

The Altimeter Setting Regions (ASRs) of the UK

Checking terrain clearance when flying at Flight Levels is more complicated than when flying on QNH. The reason is simply that when the altimeter is set to 1013mb/hPa, it is merely indicating vertical distance above the 1013 pressure level – wherever that happens to be. On the basis of the "Five Ps" (Proper Preparation Prevents Poor Performance), a little thought is required at the flight planning stage if you intend to fly at a flight level.

Example: one part of a flight passes over a range of mountains, where the properly calculated MSA is 3300ft. Track direction is 114°(T), magnetic variation is 5·5°W, and the regional QNH is 1001. Although the flight is being planned on a VFR basis, you have decided (sensibly) to conform with the quadrantal rule. What is the lowest FL usable for this part of the flight?

The first step is to apply the quadrantal rule and recall that it is based on **magnetic** track. With a true track of 114° and variation of 5·5°W, the magnetic track is 119·5°(M). This puts it into the quadrant where Flight Levels are selected at 'Odd + 500' i.e. FL35, FL55, FL75 etc.

On this day the QNH is 12mb less than standard (1013 minus 1001) which is a difference – at 30ft per millibar – of 360ft. On reaching the transition altitude of 3000ft, changing the altimeter sub-scale setting from 1001 to 1013 will increase the indicated level from 3000ft to 3360ft – i.e. FL33·6. This is the answer to the first question. On this day the lowest available FL is FL35, which is in the correct quadrantal.

So the next question is whether we will be above MSA/safety altitude at FL35? Remember that when the QNH is lower than 1013, the altitude is less than the flight level:

QNH low - look below.

The actual altitude at FL35 can be found by deducting the millibar difference (converted into feet) from the FL. Thus:

(1013mb -1001mb) = 12mb

(12mb x 30ft) = 360ft

Given that FL35 is 3500ft, (3500ft-360ft) = 3140ft

So at FL35 when the QNH is 1001, the actual altitude is 3140ft.

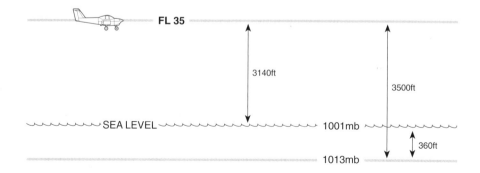

An aircraft flying at FL35,
when the QNH is 1001mb

The MSA is 3300ft. We know that with a QNH of 1001, FL35 corresponds to an altitude of 3140ft. So flying at FL35 would put you below MSA. Controlled airspace and cloud permitting, it would be better to choose the next available flight level for the track – FL55 – which will leave you at a comfortable altitude of 5140ft (FL55-360ft). This is a good safe margin above the MSA.

On days when the QNH is higher than standard (above 1013) take the FL and *add* the difference in mb/hPa to give the actual altitude. For example, let's assume that the QNH is 1025 and we're at FL60. Our actual altitude is 6000 + (12mb x 30ft) = 6360ft. When QNH is more than 1013mb/hPa, altitude is always more than the FL.

Example: the MSA is 4400ft and QNH is 1019mb/hPa. Is FL 45 above MSA?

The mental check says yes – because QNH is higher than standard, the altitude is more than the FL. To calculate the actual altitude, take the difference in mbs (6mb), multiply by 30ft (= 180ft) and add the result to the FL (4500) to give the altitude of 4680ft.

All this can look quite complicated on paper, but a few practice examples will make it easier. Don't be put off flying at flight levels just because of the need to make this calculation. Flying higher will give better radio reception, increased safety, a better view and possibly more favourable winds. It also offers more chance of avoiding assorted military machinery and less risk of encountering the hordes of VFR flights that always seem to potter along at 2500ft QNH!

▶ Checking the Altimeter

Having carefully calculated MSA and planned a safe *en route* altitude, it is worth establishing that the altimeter is working reasonably accurately before you head off.

The approved place for checking the altimeter before departure is on the airfield apron. The check is done by simply setting the airfield QNH on the altimeter sub-scale, and checking the altimeter reading against the known apron elevation. At larger airfields the apron elevation should be displayed in the Flight Briefing Unit (*q.v.*) and published in the AIP AD (Aerodromes) section. At other airfields, the best check is to set the airfield QNH on the altimeter and check the reading against the airfield elevation (which is shown on maps, published in the AIP and in flight guides). Airfield elevation is usually not vastly different from apron elevation. If you cannot obtain the QNH, set the airfield elevation on the altimeter and read the QNH on the sub-scale. This should be checked against a known regional pressure setting if possible.

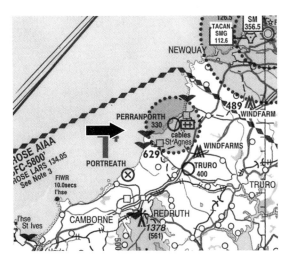

The elevation of Perranporth airfield (330ft AMSL)

As we have seen, it is important to keep the altimeter setting up-dated once you're airborne. Airfield and regional QNHs are available from ATSUs, and the regional QNH is also available on the FIR FIS frequency. Additionally, the QNH of a major airfield will be given in its ATIS broadcast, and on a VOLMET broadcast if the airfield is included.

When setting a QFE for approach and landing, check the setting against the known airfield elevation. For example if the airfield QNH is 1009mb and the airfield elevation is 300ft, expect a QFE about 10 millibars less than QNH – i.e. 999mb – on the basis that 1mb equals approximately 30ft. Some flight guides show the expected QFE/QNH difference for each airfield to save you the mental arithmetic!

The elevation of Perranporth airfield, and the representative pressure difference in millibars, as seen in the 'UK VFR Flight Guide'

ELEVATION	LOCATION	EGTP	
330ft 11mb	1.5nm SW of Perranporth N5019.90.W00510.66	**LND 114.** **BHD 112**	
PPR			

It is worth noting here that regional QNH is often different from the QNH of airfields within the ASR, and the difference often puzzles pilots. Remember the definition – *a regional QNH is the lowest QNH forecast to occur at any place within the ASR within a one-hour period*. On this basis regional QNHs tend to be a few millibars less than airfield QNHs within the ASR. Nevertheless checking QFE against even regional QNH is important, particularly to guard against a gross error. You don't really want to fly a circuit on the basis of a QFE of 981mb when it should have been 991mb, for example.

By checking and updating altimeter settings as described above, you should avoid the most common cause of incorrect altimeter readings – *barometric error*. This is a polite expression for the act of setting the wrong figure on the altimeter sub-scale. However, the altimeter reading can be in error even with the correct pressure setting on the sub-scale as a result of *temperature error*.

An altimeter is calibrated to ISA conditions, including a sea level temperature of +15°C and a lapse rate of 1·98°C/1000ft. Thus the altimeter works on the basis of ISA temperature at each pressure altitude (e.g. +13°C at 1000ft, +11°C at 2000ft, etc). At a non-ISA temperature the altimeter reading will be in error. As a general rule, when temperature is less than ISA, the altimeter will over-read (indicating a higher altitude than the true altitude) and *vice versa*. To get round this problem, the flight computer has a window that allows the calculation of true altitude, given pressure altitude and the OAT.

Example: Pressure altitude 5000ft (i.e. FL50), OAT -20°C. What is true altitude?

A mental check says that because temperature is below ISA for 5000ft, true altitude will be lower than indicated altitude. In the 'altitude' window on the conversions side of the flight computer, set the OAT (-20°C) against the pressure altitude (5000). Above indicated altitude

To calculate true altitude, the air temperature (-20°C) is set against the pressure altitude (5000ft). Above the indicated altitude on the inner scale (5000ft) the actual altitude is read off – 4540ft

4540ft true altitude
5000ft indicated altitude   -20°C at 5000ft

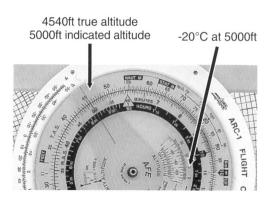

(5000ft) on the inner scale, read off the true altitude on the outer scale. The answer is 4540ft, which is rather a lot lower than 5000ft. This is one reason why MSA has to be **at least** 1000ft above the highest terrain/obstructions.

▶ Vertical Navigation Calculations

At the relatively low levels at which VFR navigation takes place, complex vertical navigation calculations are not the order of the day. Nevertheless, an appreciation of the vertical profile of the flight is helpful.

The aircraft POH/FM may contain graphs/tables for calculating climb performance. For our purposes we can consider a simple climb-gradient problem. Climb gradient is the altitude gain by distance travelled over the ground.

Example: You are departing from an airfield which has an elevation of 233ft. A hill with a spot height of 1325ft is located 6nm from the airfield and directly on track. To have a safe MSA over the hill, can you climb on track or will you need to detour around the hill? Climb airspeed will be 70kts, with a 5-knot headwind component.

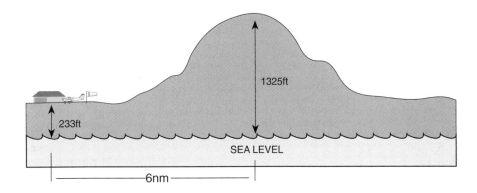

To allow for safe clearance of the hill and any obstruction on it, the MSA over the hill will be 2700ft. The airfield elevation is 233ft, which gives us our starting altitude. So we must climb (2700-233) = 2467ft by the time we pass over the hill.

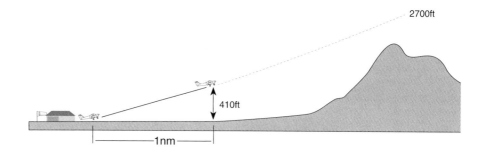

A climb gradient of 410ft/nm

2700ft

410ft

1nm

The climb gradient is the climb required divided by the ground distance (vertical distance/horizontal distance). So 2467ft divided by 6nm (do this on the flight computer for practice if you like) gives a result of 410ft. This is the minimum climb gradient (410ft/nm) necessary to reach MSA by the time you pass over the hill.

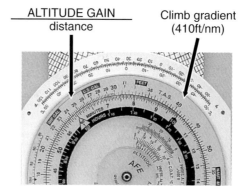

Finding climb gradient on the flight computer

ALTITUDE GAIN
distance

Climb gradient
(410ft/nm)

Unfortunately this knowledge in itself is of limited use because there is no instrument in the aircraft to measure climb gradient. However, we do have the vertical speed indicator, measuring and indicating climb *rate*. Converting one to the other is an easy job for the flight computer. Set the groundspeed of 65kts (70 - 5, the latter being the headwind) on the conversions side of the flight computer. Above the required climb gradient of 410 on the inner scale, read off the minimum rate of climb required on the outer scale. The answer is 445ft/min. If in the climb the aeroplane has an actual climb rate of less than this, you will have to divert around the hill to maintain safe terrain clearance.

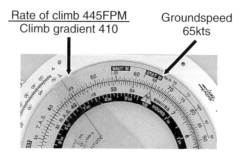

Rate of climb 445FPM
Climb gradient 410

Groundspeed
65kts

At a ground speed of 65kts, a climb gradient of 410ft/nm equates to a rate of climb of 445ft/min (feet per minute)

Vertical Navigation

We can take this calculation one stage further. If you expect a climb rate of 500ft/min, you can calculate what your altitude will be on passing over the hill. Given a distance of 6nm and a groundspeed of 65kts, the flight computer confirms that 'elapsed' time from take-off to passing over the hill will be 5·5 minutes.

Distance 6nm
Time 5·5 minutes

Groundspeed
65 knots

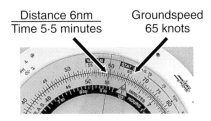

At a groundspeed of 65kts, a distance of 6nm is covered in 5·5min (i.e. 5 mins 30 seconds)

Working out (5.5min x 500ft/min) gives a climb of 2750ft. Adding this to the 233ft elevation of the departure airfield gives an altitude (AMSL) of 2983ft when passing over the hill – which is adequate for us to enjoy a good view of the summit from a safe height as we pass by.

5·5 x 500 = 2750

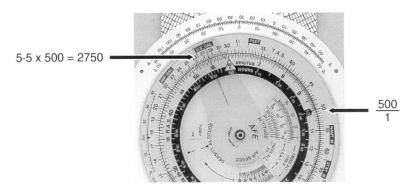

500
1

Knowing that the expected climb rate will be 500ft/min, you can use the flight computer to calculate the height gain in 5·5min (i.e. 5·5 x 500)

Descents can also be calculated on the flight computer. However, before we delve into the mechanics of these calculations, it helps to have some rules of thumb to work with.

Airliners making ILS approaches often use something like a 3° descent angle, which is a descent gradient of 300ft per nautical mile. This is a good datum for a light-aircraft cruise descent, since it allows a relatively gentle height loss without too much reduction in power (thereby being kind to the engine) whilst maintaining a manageable airspeed. To descend on a 3° slope, the required rate of descent in feet per minute is found by multiplying the groundspeed in knots by 5.

Example: at a G/S of 120kts, what is the required rate of descent to maintain a 3° slope?

G/S (120kts) x 5 = 600ft/min rate of descent.

From this you will no doubt appreciate that the higher an aircraft's groundspeed, the greater the rate of descent (ROD) required to maintain the same gradient. For example, the average light aircraft with an approach G/S of about 50-55kts will only need to descend at 275 feet per minute (ft/min) or thereabouts to maintain a 3° descent gradient. By comparison, Concorde making an approach with a G/S of perhaps 220kts needs a ROD of 1100ft/min to maintain the same gradient.

We can take this line of argument one stage further. If descending on a 3° slope, the distance required to make the descent is the height change involved (in thousands of feet) multiplied by 3.

Example: To descend from 7000ft to 1000ft on a 3° slope, what distance is required?

The required descent is 6000ft (i.e. 7000-1000). Since 6 x 3 = 18, we need to begin the descent at least 18nm from the point where you need to be at 1000ft.

Bearing in mind the first rule of thumb for calculating rate of descent to maintain a 3° slope, you will realise that with a tailwind (which will increase your groundspeed) you must either increase the rate of descent or start the descent sooner. Conversely, with a headwind – implying a lower groundspeed – you can either reduce the ROD or start the descent later.

With these rules of thumb in mind we can do more precise calculations on the flight computer.

Example: It is necessary to descend from 9500ft to 1000ft in a distance of 20nm. Given a G/S in the descent of 100kts, what is the minimum rate of descent required?

A typical descent problem. the aircraft has to descend from 9500ft to 1000ft in 20nm at a groundspeed of 100kts

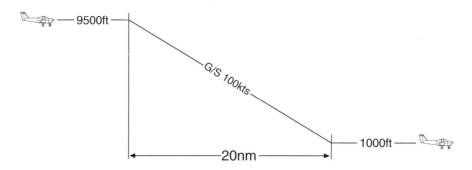

In this type of descent calculation the first step is always to find the time available for making the descent. On the flight computer you can see that at 100kts it will take 12min to cover the distance of 20nm. Now the amount of descent is calculated. The height to be lost is 8500ft (9500-1000). What remains is a simple division sum, which can be done on the flight computer as well. Dividing 8500 (feet) by 12 (minutes) on the flight computer gives a minimum rate of descent of 710ft/min.

At a groundspeed of 100kts, a distance of 20nm will be covered in 12min

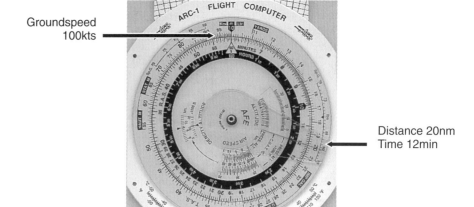

Groundspeed 100kts ➤

Distance 20nm
Time 12min

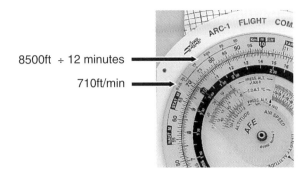

8500ft ÷ 12 minutes

710ft/min

$\frac{8500}{12}$ = 710, which is the required rate of descent (in feet per minute)

Most descent calculations are essentially basic division and variations on the standard time/speed/distance calculation. They can all be approached in the same manner. First calculate the time available for the descent, then the amount of descent, then perform the basic division of descent by time. There are several descent calculations in the revision questions for practice.

▶Revision

25 The highest point on one leg of a flight is a terrain 'spot height' of 2317ft. Assuming obstructions below 300ft are not shown on the map, what is the MSA at this point?

26 On a UK CAA 1:250 000 aeronautical chart, no terrain is depicted below 200ft AMSL and no obstructions below 300ft AGL. On a section of the chart with no terrain or obstructions marked, what is the MSA?

27 MSA is 4200ft. Track is 181°(T), variation is 2°E, QNH is 1005. What is the lowest available Flight Level if complying with the quadrantal rule?

28 At FL45 when the QNH is 995, what is the actual altitude (assume 1mb = 30ft)?

29 You are approaching the airfield at N5318 W00125. If the airfield QNH is 1015, what would you expect the QFE to be (assume 1mb = 30ft)?

30 Your position is 15nm from the destination airfield at 3000ft QNH. You want to descend to 1000ft (QFE) to be level 3nm before reaching the airfield, the elevation of which is 372ft. Your G/S in the descent will be 110kts. What ROD is required (assume 1mb = 30ft)?

31 Your airspeed in the descent will be 90kts, with an expected tailwind component of 6kts. The aircraft is at FL40, the QNH is 1025. The plan is to descend to be level at 1000ft QFE 5nm before reaching the destination airfield. The airfield QFE is 1015, and the descent will be started 25nm from the airfield. What ROD will be required to make the descent as planned?

Answers at page NAV 205

Aeroplane Magnetism

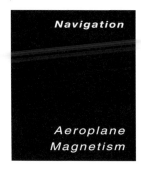

▶ **Aircraft Magnetic Field**

▶ **Compass Deviation**

▶ **Use of the Compass**

▶ **Revision**

Aircraft Magnetic Field

At the beginning of the navigation section, we looked at the earth's magnetic field, and the magnetic north pole towards which a compass points. We also saw that an aircraft has its own magnetic field. The majority of aircraft are largely constructed of metal and even those that are not – for example wooden or GRP-constructed aircraft – have enough metallic components (the engine, propeller, structural sections, etc.) to create a mini magnetic field. Likewise the instruments and radios of the aircraft will create a magnetic field which will affect the compass, and their influence is greatest when every available radio and service (e.g. pitot heat, lights etc) is turned on. One day, as an experiment, make a note of the compass reading when the aircraft is at rest without the engine running and with every service switched off, and compare this with the reading when the engine is running and every radio and service is turned on. You may be interested by the result!

Compass Deviation

Evidently, the aircraft's magnetic field will cause the compass the point in a direction that is slightly different to the actual magnetic north pole. The compass can be adjusted by an engineer to reduce these errors to a minimum, but there is usually a small difference left. This difference between magnetic north, where the magnetic north pole is, and compass north, where the compass is pointing to, is called deviation and is displayed in the cockpit in the form of a deviation card. Thus the compass reading can be adjusted by the known deviation to give a magnetic heading to fly. This calculation has already been covered in detail in the aeronautical maps chapter, so to avoid repetition you should revise this now if you are feeling unsure about how to apply deviation to the compass reading.

A typical compass deviation card

For	N	30	60	E	120	150
Steer	359	030	062	089	121	152
For	S	210	240	W	300	330
Steer	180	209	239	271	302	332
DATE						AIRPATH

▶ Use of the Compass

The Heading Indicator is the primary instrument for monitoring heading. It is best used to establish the aircraft on the heading required, which is then maintained by reference to a landmark ahead. Maintaining heading in this way helps to improve lookout and map reading. It also tends to make your flying much smoother. In normal flight the compass is used purely as a reference to cross-check the HI at regular intervals.

You may well practise navigating without reference to the HI as part of your flying training, using just the compass for heading reference. This is a useful exercise because, like any other instrument, the HI can fail. If you know or suspect such a failure, using the compass is a better bet than using an HI that may or may not be giving an accurate reading.

Aeroplane Magnetism

Navigating using the compass is not at all difficult as long as you bear in mind two principal differences between the HI and the compass:

1 The compass indication tends to move around a lot more than an HI display (especially in turbulence) even if you are holding a steady heading. It is also susceptible to turning errors and acceleration/deceleration errors.

2 The compass display is not as easy to interpret as that of the modern HI, and may lead the unwary pilot to turn the wrong way when changing direction.

Neither of these is a major difficulty if you are prepared. After all, there are plenty of vintage and small aircraft whose pilots navigate every day using only a compass for direction information.

To maintain a steady heading, the technique is just the same as for using an HI. With the correct heading showing on the compass, choose a distant landmark ahead as a heading reference. Remember that even the slightest turbulence will cause the compass card to move around a bit, so do not try to follow its every movement. Only take a reading when the aircraft is in settled wings-level, balanced flight at a steady airspeed.

To change heading, first make a mental check of the direction in which you need to turn and how many degrees to turn through. The nature of the compass-card display can easily tempt you into turning in the wrong direction. Bear in mind also that the compass reading is unreliable during the turn itself except when turning through east or west.

Assuming that you are flying in the northern hemisphere, estimate the turn using the UNOS rule – 'Undershoot North, Overshoot South'. This means that if turning on to a heading of 360°, you should roll out 30° *before reaching north* on the compass reading. Conversely, if turning on to a heading of 180°, roll out 30° *after passing south* on the compass reading. Knowing that the compass error is 30° when turning through north and south, and 0° when turning through east and west; you can guess that compass error is about 15° when passing through NE, SE, SW and NW. So you should be able to estimate the compass heading on which to roll out to achieve the desired heading. To minimise compass error, limit the rate of turn to rate 1 (about 15° of bank at average light-aircraft speeds).

UNDERSHOOT NORTH

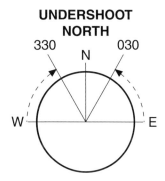

When turning on to northerly headings with reference to the compass "Undershoot North"

OVERSHOOT SOUTH

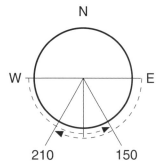

When turning on to southerly headings with reference to the compass "Overshoot South"

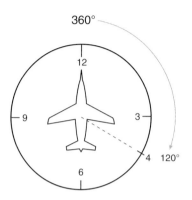

360°

12

9   3

4   120°

6

When flying on a heading of 360°, a direction of 120° is in the 4 o'clock position

As a cross-check, work out the number of degrees of the turn and convert that into a relative bearing using the clock code. For example, a turn from 360° on to 120° is a turn of 120° to the right. On the basis that each hour of the clock code is equal to 30°, the direction of 120° is in the 4 o'clock position in this case. Look out at this position for a landmark, and roll out of the turn when it is ahead. Using the clock code in this way helps to prevent gross errors, and is a good back-up to the UNOS rule. Once you have completed the turn and returned to straight flight, allow the compass to settle before checking the heading. You will almost certainly have to make some adjustment.

On the subject of the compass, it is worth briefly reviewing some aspects of the care and feeding of these devices. The reliability of a compass can be affected by all sorts of events. Some (like major maintenance, an engine change or a lightning strike) are obvious. Others are less so – such as a heavy landing, a change of radio equipment or allowing the aircraft to stand on one heading for more than a month or so. If in doubt, ask an engineer to check it out.

The compass will be influenced by even weakly magnetic materials carried in the aircraft. Some of these are mentioned in Book 2 (Air Law and RT) in the 'Carriage of Dangerous Goods' section. Compass errors caused by golf clubs, the use of 'Walkman' tape players and computers and the placing of headsets or metal ring-binders on the coaming near the compass are all well documented. The external antenna of a GPS unit can now be added to this list. Many pilots place the GPS antenna on the coaming or on the windscreen, where it has been known to deflect a compass by anything up to 30°. Undoubtedly GPS can be a blessing to aviators, but don't forget that the humble compass will still be usable when every other item of navigational and avionic equipment in the aeroplane has gone on strike – it's the ultimate back-up. So don't compromise it by placing metallic items in closer proximity than you absolutely have to.

Beware of placing objects near the compass which might affect its reading

▶Revision

32 The aircraft is on a heading of 280°. You need to turn on to north (360°). In what direction should you turn, and at what compass reading should you start to roll out of the turn?

33 You are on a heading of 020°. You need to turn the shortest way on to 110°. In what direction should you turn, and where is 110° in terms of the clock code *before* you start the turn?

34 Your heading is 140° and you need to turn the shortest way on to 350°. In which direction should you turn, and at what compass reading should you begin to roll out?

35 Your heading is 240° and you need to turn the shortest way on to 135°. Which way will you turn, and at what compass reading should you begin to roll out? Before you start the turn, what is the approximate clock-code position of the new heading?

Answers at page NAV 164

Practical Navigation:
Dead Reckoning and Map Reading

Navigation

*Practical
Navigation:
Dead
Reckoning
and
Map Reading*

▶ Dead Reckoning

▶ Map Reading Principles

▶ Practical Visual Navigation

▶ Revision

Exercise

Practical
Navigation:
Dead
Reckoning
and
Map Reading

Navigation

▶ Dead Reckoning

Although it sounds rather sinister, the term 'dead reckoning' (often abbreviated to DR) has nothing to do with the recently departed. It is an abbreviation of 'DEDuced Reckoning', which is a form of navigation known to seafarers for thousands of years. Dead-reckoning navigation is based on nothing more complicated than the triangle-of-velocities calculations already discussed. Before flight you calculate headings, groundspeeds and times as already described. In the air the emphasis is on flying accurate headings and airspeeds. At the calculated ETA you look down and, all being well, the waypoint or destination is below. Or at least it should be below – assuming the W/V was as forecast, that you flew the heading and airspeed to a high degree of accuracy and that your calculations were accurate. Nevertheless, even given these variables, DR navigation will usually take you surprisingly close to the intended destination. The early aviation pioneers made flights of thousands of miles across oceans and deserts; they relied almost solely on DR and achieved remarkable standards of navigational accuracy. Even in today's electronic age, dead reckoning is not to be consigned to the history books. If nothing else, it will always work even when every item of clever avionics in the aeroplane has ceased to function. All you need is a watch, a compass and an airspeed indicator.

Imagine that it's a sunny Sunday and you are thinking of flying across the Channel to France for the afternoon – one of the privileges of being a pilot, perhaps. For the purposes of ATC and the Full Flight Plan form (*q.v.*) an ETA is required for the London FIR/Paris FIR boundary. On the short sea crossing from Folkestone to Cap Gris Nez, the FIR boundary is over the Channel. The problem is that at mid-Channel, one wave looks pretty much like another. How will you know when you reach the FIR boundary?

Measuring a chart for the DR calculation of ETA at the FIR boundary

Looked at as a simple flight-planning exercise the solution is simple:

Example: Folkestone to Cap Gris Nez: track direction 130°(T), variation 3°W, TAS 75kts, leg distance 19·5nm, W/V 240/10. Use a map for reference if you wish

The relevant line of the flight log should look something like this:

The leg Folkestone – Cap Gris Nez as it would appear on a flight log

FROM/TO	MSA	PL/ALT	TAS	TR(T)	W/V	HDG(T)	HDG(M)	G/S	DIST	TIME	ETA	ATA
	———				/							
FOLKESTONE CAP GRIS NEZ	1900	FL 35	75	130	240 / 10	137	140	77	19.5	15		

Measuring the line from the coast at Folkestone to the FIR boundary gives a distance of 13nm. At the groundspeed of 77kts (check it out) the flight computer tells you that the FIR boundary will be reached 10min after crossing the coastline at Folkestone.

This is all pretty simple stuff. Unless some factor makes the groundspeed or track made good (TMG) grossly different from that calculated, the FIR boundary estimate is unlikely to be more than a minute or so out. Not bad, considering that this result was achieved using nothing more than basic navigation principles. No radio navigation aids, no GPS, just a modicum of navigational skill and commonsense. Moreover, if you have been monitoring the groundspeed and track prior to reaching Folkestone, the estimate can be modified if necessary. You should be able to achieve an ETA accurate to within 30 seconds (just the thing to impress ATC and maybe even your instructor!)

Dead reckoning always starts from a known point – the departure airfield, a point on the ground, the coastline, whatever. Clearly, the further you are from this known point, the greater the possible error between the calculated DR position and the actual position. Although DR is capable of giving good results on its own, it is nice to confirm its results in some way.

▶ Map Reading Principles

The other principal method of visual navigation – which, like DR, has been around since the first aircraft flew – is *map reading*.

Navigation purely by map reading is based upon the ability to relate actual ground features to their depiction on a map, and so establish the aircraft's exact position. To do this, it is necessary to know how various topographical features are depicted on the map. So we must refresh our knowledge of the map key. Mostly map symbols are commonsense and, after all, are meant to represent the actual appearance of the feature. The map symbols are explained on the map key so you have no need to guess what a symbol is. A little practice and practical application will soon fix the most common symbols in the memory.

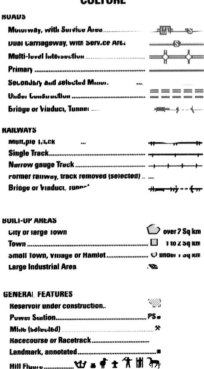

CULTURE

ROADS
Motorway, with Service Area
Dual Carriageway, with Service Area
Multi-level Intersection
Primary
Secondary and selected Minor.
Under Construction
Bridge or Viaduct, Tunnel

RAILWAYS
Multiple Track
Single Track
Narrow gauge Track
Former railway, track removed (selected)
Bridge or Viaduct, tunnel

BUILT-UP AREAS
City or large Town .... over 7 Sq km
Town .... 1 to 2 sq km
Small Town, village or Hamlet .... under 1 sq km
Large Industrial Area.

GENERAL FEATURES
Reservoir under construction..
Power Station .... PS ■
Mine (selected) .... ✕
Racecourse or Racetrack
Landmark, annotated .... ■
Hill Figure
Monument (selected) .... ▲

The standard map symbols used on UK 1:500 000 charts

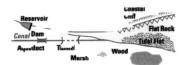

In the air, map reading is normally done 'map to ground' – that is, you select a landmark on the map and then look outside to identify that feature. Position fixing in this way is normally done in three stages:

General location. The selected landmark may have at least one major topographical feature not too far away – the coastline, an area of high ground, a city, etc. Such features are usually visible for quite some time, so you can establish that the aircraft is in the same general location as the selected landmark.

Local area. There should be several smaller features – towns, motorways, rivers, canals, railway lines, airfields, masts – around the selected landmark. By relating the position of these features relative to the landmark, the local area around the landmark can be identified.

Specific landmarks. The selected feature should be a prominent landmark – a town or an airfield, the crossing of a major line feature (a motorway, railway line etc.), a reservoir, an isolated piece of high ground, etc.

Looking for the selected landmark in this way should help to eliminate the error of mis-identifying it. A very common error in map reading is to make some ground feature fit the 'picture' you are looking at on the map. To avoid this scenario, make the assumption that each landmark has at least **three** unique characteristics depicted on the map and visible from the air. In looking at a landmark on the map, consciously search for three particular characteristics. When you look out of the window at what you presume to be the landmark itself, refer to the map and aim to identify the three unique features the landmark should have.

To identify a landmark accurately, it obviously helps to select one that will be positively identifiable and easy to recognise. Here are some basic considerations when selecting landmarks:

– Major topographical features such as coastlines, high ground and cities make excellent map-reading references for identifying the aircraft's approximate position. Line features such as motorways, railway lines, major rivers or canals – all of which should be visible for several minutes at a time – are the best features for fixing a more precise position, especially where they cross the aircraft's track. Features such as towns, reservoirs, tall masts, isolated hills etc. (especially if they have a good line feature nearby) will also enable you to make an accurate position fix.

– Minor airfields, especially grass ones, can be surprisingly difficult to spot and some private strips are only visible seasonally. Even a large airport can sometimes be less than obvious unless you look for the unique features around it. Disused airfields can vary between being very conspicuous and almost invisible. It is best not to use a disused airfield as a landmark unless you know that it is well defined. However, you could certainly use it as one of the 'three unique features' to help identify a landmark.

– Disused railway lines, minor roads and small villages (when the map does not portray their actual shape) are not reliable features on their own. Likewise woodland, small lakes and reservoirs and small rivers can be unreliable and may change seasonally.

When map reading, an appreciation of the relative bearing of ground features to each other, and to the aircraft, is essential.

Imagine a town selected as a landmark. There is high ground 10nm west of the town, a disused airfield 2nm to the north of it and a railway line running east/west through it. Forming a mental picture of what you see suggests that as you approach the town from the south, the high ground will be in view for some time. This will confirm the

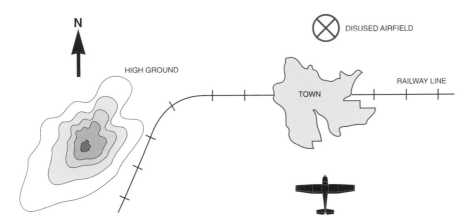

Three distinct features identifying a particular town

general location, and you know that the town is to the east of the elevated terrain. The railway line should become visible, confirming the general area, and the town should lie along the east/west stretch of the line. The disused airfield may not be clearly visible until you are almost over the town. However if the town is south of the airfield and the two other features look right, you have a positive fix.

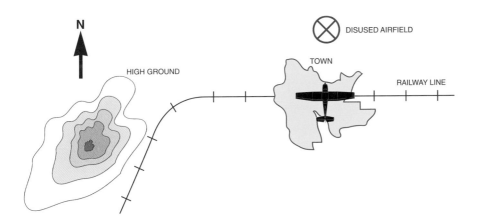

The relative bearing of the three distinct features to an aircraft which is over the town

In looking at map and ground features, you will also want to relate their relative bearings to the aircraft. This can be done using the 'clock code' as used when looking out and reporting other traffic in the air. Placing the map so that you are reading 'up-track' will make ground features appear on the map in the same relative positions as they should be seen outside, which makes map reading much easier. Going back to the previous example, by reading the map 'up-track' you can confirm your position over the selected town when the high ground is in the 9 o'clock position; when the railway line crosses under the aircraft from 9 o'clock to 3 o'clock; and when the disused airfield is in the 12 o'clock position.

Navigating purely by map reading has the advantage that provided there are enough landmarks, the pilot should always know his exact position. The disadvantages are the amount of time used in map-reading every mile of the flight, and the inevitable problems when distinct landmarks are few and far between. It's also a fact that time spent looking at the map subtracts directly from time spent looking out of the cockpit for other traffic. A pilot navigating purely by map reading will often choose to follow some distinct line feature, such as a railway, motorway or coastline, identifying landmarks as they are passed. This is fine until you want to fly to a destination which is not conveniently located next to some clear line feature. Then the flight may well proceed in a series of short legs between distinct landmarks whilst moving in the general direction of the destination. Not the most efficient way to travel!

▶ Practical Visual Navigation

Dead reckoning and map reading are two of the fundamental ways of navigating. Used in isolation, both have significant drawbacks.

Dead reckoning works well, but only on the basis that a) the flight planning has been done accurately, b) that the heading can be maintained to an accuracy of a few degrees, and speed to within a few knots of target; and c) most importantly, that the wind is close to that forecast. As soon as any one of these assumptions starts to become invalid, the aircraft will begin to deviate from its planned course and speed. The inevitable result will be a navigational error.

Pure map reading, on the other hand, implies that the pilot knows his precise position at just about any time. This is obviously not possible over the sea or a particularly featureless area, where one is reduced to flying on and waiting for an identifiable landmark to come into view. Moreover, even when constant map reading is possible, it leaves little time for other tasks. So the basic task of flying of the aircraft is almost certain to suffer – as will ancillary items such as lookout, using the radio, doing the cruise checks, or even just enjoying the flight! Map-reading every inch of the way (sometimes known as "track-crawling") is therefore not normally a practical option for a solo pilot. The only occasion on which a variation of it can be used is when you are directly following a line feature for all or part of a route.

As you might have guessed, what we are leading up to is a method combining the best of DR navigation with the certainty of map-reading position fixing.

As with all good flying, the key to good visual navigation is the planning (remember the five Ps – Proper Preparation Prevents Poor Performance). Each leg of the flight is calculated on a flight log at the planning stage, so that we start with a planned heading, groundspeed and time *en route* for each stage of the flight. The flight log also includes other information we might need whilst in flight – radio frequencies, a fuel plan, an alternate airfield, etc. In this way we won't have to search for vital information whilst also trying to fly the aircraft. The map (with the planned track marked on it) is folded so that the first leg can be viewed at a glance. If any part of the flight goes over a fold, the map should be re-folded so that it will open out into the new area. You don't need a degree in origami to do this on the ground, but you will need at least three hands to try to refold a map in-flight. You may also like to bear in mind Orville's First Law – that your destination will always be either on a fold or just off the edge of the map.

Once airborne, the flight starts from a known point – usually the departure airfield –

with the aircraft flying in a known direction (i.e. the calculated heading for the first leg) and at the planned airspeed. The basic principle is then "time, map, ground".

Time   Check that you have made a note of the airborne/overhead airfield time. Look about five or six minutes along track on the map. It is worth knowing that at average light-aircraft speeds of around 100kts, six minutes' flying time on a 1:500 000 map is represented by the top half of your thumb.

Map   At that position on the map, select prominent features and a landmark that should be coming into view, and their individual characteristics.

Ground   Look ahead at the ground to find and identify these features.

Then put the map down (yes, really) and concentrate on the actual business of flying the aircraft – maintaining an accurate heading and speed, doing the cruise checks, keeping a good lookout, operating the radio and maybe even enjoying the view! As the selected landmark comes within sight and is identified using good map-reading principles, repeat the "time/map/ground" process.

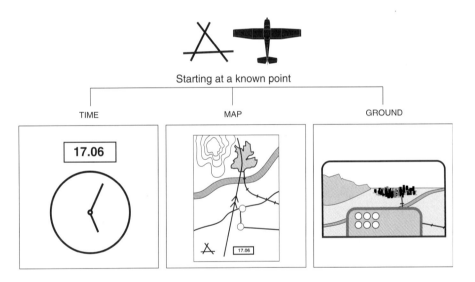

Visual navigation "Time; Map; Ground"

Time: Check that the present position is roughly in-line with the calculated groundspeed and ETAs for this leg of the flight. Review the time flown since the last turning point/fix. Look ahead on the map a further five or six minutes.

Map: Looking at this position on the map, select new features and a landmark that should be coming into view. Review their individual characteristics.

Ground: Look ahead at the ground to find and identify these features.

Maintaining the required heading and airspeed is obviously important so that we stay on track and make the ETAs accurate. Maintaining direction is best done by settling the aircraft on the correct heading using the Heading Indicator (HI). Then look ahead and choose a landmark in front of the nose which you can use to monitor the heading. This way you can maintain a constant direction without constantly referring to the HI. This allows you to improve your lookout and gives you the chance to enjoy the view and watch for the selected feature coming into sight.

▶Revision

36   You are on a cross-Channel flight, routing on a straight line from the Midhurst VOR (MID) to a point on the London/Paris FIR boundary. You pass over the MID VOR at 1123, and cross the coast (a distance of 17nm) at 1132. If the FIR boundary is 57nm from the MID VOR, what is your ETA there?

37   Looking out from an aircraft on a westerly heading you see a large town in the 9 o'clock position, a railway line parallel to track in the 2 o'clock position, and a reservoir in the 4 o'clock position. Mark the aircraft's position on the map below.

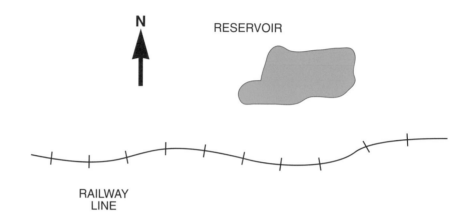

N

RESERVOIR

RAILWAY
LINE

TOWN

Answers on page NAV 205

Practical Navigation:
Departure, En-Route, and Arrival Procedures

Navigation

Practical
Navigation:
Departure,
En-Route
and Arrival
Procedures

▶ **Introduction**

'Proper Preparation Prevents Poor Performance'. The truth of this axiom is evident in many walks of life, and it is especially relevant in aviation. However, careful and meticulous flight planning is not the whole story. Once in the aircraft, it is necessary to organise your workload in a systematic way to get the best out of all your careful flight planning and calculations. A combination of Proper Preparation and an organised approach to the flight itself will make flying safer, easier and more fun.

▶ **Introduction**

▶ **Departure Procedures**

▶ **En-Route Procedures**

▶ **Turning-Point Procedures**

▶ **Arrival Procedures**

▶ **Visual Navigation – A Practical Example**

Exercise

*Practical
Navigation:
Departure
En-Route
and Arrival
Procedures*

Navigation

▶ Departure Procedures

Review the booking-out procedures before getting into the aircraft. At your home base, booking-out is likely to be second nature. At other airfields:

CHECK to be **SURE**.

At small airfields it may be sufficient to fill in the flight details on a 'booking/flight record sheet'. At a larger airfield, a visit or phone call to the ATSU may be necessary. Beware – some airfields will accept booking-out details over the radio, but others will not. A long walk back from the aircraft to the ATSU is not the best way to start a flight...

Before taxying, make sure everything is to hand. You should have a kneeboard or similar with the flight log on top, together with a chart marker and a pen, with at least one spare. The map should be to hand, folded correctly, with the first leg of the flight ready to view. If you're flying to another airfield, a flight guide will be useful. Just about all other paraphernalia – flight computers, rulers, protractors etc. – should be stowed away, so they can't get loose in the cockpit in flight.

Before take-off, check the planned heading after departure. Five hundred feet above the runway is *not* the place to be searching through the flight log for the first required heading! Whilst lining up on the runway, check the compass and HI against the known runway direction for a gross error in the HI reading and make a note of the time.

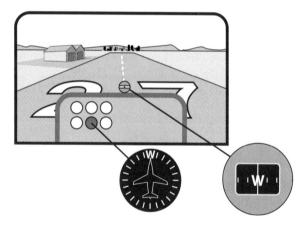

When lining up on the runway before take-off, check the compass and HI against the known runway direction

The departure procedure will vary from place to place. At smaller airfields it may be possible to turn directly on to track after take-off; or to climb and set course overhead the airfield. If you do set course from overhead the field, remember to check the time again when passing overhead and to use this for calculating the first ETA. At larger airfields a departure routing identified by a local landmark or Visual Reference Point (VRP) is more likely, in which case the route should have been planned accordingly. On reaching the initial planned level, **level out and lookout.** Confirm your present position with reference to the airfield, then look ahead – reading map to ground – to ensure you're following the correct track. Read "time, map, ground" to select the first *en route* landmark and make a note of the ETA for the first turning point. Now is a good time to do a cruise check, such as 'FREDA', and settle down to the routine of flying and navigating the aircraft. The map should

Practical Navigation:
Departure, En-Route and Arrival Procedures

be on your knee, orientated "up-track", and the kneeboard with flight log should be readily accessible underneath. If this is an early navigational exercise, take a deep breath and remind yourself that you are meant to be enjoying this!

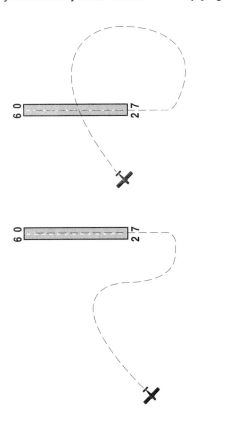

The common methods of setting course after departure

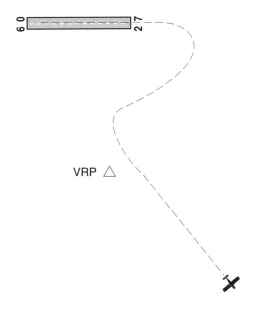

VRP △

Navigation

▶ En-Route Procedures

The first principle to apply is **ANC** – 'Aviate, Navigate, Communicate'.

This is a good moment to recall that ANC should be your order of priorities at all times. It is all too easy on a map-reading exercise to become totally engrossed in the map. You may eventually look up to find the aircraft peeling away from the planned heading and altitude. In fact, applying ANC actually helps navigation because there is less chance of the aircraft deviating from the planned heading and groundspeed. In summary:

Aviate: Confirm that the correct airspeed, altitude and heading are being flown – and *lookout.*

Navigate: Read "time, map, ground"; look for the next selected landmark and the features around it.

Communicate: This can usually wait until the top two priorities have been seen to.

The cruise checks are an important part of in-flight organisation. As well as establishing that the flight is proceeding normally at the moment, they can be used to plan ahead. Here is an example of how to use the FREDA cruise checks to reduce your workload by thinking ahead:

ITEM	CHECK	PLAN AHEAD
FUEL	Sufficient, correct tank selected, tanks in balance	What is the remaining endurance? Is there sufficient reserve for holding/diversion?
RADIO	Frequency & Volume, Transponder	When is the next report required? What will the next frequency be? Is a check of ATIS or VOLMET necessary or advisable?
ENGINE	Temperature and Pressures, mixture, carb. heat check, ammeter and suction	If changing power or altitude will the mixture need to be adjusted? Is there evidence of carb. icing? When does it next need to be checked?
DIRECTION	Correct heading being flown and HI aligned with compass	What landmark is being used to maintain heading? If approaching a turning point, what will the next heading be?
ALTITUDE	Level and pressure setting	What pressure setting is being used? Will a new level or pressure setting be needed soon? What is the safety altitude/MSA?

All this can look daunting if you're seeing it in print for the first time. You might think you're going to be working non-stop from take-off to touchdown: in fact, properly applying the thinking process will *save* you time. Planning and thinking ahead will save endless hassle in the business of flying an aircraft, and organising your in-flight workload is the best way of ensuring that things don't all happen at once. And the more you do it, the more it becomes a habit. In quiet moments, prepare for what will be happening five, ten or fifteen minutes ahead. Maybe the VOLMET service or an ATIS broadcast can be used to check the weather. If the aircraft has two radios, the next frequency you expect to use can be selected on the spare. You may want to check the ETA at the destination and review the fuel situation – will you need to refuel on arrival?

You can also use spare thinking capacity to run through theoretical 'What If?' scenarios. If you cannot land at your destination, where will you divert to? What is the nearest airfield at the moment? If the weather turned bad, what would you do?

All these elements of organising your workload are designed to avoid the situation of being caught out by an unexpected event, or a sudden increase in workload that could have been avoided by thinking and planning ahead. For example, imagine you are approaching a major airfield which is inside controlled airspace. If you have been operating on the 'Aviate, Navigate, Communicate' principle the aircraft should have the heading, altitude and airspeed you want. By navigating "time, map, ground" you should know your position, and when you expect to see the next selected landmark. You should also have an approximate ETA for the boundary of controlled airspace and the airfield itself. As part of the cruise checks, you should have already listened to the ATIS service (if there is one), contacted the approach frequency in plenty of time and set the altimeter as required. The information from the ATIS broadcast or approach controller will also have given you the runway and arrival pattern to expect. If you have been thinking 'what if?' you will already have considered your options if the airfield becomes suddenly unavailable, or if you cannot establish radio contact. All in all, you should feel that everything is well under control and you will have the spare capacity to build up your *situational awareness* and actually enjoy your flying. And all of this is possible because you have been thinking and planning ahead – not leaving everything until you arrive at the zone boundary!

Situational awareness is a state of mind that all pilots try to achieve, and is largely obtained through:

Awareness of the present situation, inside and outside the cockpit.

Preparation for tasks and situations that will occur soon.

Anticipation of problems, workload peaks and changes of plan.

Situational awareness is achieved largely by applying the principles already covered. At first, this may require a fair amount of concentration and mental discipline. However, action and preparation to make a flight pass more smoothly and professionally should soon become almost instinctive. It will probably feel as if you have much more time available to fly the aircraft, whereas in fact all you have done is organise your workload and planned ahead.

To sum it all up, the conscious steps to apply are:

– Establish your priorities: Aviate, Navigate, Communicate.

– Navigate by "time, map, ground".

– Use regular cruise checks to increase situational awareness and plan ahead.

– In quiet moments consider "what if?".

▶ Turning-Point Procedures

Most flights involve a number of legs, which end in *turning points* (also known as *waypoints*). At each turning point, apply the four Ts:

Time: Check the actual time over the turning point and note this as the ATA (Actual Time of Arrival) in the flight log.

Turn: Lookout and turn on to the new heading. When established on this heading, note a distant landmark for monitoring direction.

Talk: Report your position and new heading if necessary.

Task: Calculate the ETA at the next turning point/waypoint and attend to any other task necessary on this new leg – a change of altitude, a change of radio frequency etc.

▶ Arrival Procedures

The arrival procedure will vary from airfield to airfield, and may even vary at the same airfield depending on whether ATC is in operation or not. The golden rule is still to plan ahead.

Identification of the airfield is done initially from the map, applying the standard "time, map, ground" and "three unique characteristics" principles. It is particularly important to be careful about identifying the airfield. At the end of a flight, on seeing an airfield approximately where you expect it to be, it is very easy to put the map away and prepare for landing without looking objectively at it and positively ensuring that it really *is* the correct airfield. Approaching or even landing at the wrong place is by no means unknown where two airfields are close together – or even quite far apart! Well known examples in the UK include aircraft landing at RAF St Athan instead of Cardiff; Langar (parachuting site) or RAF Syerston instead of Nottingham; Cambridge instead of Duxford; North Weald instead of Stapleford; RAF Shawbury instead of Sleap; and RAF Cosford instead of Wolverhampton airfield. Even airliners are said to have landed at Woodford instead of Manchester, RAF Northolt instead of Heathrow and Wymeswold disused airfield instead of East Midlands. To avoid this sort of embarrassment – how would you tell a cabin full of passengers that you had just landed at the wrong airfield? – apply the 'three unique characteristics' principle to an airfield and check the ETA, just as you would with any other landmark. It helps to have a flight guide which will have a plan of the airfield layout.

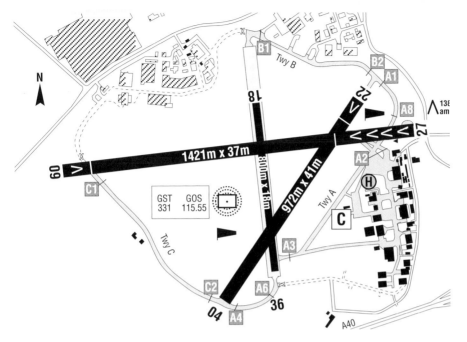

The runway layout of Gloucestershire airport as seen in the UK VFR Flight Guide

An overhead join is often standard at smaller and non-radio airfields, so envisage beforehand how you will fly this in relation to the runway in use. At larger and busier airfields it is not uncommon to be instructed to join straight into the circuit, either on downwind, base leg or finals. Listen out to acquire a picture of the other

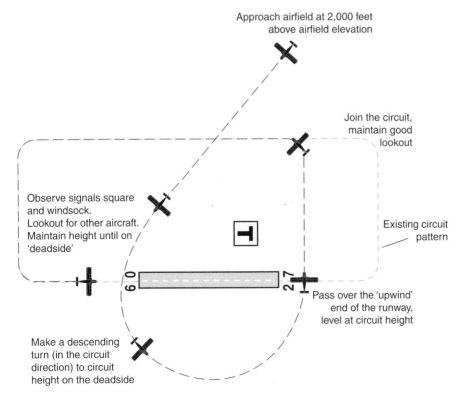

The standard overhead join to a left-hand circuit

traffic around the airfield, and plan ahead to decide how you will proceed. Above all, keep a good lookout and do not be afraid to query an instruction or advice you are not happy with. If the runway in use has a 15-knot crosswind but there is a runway available into wind, why not ask for it? If ATC asks you to route via a landmark not shown on the map, query it. If you are instructed to join number two to another aircraft and you cannot see it, ask for its position. If in doubt, shout.

Where an airfield has special arrival routes or procedures, these can be checked in the AIP or flight guide during flight planning. Doing so will avoid surprises at this late stage of the flight. Once in the circuit, concentrate on flying a safe approach and landing.

Having arrived on the ground, a flight guide will be useful for finding your way around the airfield. Once again don't hesitate to query an instruction you do not understand, or ask for help if you are not sure of where you are and where you should go. After parking, remember to book in with the ATSU or airfield management. If you require fuel, make early arrangements for it just in case the refueller is about to take a lunch break or go home! Be present whilst the aircraft is being refuelled and be sure that the correct amount and grade of fuel is going in. Above all **do not** put off refuelling because of perceived time pressures. In the majority of accidents caused by running out of fuel, the aircraft could quite easily have been refuelled before flight, but the pilot rationalised the fact that he was in a hurry (or that someone else was) by deciding that refuelling wasn't really necessary or worthwhile. Don't forget your own 'refuelling' either. A 'refuel' of a sticky bun and a cup of tea can work wonders in putting you in the right frame of mind for the next sector, if there is one.

With the aircraft taken care of, you can check the weather if you are planning to fly onward shortly. It may even be worth checking the weather if the aircraft is staying on the ground for a day or two, in case bad weather or strong winds are forecast.

▶ Visual Navigation - A Practical Example

So much for the theory of visual navigation and organising in-flight workload. What follows is a practical example of a straightforward VFR flight from Manchester (N5321.22 W00216.50) to Gloucestershire (N5153.65 W00210.03) via a turning-point at Wolverhampton Business Airport 'WBA' (N5231.05 W00215.58). You might like to plan the flight and compare your results with the flight log overleaf. The aircraft's CAS is taken to be 105 knots, and forecast w/v are taken from the METFORM 214. The time for the first leg (Manchester to Sandbach) includes a two minute allowance for the climb to 1500ft and the turn on to heading.

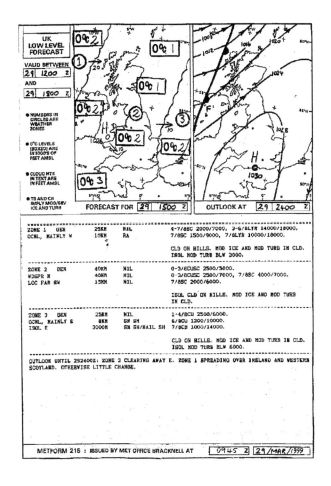

LEFT> The METFORM 215 covering the period of the flight. As can be seen, there is an area of high pressure centred just off the Welsh coast. The flight will take place within Zone 2, where conditions are forecast to be very much VFR. However, on the outlook there is a warm front approaching, which will be a factor if we are thinking of making the return flight the following day

RIGHT> The routing Manchester (EGCC) to Gloucestershire (EGBJ) via Sandbach and Wolverhampton airfield

VFR FLIGHT LOG

Airplan Flight Equipment
1a Ringway Trading Est. Manchester M22 5LH
Tel: 0161 499 0023 Fax: 0161 499 0298
www.airplan.u-net.com

DATE 29 / 3			
PILOT SELF	A/C G-BGVU	ALTERNATE BRIZE NORTON	
FROM MANCHESTER EGCC		DISTANCE 23	FLIGHT TIME 13
TO GLOUCESTERSHIRE EGBJ		SUNSET 18:38	VAR. 5° W
DISTANCE 89	FLIGHT TIME 0.44	2000' w/v 360/20	TEMP. -2

	FUEL CONSUMPTION	7FG	5000' w/v 020/20	-7
F FUEL				
R RADIO	TOTAL REQUIRED	5+1	DEPARTURE INFO. "O"	
E ENGINE	FUEL ON BOARD	40	1150 24 360/06 50K NSW	
D DIRECTION	RESERVE	34	SCT/037	
A ALTIMETER	TOTAL ENDURANCE	5:34	+6/-4 Q1022	

BRAKES OFF		TAKE OFF		LANDING			BRAKES ON		

FROM/TO	MSA	PL/ALT	TAS	TR(T)	W/V	HDG(T)	HDG(M)	G/S	DIST	TIME	ETA	ATA
MANCHESTER SANDBACH	2000	1500	106	198	360/20	201	206	124	13	8		
SANDBACH WBA	2200	FL 35	107	173	010/20	170	175	126	38	18		
WBA GLOUCESTERSHIRE	2700	FL 40	107	176	010/20	172	177	127	38	18		
GLOUCESTER BRIZE NORTON	2400	FL 35	106	110	010/20	099	104	108	23	13		

DISTRESS 121.50 TRANSPONDER DISTRESS 7700 COM FAIL 7600 CONSPICUITY 7000

STATION	SVC	FREQ.	CLEARANCE/OBSERVATIONS
MCR	GND	121.70	
MCR	TWR	118.625	
MCR	APP	119.40	
SHAWBURY	LARS	120.775	
COSFORD	TWR	122.10	
WBA	AFIS	123.00	
GLOSTER	ATIS	127.475	
GLOSTER	APP	125.65	
GLOSTER	TWR	122.90	
BRIZE	LARS	134.30	

The VFR Flight Log for the flight Manchester – Gloucestershire. The departure information obtained from the ATIS broadcast has been entered in the 'DEPARTURE INFO.' box

Before requesting taxying instructions, the ATIS broadcast is monitored and the information noted. Amongst other things, the airfield QNH quoted in the broadcast allows a check of the altimeter against the known airfield elevation of 256ft. Taxying, power and pre-take-off checks are normal, and as we line up on runway 24 we check the compass and HI readings against the runway QDM. We note the time of take-off as 1232. Once more than 500ft above the runway the aircraft is turned on to the heading for Sandbach of 206° as the after-take-off checks are completed. These include checking that the requested 'squawk' of 3636 is correctly set on the transponder. Established on heading, the first prominent landmark – the Jodrell Bank radio telescope – is clearly visible, confirming that the heading is generally

A ALTIMETER	TOTAL ENDURANCE 5:34			+6/-4 Q1022						
BRAKES OFF **1225**	TAKE OFF **1232**			LANDING				BRAKES ON		
FROM/TO	MSA	PL/ALT	TAS	TR(T)	W/V	HDG(T)	HDG(M)	G/S	DIST	TIME	ETA	ATA
MANCHESTER SANDBACH	2000	1500	106	198	360/20	201	206	124	13	8	**40**	
⎯⎯⎯⎯					/							
SANDBACH WBA	2200	FL 35	107	173	010/20	170	175	126	38	18		
⎯⎯⎯⎯					/							
WBA GLOUCESTERSHIRE	2700	FL 40	107	176	010/20	172	177	127	38	18		
GLOUCESTER BRIZE NORTON	2400	FL 35	106	110	010/20	099	104	108	23	13		

DISTRESS 121.50	TRANSPONDER	DISTRESS 7700	COM FAIL 7600	CONSPICUITY 7000

STATION	SVC	FREQ.	CLEARANCE/OBSERVATIONS
MCR	GND	121.70	**VFR 1500ft SANDBACH Q1023 SQ3636**
MCR	TWR	118.625	

The departure clearance is noted, together with the 'brakes off' time and the take-off time, which is used to calculate the ETA at Sandbach

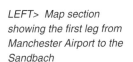

LEFT> Map section showing the first leg from Manchester Airport to the Sandbach

TOP RIGHT> Jodrell Bank radio telescope

MIDDLE> A particularly good visual fix can be made where two distinct line features cross. Here the north/south railway line from Manchester to Crewe crosses the M6 just north of Sandbach

BOTTOM> Approaching Sandbach, note the railway junction just north of the town

correct. The ETA at the first turning point is noted on the flight log, and as expected ATC instructs a frequency change from Manchester Tower to Manchester Approach. This second frequency had already been selected on the second radio before departure.

With Jodrell Bank identified (being the largest steerable radio telescope in the world, it is rather distinctive) the next *en route* landmark is selected – Sandbach. According to the flight log, our ETA there is 1240. So we can now consider three unique characteristics we can expect to see at Sandbach. These might be the larger town of Crewe 3 miles to the SW; the north/south motorway (the M6) passing around the town to the north and east, with a service station directly east of the town; and the Manchester-Crewe railway line passing by the town, with a second railway line joining from the right just north-west of Sandbach.

Levelling at 1500ft we can concentrate on flying the aircraft and making the first FREDA check – not forgetting a good lookout. Even though we are inside controlled airspace, good airmanship dictates that lookout and collision avoidance are first and foremost the pilot's concern. After all, if we hit something it will hurt us rather more than it will hurt the controller.

Reading 'time, map, ground' and looking for the three characteristics, we identify Sandbach from a few miles away. This gives us the chance to consider what will be happening after that turning-point. As we pass overhead the railway junction, we can apply the 'Four T's':

Time – the ATA of 40 is noted.

Turn – the new heading is 175°.

Talk – our position is reported to Manchester.

Task – as expected, Manchester clears us to change frequency and instructs us to squawk standby. The ETA for the next turning point, Wolverhampton airfield, is calculated as 1258 and a climb is initiated. Due to the CTA above us, this climb may have to be curtailed at 2400ft until we have passed east abeam Crewe. After that, we can continue to the planned level of FL35.

The ATA overhead Sandbach is 40, so the ETA for Wolverhampton airfield (WBA) is 58. The regional QNH for the Barnsley ASR is noted as 1017mb/hPa

BRAKES OFF 1225		TAKE OFF 1232				LANDING				BRAKES ON			
FROM/TO	MSA	PL/ALT	TAS	TR(T)	W/V	HDG(T)	HDG(M)	G/S	DIST	TIME	ETA	ATA
MANCHESTER SANDBACH	2000	1500	106	198	360/20	201	206	124	13	8	40	**40**
					/							
SANDBACH WBA	2200	FL 35	107	173	010/20	170	175	126	38	18	**58**	
					/							
WBA GLOUCESTERSHIRE	2700	FL 40	107	176	010/20	172	177	127	38	18		
GLOUCESTER BRIZE NORTON	2400	FL 35	106	110	010/20	099	104	108	23	13		

DISTRESS 121.50 TRANSPONDER DISTRESS 7700 COM FAIL 7600 CONSPICUITY 7000

STATION	SVC	FREQ.	CLEARANCE/OBSERVATIONS
MCR	GND	121.70	VFR 1500ft SANDBACH Q1023 SQ3636
MCR	TWR	118.625	**BARNSLEY Q1017**
MCR	APP	119.40	

The point east abeam the village of Woore is selected as the next landmark, being about five minutes ahead. Looking at the map, obvious characteristics around Woore are the higher ground to the south, the railway line running NNW/SSE and the distinctive curve of the motorway to the east. We change frequency and call the next ATSU, which is Shawbury LARS – with whom we establish a radar information service. After levelling-out at the top of climb, looking out and establishing in the cruise, it's time for another FREDA check. The transponder is set to the 'conspicuity' code of 7000.

Reading 'time, map, ground' we confirm our position abeam Woore at 45. The next landmark is selected as a point east abeam the town of Newport, about six minutes

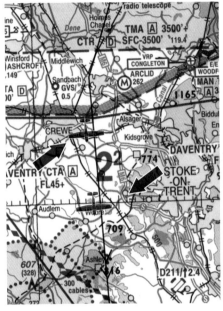

TOP RIGHT> The large town of Crewe passing on the right-hand side of the aircraft

BOTTOM> The distinctive curve in the M6 motorway as seen from abeam Woore

ahead. On the map the large conurbation of Telford, together with high ground behind it, is noted five miles to the south-west of Newport. The shape of Newport town and its position in open country are distinctive, as is the large lake about a mile WNW of the town. The five minutes or so approaching Newport are over mostly open countryside, the only good map-reading features being the high ground just south of Woore and point where our track crosses the canal running NNW/SSE. Since the visibility is good, we should also see the high ground known as the Wrekin to the south-west – a prominent landmark for aviators in this area. And so we continue; concentrating on flying the aircraft, doing a FREDA check, and planning ahead for what will be happening after passing abeam Newport.

The time and place at which the heading is revised is noted, together with the new ETA for Wolverhampton airfield (WBA)

DRIZE NORTON ⎹ / 20

DISTRESS 121.50			TRANSPONDER	DISTRESS 7700	COM FAIL 7600	CONSPICUITY 7000
STATION	SVC	FREQ.	CLEARANCE/OBSERVATIONS			
MCR	GND	121.70	VFR 1500ft SANDBACH Q1023 SQ3636			
MCR	TWR	118.625	BARNSLEY Q1017			
MCR	APP	119.40	**50 NEWPORT, NEW HEADING 170, NEW ETA WBA 1300**			
SHAWBURY	LARS	120.775				
COSFORD	TWR	122.10				

TOP RIGHT> The large lake just ENE of Newport. This position fix confirms that the aircraft is slightly right of track

BOTTOM> The town of Telford, and the high ground of the Wrekin behind it (summit 1334ft AMSL) are visible from some distance

The high ground (including the peak of the Wrekin) and the urban sprawl of Telford are good features to help identify Newport, with the distinctive lake acting as a confirmation of position. By now it is evident that we are right of track by about a mile, and from the elapsed time we can see that our groundspeed must be less than expected. Both of these factors imply that rather than being behind us, giving a strong tailwind component, the wind is more from the left (easterly). We apply a heading correction using the 1 in 60 rule (*q.v.*) and revise our ETA at Wolverhampton airfield to allow for the lower than planned groundspeed.

The next landmark selected is RAF Cosford. As an active airfield, it should be a prominent feature. A look in the flight guide shows a single tarmac runway, and on the map we note that a motorway and railway line pass just to the north. Cosford is also ten miles east abeam the Wrekin, which we now have clearly in sight.

Although at FL35 we will pass above the Cosford ATZ, we decide to change frequency to call them for traffic information – not least because they may be operating assorted light aircraft and gliders which Shawbury radar might not be able to see. We inform Shawbury of our intention to change frequency and the radar information service is terminated. The frequency change provides a good reason for another FREDA check. The call to Cosford reveals nothing to affect our flight, but we decide to remain on the frequency until we have passed the airfield.

At 1255 we pass over Cosford, apparently closing the desired track on the new heading. The simple application of the 'three unique characteristics' and 'time, map, ground' principles mean that any possible confusion with Wolverhampton airfield is unlikely. With Cosford positively identified, Wolverhampton airfield is the next landmark and also the next turning point. The large conurbation of Wolverhampton just a few miles to the east, and the high ground to the west, will confirm the approximate location of the airfield. The main road running east-west a couple of miles to the north and the town of Bridgnorth 5nm WNW will help narrow down the location. Perhaps one of the best aids will be the ETA, based on the flight's progress so far. The flight guide shows a typical three-runway layout, which we can look for when the airfield is in sight.

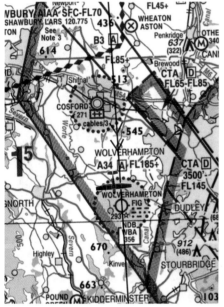

RIGHT> RAF Cosford

RIGHT> Wolverhampton airfield

As part of the FREDA check, frequency is changed to Wolverhampton airfield to request traffic information.

Wolverhampton airfield is identified by 'time, map, ground' and overhead the 'Four Ts' are applied again:

Time – the ATA of 1301 is noted.

Turn – the new heading of 170 is taken up. This has been slightly modified from the calculated heading to take account of the actual W/V we are experiencing.

Talk – we report overhead the airfield.

Task – the ETA for Gloucestershire is calculated. An extra 2min is added to allow for the slower-than-expected groundspeed. Because our magnetic *track* has changed, it is necessary to change level to continue to comply with the quadrantal rule. FL40 is chosen.

The ATA over Wolverhampton airfield (WBA) is noted as 01. The ETA for Gloucestershire is calculated at 21, making allowance for the slower than planned groundspeed. The heading for the next leg is also revised to allow for the actual W/V

SANDBACH ———— WBA	2200	FL 35	107	173	010/20	170	175	126	38	18	58	**01**
————					/							
WBA GLOUCESTERSHIRE	2700	FL 40	107	176	010/20	172	177	127	38	18	**21**	
GLOUCESTER ———— BRIZE NORTON	2400	FL 35	106	110	010/20	099	104	108	23	13		

DISTRESS 121.50		TRANSPONDER	DISTRESS 7700	COM FAIL 7600	CONSPICUITY 7000
STATION	SVC	FREQ.	CLEARANCE/OBSERVATIONS		
MCR	GND	121.70	VFR 1500ft SANDBACH Q1023 SQ3636		
MCR	TWR	118.625	BARNSLEY Q1017		
MCR	APP	119.40	50 NEWPORT, NEW HEADING 170, NEW ETA WBA 1300		
SHAWBURY	LARS	120.775	**13:01 HDG 170 TO GLOSTER**		
COSFORD	TWR	122.10			

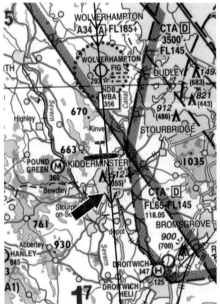

RIGHT> The town of Kidderminster

The next landmark is the town of Kidderminster, about five minutes ahead. We note the high ground and river to the west and the large conurbation of Birmingham to the east. We note that a railway line runs approximately north-south through the town (with a junction for the Severn Valley Railway to the west – we may see one of the preserved steam trains) and a canal passing NNE/SSW through the town. Time for another FREDA check, which includes changing over fuel tanks to keep them in balance.

Kidderminster appears on time and on track, confirming that the new heading and estimated groundspeed are about right. The next landmark is the town of Worcester about six minutes ahead. The north-south motorway passing just to the east (the M5) and the River Severn and railway line both passing north-south through Worcester will be distinct characteristics. Now that we are ten miles from

Wolverhampton airfield, with no traffic to affect us, we decide to change frequency. But who shall we talk to? Birmingham Approach is one possibility (for a radar service) but we decide to check the Gloucestershire ATIS broadcast instead. This will give us advance information about our destination and keep the workload light – allowing more time to enjoy flying the aircraft and the splendid view.

DISTRESS 121.50			TRANSPONDER DISTRESS 7700 COM FAIL 7600 CONSPICUITY 7000
STATION	SVC	FREQ.	CLEARANCE/OBSERVATIONS
MCR	GND	121.70	VFR 1500ft SANDBACH Q1023 SQ3636
MCR	TWR	118.625	BARNSLEY Q1017
MCR	APP	119.40	50 NEWPORT, NEW HEADING 170, NEW ETA WBA 1300
SHAWBURY	LARS	120.775	13:01 HDG 170 TO GLOSTER
COSFORD	TWR	122.10	
WBA	AFIS	123.00	"G" 04L 1250 340/09 50K NSW
GLOSTER	ATIS	127.475	SCT/040 1020/1023 +9/+1

Gloster information "Golf", as taken from the ATIS broadcast

Worcester appears ahead, on time, and the racecourse turns out to be a surprisingly prominent feature. Just north of the town, the dual carriageway crossing the railway line and joining the motorway is the sort of landmark that allows precise visual position-fixing. The timings are looking good, and the next landmark is chosen where the east-west motorway (M50) crosses the river Severn. The north-south motorway and river are good line features approaching this landmark. We also note that by staying about mid-way between them, we should remain clear of the HIRTA at Defford.

TOP RIGHT> Worcester, as seen from a few miles to the north

MIDDLE> The dual carriageway crossing the railway line and joining the motorway (M5) permits an exact position fix just north of Worcester

BOTTOM> The view south of Worcester. Note the line features of the motorway to the left, and the river Severn to the right

Another good point for an exact position fix, the M50 motorway crossing the river Severn

A close-up view as the aircraft passes overhead

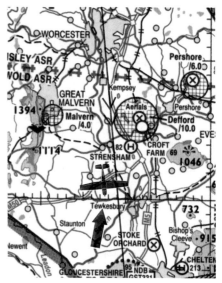

Now is the time to contact Gloucestershire ("Gloster Approach"), confirm receipt of the ATIS broadcast, pass our ETA and request joining instructions. We are given the runway in use and circuit direction. Listening out, we can also build up a picture of the traffic situation. As part of the FREDA check we can consider where to begin our descent. Since we will be joining overhead the airfield at 2000ft QFE (which is 2095ft QNH) it is clear that we can start the descent at the next landmark (where the east-west motorway crosses the river Severn, 8 miles from the destination) to allow plenty of time for a cruise descent.

The town of Tewkesbury

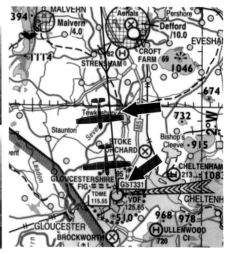

First view of Gloucestershire airport

The M50 motorway crosses the river Severn on a large bridge, making the this landmark quite prominent. The time overhead is 13:15, so our ETA for Gloucestershire seems to be correct. A cruise descent is initiated. We are maybe half a mile right of track, but with only eight miles to run to Gloucestershire this is not a problem. We can expect the airfield to appear slightly left of dead ahead, which might actually help in seeing it. We note from the map that the airfield itself is just west of the north-south M5 motorway, a couple of miles west of Cheltenham and on the north-east outskirts of Gloucester. There is a large area of high ground rising five miles south-east of the airfield, and an isolated hill with a spot height of 509ft (more than 400ft above airfield elevation) just two miles south of the airfield. Passing west abeam Tewkesbury, confirmed by the River Severn passing through it and the motorway to the east, is a good time for the 'approaching airfield' checks in the form of FREDA.

The motorway is clearly visible on the left, and looking along this whilst gauging the relative bearings of the other features brings Gloucestershire airfield nicely into view. The time agrees with the ETA, and level at 2095ft QNH we use an airfield guide to confirm the airfield layout. With the airfield positively identified we can change to QFE and plan the overhead join. Passing overhead the airfield allows us to check the windsock (and therefore the surface wind) in relation to the runway in use. And now we can put the map away, concentrate on lookout and fly the aircraft to an uneventful overhead join, circuit and landing.

The view of the airport as the aircraft joins overhead

Practical Navigation:
Off-Track Calculations and Track Marking

Navigation

Practical
Navigation
Off-Track
Calculations
and
Track Marking

▶ Introduction

Life being what it is, the actual W/V is never exactly the same as that forecast. Equally, it is not possible to fly a heading manually to within a degree or two for any length of time. Weather or ATC may take you off the planned track, or an error in checking or setting the HI against the compass may lead to you flying a different heading from that planned. In short, aircraft (and pilots) inevitably deviate from the planned track. When this happens it is necessary to alter the heading, either to regain the desired track or to head directly to the destination. However, any alteration of heading cannot be a 'hit-and-miss' affair, since this may well make the situation worse. A logical calculation is required.

Practical
Navigation
Off-Track
Calculations
and
Track Marking

▶The One in Sixty Rule

The various ways of calculating an alteration of heading are all based around the *one in sixty* rule. The basic premise of this rule is that for each 1° difference between planned track and actual track ('Track Made Good' or TMG) the aircraft will be one nautical mile off-track after flying 60 nautical miles.

Imagine an aircraft following an actual track (TMG) that is 5° different from that required. After 30 nautical miles, the aircraft will be 2·5 nautical miles off-track; after 60nm, 5nm off-track; after 90nm, 7·5 nm off-track; and so on.

The 1 in 60 rule. For each 1° of track error, the aircraft will be 1nm off-track after 60nm

When making an off-track calculation, the first stage is to assess the *Track Error* – the angle/distance off-track.

If you know the distance off-track, track error can be calculated using the following formulae:

$$\frac{\text{Distance off-track (in nm)}}{\text{Distance gone (in nm)}} \times 60 = \text{track error (in degrees)}$$

Your mental arithmetic will have to be pretty good to do this calculation in your head. For the rest of us, the flight computer comes in handy.

Example: an aircraft is heading 090°. After flying 20nm, the aircraft is 3nm off-track to the north. What is the track error (TE) angle?

A quick mental check says that if the aircraft is 3nm off-track at 20nm, it will be 9nm off-track at 60nm. So TE = 9°. On the conversions side of the flight computer, place the distance flown (20nm) on the inner scale under the distance off-track (3nm) on the outer scale. Above the 60 arrow, read the track error on the outer scale. It should be 9°.

The basic flight computer set-up to calculate track error

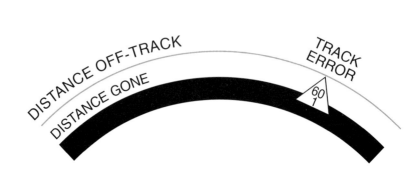

Practical Navigation:
Off-Track Calculations and Track Marking

Distance off-track
―――――――――――
Distance gone

Track error = 9°

Using the flight computer
to find track error

But TE is only the beginning of the story. By altering heading by the amount of TE, the aircraft will begin to fly in the correct direction. However, it will now be flying *parallel* to the required track, not *along* it. To regain track, or to fly directly to the destination, the closing angle (CA) needs to be calculated.

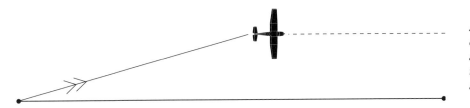

*Adjusting heading by track error only will leave the aircraft flying **parallel** to the required track - not along it*

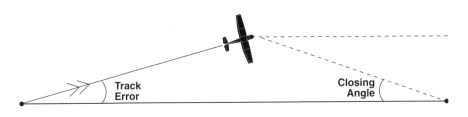

Track
Error

Closing
Angle

A further correction by the closing angle is necessary to reach the destination

Again we are in the realms of the 1 in 60 rule, which states:

$$\frac{\text{Distance off-track (nm)}}{\text{Distance to go (nm)}} \times 60 = \text{closing angle (in degrees)}$$

DISTANCE OFF-TRACK

DISTANCE TO GO

CLOSING ANGLE

60
1

The basic flight computer set-up to calculate Closing Angle

Example: the aircraft which is 3nm off-track in the previous example is 45nm from the destination. What is the closing angle to the destination?

A mental check gives a closing angle of around 4°. On the flight computer, set distance to go (45nm) under distance off-track (3nm). Above the 60 arrow, read the closing angle of 4° on the outer scale.

Using the flight computer to find closing angle

Distance off-track
—————————————
Distance to go

Closing angle = 4°

To find the total heading correction needed to fly directly to the destination add the closing angle to the track error. In other words, 9° + 4° = 13°. The aircraft is left of track, so logically enough the heading must be altered to the right. Given that the original heading was 090°, the heading required to fly directly to the destination is (090 + 13) = 103°.

Having calculated the heading correction and applied it, the aircraft may regain track before reaching the destination. In this case return to the original heading – plus or minus the track error correction – to maintain the original track.

A simple rule-of-thumb comes in handy when doing a 1 in 60 rule calculation. By doubling the track error and correcting heading by that amount, you should regain the desired track in the same distance as it took to leave it.

Double Track Error

If you double the track error, and alter heading by that amount, you will (in theory) regain track in the same distance as you took to leave it

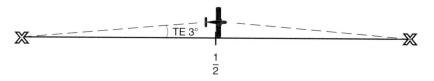

Alter heading by 6°

Even so, we might as well face the fact that calculating track error and closing angle whilst in flight is not especially easy for most of us. It would help if we could estimate angles directly on the map, without any mental arithmetic or needing to use the flight computer. This is where *track markings* come in useful.

▶Track Markings

To help estimate angles, *fan lines* can be drawn at 5 and 10° to the track. These 'fan out' from the departure point and into the destination. Using these lines you can make a good estimate of off-track errors and closing angles.

Markings can also be made along the track line itself to estimate distances and times.

Distance markings on a track line at 10nm intervals

Distance markers, typically every 10 miles, can aid estimation of distances.

Time markers along track will help ETA calculations. These markings may be added at set intervals (say every five or six minutes) based on the calculated groundspeed for the leg. Over very featureless terrain it is better to mark any prominent landmarks with the estimated elapsed time to that point.

6min	12min	18min	24min

Time markings on a track line at 6min intervals

Fraction markings are also common – marked typically at the quarter, half and three-quarter-way points. These are useful in ETA checking. For instance, at the half-way point, simply double the elapsed time to give the estimated elapsed time, and compare this with the ETA. Checking the time further at the three-quarter mark gives a very accurate ETA.

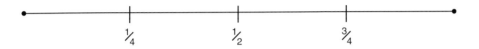

$\frac{1}{4}$ $\frac{1}{2}$ $\frac{3}{4}$

Fraction markings on a track line

Fraction markings can also be used in conjunction with fan lines to give very easy heading correction calculations, thanks again to the 1 in 60 rule.

10°
10°
$\frac{1}{4}$ $\frac{1}{2}$

A track line with fractions markings and 10° fan lines

The off-track angle (TE) is estimated at the quarter, half or three-quarter-way point by reference to fan lines out from the departure point. The TE angle is then multiplied by a factor to give the total heading change necessary to reach the destination:

At the $\frac{1}{4}$ point – TE x 1·5 = heading correction required

At the $\frac{1}{2}$ point – TE x 2 = heading correction required

At the $\frac{3}{4}$ point – TE x 3 = heading correction required

For example, if the aircraft is estimated to be 4° off-track at the quarter-way point, the total heading correction required is (4 x 1·5) = 6°.

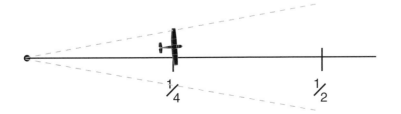

$\frac{1}{4}$ $\frac{1}{2}$

The use of fan lines to estimate track error abeam the 1/4 point: 4°. 4° x 1·5 = 6° which is the TOTAL heading change necessary to reach the destination

Strictly speaking, this method of heading correction is not as accurate as the full application of the 1 in 60 rule. However, for practical purposes it is much easier to calculate in the air and gives an answer accurate enough for most of us.

Of course, too many markings on the map can easily obliterate some important map detail (such as a mast or railway line). There may even be so many markings that the track line gets mixed up with fan lines, distance markers etc; the result is confusion all round. Moreover, ask ten instructors how they like to mark track lines and you will probably receive at least fifteen answers! The only realistic solution is to keep the markings to a minimum. During the PPL course it is best to use your instructor's selected method of track marking, which will probably be one of those just described or a variation thereof.

▶Revision

38 After 17nm, the aircraft's position is fixed as being 2nm off-track. What is the TE angle (to the nearest degree)?

39 An aircraft is 6nm right of track after flying 40nm. If the heading has been 075°, and the destination is 50nm away, what is the new heading required to fly direct to the destination (to the nearest degree)?

40 Half-way along a 90nm leg, the aircraft is 4nm east of track. If the heading has been 020°, what is the new heading to reach the destination (to the nearest degree)?

41 You started a leg of a flight at a time of 1242. At the three-quarter-way point of the leg, the time is 13:03. What is the ETA at the destination?

Answers at page NAV 206

Practical Navigation: Diversion Procedure

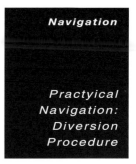

▶ Reasons For Diverting

▶ Diverting Around Weather or a Hazard

▶ Diverting to an Airfield or Landmark

▶ Reasons For Diverting

The most common reasons for diverting from the planned track are meteorological. It may be necessary to divert around bad weather (such as an isolated shower or active CB) or to avoid high ground covered by cloud. Alternatively you may need to divert to a different airfield from your planned destination. Again weather is the most common reason for this, although closure of the destination airfield, the need to refuel or the requirement to land before nightfall are other possible causes. You will practice in-flight diversions during your navigation training. Your instructor may dream up some outlandish reason for needing to divert to a nearby airfield – suspected heart attacks or sudden bouts of vertigo are particular favourites, although more sadistically inclined mentors may come up with imaginary hijackers or time-bombs to keep themselves amused.

▶ Diverting Around Weather or a Hazard

This type of diversion assumes the need to route around an in-flight hazard, such as an isolated thunderstorm or shower. The first rule of a diversion is to start from a known point. If you have seen the hazard from some distance, you should have time to pick a good point from which to start the diversion without getting too close to the hazard. Note the time overhead this point in the flight log. The ideal is to then turn on to a track 45° left or right of the original, provided that this angle is sufficient to avoid the hazard. The choice of left or right turn will probably be dictated by terrain, weather, controlled airspace or ground features suitable for map reading. As you turn, apply the standard turning-point procedure:

Time, Turn, Talk, Task.

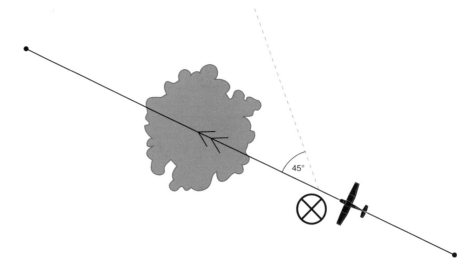

Diverting from track to avoid a weather hazard

45°

The task is to draw the diversion line on the chart. A 45° angle should be fairly easy to estimate using the 'halving' method of angle calculation as shown below:

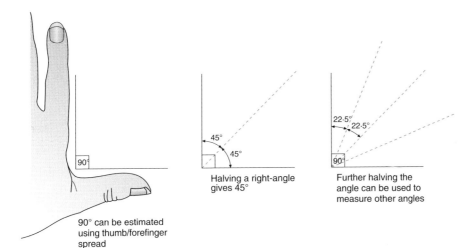

90° can be estimated using thumb/forefinger spread

Halving a right-angle gives 45°

Further halving the angle can be used to measure other angles

Most people can free-draw a right-angle very close to 90°. With just this you can measure angles close to 0° and 90°. Halve the right angle and you can also measure angles near to 45°. Halve the resulting angles and you can further measure near 22·5° and 67·5°

Mentally estimate the heading required to follow this new track (allowing for the W/V). Then enter it into the flight log and establish this heading. Then read "time, map, ground" to ensure that you are following the new track. Almost certainly a heading change will be needed to stay on track. Monitor your progress in relation to the hazard, looking for the point where a 90° turn will return you to track whilst remaining clear of the hazard. This can be 'eyeballed' by simply looking at the left or right wingtip (9 o'clock or 3 o'clock position) and waiting until it has cleared the hazard. Then, again aiming to start from an identified landmark, draw a line at 90° to the present track back to the original. Turn on to this track over the landmark (remember the 4 Ts), again making allowance for the W/V, and read "time, map, ground" back to the original track.

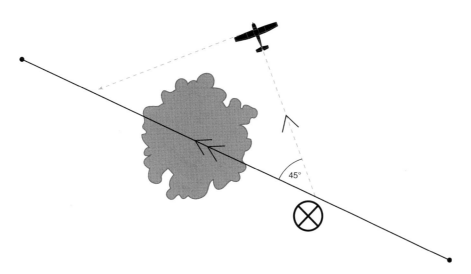

In this case, when the left wing has cleared the hazard, a 90° track alteration should take you back to the original track avoiding the hazard (don't forget to make allowance for the wind!)

Navigation

As with so much in navigation, the description is much more complicated than the act itself – as a few practice diversions will quickly demonstrate. It helps to spend a few minutes drawing lines on a piece of paper and estimating their direction using the 'halving' method, then checking your estimate with a protractor. With a few attempts you should be able to 'eyeball' a track line direction to within 10° or so.

An alternative way to estimate track direction is to compare it with a VOR compass rose near to track. One advantage is that VOR compass roses are orientated to magnetic north, so no further allowance for variation is necessary. You might even choose to put 'stick-on' compass roses onto your map. However, it is unlikely that you will achieve much greater accuracy this way than by using the 'halving' method of direction calculation, although using the two together is a useful double-check to avoid gross errors.

The compass rose around a VOR radionavigation beacon is orientated to magnetic north and can be used for estimating a track direction

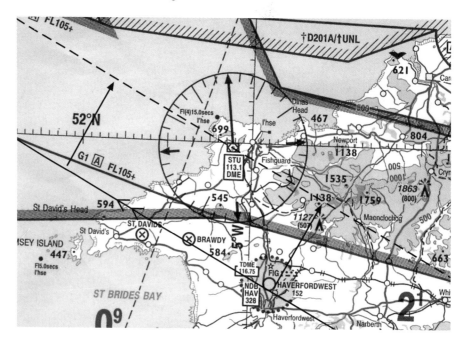

▶ Diverting to an Airfield or Landmark

Estimating track direction using the 'halving' method

45°
22·5°
7·5°

TRACK APPROX 075°
45+22·5+7·5 = 75°

The basics of diverting to an airfield or landmark are much the same. Start from a known point, marked by a landmark which can be positively identified. Draw a line from this landmark to the chosen diversion. Then estimate track direction and a heading necessary to follow it.

NAV110

Practical Navigation: Diversion Procedure

Having identified the landmark from which to begin the diversion, apply the normal turning-point procedure – Time, Turn, Talk, Task. One of the tasks is to calculate an ETA. To do this you must first measure the track distance to the diversion. Unless you have a spare hand to use a scale rule, there are two practical ways to measure distance:

1   Use the distance scale printed along the edge of the flight-log page, or carved along your pencil.

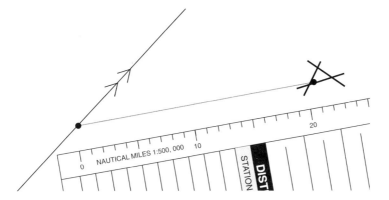

Measuring the distance of a diversion using a suitably marked flight log

2   Use the top half of your thumb. On a 1:500 000 scale chart, it will be about 10nm long.

Don't attempt too many elaborate calculations just as you're starting the diversion. Concentrate on flying a heading which will keep the aircraft on course and read "time/map/ground" to check that you're following the new track. Then make any heading correction necessary. Once established on the diversion track, the ETA can be calculated. Given the distance to the diversion and an estimated groundspeed, you may be able to make the necessary mental calculation. As an alternative, go back to your thumb.

Based on the 'standard' 10nm half-thumb (on a 1:500 000 chart) a little thought and some twiddling on the flight computer reveals that:

>   At 60kts, one thumb-half = 10 minutes
>   At 90kts, one thumb-half = 6·5 minutes
>   At 120kts, one thumb-half = 5 minutes.

ON A 1: 500 000 CHART

10 mins	6.5 mins	5 mins

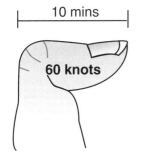

60 knots

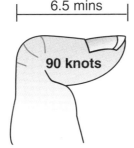

90 knots

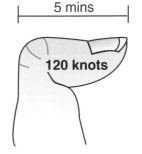

120 knots

'Rules of thumb' for estimating ETAs on a 1:500 000 map

Given a good estimate of groundspeed, you should therefore be able to come up with a reasonable estimate of time *en route* by the number of thumb halves along track. Add this estimated time to the time you started the diversion (you did remember to note that, didn't you?) and you have an ETA. Progressing along the diversion, an *en route* landmark – ideally one at the half-way mark – can be used to check elapsed time and update the ETA if necessary.

If the diversion has been made necessary by poor weather, workload is bound to be high. This is a good time to re-iterate your priorities, namely:

Aviate

Navigate

Communicate

If your diversion is taking you well off the planned route, look along the track for high ground and obstructions. MEFs are a good basis for MSA on UK 1:500 000 charts. Find the MEF(s) in the area of the diversion track and add 1000ft to give a rough-and-ready MSA.

During the PPL course you will be trained to be purely self-reliant in making a diversion. In later life the same principles apply, but you can also make use of any outside agency who can help – belt and braces, if you like. For instance, if the ATSU you are talking to does not have radar, consider changing to an ATC unit which can offer a radar service. You can then use this as a back-up to your own visual navigation. If the airfield you are diverting to has a VDF facility, consider asking for QDMs to verify your track to the airfield. Likewise if the airfield has an NDB, VOR or DME (described shortly) do not hesitate to use these as an aid to your visual navigation to take you to your destination. In a real diversion situation, there is no sense in not making use of a service if it is there for the asking.

Practical Navigation:
Lost Procedure

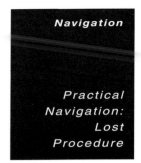

▶ **Why Do Pilots Get Lost?**

▶ **Uncertain of Position Procedure**

▶ **Lost Procedure**

▶ **If All Else Fails**

Navigation

▶ Why Do Pilots Get Lost?

There are two types of pilots: those who have been lost and those who will be. Being lost is usually an avoidable situation. Lack of flight planning, errors in heading or time calculations, flying into bad weather or a gross navigation error (such as flying the wrong heading for the leg to be flown, or totally mis-identifying a landmark) are all common causes of becoming lost. More often than not, getting lost is the consequence of a combination of factors. None of this will be of the slightest consolation if it happens to you. However, on the basis that prevention is better than cure, here are some common causes of becoming lost – and possible remedies.

CAUSE	REMEDY
Poor flight planning, or even none at all – usually because "…there wasn't time".	If there isn't time to do proper flight planning – don't go. **Never** allow **anyone** to pressure you into getting airborne if you are not happy to go.
Gross errors in flight planning.	Before flying, check the flight log. Do the planned headings and times look sensible? Have any numbers been transposed, or the W/V applied in the wrong direction?
Gross errors in flight.	Ensure that you are flying the correct heading for the leg you are on. It is particularly easy to confuse 300°, 330° and 030°; 010° and 100°; 020° and 200°. Are you using the correct ETA? Is the HI synchronised with the compass?
Mis-identifying landmarks.	Read "time, map, ground" and use the "three unique characteristics" principle to avoid mis-identifying landmarks.
Poor weather makes visual navigation difficult.	Turn back or divert. Visual navigation is not a practical proposition in much less than 5km visibility unless you know the area well.
An ATC unit (particularly a radar unit) takes you off your chosen route.	Ask for a Radar *Information* Service (RIS) so you can stay on track. If you have to deviate, do not be fobbed off with "Resume your own navigation". Ask for a position check and track/distance to your next turning point/landmark. Do not leave the frequency until you are happy. If ATC took you off track, they can put you back on. If in doubt – shout.

▶ Uncertain of Position Procedure

There is a big difference between being uncertain of position and being totally lost. Being uncertain of position might happen if – for instance – you fail to spot a selected landmark on time. Once five or ten minutes have passed since you expected to see the landmark, you can reasonably suppose that you have either passed it or missed it. This can happen if you are slightly off track. Maybe the landmark passed close by on the other side of the aircraft; maybe you were distracted and missed it. In either case, you are a long way from being lost.

Once you realise you're uncertain of your position, look back on the map to the last landmark you're confident of having identified correctly. Mark it on the map, together with the approximate time you were there. Now carry out a FREDA check, paying particular attention to checking the HI against the compass. Check on the flight log that you have been flying the correct heading. Had the flight been going according to plan up until now? Make a note of the time.

Now estimate the time since the last positive position fix. Continue a line forward from that point based on heading, time and groundspeed to give a dead-reckoning position. Make a mark on the map at the approximate DR position and draw a circle around it about 10nm in diameter (i.e. about the size of an average MATZ). At average light-aircraft speeds, assuming your last positive fix was within the last 15min or so, your position should be somewhere within this circle.

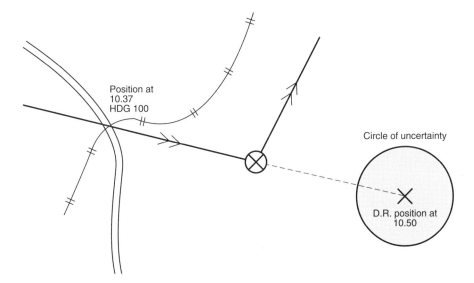

Position at
10.37
HDG 100

Circle of uncertainty

D.R. position at
10.50

An estimated DR position and circle of uncertainty based on direction flown and time since last positive fix

If you have been manoeuvring rather than flying a straight line, you are likely to have drifted downwind. Estimate the DR position based on time elapsed since the last known fix, using the estimated wind drift and wind speed in place of heading and groundspeed. For example a W/V of 360/30 will drift a block of air southwards by 30kts. Make a 20nm diameter circle around the DR position.

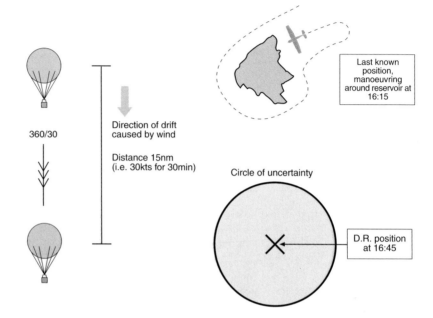

An estimated DR position and circle of uncertainty based on W/V and time since last positive fix. The balloon represents the movement of the 'block of air' the aircraft has been manoeuvring in

360/30

Direction of drift caused by wind

Distance 15nm (i.e. 30kts for 30min)

Last known position, manoeuvring around reservoir at 16:15

Circle of uncertainty

D.R. position at 16:45

If the calculated DR position on the map does not relate to any ground features you can see, start widening your search within the circle. Switch to reading 'ground to map'. Look outside for major topographical features – cities, high ground, a coastline or something similarly prominent – and search within the circle on the map for anything that matches. Large towns, large lakes or reservoirs and major line features are good characteristics to correlate 'ground to map'. If you see a particularly good landmark on the ground (e.g. a major reservoir, two prominent line features crossing, a large town with prominent line features nearby, etc.) consider circling it whilst you look on the map for the same features.

Most importantly, *do not* wander around aimlessly hoping something will appear. Work to a plan and review your options every 10min or so. Above all, **don't panic**. Being uncertain of position is not in itself dangerous – and if you follow the basic principles above, the chances are that you will re-locate yourself in a reasonably short time. And even if you don't, there are plenty of options left.

▶ Lost Procedure

As already said, there's a big difference between being uncertain of position and being lost. To be lost you must by definition have initially been uncertain of position. So you should have already gone through the 'uncertain of position' actions described. If you have failed to locate your position using this procedure, the chances are that it is now something like 25 or 30 minutes since your last definite position fix. Over terrain where features are relatively close together, flying for this amount of time without a positive position fix amounts to being lost. The unfortunate fact is that you are, at average light-aircraft speeds, anything up to 50 miles from your last known position.

Here again, the important thing is to have a plan of action. Don't wander about aimlessly, and don't let panic get a hold. It won't if you just take a little time to think about what to do next.

1   Do a **FREDA** check. Pay particular attention to fuel remaining, and convert this into endurance. Look at the weather and decide if daylight remaining is a consideration.

2   Note the **time.** Re-check your last known position and the approximate time there. Reduce speed to a slow, safe cruise and lean the mixture in accordance with the recommendations in the POH/FM to increase endurance. There's no point flying around at warp speed if you don't know where you are.

3   **Climb; Confess; Comply.**

"Climb; Confess; Comply" is the golden rule when you are lost, so let's look at it in more detail.

Climb. If you are not already there, climb to MSA or above. This will keep you clear of the ground, improve the view, and increase radio range and radar visibility. Of course if you don't know where you are, MSA can be a bit of a problem. Here the CAA has come to the rescue with a handy card showing the MSA of each Altimeter Setting Region as a Flight Level, at different QNH settings. Climb to the MSA for the ASR (or group of ASRs) you think you are in, *provided you can remain in visual contact with the ground.* Unless you have instrument qualifications, and the aircraft has serviceable instruments for flying in cloud, **stay VMC at all costs.**

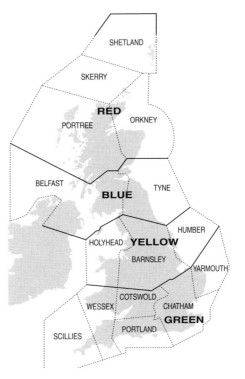

The Altimeter Setting Regions (ASRs) of the UK, and the coloured groups

The CAA's Terrain Clearance Table can be used to find the Minimum Safety Altitude for the ASR you in. Alternatively you can use it to find the minimum safe Flight Level, depending on the regional QNH. For example, within the Chatham ASR the MSA is 2300ft. If the QNH is 1005, this equates to a minimum flight level of FL30

If you do not know which ASR you are within, you should be able to estimate which group of ASRs you are in. Take the QNH, and follow the correct QNH band across the table to find the highest FL, this becomes your minimum FL. For example if you are believed to be within the YELLOW ASR group, and the QNH is 1020, the minimum flight level is FL50 (the highest within the group)

TERRAIN CLEARANCE TABLE

ASRs	WESSEX	Scillies	Cotswold	Portland	Chatham	Yarmouth	TYNE	Belfast
Highest Obstacle	2907ft	1322ft	2660ft	1995ft	1300ft	1217ft	2930ft	2868ft
Minimum Altitude	4000ft	2400ft	3700ft	3000ft	2300ft	2300ft	4000ft	3900ft
REGIONAL QNH	GREEN						BLUE	
1032 or Above	FL35	FL20	FL35	FL25	FL20	FL20	FL35	FL35
1014 - 1031	FL40	FL25	FL40	FL30	FL25	FL25	FL40	FL40
995 - 1013	FL45	FL30	FL45	FL35	FL30	FL30	FL45	FL45
977 - 994	FL50	FL35	FL50	FL40	FL35	FL35	FL50	FL50
960 - 976	FL55	FL40	FL55	FL45	FL40	FL40	FL55	FL55
943 - 959	FL60	FL45	FL60	FL50	FL45	FL45	FL60	FL60
927 - 942	FL65	FL50	FL65	FL55	FL50	FL50	FL65	FL65

IMPORTANT - SET 1013mb ON THE ALTIMETER SUB-SCALE TO FLY AT A FLIGHT LEVEL.

ASRs	PORTREE	Orkney	Skerry	Shetland	HOLYHEAD	Barnsley	Humber
Highest Obstacle	4406ft	3791ft	1421ft	1477ft	3559ft	3116ft	473ft
Minimum Altitude	5500ft	4800ft	2500ft	2500ft	4600ft	4200ft	1500ft
REGIONAL QNH	RED				YELLOW		
1032 or Above	FL50	FL45	FL20	FL20	FL45	FL40	FL15
1014 - 1031	FL55	FL50	FL25	FL25	FL50	FL45	FL20
995 - 1013	FL60	FL55	FL30	FL30	FL55	FL50	FL25
977 - 994	FL65	FL60	FL35	FL35	FL60	FL55	FL30
960 - 976	FL70	FL65	FL40	FL40	FL65	FL60	FL35
943 - 959	FL75	FL70	FL45	FL45	FL70	FL65	FL40
927 - 942	FL80	FL75	FL50	FL50	FL75	FL70	FL45

1. REMEMBER: Although you use the Regional QNH to obtain the Terrain Clearance Flight Level you must set 1013mb on the altimeter sub-scale to fly at that Flight Level.
2. IMPORTANT: When lost or uncertain of your position always call the Distress and Diversion cell on 121·5MHz at the earliest opportunity.
3. For information on how to use this table refer to AICs.

Confess. You are lost. So tell somebody. Start with the last frequency used, or a radar ATSU in the general area you think you might be in. If you think you might be in controlled airspace, call the controlling ATSU. Do not mince words; don't pretend that you want to 'confirm position' or something similarly vague. Say you are lost and give your qualifications (solo student pilot, PPL without instrument qualifications, etc.) so that ATC can tailor their service to your experience. If you have some additional problem such as fuel shortage or poor weather, consider making a PAN call. If you cannot make contact, change to the VHF emergency frequency of 121.5MHz and try again. If the aircraft has a transponder, say so. With the assistance of a transponder, you can probably be located anywhere in the UK and most of Europe in less than a minute.

Comply. Having made contact with an ATC unit, comply with their instructions and advice unless doing so would conflict with the safety of the aircraft. ATC will do their best to help you and have many resources at their disposal. Having located you, the Distress and Diversion cell will be able to guide you to overhead a suitable airfield for landing if necessary. Incredibly, experience has shown that a 'found' pilot has occasionally left the emergency frequency *against the controller's advice* and continued on his way. In more than one case, this only led to the hapless pilot becoming lost again.

Above all, make the decision to "Climb, Confess and Comply" in plenty of time. The sooner you call, the better your chances of being found before the situation gets out of hand.

▶If All Else Fails

As the old saying goes, troubles never come singly – and aviation is no exception. If you really are having a bad day, getting lost might coincide with some other problem. Maybe the radio has failed (or you are perhaps flying a non-radio aircraft). Possibly the weather has turned bad, or nightfall is approaching. Or perhaps fuel is getting critically low. If you cannot get help from ATC, you are going to have to rely on your own resources.

Having run through the 'uncertain of position' procedure, and the lost procedure, you should have a good idea of your situation in respect of weather, fuel and daylight remaining. If you are completely lost and unable to contact anybody to fix your position, the next option to consider should be a precautionary landing. Accepting that this is a major step, make a positive decision to act whilst weather, fuel and daylight are still on your side. If you delay too long, one of these factors could turn against you and make a safe landing more difficult.

If you spot a prominent line feature, such as a motorway, a railway line or a major river, follow it and search for a landmark. As always, maintain an awareness of fuel, weather and daylight remaining, and plan to land with plenty of all three in hand. If you see an airfield where you can make a safe landing, do so whilst keeping an especially good lookout. Don't worry in the slightest about whether it's private, civil, military or even a major airport – just go for it. You can sort out the niceties when you are safely on the ground; as captain of an aircraft with an emergency, your action in landing at **any** airfield is unlikely to be faulted. And what's a bit of debate and paperwork as long as you're back on *terra firma* in one piece? In the absence of an airfield, plan a precautionary landing at a suitable site in accordance with the Flight Exercise 17 (Precautionary Landing) which you should revise now in PPL1.

Above all, *stay calm and keep your options open.* As long as the aircraft is serviceable, the very worst you should fear from a forced landing with power is a landing you will walk away from.

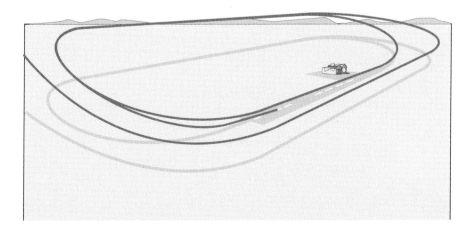

The surface inspection circuits of the 'forced landing with power' procedure

Flight Planning: Fuel Planning

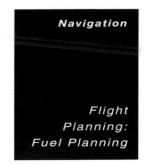
▶ How Not to Run Out of Fuel

▶ Fuel Planning

▶ Fuel Volume Conversions

▶ Specific Gravity Calculation

▶ Revision

*Flight
Planning:
Fuel Planning*

▶ How Not to Run Out of Fuel

The shameful fact is that every year a significant number of engine failures in light aircraft are caused by quite simply running out of fuel.

Running out of fuel is something which most drivers have done at least once in a car. At worst it is inconvenient and time-consuming, and most people resolve not to do it again. In an aeroplane the possible consequences are patently more serious. There are three simple steps to take to avoid this happening to you:

If at all possible, fuel contents should always be checked visually before flight

1   Make a proper fuel plan during the flight planning, so that you know how much fuel is going to be required and how much reserve will be available.

2   Before flight, ensure that there is more than enough fuel on board – check visually if possible – and monitor the fuel situation during flight. If necessary, land and refuel rather than taking a chance and pressing on.

3   Never, ever, rely completely on a fuel gauge.

▶ Fuel Planning

Fuel planning begins in the aircraft's POH/FM with graphs or tables of fuel consumption. These figures should be treated with caution because they are normally based on the manufacturer's recommended mixture-leaning technique. If this is not used, fuel consumption may be as much as 25% more than the figures shown. During the PPL course, your instructor is the best source of information about the aircraft's fuel consumption.

It is a simple matter to calculate fuel required on the conversions side of the flight computer, given the flight time and the fuel consumption. The principle of this computation follows on from time/speed/distance calculations. For fuel-consumption calculations, fuel is read on the outer scale and time on the inner scale.

The basic flight computer set-up for time/fuel used/fuel consumption calculations

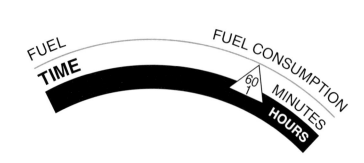

Flight Planning: Fuel Planning

Example: flight time 2hr 37min; fuel consumption 5 imp gal/hr; allowing 1 imp gal for taxying and power checks, how much fuel is required?

A mental check suggests a figure of about 13·5imp gal. On the conversion side of the flight computer, place the time index of the inner scale under the fuel consumption (5) on the outer scale. Above the flight time on the inner scale, read off the fuel required on the outer scale. The answer is 13·1imp gal. Add to this the one-gallon taxying allowance and we have 14·1imp gal. This of course does not allow for any reserve, of which more in a minute.

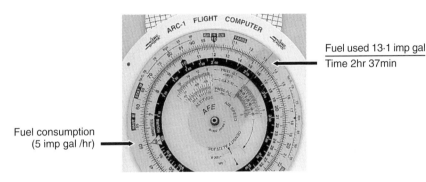

Fuel used 13·1 imp gal
Time 2hr 37min

Fuel consumption (5 imp gal /hr)

At a fuel consumption of 5 imp gal/hr, the Flight Computer shows that in 2hr 37min 13·1 imperial gallons of fuel will be used

Using much the same method as above, endurance can be calculated if we know fuel consumption and fuel on board. This is the maximum time for which the aircraft can remain airborne.

Example: fuel on board 33 imp gal; fuel consumption 7 imp gal/hr. What is the airborne endurance (allowing 1 imp gal for taxying and power checks) without reserves?

A mental check puts the figure at about 4.5 hours. On the flight computer, place the time index (inner scale) under consumption (7). We know that the fuel on board once airborne is 32 imp gal (i.e. 33 imp gal minus 1 imp gal taxying allowance) and this is located on the outer scale. Endurance can then be read off on the inner scale under 32, and turns out to be 4hr 34min.

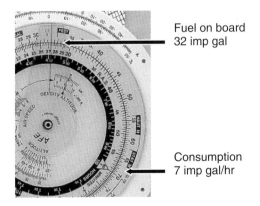

Fuel on board
32 imp gal

Consumption
7 imp gal/hr

At a fuel consumption of 7imp gal/hr, a fuel load of 32 imp gal will give an endurance of 4hr 34min

If you understand the principles involved here, calculating fuel consumption given the fuel used in a specific time should be simple. Attempt the following example at first without looking at the instructions to see if you have the right idea.

Example: In the course of a flight lasting 3hr 25min, a total of 127ltr of fuel were used. What was the fuel consumption?

A mental check suggests an answer of about 40ltr/hr. On the flight computer, remember that time is on the inner scale and fuel on the outer scale. On that basis the method of calculation should be simplicity itself. Place time (3hr 25min) under the fuel used (127). Above the time index (remember that this represents 60min or 1hr) read off fuel consumption on the outer scale. The answer is 37 ltr/hr.

To find consumption, fuel used is placed over time. Consumption can be read off above the time index (representing one hour)

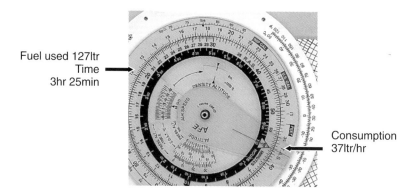

Fuel used 127ltr
Time
3hr 25min

Consumption
37ltr/hr

These calculations are pretty simple and, given the importance of fuel planning, it is well worth while spending a little time practising the various fuel calculations for fuel required, endurance and consumption. A few examples should soon make the process second nature.

▶Fuel Volume Conversions

Having decided how much fuel is required, there is the matter of making sure that there is sufficient fuel on board. Here the question of conversion arises again, since fuel volume can be measured in at least three different units.

The standard units of volume are:

US gallons.

Imperial gallons.

Litres.

The approximate relationships are:

1 imperial gallon = 1·2 US gallons = 4·5 litres.

The relationship between imperial gallons, U S gallons and litres

| 1 IMPERIAL GALLON | = | 1·2 US GALLONS | = | 4·5 LITRES |

Unfortunately it is not uncommon to find one set of units used in the fuel calculation (for instance US gallons in the POH/FM) but a different set of units in use at the refuelling pumps (e.g. litres). So the ability to convert quickly and accurately between these units is essential. The conversions side of the flight computer has markings to make this process simple.

Example: convert 25 imperial gallons into US gallons and litres.

A mental check based on the factors above gives an estimate of 30 US gallons and 110 litres. On the conversion side of the flight computer place 25 under the 'imp gal' line. Use the cursor if necessary to line up accurately. Without moving the scales use the cursor to accurately read off the numbers on the inner scale. Under the "US gal" line you should see 30 US gallons on the inner scale, and under the "Ltr" line 113·8 litres. As always, the

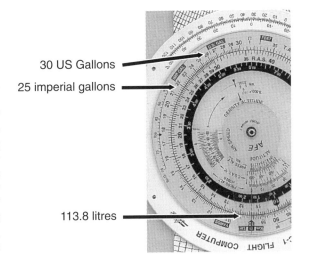

30 US Gallons

25 imperial gallons

113.8 litres

Converting 25 imp gal into US gal and litres

mental check is important and you should always double-check the units in use: **CHECK** to be **SURE**. There is a world of difference between putting 30 litres into the fuel tanks and 30 gallons, as more than one pilot has discovered the hard way!

In calculating fuel required, it is common practice to allow at least one gallon (or five litres) for taxying and power checks prior to take-off. The fuel reserve (the excess of fuel on board over fuel required) is there to cover a diversion from overhead the intended destination to a suitable alternate, and a holding time of at least 45 minutes fuel on arriving over the alternate. Be realistic in selecting the alternate airfield. If you are flying to Denham, for example, there is little point in planning Heathrow as the alternate even if it is only seven miles away. On a particularly long flight, or if suitable diversion airfields are few and far between, consider a larger fuel reserve than standard. The RAF have a saying to the effect that the only time you've only got too much fuel on board is when you're on fire. There's a lot of truth in that. There is also a saying that one of the most useless things in aviation is the fuel left behind in the bowser.

If at all possible, fuel quantity should always be checked visually before flight. Some aircraft have a 'step' in the fuel tank indicating a specific fuel level, and many operators provide a dipstick to help estimate fuel contents. If you're wise, you'll also check whether it's the appropriate fuel for your aeroplane. When you open the fuel cap, the smell of the fuel is just about unavoidable. AVGAS, either in its 80/87 or 100LL forms, smells highly aromatic with a very characteristic 'top note' of benzene. MOGAS has a heavier and slightly metallic odour. Fuel for jet engines (AVTUR or JET A-1) smells quite strange, rather like slightly rancid paraffin with a hint of diesel. It's easy to slip on as well if the refueller has spilt any.

In case you think that sniffing the fuel is going a bit far, be well aware that piston engines run very badly indeed on AVTUR and it's the last thing you want in the fuel tank of the average light aircraft. A quick 'sniff' of the fuel is a good way to ensure that the bowser disappearing round the corner has left you with the right fuel in the tanks. Ideally, of course, you should have been present when the aircraft was refuelled anyway.

Fuel gauges in light aeroplanes are notoriously unreliable, and should **never** be relied upon instead of a visual check of fuel contents. During flight, maintain an awareness of the fuel state and the effect that changed routings or slower-than-expected groundspeeds will have on the fuel situation. Monitor the fuel gauges as part of the cruise checks; if you begin to doubt whether the fuel on board is sufficient to reach the destination with safe reserves, make an early decision to land at an airfield where more fuel can be uplifted. The extra time involved is nothing compared to the wear and tear on your nerves of continuing with ever-diminishing fuel reserves, wondering why stronger-than-forecast headwinds always occur when you choose not to fuel-up!

▶ Specific Gravity Calculation

Having calculated the volume of fuel necessary to complete the flight (with sensible reserves) you need to consider how the weight of this fuel will affect the aircraft's performance. Contrary to what you might think, it is often not possible to occupy all the seats of the average light aircraft with reasonably-sized adults, fill the baggage compartment to its weight limit *and* carry full fuel whilst remaining within the aircraft's weight and balance limits.

Before considering performance in detail, we need to be clear about one of the units. In everyday speech we talk about the 'weight' of objects and have little difficulty with the notion of buying things by the pound or kilogram. Aviators, however, need to bear in mind that there is a distinction between *weight* and *mass*. A two-pound bag of sugar on the supermarket shelf 'weighs' 2lb and also has a 'mass' of 2lb. However, if we now buy the sugar, take it in an aircraft and perform a level 60-degree banked turn, we are subjecting it to an *acceleration* of 2g. In these circumstances it will still possess a mass of 2lb but its weight will now be 4lb. In other words, weight is mass multiplied by acceleration.

Unless you are an aerobatic pilot habitually subjecting yourself to high values of g – in which case you will know how 'heavy' your limbs can feel when you move them during manoeuvres – the distinction between weight and mass may seem rather academic. However, in recent years aviation has tended towards the use of 'mass' rather than 'weight' in performance calculations, and terms such as "all-up mass" are finding their way into POH/FMs. In this book we have chosen to use weight rather than mass simply because the majority of pilots are more familiar with the former term. It may be, however, that the position will change in the future.

Returning to the matter in hand, fuel *volume* is converted into fuel *weight* (or *mass*) using the specific gravity (SG) of the fuel. Specific gravity is the ratio of the density of a substance to the density of water.

Water has a specific gravity of 1, which means that:
1 litre of water weighs 1kg; 1 imperial gallon of water weighs 10lb.

AVGAS has a specific gravity of 0·72. Hence:

1ltr of AVGAS weighs 0·72kg; 1 imp gal of AVGAS weighs 7·2lb.

WATER Specific Gravity 1·0

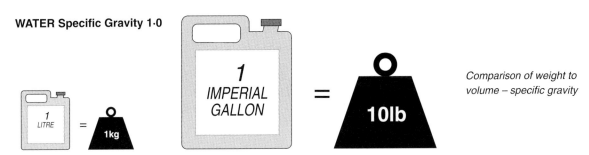

Comparison of weight to volume – specific gravity

The specific-gravity calculation can be done on the flight computer.

AVGAS Specific Gravity 0·72

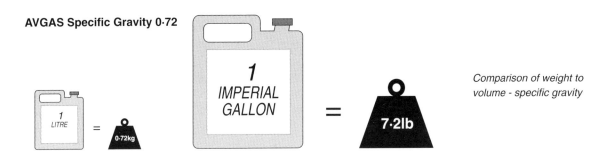

Comparison of weight to volume - specific gravity

Example: the calculated fuel requirement is 78ltr of AVGAS. How much does this fuel weigh in kilograms, given a SG of 0·72?

A mental check puts the figure at about 50kg. On the conversion side of the flight computer, set the fuel volume in litres (78) on the inner scale under the 'Ltr' line on the outer scale. Find the 'Sp.G. kg' index on the outer scale and use the cursor to locate the 0·72 point. Along the cursor line on the inner scale, read off fuel weight in kilograms. The answer is 56·3kg. Without moving the scale, if you take the cursor over to the 'Sp.G. lb' scale and locate the 0·72 point, you can read off the weight in pounds on the inner scale. It is 124lbs.

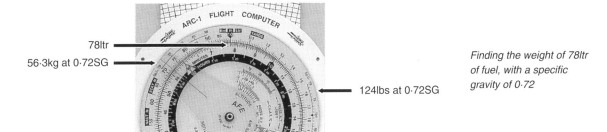

Finding the weight of 78ltr of fuel, with a specific gravity of 0·72

Navigation

►**Revision**

42 Complete the following table, no allowance is made for taxying or reserves:

Flight Time/Endurance	Fuel Consumption	Fuel On Board/Fuel Required/Fuel Used
1hr 58min	12·2 imp gal/hr	24
3hr 23min	46·3	159ltr
1 28	17 US gal/hr	25 US gal
5hr 10min	8·5 imp gal	44

43 With a flight time of 3hr 45min, and a fuel consumption of 47ltr/hr, how much fuel is required (allowing 5ltr for taxying) to have 25ltr reserve fuel on landing?

44 You have a planned flight time of 3hr 6min, plus a diversion allowance of 45 min, with a fuel consumption of 6·5 imp gal/hr. The aircraft presently has 10 US gallons of fuel on board; the refuelling pumps read in litres. Allowing 1 imp gal for taxying, and allowing a reserve 7 imp gal of fuel on landing at the diversion airfield, how many litres of fuel do you need to uplift (rounding up to the nearest litre)?

45 In a flight time of 2hr 40min, 20 US gal of fuel are used. Based on this fuel consumption, for the next flight of 4hr 24min, how much fuel is required (in litres) including an allowance of 10ltr for taxying and 65ltr on finishing the flight?

46 Your aircraft has total usable fuel of 40 US gal. Given a fuel consumption of 7 imp gal, and allowing 1 imp gal for taxying, what is the aircraft's airborne endurance?

47 You took off at 1433 with an estimated 91ltr of fuel on board. The time is now 1605. Given an estimated consumption of 21ltr/hr, what is the remaining endurance?

Answers at page NAV 206

NAV128

Special Navigation Situations

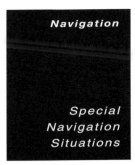

Navigation

Special
Navigation
Situations

▶ **Navigation at Minimum Level**

▶ **Navigation Over Featureless Terrain**

▶ **Transits**

▶ **Revision**

▶Navigation at Minimum Level

Navigation at minimum level (below 1000ft AGL) is not the sort of thing you usually plan to do in civilian flying. The only exception is when using certain entry and exit lanes in controlled airspace. Otherwise, operation at minimum level might be necessary if you have been forced to descend in order to maintain good visual flight conditions. It must be stressed that *for a non-instrument-rated pilot, maintaining VMC must be an absolute priority.* By staying in VMC you can still control and navigate the aircraft, whilst avoiding hazards such as high terrain and obstructions.

The practical aspects of flying an aircraft at minimum level are covered at Exercise 18b in PPL1, which is worth revising now. The differences from a navigational viewpoint mostly concern the change of perspective at lower levels.

When map reading from two or three thousand feet, it is relatively easy to relate the shape of towns, lakes or high ground to their depiction on the map. Likewise, the directions and turns of line features and the relative bearings of one ground feature to another are generally quite obvious. At minimum level much of this view is lost. The general outlines of towns, water features and so on are more difficult to appreciate because you are viewing them at a shallower angle. The visible horizon is nearer, so features will be in view for a shorter time. Landmarks may be hidden behind terrain; line features running through valleys, deep cuttings or woodland might be lost altogether.

When flying at minimum level, landmarks and map reading features may be hidden by terrain

On the positive side, contours are much easier to appreciate at low level. Small hills and valleys which tend to blend into the countryside when viewed from 5000ft will be quite prominent at 1000ft AGL. By the same token, relatively low obstructions will also be more prominent, particularly where they are on top of high ground.

Some pilots claim that navigation at minimum level is actually easier than at higher altitudes; there is something in this, although the differences are chiefly ones of technique and it depends what you are most practised at doing. Nevertheless, the fact remains that, for practical purposes, navigation at minimum level is usually forced on civilian pilots by the weather, which probably means reduced visibility (and possibly low cloud or precipitation) obscuring landmarks and ground features. Therefore practising navigation at minimum level is mostly intended to prepare you for the situation where a need to remain VMC brings you lower than you had planned. In this situation, remember to stay well clear of cloud, bad weather and high ground, even if that means deviating from the planned track.

▶Navigation Over Featureless Terrain

If navigating visually over particularly featureless terrain, the integration of dead reckoning and map reading is especially important. If possible, plan all or part of the route to follow a prominent line feature, even if this increases the distance flown. Otherwise mark the map with the expected elapsed times when passing prominent landmarks – especially line features. It may be worth making a note of the distance between these landmarks so that you can check the actual groundspeed against the flight-log calculation.

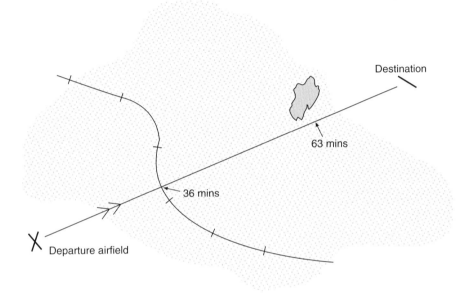

Marking distinct landmarks with estimated elapsed time when flying over particularly featureless terrain

If the terrain is particularly hostile, carefully consider the survival aspects of the flight. A longer routing may keep you closer to civilisation than a 'short cut' across hostile terrain and an unpopulated area. If possible seek the advice of pilots who know the area well. In flight, try to maintain radio contact with an ATSU or, alternatively, with other aircraft in the same area. These aircraft may well be able to relay messages between yourself and an ATSU.

▶Transits

The use of *transits* is a technique well known to inshore sailors which has its own application to aviation. This technique is particularly useful when flying at minimum level, or over relatively featureless terrain. Imagine for a moment that you are flying to a small grass airfield, located amongst lots of other small grass fields. In the absence of a prominent landmark next to the airfield, look for landmarks in the area which are *lined up* when seen from over the airstrip. For example, there might be a tall TV mast a few miles ahead which, when lined up with a small lake, puts you on a line directly through the airstrip. Now look for another transit at something like a right angle (90°) to the first – say a motorway junction behind a village. When both these sets of transits line-up, you should be over the airstrip. If in doubt, fly along one (using the relative positions of the landmarks to stay on track) whilst waiting for

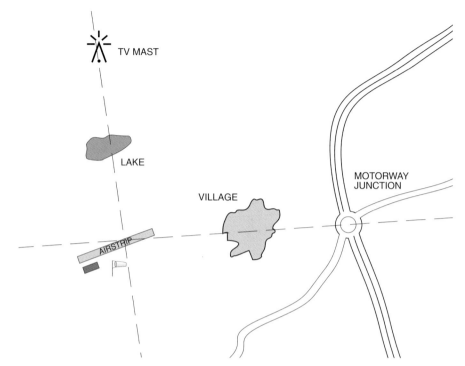

The use of transits in locating a point on the ground

the other transit to line-up. Incidentally this technique is also pretty useful when you park your car in the middle of a huge car park. Before you leave the car, look for a couple of transits – for instance the edge of a building lining up with a tree in one direction, a signpost lining up with a street lamp in the other. To return to your car, establish one transit and walk along it until the other comes into line. You should now be standing next to your car – unless somebody has stolen it (something which rarely happens to airfields).

Flight Planning: Performance

▶Introduction

During your initial flying training, the performance of your aircraft is more or less taken for granted. You will know that the aircraft can get airborne safely with yourself, your instructor and a reasonable fuel load on board. You will soon learn whether all the runways at your home airfield are long enough to use at any time or whether one might have to be saved for a particularly windy day. By and large, a standard training flight from your home airfield in your usual aircraft type is not likely to require extensive performance calculations beforehand.

As you begin flying to different airfields in different aircraft, and planning more ambitious flights, the question of performance becomes far more important. If you are planning a flight with a couple of passengers, to a new airfield, perhaps in an aircraft type which is relatively new to you, performance calculations should be very high on your list of flight-planning priorities.

▶**Introduction**

▶**Mass and Balance**

▶**Take-Off and Landing Performance**

▶**Crosswind Component**

▶**Revision**

Navigation

▶ Mass and Balance

All aircraft have a maximum authorised weight, and also forward and aft centre-of-gravity (CG) limits. The limits for the individual aircraft you are planning to fly will be found in the aircraft's POH/FM.

For the purposes of the navigation syllabus, we will put questions of balance (centre of gravity position) to one side and concentrate on the aircraft weight or mass. This can be divided into three categories:

Basic Weight   This will be noted in the aircraft's weight schedule and normally includes full oil and unusable fuel. This weight is fixed; short of taking a hacksaw to the aircraft, there is nothing the pilot can do about it.

Variable Load   The weight of the flight crew. During training, this weight will be that of yourself and the instructor, or just yourself for solo flights. Unless you or your instructor decide to diet, there is little you can do about this weight either.

Disposable Load   This is where you do have a choice. In essence, disposable load consists of items such as passengers, fuel or baggage which can be left behind.

A common weight calculation is to find the maximum fuel the aircraft can carry, or to find the maximum payload that can be loaded with a given fuel load already on board, whilst remaining within the weight limitation. You will need to know the basic weight, variable load and disposable load.

Example: You are planning a flight in a C152, which has a maximum authorised weight of 757kg. The basic weight of the aircraft is 530kg (including full oil and unusable fuel). Yourself and the instructor together weigh 150kg, and there are 10kg of baggage. Ignoring balance considerations, what is the maximum amount of fuel (in litres) the aircraft can carry and remain within the weight limit? Assume that AVGAS has an SG of 0·72.

To find the solution, a simple table will help:

Aircraft basic weight	530kg
Pilots	150kg
Baggage	10kgs
Sub-Total	690kg

Total authorised weight less the sub-total figure = payload available:

(757-690) = 67kg.

A mental check suggests that the answer will be about 90. On the flight computer, place the maximum allowable fuel weight (67kg) on the inner scale under the 0·72 point on the 'Sp.G. kgs' scale. Below the 'Ltr' line on the outer scale, read off the fuel volume in litres on the inner scale. The answer is 93.

Flight Planning: Performance

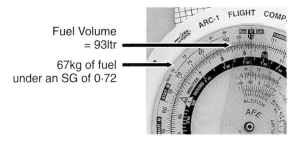

Fuel Volume
= 93ltr

67kg of fuel
under an SG of 0·72

Finding the volume of 67kg of fuel at a S/G of 0·72

If you fly the C152, you may well know that 93 litres happens to be the maximum usable fuel capacity with standard tanks. So if the basic aircraft, the occupants or the baggage weigh more than the figures above, you will not be able to take full fuel. This is a very common situation in light aircraft, and one which may well apply to whatever you usually fly. So be careful.

▶Take-Off and Landing Performance

You should already have an appreciation of the average take-off and landing distance of the aircraft you normally fly. If not, ask your instructor and try gauging the take-off and landing distance against runway markings (if there are any) next time you get airborne.

The aircraft's POH/FM will contain graphs or tables for calculating take-off and landing distance under certain conditions, although it has to be said that some POH/FMs are more comprehensive than others in this respect. This is not the place to explore these graphs and tables fully; the important thing to appreciate is that weather conditions and runway surface have a marked effect upon take-off and landing distances. The CAA has published a very useful pair of tables giving various parameters to take into account when calculating take-off and landing performance. There is no point trying to memorise them, but they do give a vivid appreciation of how much a factor such as wet grass can lengthen both take-off and landing distances.

Take Off Distance Factors

VARIATION	INCREASE IN TAKE-OFF DISTANCE (to 50')	FACTOR
10% increase in aircraft weight	20%	1.2
Increase of 1000' in runway altitude	10%	1.1
Increase in temperature of 10°C	10%	1.1
Dry Grass		
- Up to 8 inches	20%	1.2
Wet Grass		
- Up to 8 inches	30%	1.3
2% uphill slope	10%	1.1
Tailwind component of		
10% of lift off speed	20%	1.2
Soft ground or snow *	at least 25%	at least 1.25

The CAA recommended take-off distance factors

Landing Distance Factors

VARIATION	INCREASE IN LANDING DISTANCE (from 50')	FACTOR
10% increase in aircraft weight	10%	1.1
Increase of 1000' in runway altitude	5%	1.05
Increase in temperature of 10°C	5%	1.05
Dry Grass		
- Up to 8 inches	20%	1.2
Wet Grass		
- Up to 8 inches	30%	1.3
2% downhill slope	10%	1.1
Tailwind component of		
10% of landing speed	20%	1.2
snow *	at least 25%	at least 1.25

The CAA recommended landing distance factors

Imagine your home base is a sea-level airfield which has a tarmac runway. From experience, you know that in average (ISA) temperature conditions and zero wind, the take-off distance (from brake release to 50ft above the runway) is about 450m. You plan to visit a nearby airfield with a 600m grass runway; because it has recently been raining, you expect the surface to be wet. The airfield has an elevation of 1000ft and the temperature is +25°C. Even if the aircraft's flight manual does not allow for all these factors, the CAA tables show that the take-off distance at this airfield is going to be at least 650m. This is something like *half as much again* as at your home base. If the runway is only 600m long, you are obviously asking for trouble by going there.

With the increasing number of small airfields and private airstrips in the UK, performance-related accidents seem to be on the increase. In most cases a simple calculation by the Air Accident Investigation Branch (AAIB) after the accident shows that the runway simply wasn't long enough for the aircraft trying to take-off or land. Why the pilots didn't perform these calculations *before* the flight, thereby saving the AAIB the trouble and themselves the subsequent expense, is a matter for conjecture.

▶ Crosswind Component

The other element of take-off and landing performance to consider is the **crosswind component**. All aircraft have a maximum demonstrated crosswind component, which should be noted in the flight manual. This crosswind component is usually (but not always) the same for take-off and landing. The FTO or your instructor may impose a more stringent crosswind limit on you than that in the POH/FM.

The crosswind component can be calculated using several rules of thumb (which are described in Book 1 – Flying Training) or a crosswind component table. For the purposes of the navigation syllabus, precise crosswind component calculations are done on the wind grid of the flight computer.

Example: the surface wind is 260/20, the runway in use is 21. What is the crosswind component on this runway?

On runway 21 with a W/V of 260/20, the angle between runway direction and wind direction is 50°

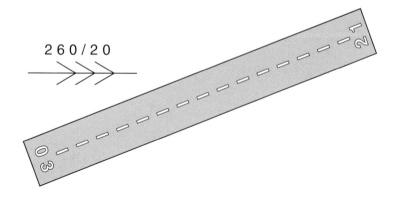

260/20

Flight Planning: Performance

A mental check using a rule of thumb indicates about 15kts. On the wind-slide side of the flight computer, rotate the plotting disk to put the wind direction (260) under the index. Place the centre dot at the top of the wind grid and make a mark at 20 (knots). Now rotate the plotting disk to put the runway direction (210) under the index. The horizontal distance of the wind cross from the centreline is the crosswind component – 15kts. The vertical distance from the top of the grid to the wind cross is the headwind component – 13kts. If the wind cross is above the wind grid, there is a tailwind component.

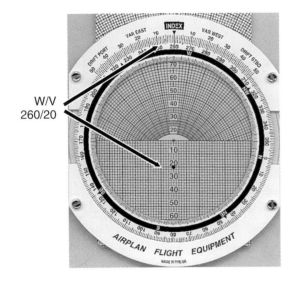

W/V
260/20

Setting the W/V of 260/20 on the wind grid

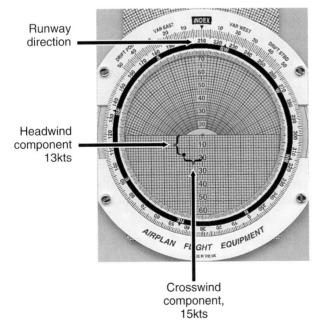

Runway
direction

Headwind
component
13kts

With the runway direction set at the index, crosswind and headwind component can be read off

Crosswind
component,
15kts

You can also use the wind grid to calculate the maximum angle you can accept between the runway and wind direction, given a wind speed.

Example: the surface W/V is varying between 180° and 280° at 15kts. The runway in use is 19, and the maximum demonstrated crosswind component is 12kts. What is the maximum angle between wind direction and runway that you can accept whilst staying within the crosswind limit?

A mental check suggests that at 15kts, a 12-knot crosswind component will occur at an angle of about 50 or 60 degrees.

On the flight computer, set the runway direction of 19 (190°) at the index. With the centre dot at the top of the wind grid, make a mark at 15kts. Now rotate the plotting disk until the wind cross reaches the crosswind limit of 12kts. At the index the direction is 240 (or 140 if you rotated the other way) implying a maximum angle of 50°. So, to remain within the crosswind limit at this wind speed, the wind direction must be within the 140° - 240° arc.

Runway direction is set under the index, and the windspeed marked down the wind grid

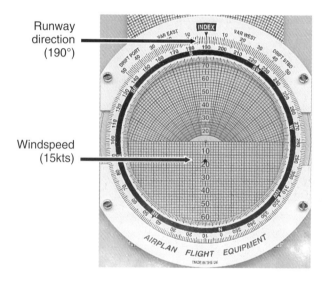

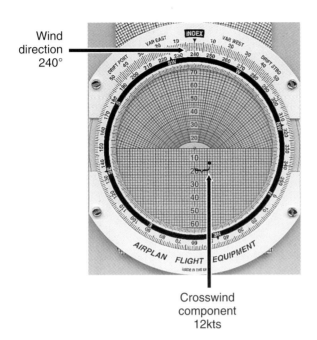

Wind direction 240°

Crosswind component 12kts

The plotting disk is rotated until the wind mark reaches the crosswind limit of 12kts. This happens at 240°...

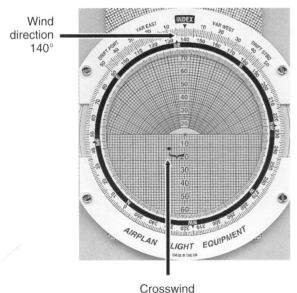

Wind direction 140°

Crosswind component 12kts

...and 140°

The wind reported by the ATSU is usually in degrees magnetic, whilst wind direction on a METAR, TAF or other forecast is usually in degrees true. In principle, an allowance should be made for variation. That said, runway directions (which are magnetic) are always rounded up or down to the nearest 10°. So unless variation is more than about 10°, the difference between magnetic and true wind direction is not significant. Surface-wind direction tends to be more than somewhat variable in any event, and may not be quite the same at the threshold as it is at the anemometer.

▶Revision

48 Aircraft basic weight is 1267lb. The pilots' joint weight is 320lb and they have 20lb of baggage. If the maximum permitted weight is 1750lb, what is the maximum amount of fuel (in litres) that can be carried (using a specific gravity of 0·72)?

49 Aircraft basic weight is 750kg. The pilot weighs 75kg and the aircraft is carrying 46 imp gal of fuel. Given a maximum permitted weight of 1150kg, what is the maximum payload that can be carried (assuming the fuel has a specific gravity of 0·72)?

50 Aircraft basic weight is 950lb. The pilot weighs 160lb and there are 10lb of baggage. For the planned flight a minimum of 167ltr of fuel is required (including reserves). Given a maximum permitted weight of 1400lb, and a specific gravity of 0·72, can enough fuel be carried to complete the flight without refuelling *en route*?

51 The aircraft's take-off distance required from a tarmac, sea-level runway in ISA conditions and nil wind is 1400ft. You plan to use a 600m runway with a grass surface, a 2% uphill slope and an elevation of 1000ft. Assuming nil wind, ISA temperature and using the factors below, is the runway long enough to allow a safe take-off?

Grass	1·2 (+ 20%)
2% uphill slope	1·1 (+10%)
Increase in runway elevation of 1000ft	1·1 (+10%)

52 An airfield has runways 10/28 and 17/35. The surface wind is 240/15. The crosswind limit is 10kts and you cannot accept a tailwind. Which runway(s) are within the crosswind limit?

53 An airfield has runways 08/26 and 14/32. The surface wind is 290/20. The crosswind limit is 12kts and you cannot accept a tailwind; to use 14/32 you must have a minimum headwind component of 10kts. Which runways are usable?

Answers at page NAV 206

Flight Planning: The Aeronautical Information Service

Navigation

Flight
Planning:
The
Aeronautical
Information
Service

▶ The Aeronautical Information Service

▶ The Aeronautical Information Circulars (AICs)

▶ The Aeronautical Information Publication (AIP)

▶ Pre-flight Information Bulletins

▶ Obtaining AIS Information

▶ Revision

Exercise

*Flight
Planning:
The
Aeronautical
Information
Service*

Navigation

▶ The Aeronautical Information Service

The Aeronautical Information Service (AIS) publishes and distributes information about airfields, air-traffic services, airspace and many other matters that concern pilots. The two main AIS publications are:

- the AICs (Aeronautical Information Circulars)

- the AIP (Aeronautical Information Publication)

Up-to-date copies of these publications should be available at any FTO or ATSU, although they may not be available at smaller airfields without a flying school or ATSU.

▶ Aeronautical Information Circulars (AICs)

AICs are issued monthly and are collated into a large ring binder. They contain information of interest to pilots, and are colour-coded as follows:

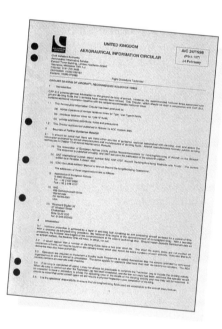

Pink AICs concern safety matters

White	Administrative
Yellow	Operational (including Air Traffic Services & Airspace)
Pink	Safety
Mauve	Airspace restrictions, danger areas etc.
Green	Maps and Charts

AICs come with regular indexes, so that you can quickly find those that directly concern you. It is also useful to check new AICs when they arrive because they have a habit of containing important information – changes in controlled airspace, changes to danger areas, Red Arrows displays, major restrictions of flying (such as flypasts and air displays), new met. services and so on. Other AICs are of a more general nature; instructions for completing a flight-plan form, cross-Channel flight planning, use of portable telephones in aircraft, etc.

All AICs are worth checking but pink AICs (safety matters) make particularly good reading on non-flyable days and contain a lot of invaluable advice.

Flight Planning:
The Aeronautical Information Service

▶ The Aeronautical Information Publication (AIP)

The AIP is also known (at least to aviators beyond a certain age) by its old name of the 'Air Pilot'. The AIP is **the** primary reference source for information during flight planning. To be able to find your way around the AIP quickly, a basic knowledge of the sections helps:

GEN   GENERAL - information on national procedures, entry and departure procedures, 'differences' from ICAO procedures, abbreviations, encodes & decodes, sunrise & sunset tables, charts, AIS organisation, air traffic services, met services, Search & Rescue organisation and procedures etc.

ENR   EN ROUTE - VFR & IFR procedures, airspace classifications, rules & procedures, LARS & MATZ, flight plans, interception procedures, ATS routes, radionavigation aids, Prohibited, restricted and danger areas (ENR 5), obstructions and hazards etc.

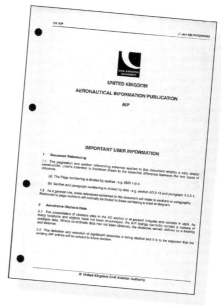

*The AIP (as amended and up-dated) is **the** authoritative source of aeronautical information*

AD   AERODROMES - Each licensed airfield is listed, with details of runways, radio frequencies and radionavigation aids, procedures, airfield charts, VRPs, obstructions and warnings, facilities, opening hours, telephone numbers etc.

It is worth noting that the AD section does not list all the airfields in the UK, in fact it is largely restricted to licensed 'public use' civilian airfields. Thus details of other airfields such as military airfields, smaller airfields and private strips, private helipads etc. must be obtained from elsewhere. The most common source of this type of information will be some form of commercially produced flight guide. If using such a flight guide you should bear in mind that they should be used as a guide only, not an authoritative document, and that they may not be amended as regularly or comprehensively as the AIP.

The AIP is a heavyweight document consisting of at least three large binders weighing about 5kg apiece. Knowing it off by heart is out of the question, and it is certainly not bedtime reading. The AIP is intended as a reference source, and the only practical method of learning your way around it is to use it on a regular basis. Happily the AIP has a comprehensive contents list and index sections which make its use quite easy with a little practice.

Apart from the fact that the AIP is the official source of aeronautical data and information, becoming conversant with its format is especially useful if you become adventurous and start flying to other countries because the layout of AIPs is being standardised internationally. Once you know where to find information in one AIP, you should be able to make a good start with another country's AIP.

Navigation

Life would be quite simple for pilots and the AIS if the information in the AIP didn't change very often. However, as you know by now, aeronautical information can – and does – change constantly. Having found information in the AIP, you need to know if any of it has changed or is about to change. Updated information is available in a number of documents, the common thread being that update information is in the form of printed pages posted to AIP owners.

– *AIRAC*. The primary means for updating the AIP is the AIRAC system of amendments. AIRACs are issued every 28 days, and are usually replacement pages to be inserted into the AIP on a set date. AIRACs should give at least 6 weeks notice of *major* changes to the AIP. UK AIRACs have a pink cover sheet.

– *AIP Amendments*. These are replacement pages for the AIP, usually to be inserted on receipt, which contain information of a more minor nature than that found in AIRACs. AIP amendments often concern changes at smaller airfields, and hence are of greater interest to general aviation pilots.

– *AIP Supplements*. These documents contain information of a temporary nature; changes likely to last for a few months; or information that has some other importance such as temporary closure or re-activation of airfields, etc. UK AIP supplements are printed on green paper.

Having used the AIP, you should then refer to the AIRACs, amendments and supplements (which are usually kept in a separate binder) to ensure there are no changes to affect the flight.

If the AIRACs, amendments or supplements are more than a month or two old – or are missing altogether – it's wise to wonder why. The AIP can only be kept up to date if:

– the AIP owner pays the annual subscription to receive updates.

– somebody is actually inserting the updated information.

TOP> An AIRAC giving at least six weeks' advance warning of a major change to the AIP

MIDDLE>
An Amendment to the AIP

BOTTOM> An AIP Supplement

Needless to say, in the absence of a dedicated operations person, this task (and that of regularly cross-checking it, using a gruesome form of AIS-devised torture known as the "Checklist of AIP Pages") tends to be delegated to those perceived as having time on their hands. If there is no such victim, the job can go unfinished for some time – so beware!

At the time of writing the AIS are testing a CD-ROM version of the AIP which is expected to be commercially available shortly. This will be a major leap forward for the AIP, not least because it will be updated by simply issuing a new CD-ROM to coincide with each AIRAC release. Arguably information will be easier and quicker to find too and the product is expected to be significantly cheaper than the 'hard copy' version of the AIP. Of course, it does mean that flying schools will have to find something new to occupy their junior operations staff and instructors…

▶ Pre-flight Information Bulletins

As the name implies, 'Pre-flight Information Bulletins' are designed to be the last documents to be checked immediately before flight, they are essentially a collection of NOTAMS covering a period of a few days or shorter. Examples of information found within a Pre-flight Information Bulletin are the temporary withdrawal (or implementation) of a service or facility; air displays; military exercises; work in progress at airfields; lights temporarily out of service; recent frequency changes, etc.

Until recently, the AIS have published a number of pre-flight information bulletins, each one containing information for a specified area or a specified group of airfields. However, the way in which Pre-flight Information Bulletins are presented is changing, as described in the next chapter.

A pre-flight information bulletin

Navigation

Pre-flight Information Bulletins are written as far as possible in plain language, but they inevitably contain a certain number of abbreviations. Many are commonsense or standard aviation abbreviations, but the following is a list (which may not be completely comprehensive) of those often found in bulletins:

acft	aircraft		exc	except
AD	Aerodrome		flts	flights
airex	air exercise (usually by military aircraft)		fm	from
			freq	frequency
alt	alternate or alternative		gnd	ground
alt	altitude		H24	24 hours
amdt	amendment		HEL	helicopter
apch	approach		hgt	height
aprx	approximately		HJ	Hours Day – sunrise to sunset
ARP	Aerodrome Reference Point (The ARP is marked on the airfield chart in the AD section of the AIP)		HN	Hours Night – sunset to sunrise
			hr(s)	hour(s)
ARR	Arrival		intxn	intersection
authy	authority		ldg	landing
avbl	available		LFA	Low Flying Area (see AICs)
awy(s)	airway(s)		LFZ	Local Flying Zone
bdry	boundary		lgts	lights
blks	blocks (usually referring to sections of apron or manoeuvring area)		M/mag	magnetic
			m	metres
			mil	military
brg	bearing		mkd	marked
btn	between		mvmt	movement
c/l	centre line		no	number
c/s	call sign		O/H	Overhead
cas	controlled air space		o/r	on request
chg	change		obst	obstruction
chk	check		opr	operating
clsd	closed		ops	operation
com	communication		perm	permanently
deg	degree(s)		ph	public holidays
dep	departure(s) or departing		PJE	Parachute Jumping Exercise
dist	distance		PN	Prior Notice
dly	daily		proc	procedure
elev	elevation		psn	position
eqpt	equipment		pt	point
est	established		pwr	power

rad	radius	tbn	to be notified
rcl	runway centre line	temp	temporary
rcvd	received	tfc	traffic
ref	reference	thr	threshold
RFF	Rescue and Fire Fighting (category)	til	until
		tkof	take-off
rtf	radiotelephony	trk	track
rwy	runway	trng	training
SAR	Search And Rescue	twy	taxiway
sched	scheduled	tx	transmission or transmit
sec	sector	u/s	unserviceable
sfc	surface	unl	unlimited
shld	should	w/d or wdn	withdrawn
ssr	secondary surveillance radar		
stn	station	wef	with effect from
svce	service	wi	within

▶ Obtaining AIS Information

AIS information for the UK originates from the AIS headquarters at London Heathrow, with two smaller AIS 'outstations' at Manchester and Prestwick. Unless you have direct access to one of these units, you are likely to obtain AIS information from a *Flight Briefing Unit*.

Flight Briefing Units (FBUs) are found at most airfields, and vary from a large room (containing comprehensive met. and AIS information and dedicated AIS personnel) to a notice-board in an FTO. In all cases the basic principle, as with met. information, is one of self-briefing.

If you have a specific query regarding an item in a pre-flight information bulletin or NOTAM, you can telephone AIS headquarters for clarification – the telephone number is given in AICs and flight guides. As well as NOTAMS and pre-flight information bulletins, a freephone telephone service is available which gives up-to-the minute details of Royal Flights; Red Arrow displays and other Temporary Restricted Airspace. It also gives information on any airspace covered by an Emergency Restriction of Flying – such as the scene of a major incident– in the form of a recorded message of a couple of minutes duration. The message is updated twice daily (or more frequently if an Emergency Restriction of Flying is issued) and is available in the UK on 0500 354802.

The only other AIS message that might directly affect a pilot is the *Class One NOTAM*. These are issued when an urgent AIS message needs to be distributed quickly – for example, the unexpected closure of a major airfield. Class One NOTAMs are distributed via the AIS communications network to AIS centres and those FBUs connected to the system. These units then distribute it by the fastest possible means to all interested agencies – ATC units, airfield operators, airlines, etc.

A Class One NOTAM:

A EGCC – issued by Manchester Airport (EGCC is its ICAO code)

```
NZCO11 280303
GG EGZZNOFA EGZZINTA EGZZEGCC
280301 EGGNYNYX
(AO621/95 NOTAMN
Q) EGTT/QMRLC/IV/NBO/A /000/999
A) EGCC B) 9504280301 C) 9504280600 EST
E) RWY CLOSED DUE DISABLED ACFT)
```

B 9504280301 – issued at 0301UTC 28/04/95

C 9504280600 EST – valid until 0600UTC 28/04/95 (estimated)

E RWY CLOSED DUE DISABLED ACFT – Runway closed because of a disabled aircraft

At many smaller FBUs you may still find the majority of AIS information (the AIP, NOTAMS, Pre-flight Information Bulletins) presented in 'hard copy'. However, the AIP is now available in CD-ROM format – which allows much more sophisticated search facilities as well as being considerably easier to move around. Moreover, there is an excellent AIS website at:

www.ais.org.uk

At this site you view and download most (but not all) of the AIP, as well as AIP supplements, AICs and other aeronautical information. Pre-flight Information Bulletins can also be accessed at this website, and indeed in the foreseeable future the website is likely to become the sole source of Pre-flight Information Bulletins.

The availability of AIS information via the Internet means that anybody with access to the web can carry-out much of their pre-flight planning before they reach the airfield. As with Met. Information, the 'on-line- access to AIS information is improving all the time, and you should be able to keep abreast of developments in the aviation press and in official and safety publications.

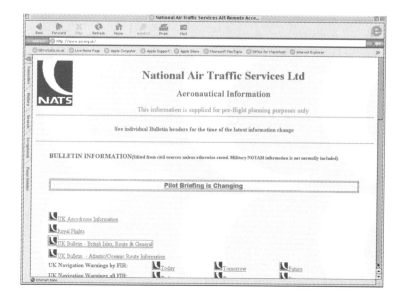

The AIS website

▶Revision

54   What class of information does a pink AIC contain?

55   Which section of the AIP contains information about specific airfields?

56   Where would you find the up-to-date radio frequency for an airfield ATSU (other than a LARS unit)?

57   Where would you find the up-to-date radio frequency for a LARS unit?

58   Which update service gives advance notice of major changes to the AIP?

59   Decode the following item from a pre-flight information bulletin:

    OBST   Til 14 JUL 1600 Tower crane 299 deg M 535m ARP 66ft AAL length of boom 150ft, top of crane and end of boom lit. (A585/95)

60   Decode the following item from a pre-flight information bulletin:

    AB5152   13 May   1400-1430   12000FT   WESTON ON THE GREEN: PJE N5152 W00112 rad 2nm.

61   What is the vertical limit of the danger area notified in the following item from a pre-flight information bulletin, and what is the designation of the danger area?

    D115B   0800-1800   40000ft   Active, upper limit raised

62   Other than in pre-flight information bulletins, where could you obtain information regarding Royal Flights, Red Arrows displays, Temporary Restricted Airspace and Emergency Restrictions of Flying?

    Answers at page NAV 207

Radio Navigation

▶ **Ground Direction Finding (DF)**

▶ **Ground Radar**

▶ **Secondary Surveilance Radar (SSR)**

▶ **Automatic Direction Finding (ADF)**

▶ **VHF Omni-directional Range (VOR)**

▶ **Distance Measuring Equipment (DME)**

▶ **Global Positioning System (GPS)**

BACKGROUND BRIEFING

▶ Ground Direction Finding (DF)

Direction Finding (DF) is based on the principle that a radio receiver can take a bearing on a radio transmission, and so determine its direction in relation to the receiving radio. In civilian aviation, a radio receiver that can determine direction in this way will be a ground-based Air Traffic Service Unit (ATSU), utilising the VHF band as used for civil aviation communications. Such VHF Direction Finding is abbreviated to VDF. When an ATSU receives a radio transmission on a VDF frequency, bearing information is displayed to the controller/information officer. Although the differing types of display need not concern pilots too greatly, the bearing (direction) may be displayed as a 'trace' against the appropriate direction on a Cathode Ray Tube (CRT), or may be displayed digitally.

A VDF display in an ATSU

It is important to appreciate that not all ATSUs can offer a VDF service; the steadily decreasing number that do are noted in the AIP and flight guides using the designation 'VDF' next to the frequency on which the ATSU offers that service. Even then, you cannot assume that a VDF service is available instantly – it is not unknown for an ATSU to need some warning in order to switch on the VDF equipment and have it ready for use. Assuming that all are ready, as the pilot you will need to decide whether you want to know your direction from the VDF unit, or your direction to it. In theory, you might also have a choice of whether you want to be given bearing information as a magnetic direction, or a true direction. These combinations give four possible options, each of which is allocated a 'Q' code as follows:

QDM The aircraft's magnetic track to the VDF station – in other words the magnetic heading that, if there was no wind, would take the aircraft to the VDF station.

QDR The aircraft's magnetic track from the VDF station – in other words if you draw a line from the VDF station in this magnetic direction, the aircraft is somewhere along it.

QUJ The aircraft's true track to the VDF station.

QTE The aircraft's true track from the VDF station.

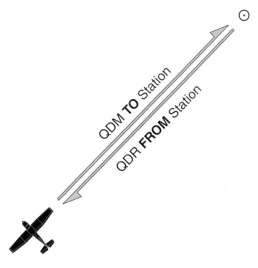

A QDM is a magnetic direction to the station, a QDR (radial) is a magnetic bearing from the station

There were far-off and rose-tinted days when VDF information was used for en-route navigation, and one can almost imagine the navigator hunched over his plotting table as the wireless operator passes back scraps of paper that read "Newtown QTE 120° at 1000 hours" and the like. From a series of such bearings and cross-cuts positions could be plotted and an early form of radio navigation could be achieved. In the 21st century, where VDF is in use (and the number of ATSUs that can offer VDF is tending to decrease year-on-year), it is based on an airfield and used to allow an aircraft to 'home' to the airfield by requesting a 'QDM' – the aircraft's magnetic track to the airfield. The technique for using a series of QDMs to track to an airfield is described in some detail at exercise 18c of PPL1, which you should revise now. In principle, in conditions of nil wind you can simply fly a QDM as a heading to reach the airfield. In more common wind conditions you must adjust the heading for wind drift, and then re-check the QDM every few minutes to see that you are maintaining a constant track to the airfield. To properly visualise the direction, you should imagine the QDM on the Heading Indicator. If the QDM begins to move to the right, you should adjust heading to the right, and vice versa. The Communications section of PPL2 contains more detailed information about ATC and RT procedures in relation to VDF.

As already seen, an ATSU frequency which can offer a VDF service is listed in aeronautical information publications using the prefix 'VDF', and this information is also noted on aeronautical charts. The times when the service is available are listed in the AIP and some flight guides, although they normally coincide with the ATSU hours of watch these may not be the same as the operating hours of the airfield itself.

	Gloucester	
ATIS	127.475	
APP	125.65	
RAD	120.975*	
VDF	125.65	122.90
TWR	122.90	
FIRE	121.60	
*RAD not continuously manned		
NDB	GST 331**	
DME	GOS 115.55***	
**on A/D range 25nm		
***Co-located with NDB		

The VDF service at Gloucestershire operates on 125.65 MHz

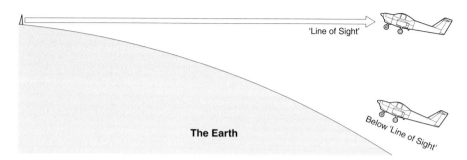

'Line of Sight'

The Earth

Below 'Line of Sight'

VHF signals travel in straight lines and so the aircraft needs to be in 'line-of-sight' to receive a VHF transmission

The range at which a VDF service can operate is theoretically set by the 'line of sight' principle which applies to radio waves in the VHF frequency band and above. This means that range can be increased by either increasing the height of the aircraft, or increasing the height of the VDF transmitter. However, in practical terms the truth of the matter is that if you can establish satisfactory two-way communications on a frequency with VDF capability, the ATSU should be able to offer a VDF service. The accuracy of a VDF bearing does not vary by day or night, however it may be subject to factors which can affect VHF waves, namely site error and propagation error. Site error can be caused by reflective surfaces (such as buildings or hills) scattering radio waves in the vicinity of the VDF aerial. Propagation error can be a problem if the aircraft is at a considerable range from the VDF station, at low altitude, and the VHF signal is travelling over irregular terrain (such as hills) where, again, the VHF wave can be reflected or scattered.

The accuracy of VDF bearings is graded into four classes:

Class A	Accuracy +/- 2°
Class B	Accuracy +/- 5°
Class C	Accuracy +/- 10°
Class D	Accuracy worse than class C

When giving VDF bearings, the ATSU should state the class of bearing. In practice, class A accuracy is almost unheard of, whilst class D is usually considered too unreliable to pass on to a pilot except in dire circumstances.

▶ Ground Radar

The term 'radar' was determined from '**ra**dio **d**etection **a**nd **r**anging', which describes well the principle on which the system operates. A radar system transmits a beam of radio pulses on a frequency above the VHF band. These pulses of radio energy travel out from the radar antenna at the speed of light (300,000km per second). Depending on the characteristics of the radio pulses (a subject which need not detain us), certain objects in their path will scatter and reflect or 'echo' these pulses. The receiving part of the radar system measures the return of these 'echoes'. The time taken for the pulse to travel out to an object and be reflected back to the antenna allows the distance of the object to be calculated, as the radio waves are travelling at a known speed – the speed of light. Therefore if an echo is received back one thousandth of a second after it was transmitted, it has travelled 300km. This is the distance out to and back from the object which reflected the echo, so halving this figure gives the range – in this case 150km. The direction of the antenna when the returning pulse is received gives the direction of the object. Because radar operates at higher radio frequencies, like VHF it follows the 'line of sight' principle. If an object is over the horizon, or very close to the ground, it may not reflect an echo back to the radar echo back to the radar. Thus, the range of a radar system can be increased by placing it on a high point (which is done wherever possible), and a high-flying aircraft can be 'seen' by radar at a greater range than a low-flying one. However, an object directly over the radar site is likely to be outside the radar beam and so it is not uncommon for an ATSU to lose radar contact as an aircraft flies through its overhead.

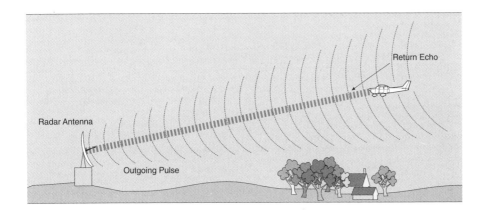

The principle of radar

Radar information is normally displayed on a CRT screen known as a Plan Position Indicator (PPI). The PPI is commonly a circular screen on which the radar antenna is represented by the centre of the disc. As the radar antenna rotates, a trace (known as the 'time base') rotates around the centre of the display, and echoes (known as 'targets' or 'returns') show as bright plots. These fade slowly after the time base has moved over them, being re-illuminated on the next pass of the time base: most displays allow an number of successive plots of each target to be displayed so that its track is evident. The display has a north reference, so that target's position around the circle gives its direction, the distance out from the centre is its range. On most radar displays the scale can be adjusted and on virtually all modern units there is an overlay of airfields, controlled airspace etc.

An airfield ATSU offering a radar service often has the callsign "Radar" or "Approach", abbreviated to RAD and APP respectively in the airfield entry in the AD section of the AIP, on aeronautical charts and in flight guides. Additionally, the En-Route (ENR) section of the AIP contains details of other radar services for en-route traffic, such as the Lower Airspace Radar Service (LARS), and LARS frequencies are marked on aeronautical charts also. To use a radar service, a pilot must make a specific request for a specific service. You can never assume you are receiving a radar service until the controller has confirmed it to you. The two principal radar services are:

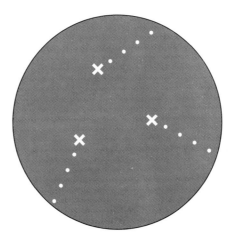

A series of radar returns displayed on a basic Plan Position Indicator (PPI)

Radar Information Service (RIS) – the controller passes details of any other traffic and the pilot decides on avoiding action.

Radar Advisory Service (RAS) – the controller passes details of other traffic and gives avoidance advice. If you choose not to take this advice, you must inform the controller.

These services, and radio phraseology for use with a radar service, are described in more detail in the Communications section of PPL2.

The LARS service at Exeter

Exeter	
APP/LARS	128.15
RAD	128.15 119.05
VDF	128.15
TWR	119.80
ILS/DME	I-XR 109.90 Rwy26
ILS/DME	I-ET 109.90 Rwy08
NDB	EX 337*
	range 15nm
	*EX 261/4.12 to Thr26

Because radar works in the frequency bands above VHF, the basic 'line-of-sight' principles of range and visibility apply: these have been sufficiently covered already so there is no point repeating them verbatim. If a target is below the horizon visible to the radar, or if it is shielded behind some solid object such as a mountain, it will not be struck by the radar pulses and so cannot echo any back to the radar antenna. Terrain in general can reflect a lot of echoes back to a radar unit, leading to areas of permanent 'clutter' on the radar display. Thus it is that a low-flying aircraft can be lost within this clutter and to all intents and purposes be invisible to radar. Radar range and the visibility of radar targets are also effected by the power of the radar transmission and the characteristics of the target. A metallic target showing a large area to the radar beam will give a stronger return than a small wood or composite object for example. It is also worth knowing that modern radar units have 'filters' to reduce returns from atmospheric phenomena (known to controllers as angels). This means that a very slow moving object might be removed from the display by such a filter, and an aircraft with little metal in its construction may make a very faint target on the PPI. Although radar is thought of as being an 'all weather' aid – in that it can see through cloud and fog, it is not totally unaffected by weather. Intense precipitation and thunderstorms may 'clutter' a radar display by creating a large area of returns, and short range radar such as that used exclusively for radar approaches is likely to be the worst affected in this way.

The 'basic' radar discussed above is known as 'primary' radar. In essence the radar controller knows that an object is in a certain place and moving in a certain direction. This still leaves the question of exactly who or what the target is. To establish this on the radar screen, a more advanced radar system is required.

▶Secondary Surveillance Radar (SSR)

Secondary Surveillance Radar (SSR) in civilian aviation is a ground-based radar usually used in conjunction with a primary radar unit – although it is important to appreciate that not all radar units automatically have SSR capability. SSR transmits a series of coded pulses on a frequency, which are received by any transponder within radio range. The transponder replies on a different frequency with a set of information for the ground-based SSR. At its most basic this information will be the four numbers selected by the pilot on the transponder. If the transponder has altitude encoding capability (known as mode C), and this mode is selected by the pilot, the aircraft's flight level can also be transmitted back to the ground-based SSR unit. SSR information is displayed on a PPI next to the 'primary' radar return for the aircraft. In this way the radar controller is able to identify the radar contact with a greater certainty than with a primary return alone.

SSR as it appears on a controller's radar screen. The code is displayed next to the primary return, with the flight level read out underneath – in this case FL020.

ATC liaison and RT phraseology in relation to SSR is discussed in some detail in the Communications section of PPL2, however a quick revision of the main points is not out of place.

Controller request	Pilot action
Squawk standby	Set the transponder to the 'standby' position.
Recycle squawk	Set the transponder to 'standby', check that the correct code is selected and set the transponder to 'on' again.
Squawk ident	Press the transponder 'ident' button. This causes the code displayed on the controller's radar screen to highlight and flash, remaining highlighted for several seconds.

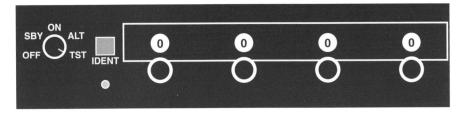

A typical transponder unit. The four-figure code is selected using the dial under each window. The "Ident" button is usually under the ident light – which illuminates when the transponder is interrogated by ground based SSR.

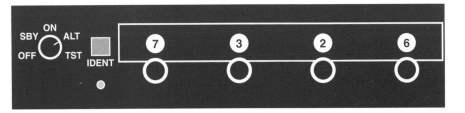

The code '7326' set on the transponder, in this case with Mode C selected.

The most frequently used transponder code is the conspicuity code – 7000. This code can be used when outside controlled airspace and if no other code has been allocated to you by an ATC unit. Select Mode C ('Alt') if this is available on the transponder. Remember to set the transponder to 'standby' before entering controlled airspace, if no other code has been allocated to you. The transponder should also be set to 'standby' when operating within the circuit and whenever changing codes. If you are allocated a transponder code by an ATC unit during flight, you will normally be instructed to 'deselect' it (e.g. squawk standby) on changing to an en-route frequency. There are three emergency transponder codes. When these are used, alarms will go off at all receiving stations and you are guaranteed instant attention. Only set an emergency code if you require assistance:

7700 – Emergency (i.e. Mayday situation)

7600 – Communications failure

7500 – Unlawful Interference

The use of Mode C for altitude reporting has already been discussed. A transponder without altitude reporting capability is sometimes referred to as Mode A. You might also hear talk (particularly in the airliner world) of Mode S. This is a development to provide a data link which will allow a suitable transponder to transmit more information about a flight, but is unlikely to be available to General Aviation for some time.

One of the great advantages of SSR is that the radio pulses it utilises only have to make a one-way journey. Once the coded pulse from the ground station has been received, a new transmission is sent from the transponder. This means that an SSR array has a greater range than a primary radar array with the same transmitter power – the typical range of an SSR unit is 200nm. SSR, as with primary radar, works at frequencies above VHF but unlike a primary radar return it gives a fairly unambiguous response to the ground unit and SSR information can often be seen on a display in circumstances where the primary radar return cannot. One of the few disadvantages of SSR is that the aircraft has to carry the necessary transponder. Although an aircraft operating VFR below FL100 is not required to carry a transponder in the UK and most JAA states, life in and around controlled airspace becomes infinitely easier if you have SSR capability and you want something from a radar controller. Likewise if you become lost or have a serious problem, a transponder should allow you to be located within a minute or so, whereas without a transponder location using VDF triangulation and primary radar can be a much more protracted affair.

▶ Automatic Direction Finding (ADF)

One of the oldest and most basic forms of radionavigation, the Non-Directional Beacon (NDB) is nothing more sophisticated than a radio transmitter similar to that used by any AM commercial radio station. When that station's frequency is selected on the aircraft's receiver (known as the Automatic Direction Finder – ADF), the ADF antenna system determines the direction of the transmission relative to the aircraft. This antenna system drives a needle that automatically points to the NDB. It is a simple system, but its use and interpretation by the pilot need careful consideration.

The ADF needle is usually presented over a vertically mounted compass card, hence the original term for this dial, a Radio Compass. Nowadays, the same display is referred to as an RBI – Relative Bearing Indicator – because the needle is showing the direction of the NDB station relative to the aircraft. To be any use, this relative bearing has to be converted into an actual direction to or from the station. The simplest way to do this is to transfer the needle position to the Heading Indicator (HI), for example by placing a pencil over the needle, aligned in the same direction, and then moving the pencil to the HI. The nose of the needle is indicating the magnetic track to the NDB – in other words the QDM. The tail of the needle is indicating the magnetic direction of the aircraft from the NDB – the QDR or radial. Of course, transposing the needle position over to the HI was not likely to be a long-term practical proposition, so beneath the ADF needle there is a compass card. In its most basic form the compass card of the RBI is fixed, with North straight ahead (i.e. in the 12 o'clock position), South directly behind in the 6 o'clock position, etc.. If the needle is pointing 45° right of dead ahead, this position can be

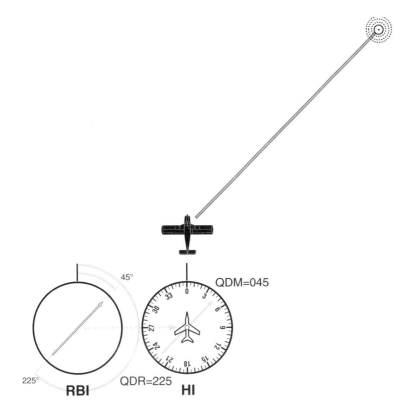

Converting a relative bearing into a QDM: Heading (000) + Relative Bearing of needle nose (045) = QDM 045

Converting a relative bearing into a QDR: Heading (000) + Relative Bearing of needle tail (225) = QDR (radial) 225

carried across to the HI to give a reasonably accurate QDM. More common than the fixed compass card is the RBI with a compass card that can be rotated by a setting knob. In this way the present heading can be set at the 12 o'clock position (as per the HI), and the direction to the station (QDM) can be read straight off the RBI dial at the nose of the needle. The direction of the aircraft from the station can be read off at the tail of the needle.

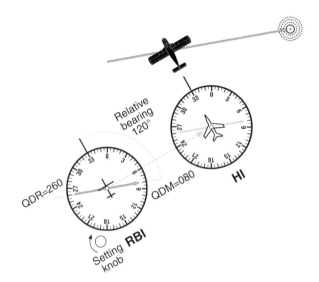

The relative bearing of the nose of the needle is 120, thus heading 330 + 120 gives a QDM of 080. Alternatively, set the heading at the top of the RBI and simply read-off the QDM at the nose of the needle (much easier, no?). Of course, it is vital to reset the RBI if the heading changes

You may already have thought that the needle presentation would be even easier to interpret if the ADF needle was simply placed over a real HI. No need to transpose needles or set RBI compass cards. Such a presentation is easy to read, and is available if the ADF receiver is linked to a Radio Magnetic Indicator – RMI. However, the cost of an RMI means that it is rarely found outside the ranks of business and serious touring aircraft.

Aviation NDB stations are listed in the AIP and commercial flight guides with their frequencies, identification letters, exact position and range. The range may vary in different directions from the NDB. Although most NDBs transmit on an 'H24' basis, they may have regular maintenance periods, and can be unavailable as notified by NOTAMs and Pre-flight Information Bulletins. Low-powered NDBs provided specifically as an aid to finding an airfield or as part of an instrument approach are known as Locators (abbreviated to L), but are otherwise identical to other NDBs. Aviation NDBs are marked on aeronautical charts although, if they are based on an airfield, the NDB symbol may be omitted for clarity. Other NDBs, such as the

Details in the AIP of the Chiltern NDB

ENR 4-1-1-2 (18 Jun 98)   UK AIP

ENR 4.1 — RADIO NAVIGATION AIDS — EN-ROUTE						
Name of Station (VOR set Variation)	IDENT	Frequency (Channel)	Hours of Operation (Winter/Summer)	Co-ordinates	DME Aerial Elevation	Remarks
1	2	3	4	5	6	7
Chiltem NDB	CHT	277.0 kHz	H24	513723N 0003107W	—	Range 25 nm.

Shipdham NDB, identification letters SDM, transmitting on 348.5 kHz

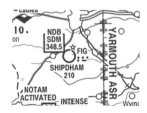

transmitters for commercial AM radio stations, tend not to be marked on charts, although pilots often know the frequency of those in their local area. Be aware, however, that the sound quality of music through an ADF receiver is appalling!

The principle limitation in selecting an NDB is range, as many NDBs and Locators are limited to only 10 or 15 miles range, which does tend to restrict the choice somewhat. Having chosen an NDB, and selected its frequency on the ADF receiver, the next step is to identify it. The importance of this cannot be over-stated. If the pilot does not identify the NDB station, there is no guarantee that the ADF is receiving any signal at all, let alone that from the correct station. A lazily meandering ADF needle can lead a pilot a merry dance in any direction with comic, or tragic, consequences. NDBs and Locators identify themselves by transmitting their two or three letter identification in morse code, several times a minute. The usual method to listen to this morse identification after selecting the NDB's frequency is to switch the ADF mode selector to 'ANT' (antenna) and adjust the volume control (you may also need to select the ADF receiver on the audio selector panel if the aircraft has one). The ANT mode gives the best audio reception for the incoming NDB signal but, because it bypasses part of the antenna system, it also means that the ADF needle cannot provide any bearing information while it is selected. Therefore it is vital that after identifying the NDB the mode selector is returned to 'ADF'. The mode selector will probably also have a 'BFO' mode. This is used for identifying the very small number of NDBs that have continuous wave (CW) transmissions. These are also known as N0N A1A transmissions, but are generally out of favour today for aviation NDBs and declining in number.

A typical ADF receiver

Symbol	Name	Sound
•	DOT	"DIT"
–	DASH	"DAH"

A Alpha	• –	DIT DAH
B Bravo	– • • •	DAH DIT DIT DIT
C Charlie	– • – •	DAH DIT DAH DIT
D Delta	– • •	DAH DIT DIT
E Echo	•	DIT
F Foxtrot	• • – •	DIT DIT DAH DIT
G Golf	– – •	DAH DAH DIT
H Hotel	• • • •	DIT DIT DIT DIT
I India	• •	DIT DIT
J Juliett	• – – –	DIT DAH DAH DAH
K Kilo	– • –	DAH DIT DAH
L Lima	• – • •	DIT DAH DIT DIT
M Mike	– –	DAH DAH
N November	– •	DAH DIT
O Oscar	– – –	DAH DAH DAH
P Papa	• – – •	DIT DAH DAH DIT
Q Quebec	– – • –	DAH DAH DIT DAH
R Romeo	• – •	DIT DAH DIT
S Sierra	• • •	DIT DIT DIT
T Tango	–	DAH
U Uniform	• • –	DIT DIT DAH
V Victor	• • • –	DIT DIT DIT DAH
W Whiskey	• – –	DIT DAH DAH
X X-Ray	– • • –	DAH DIT DIT DAH
Y Yankee	– • – –	DAH DIT DAH DAH
Z Zulu	– – • •	DAH DAH DIT DIT

The morse code

Example, NDB MCH on 428kHz:

M Mike	– –	DAH DAH
C Charlie	– • – •	DAH DIT DAH DIT
H Hotel	• • • •	DIT DIT DIT DIT

Morse decode for the NDB 'MCH'

The quality of the morse ident you hear will tell you something about how reliable the signal is. A very weak signal, or excessive static and 'noise', are all signs that the signal may not be very reliable. In many ADF installations, when 'ANT' is selected, the ADF needle automatically swings to a fixed 'three o'clock' position on the dial. The speed and certainty with which the needle returns to the QDM when 'ADF' is re-selected is also an indication of how good the incoming signal is. Alternatively some ADF receivers have a 'Test' mode which deflects the ADF needle around the dial. Once again, the movement of the needle back to the QDM when 'Test' is de-selected is a useful indication of signal reliability.

Navigation

Some pilots choose to identify NDBs with the ADF receiver still in 'ADF' mode. This is quite possible and, although the morse ident may be less clear, it does remove the possibility of leaving the mode selector at 'ANT' and being left puzzling at an immobile ADF needle.

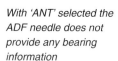

With 'ANT' selected the ADF needle does not provide any bearing information

RBI

With "ANT" selected, the ADF needle is FIXED on the RBI, it is not showing the correct QDM/QDR

NDB stations transmit in the LF (Low Frequency – 30-300 kHz) and MF (Medium Frequency – 300-3000kHz) bands, and the characteristics of radio signals in these bands define many of the factors that restrict NDB range and accuracy. LF and MF radio transmissions are not limited by the 'line-of-sight' principle that applies to the VHF band. Therefore the transmissions are capable of much greater range than VHF although in practice, limits on transmitter power and environmental factors that effect the LF and MF bands, mean that most NDBs have a relatively short range. All aviation NDBs have a promulgated range, and pilots should not attempt to use an NDB outside that range. This caution aside, there are some environmental factors that will effect the range of NDB transmissions, these are:

Surface – NDB transmissions travel further over a smooth sea than over an irregular land terrain: over the sea effective range may be doubled.

Precipitation Static – precipitation such as rain and snow, or even flight in cloud, can cause a build up of static electricity on the aircraft that may weaken the received NDB signal and effectively reduce range.

Environmental factors that can effect the accuracy of ADF bearings include:

Terrain – mountainous terrain between the NDB and the ADF receiver, especially if the aircraft is at low level, can deflect the NDB signal.

Precipitation Static – discussed above, this reduces the accuracy as well as the range of ADF bearings.

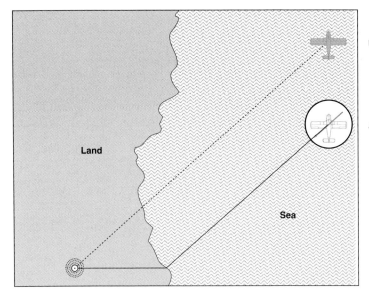

Pilot thinks he is here

Aircraft is here

Land

Sea

Coastal refraction of an NDB signal

Coastal Refraction – where NDB signals cross the coastline, the signal can be deflected. This effect can be minimised by using an NDB that is close to the coast and using it where the signal is crossing the coastline at an angle as close to 90° as possible.

Night Effect – changes at night in the ionosphere (an electrically charged region 50-350km above the surface) can result in NDB signals being reflected back to earth some distance from the NDB station. This can lead to unreliable bearings to the NDB in use, or *station interference* from a different NDB many miles away. The inaccuracies are generally worse around sunrise and sunset, and station interference is worse at night. For this reason NDB ranges and accuracy are not guaranteed at night.

A fast-developing Cumulonimbus (CB), very attractive to an ADF needle!

Thunderstorm

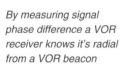

ADF needle is diverted towards a thunderstorm

Thunderstorm Effect – an active thunderstorm can be an enormous generator of electromagnetic energy. This is peculiarly attractive to an ADF receiver and it can be said that in thundery conditions, the best use for the ADF needle is to point to the nearest and most active thunderstorm! Excessive static and the 'crashes' of lightning discharges may be quite audible when listening to the NDB signal in these conditions and act as a warning not to rely on ADF bearings.

The accuracy of the ADF can be checked before flight if there is an NDB on the airfield or close enough to be received from the ground. The QDM and QDR shown on the RBI can be compared with the known direction of the NDB from the aircraft.

The limitations and possible error factors of NDB signals are underlined by the fact that the ADF receiver lacks an conspicuous failure warning system. If the NDB signal fades, if the aircraft moves out of range, or if the signal suffers interference, the most likely effect is that the ADF needle will begin to wander, become fixed or point away from the NDB. In these circumstances the failure of the signal is not obvious or apparent to the pilot. This is why it is particularly important that the NDB ident is re-checked at regular intervals whenever it is being used as a navigation aid.

▶ VHF Omni-directional Range (VOR)

In the 1960s the NDBs that had defined airways and routes for many years began to be replaced by a new type of beacon, the VHF Omni-directional Range (VOR). A VOR station transmits two signals, a reference signal and a directional signal. The VOR receiver measures the 'phase difference' between these two signals, which are aligned with magnetic north at the VOR. A 90° phase difference occurs

By measuring signal phase difference a VOR receiver knows it's radial from a VOR beacon

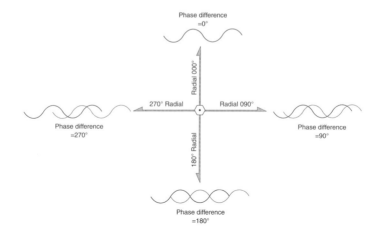

directly magnetic east of the VOR, a 180° phase difference occurs directly magnetic south of the VOR etc. One can imagine a series of tracks or radials, spokes if you like, radiating out from the VOR. In theory a VOR produces an infinite number of radials, but in practice we assume that there are 360 radials. The VOR receiver measures the signal's phase difference and converts this into the radial of the receiver from the VOR. Thus a pilot can determine the current radial from a VOR and its reverse, the bearing to the VOR.

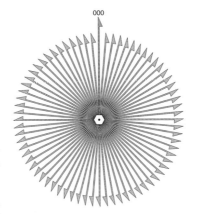

Radials 'radiating' out from a VOR beacon

In most light aircraft the information from a VOR receiver is displayed on an indicator with three main components:

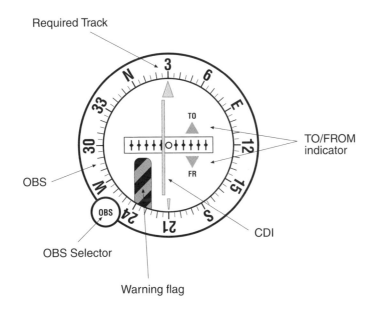

An Omni Bearing Selector – OBS

A Course Deviation Indicator – CDI

A TO/FROM flag, sometimes combined with a warning flag.

The OBS is used to select a radial from the VOR, or a bearing to it.

The CDI bar displays angular deviation from the track selected on the OBS. There are usually five dots across the dial (the outer edge of the centre circle may represent the first dot). When tuned to a VOR, each dot is equivalent to 2° of deviation from the selected track, so at full deflection the CDI bar is displaying a deviation (or Track Error) of 10° or more. The centre circle represents the aircraft, the CDI bar represents the selected track. When the CDI bar is centred, the OBS is displaying the present magnetic track to or from the station.

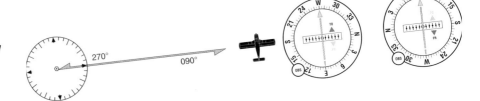

The 090 radial from the VOR is also the 270 QDM to the VOR

The TO/FROM flag indicates if the track selected at the top of the OBS is a track to or a track from the VOR. The importance of this apparently insignificant indicator cannot be overstated. The VOR display is totally independent of the aircraft's heading. For the CDI to give correct indications (in other words show a fly left indication to regain track when the aircraft is to the right of track, and vice versa), the aircraft must be heading generally in the same direction as the selected track. Imagine an aircraft orbiting to the left of the 090° radial from a VOR. To fly to the VOR, the pilot wants to follow a track of 270°. With 270° selected on the OBS, and the TO flag showing, the CDI shows a 'fly right' indication. However, it will continue to show this whatever the aircraft's heading. Clearly at some parts of the orbit, for example when the aircraft is heading east, this fly right indication might lead the unwary pilot in completely the wrong direction! To reduce the chances of confusion when tracking to or from a VOR, always check the TO/FROM flag, and transpose the selected track onto the HI to see that you are generally heading in the same direction as the selected track.

With 270 selected on the OBS, the CDI shows a 'fly right' indication regardless of the aircraft's heading

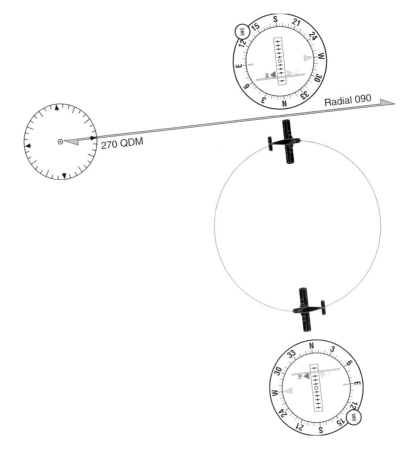

In more sophisticated aircraft VOR information can be displayed on an RMI (Radio Magnetic Indicator) as already described, which often has one 'VOR' needle and one 'ADF' needle; the VOR needle points to the QDM to the selected VOR beacon. VOR information can also be displayed on a Horizontal Situation Indicator – HSI. This puts the CDI bar directly over a Heading Indicator, the required track is selected by moving the nose of the needle around the HI. One advantage of the HSI is that the selected course and present heading can be seen at a glance, rather than having to look between two instruments.

A Horizontal Situation Indicator (HSI)

During pre-flight planning, VORs can be selected taking into account their Designated area of Operational Coverage – DOC. This information is given in the AIP (together with location, frequency, ident etc.). The DOC is a radius and height within which the VOR signals are considered reliable; the radius of the DOC may vary in certain directions. Although VORs transmit on an 'H24' basis, they may have regular maintenance periods which are shown in the AIP. They may also be 'off the air' as notified by NOTAMs and Pre-flight Information Bulletins. The AIP

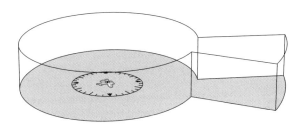

A Designated area of Operational Coverage – DOC

also lists 'localisers'(LLZ), which may operate independently or as part of an Instrument Landing system (ILS). As opposed to the infinite radials of a VOR, a localiser transmits a single radial, aligned with the final approach track of an instrument approach to a particular runway. When a localiser is selected on the aircraft's VOR receiver, the CDI bar operates solely in respect of the single radial of the localiser, in the sense of the QDM to the threshold. The pilot cannot select a QDM or QDR in relation to the localiser, the CDI operates only with reference to the single direction fixed by the localiser. The CDI needle also becomes more sensitive: each one dot across the CDI face equals just half a degree of Track Error when a localiser is selected.

Navigation

VORs operate in the VHF (Very High Frequency) band – 30-300 MHz. In general VHF radio signals are considered to be free of many of the errors that can afflict low frequency radio transmissions. This means that in particular VOR bearings are virtually unaffected by weather and static, time of day, etc. Unlike an NDB, the range and accuracy of a VOR is equally valid by day or night. In limited circumstances a very strong temperature inversion in the lower atmosphere (such

Details in the AIP of the Clacton VOR (which is co-located with a DME)

ENR 4-1-1-2 (18 Jun 98)   UK AIP

ENR 4.1 — RADIO NAVIGATION AIDS — EN-ROUTE						
Name of Station (VOR set Variation)	IDENT	Frequency (Channel)	Hours of Operation (Winter/Summer)	Co-ordinates	DME Aerial Elevation	Remarks
1	2	3	4	5	6	7
Chiltern NDB	CHT	277.0 kHz	H24	513723N 0003107W	—	Range 25 nm.
Clacton VOR/DME (3.2°W - 1995)	CLN	114.55 MHz (Ch 92Y)	H24	515055N 0010851E	100 ft amsl	DOC 100 nm/50000 ft (150 nm/ 50000 ft in Sector 321°-051°M).

as that which may occur during a prolonged summer anticyclone) can cause VHF radio signals to travel many hundreds of miles close to the surface. Aside from these unusual and quite rare conditions, VHF radio waves travel in a straight line and so, if you ignore factors such as transmitter power and receiver sensitivity, the range of VHF is defined by the 'line-of-sight' principle. If you could theoretically see to the VOR station on a perfectly clear day (e.g. it is not below the horizon in unlimited visibility), you should be able to receive its transmissions. Therefore the higher an aircraft is flying, or the higher the VOR beacon is sited, the greater the effective range at which VOR information can be received.

Because there are only a limited number of frequencies available for VOR stations, this 'line-of-sight' principle could lead to a high-flying aircraft being able to simultaneously receive signals from two VORs with the same frequency. This should not happen if the pilot observes the notified DOC of each VOR, which may be limited by the nearest VOR using the same frequency. For example, Glasgow VOR in Scotland and Caen VOR in northern France both have the same frequency. In theory an aircraft flying halfway between the two at 18,000ft or higher would be able to receive signals from both, although it would be outside their respective DOCs.

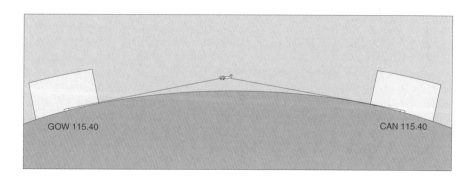

Although VOR signals are generally regarded of being very accurate, errors in bearing information may occur if the area around the VOR beacon contains reflective surfaces (such as buildings or obstacles) which can deflect the VOR transmissions – so-called site error. Site error can be minimised by locating the VOR beacon on flat terrain and as far as possible from buildings or obstacles. Additionally, propagation error (also known to pilots beyond a certain age as the 'bends' or 'scalloping') may occur if the VOR signal is travelling over hilly terrain and the receiver aircraft is at relatively low level – especially if it is also towards the edge of the DOC. The consequent uneven propagation of the VOR signal can cause a bearing error in the VOR signal received at the aircraft. Where such errors have been measured with regard to a specific VOR, or are a known or common problem, warning information may be found in the AIP. In general, VOR information displayed to the pilot is considered accurate to within +/-5°, which still means that at a range of 60nm from a VOR, an aircraft could be up to 5nm off-track although the CDI is centred on the desired QDM/QDR. This only goes to illustrate why for VFR navigation, VOR (as any other radionavigation aid) should be used as a back-up to visual navigation and identifying ground features.

The accuracy of the VOR receiver can be checked before flight if there is a VOR beacon on the airfield or close enough to be received on the ground. By identifying the VOR and checking the QDM/QDR, the pilot should be able to assess the accuracy of the bearing information displayed.

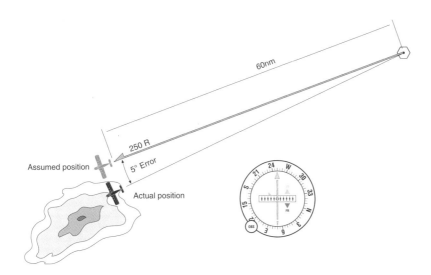

At 60nm from a VOR, a 5° Track Error puts the aircraft 5nm off-track

▶Distance Measuring Equipment (DME)

Distance Measuring Equipment (DME) in an aircraft gives the pilot the option of knowing the exact distance to a DME station. The DME transceiver in an aircraft transmits a code pulsed signal on the selected frequency. If this signal is received at a ground DME station, the signal is re-transmitted. When this transmission reaches the aircraft, the DME recognises its own coded pulses. Because radio

A typical DME display

waves travel at a set speed (the speed of light, 186,000 miles per second), by knowing the time interval between sending and receiving back its signal, the aircraft's DME transceiver can calculate distance to the DME station.

Most DME indicators will give a permanent display of distance to the selected DME. DMEs can normally also be set to show groundspeed, which is calculated based on the rate of change of distance from the DME. Given distance and groundspeed, DMEs can also display Time To Station, allowing an accurate ETA to be determined if you are flying towards a DME.

DMEs are often 'co-located' with a VOR, so that accurate range and bearing information to and from a specific point can be displayed. Although DME actually operates in the Ultra High Frequency (UHF) band, 300-3000MHz, DME frequencies are listed in the AIP and commercial flight guides as VHF values. This is possible because DME frequencies are 'paired' so that when the listed VHF

LEFT> A co-located VOR/DME

MIDDLE> A DME which is associated with an NDB, hence the prefix 'T'

RIGHT> A TACAN with the identification letters PEM

frequency is set on the aircraft's DME, the correct UHF frequency is automatically selected. Combined VOR/DMEs are listed in the AIP, and share a DOC. DMEs can also be located with or close to an NDB, and in conjunction a localiser or ILS. In these latter two instances the DME distance information is normally with reference to the threshold of the instrument runway in use; in other words the aircraft's DME will read zero at the instrument runway threshold. DME information is also available from military TACAN beacons, the appropriate VHF frequency is shown on aeronautical charts and in commercial flight guides.

DME stations are generally considered to operate H24, with the usual provisos regarding scheduled and unscheduled maintenance. DMEs transmit their ident letters in morse code every 30 seconds. UHF radio waves are similar to VHF in that they are largely immune to interference from static, weather, time of day etc. and their theoretical range is governed by the 'line-of-sight' principle.

It is important to appreciate that DMEs measure and display the direct distance between the aircraft and the DME station – known as 'slant' range – rather than the ground distance between the two. Thus the DME in an aircraft flying at 12,000ft (2nm) will read 2nm when the aircraft is directly over a DME station. At lower altitudes and at any respectable distance from a DME, the difference between 'slant' range and the actual distance over the ground is very small, for example at 6000ft and 30nm 'slant' range from a DME, the actual ground distance from the DME is 29.98nm. It should be appreciated that the groundspeed function will only give an accurate reading if the aircraft is maintaining a constant bearing relative to the DME (i.e. flying directly towards or directly away from it). The groundspeed

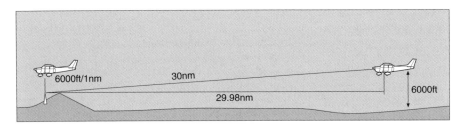

The aircraft's DME reads 'slant' range to the DME beacon

readout is only based on the rate of change of distance relative to the DME: if the aircraft is not flying directly to or from a DME station the indicated groundspeed will be less than the actual figure. It follows that the Time To Station (TTS) function is also only reliable when the aircraft is flying directly towards a DME. In addition, as an aircraft passes over a DME, the groundspeed value will fall to almost zero for a short time as the rate of change in distance becomes very small.

DME information is considered to be very accurate – within 0·25% of actual slant range – once the aircraft's DME has 'locked onto' a DME station within its DOC. However, the fact that the DME station is receiving and re-transmitting signals from many aircrafts' DMEs places a practical limit on how many DMEs can 'lock on' to a single DME station at any one time. Most existing DME stations can cope with no more than around 100 aircraft (although new DME stations may be able to handle more). When this limit is reached, the DME station will begin to disregard the weaker signals (which will normally be those furthest away). Thus the aircraft's DME may be unable to obtain information from a DME station even though both are functioning properly; this is a situation is known as 'beacon saturation'. As you might expect, beacon saturation is most prevalent at DME beacons around busy airports and terminal airspace, and at peak periods of air traffic flow.

Although many airfields do have a DME, it can be quite difficult to check the aircraft's DME accuracy on the ground as the distance from the aircraft to the DME beacon may be too small. Nevertheless, the pilot should be able to tune and identify a nearby DME on the ground, with a view to re-checking the aircraft's DME once airborne.

▶Global Positioning System (GPS)

It is no exaggeration to say that the Global Positioning System – GPS – has the capability to revolutionise aviation navigation, and for that matter most forms of surface navigation too. GPS is based on information from 24 NAVSTAR satellites orbiting 10,900nm above the earth. Each satellite constantly transmits its orbital position and the precise time that the transmission left the satellite. A GPS receiver has its own very accurate clock, and it can therefore measure the exact

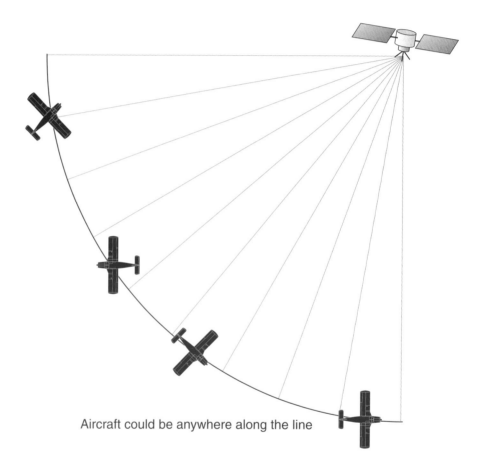

Aircraft could be anywhere along the line

time taken for the satellite's transmission to reach it. Because radio waves travel at a known speed – the speed of light – this time can be converted into an exact range from the satellite. It is useful to think of this known distance as a radius (although it's actually the surface of a sphere); the GPS receiver knows that it is somewhere along that line, but that still leaves a lot of possible positions!

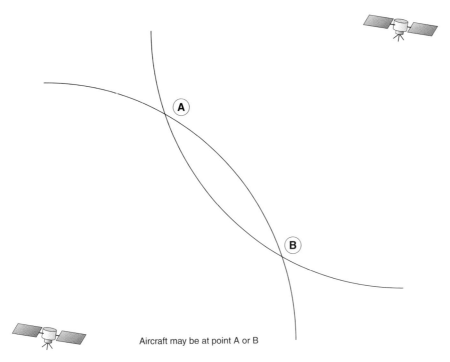

Aircraft may be at point A or B

By knowing the exact distance from a second satellite, the GPS receiver can narrow down its position to those points where the two radii cross. If the GPS receiver knows its exact distance from a third satellite, this ambiguity is resolved and a position is arrived at. Thus in practice the GPS receiver must receive signals from at least three satellites for two-dimensional navigation, and four satellites for 3-d navigation (i.e. altitude as well as position over the surface).

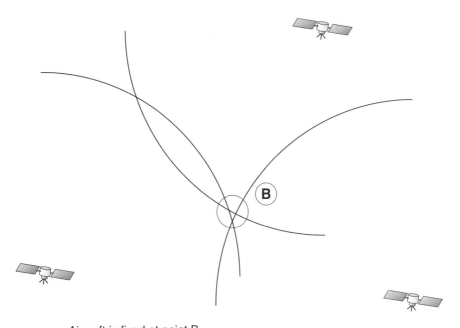

Aircraft is fixed at point B

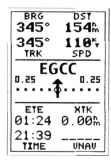

A GPS display showing bearing, actual track and distance to a waypoint, with a CDI too

An 'HSI' type display on a GPS unit

At its most basic, a GPS receiver can display its current position, for example as a latitude and longitude co-ordinate. Of course, this on its own is of limited use in a moving aircraft and so it is more common for the GPS user to navigate by reference to 'waypoints' – a fixed position on the earth. If the GPS knows its present position, it can display the range and bearing to any other selected waypoint. This is only the beginning; by knowing how its own position is changing the GPS receiver can also compute the present track (or Track Made Good – TMG), groundspeed, ETA at waypoint etc. Most GPS receivers offer a choice of displays: you may wish to see the bearing to (QDM) your waypoint, and the current TMG: match the two and you are tracking directly towards the waypoint. You may be able to select a display that shows any deviation from a track between two points, rather like a CDI bar. You may prefer a stylised HSI, or an arrowhead that points towards the selected waypoint. The latest generation of GPS receivers now have in-built maps, giving the user a moving map display with the aircraft's current position, planned route (if there is one) and actual track (TMG) over the ground. On the face of it all this is available to anyone able to obtain a GPS receiver and turn it on; there are no beacons to tune, no morse idents to decode, no ranges to check and no radial or relative bearings to interpret. Turn on the box at wait for it to find itself: simple!

Well, of course, it is not quite that simple. The database of waypoints stored in the GPS is made up of those input by the manufacturer, and those which the user can add. Waypoints input by the manufacturer are normally known aeronautical features: airfields, radionavigation beacons etc. Airfields are normally accessed by their four-letter ICAO code, navigation aids by their identification letters. It follows that an airfield without an ICAO code will probably not feature in the GPS receiver's database. Likewise the information on radionavigation aids will only be current at the moment of manufacture. New airfields, new navigation aids, changes of position, new identification letters etc. will not be known to the GPS receiver unless the user updates the database in some way, and the practicalities and cost of such updating are still evolving. Additionally, because many modern GPS receivers have databases covering a very large area, there can be several radionavigation aids in the database with identical identification letters: 'TRN' could be a VOR in Scotland, Iran or Thailand; 'LON' identifies a VOR at London Heathrow and an NDB at Svalbard in Norway. Select the wrong waypoint and follow the GPS blindly and you could end up very far from where you intended! The map databases tend to be quite limited in terms of the topographical information and what types of airspace are displayed and, once again, the map can only represent the information current at the moment of manufacture unless it is updated.

When inputting a 'user' waypoint, the usual computer maxim of 'rubbish in, rubbish out' still applies. Input the wrong co-ordinates, maybe 51S instead of 51N, and your GPS receiver will quite happily accept that your farm strip is somewhere in the middle of the South Atlantic.

The limitations of GPS are still being defined. The satellites transmit in the UHF band and the transmissions seem, apart from possible sunspot interference, to be very reliable. Any number of GPS receivers can listen to transmissions, so there is no danger of the system becoming saturated. Some aerial systems on portable units seen susceptible to interference from certain VHF frequencies, and can be blocked by the aircraft's structure, but fitted aerials largely solve these problems. The GPS receiver needs to be able to 'see' at least three satellites above the horizon, and its view may be blocked on the ground by buildings or mountains. In practice, the number of satellites now in orbit means that it is rare that an airborne GPS receiver fails to find enough satellites for at least 2-d navigation. GPS is useable worldwide, from and to any point on the globe. If you tell a GPS receiver that you want to go to a point on the other side of the world it will faithfully record the bearing required, distance to go and present groundspeed. Be aware, however, that it can only give an accurate ETA if you are heading directly towards the selected waypoint; if you are moving at an angle to it the time to go value will be in error, although the groundspeed readout will be correct. Civilian GPS receivers are considered to give a position accurate to 100m at least 95% of the time, although many users claim a much better average accuracy.

So, if this system really is a dream come true for pilots, what's the catch? The catch is largely political rather than practical. The NAVSTAR satellites that provide GPS information have been thoughtfully provided by the American military, at a cost of many billions of dollars. This means that, not unreasonably, they retain control of the whole system. (Incidentally, there is a CIS equivalent system, called GLONASS – Global Orbiting Navigation Satellite System – but most commercially available receivers use GPS information). So, if the military control the system they have the option to turn it off, degrade its accuracy (which in fact they already do, military GPS units have a much better accuracy than civilian), or even jam the signals in selected areas. The portable GPS receivers that most GA pilots use also have their own built-in limitations. Apart from the question of the currency of the database, the

small aerial of a portable unit gives noticeably worse performance than a fixed aerial. Most hand-held GPS receivers are not very easy to re-program in flight, and they all suffer from basic frailty in that, if the electrons stop flowing to the unit, it goes on strike very quickly indeed. Given that most portable GPS receivers work on alkaline batteries, which only give around four hours usage, this is a much more common problem than you might think. It is no fun trying to replace the batteries in a small GPS unit, not forgetting also to properly aviate, navigate and communicate, whilst flying single crew in a light aircraft with no autopilot.

A typical 'handheld' GPS receiver with small aerial

Checking the accuracy of a GPS unit before flight is largely a matter of turning it on and allowing it a minute or so to give its present location. This location, whether it is displayed as a map, a latitude and longitude co-ordinate or whatever should be subject to a normal common-sense check to ensure that the GPS really does know where it is and where you want to go. At this stage it is also prudent to check the battery state for the reasons just covered.

There is little doubt that the potential accuracy and ease of use of GPS makes it the navigation system of the future, but much remains to be done before it replaces any of the more traditional radionavigation aids. Although the authorities caution that GPS should only be used as an aid to visual navigation, there have already been instances of pilots getting lost by relying totally on the comfort of a GPS readout. It is all very interesting to know that you are heading towards a waypoint on a track of 143° at 107 knots and you have 67.32nm to go. But if you don't realise that this position puts you inside controlled airspace, which you didn't intend, or if you fail to spot that this track will take you straight through an active danger area, or a busy ATZ, this apparent accuracy is of limited use. Having an accurate mental picture of where you are, and where you are going, in relation to the real world outside the window has always overridden the advice of the latest navigation box of tricks – and it always will.

▶Revision

63 VHF radio, as used in VDF, is <u>not</u> subject to which of the following errors?
   – Line-of-sight error
   – Propagation error
   – Night effect

64 What is the definition of QDM?

65 What class of VDF bearing is classified as being accurate to within +/- 10°?

66 In relation to primary radar, how (if at all) will increasing the height of the radar antenna above the surrounding terrain alter the radar range?

67 Will a radar operator generally consider terrain 'clutter' on the PPI to be useful in relation to low flying aircraft?

68 Primary targets are normally displayed on what piece of radar equipment?

69 What is the name of the <u>aircraft</u> equipment required for SSR?

70 Where is SSR information normally displayed to an Air Traffic Controller?

71 If you are 'squawking' mode C, what particular SSR information will you expect the ground-based SSR receiver to display?

72 What is an NDB?

73 How is ADF information displayed in its simplest form?

74 List at least three <u>environmental</u> factors that effect the range and accuracy of an NDB/ADF bearing.

75 What does the abbreviation VOR stand for?

76 VOR bearings are measured in relation to what datum?

77 During what times of the day is a DOC guaranteed?

78 If you are not flying directly towards a DME, which DME measurements, as displayed to the pilot, will not be accurate?

79 If the aircraft's DME reads an in-flight range of 25.4nm, is this the ground distance from the aircraft to the DME station?

Answers at page NAV 207

The Full Flight Plan

▶ When to File a Full Flight Plan

▶ The 'Full Flight Plan' Form

▶ Filing a Full Flight Plan

▶ Revision

Exercise

The
Full
Flight
Plan

▶When to File a Full Flight Plan

A flight plan is a message from a pilot to the Air Traffic Service giving details of his intended flight. In this context we are looking at the 'Full Flight Plan', as opposed to the process of 'booking-out' before departure or the flight details given by radio when seeking to enter controlled airspace.

A full flight plan is normally filed on a standard form (CA48). The circumstances when a full flight plan must be filed are covered in the 'Air Law' section of the PPL course (Book 2) but in summary:

A flight plan **may** be filed for **any** flight, even if you are just going for one circuit!

It is **advisable** to file a flight plan for a flight routing over the sea; more than ten miles from the coast; or over a sparsely populated area where SAR operations could be difficult.

Land areas of the UK considered difficult for Search And Rescue (SAR) operations

It is **mandatory** to file a flight plan:

– for a flight in Class A airspace,

– for an IFR flight in controlled airspace (Classes A to E),

– for a VFR Flight in Classes B, C, and D airspace (this requirement can be satisfied by contacting the ATSU controlling the airspace and obtaining permission to enter),

– when wishing to use an air traffic advisory service in advisory airspace,

– for a flight which will cross an international FIR boundary,

– for a flight where the destination is more than 40km from the departure aerodrome and the aircraft is more than 5700kg MTWA.

A full flight plan for a VFR flight must be filed at least 60min before start/taxi clearance is requested. Flights planning to use controlled or advisory airspace controlled by London, Manchester or Scottish Control must also give 60min notice. Other flights can give 30min notice.

An airborne flight plan can be filed with an FIR controller on the notified FIS frequency. The pilot must give at least 10min notice of an intention to enter controlled airspace.

Thus, if you are intending to file a full flight plan you need to allow plenty of time for flight planning in order to file the plan in advance. Practical experience has shown that it is sometimes possible to file a VFR full flight plan giving less than 60min notice, but there is no guarantee that it will be accepted.

▶ The 'Full Flight Plan' Form

The full flight-plan form (CA48) is a standard form completed using certain abbreviations and conventions. The increasing automation of ATS communications means that mistakes in completing the form can lead to the flight plan being rejected, and an inevitable delay. Detailed instructions for completing a flight-plan form are found in AICs, flight guides, and even on wall posters at the FBU. Following are the basic conventions used when filing a flight plan.

Block capitals should be used throughout, and all clock times should be in four-figure UTC format. The section to be completed by the pilot starts with item 7.

7: **Aircraft Identification**. The aircraft's RT callsign. For most VFR flights this will be the aircraft's registration. Registration is also inserted for a non-radio aircraft.

8: **Flight Rules/Type of Flight.** The flight rules under which the aircraft will operate. I = IFR, V = VFR. Type of flight is normally G (General aviation) for a private flight.

9: **Number** and **Type of Aircraft, Wake Turbulence Category**. The number of aircraft is inserted only if there is more than one. The aircraft type is entered as the ICAO aircraft type designator (as listed in good flight guides and the ICAO decode booklet possessed by most ATSUs). If the aircraft has no designator, enter "ZZZZ" and specify the type of aircraft in Item 18 preceded by TYP/. For a general-aviation aircraft, the wake-turbulence category is usually L (Light, MTOW 7000kg or less).

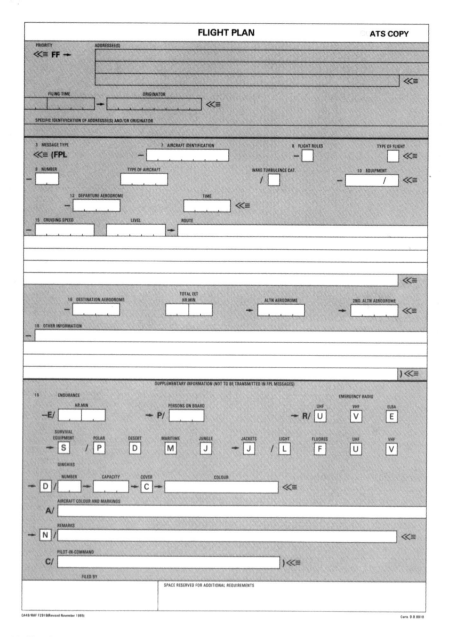

The ICAO full flight-plan form

10: **Equipment**. N = no com/nav equipment; S = standard com/nav equipment (VHF RTF, ADF, VOR, ILS); V = VHF communication radio. SSR equipment is inserted after the slash (/) N = None; A = Transponder Mode A; C = Transponder Mode C (i.e. altitude encoding).

13: **Departure Aerodrome** and **Time**.
The ICAO four-letter designator for the departure aerodrome is inserted. This can be found in the AIP and in flight guides. If no ICAO designator exists, "ZZZZ" is entered and the airfield name is given in Item 18, preceded by DEP/.

The estimated time of taxying (off-block time) is entered in four-figure UTC format.

15: **Cruising Speed, Level** and **Route**. The cruising TAS is given as a four-figure number preceded by N (kNots) or K (Kilometres).

Cruising level is normally given as Flight Level (F followed by three numbers) or Altitude (A followed by three figures). VFR can be inserted for a VFR flight with no specific cruising level.

A route outside designated ATS routes (i.e. airways) should be given as one of the following:

– the coded designator of each waypoint/turning point as a navigation aid (e.g. a VOR or NDB) or reporting point,

– lat./long. co-ordinates,

– bearing and distance from a navigation aid.

DCT (Direct) can be used to join successive points unless both points are defined as geographical co-ordinates or bearing and distance from a navaid. For a VFR flight 'DCT' is usually inserted before the first waypoint/turning point.

16: **Destination Aerodrome, Total Elapsed Time, Alternate Aerodrome** and **Second Alternate Aerodrome**.

The ICAO four-letter designator of the destination airfield is inserted. If no ICAO designator exists, enter "ZZZZ", and specify the airfield name in Item 18 preceded by DEST/.

The Total Elapsed Time (i.e. expected flight time) is given in four figures denoting hours and minutes.

The alternate aerodrome(s) is given as the ICAO designator. If no designator exists, insert "ZZZZ" and specify alternate name in Item 18 preceded by ALTN/.

18: **Other Information**. Insert 0 if None. EET/ is used for the elapsed time to a significant point(s) or FIR boundary designator(s) as required. RMK/ = any other plain-language remarks (e.g. request SVFR etc.).

19: **Supplementary Information**.

Endurance:
E/ – fuel endurance in a four-figure group to express hours/minutes.

Persons on Board:
P/ –

Emergency Radio:
R/(Radio) – cross-out those facilities which are *not* available, e.g. cross out '**U**' if UHF 243MHz is not available.

Survival Equipment:
S/(Survival Equipment) – cross-out indicators of survival equipment *not* carried.

Jackets: J/(Jackets) – cross out all indicators if no life-jackets are carried. Cross-out **L** if life-jackets are not equipped with lights; cross-out **F** if life-jackets are not equipped with fluorescein; cross-out **U** or **V** to indicate radio capability (or not) of life-jackets.

Dinghies: (Number) – Cross out indicators **D** and **C** if no dinghies are carried, or insert number of dinghies.

(Capacity) – Insert total capacity, in persons, of dinghies carried.

(Cover) – Cross out **C** if dinghies are not covered.

(Colour) – Insert colour of dinghies carried.

Aircraft Colour and Markings:

A/(Aircraft colour and markings) – insert colour of aircraft and any significant markings.

Remarks. N/(Remarks) – Cross out indicator **N** if no remarks, or indicate other survival equipment/remarks.

Pilot in Command: C/(Pilot) – Insert name of pilot in command.

▶Filing a Full Flight Plan

The completed full flight-plan form can be given to the ATSU at most airfields which possess one. It will then be passed on to the relevant unit. If there is no ATSU at the departure airfield, or if the ATSU cannot pass on the flight plan, it has to be filed directly with a 'parent' ATSU. These are mostly flight-briefing units at the larger airports. At present there are nine parent ATSUs in the UK. A full flight plan can be filed by fax or by phone, and the relevant numbers are found in the AIP, AICs and flight guides.

Once a full flight plan has been filed, you have in effect committed yourself to flying a set route and departing at a set time. If the flight is cancelled or its departure is delayed by more than 30min (or if flight-plan details change) the departure or parent ATSU must be informed.

Having filed a full flight plan, the aerodrome ATSU will inform the parent ATSU of your time of departure. This time is used to 'activate' the flight plan and is the basis of calculating your ETA at the destination. If the aerodrome does not have an ATSU, you should nominate a 'responsible person' to telephone the parent ATSU once you are airborne and pass the airborne time. If this is not possible you can contact an FIR controller (on the FIS frequency), pass on the airborne time and request them to 'activate' your flight plan.

Filing a full flight plan actually makes little difference to the progress of the flight until your arrival at the destination. This is because probably the prime purpose of filing a flight plan for a VFR flight is to ensure that somebody (usually the ATSU at the destination) is watching for your safe arrival.

The ATSU at the destination airfield will 'close' the flight plan when you arrive; in other words, the ATSU knows that your flight has arrived safely. If you do not arrive within 30min of the flight-plan ETA, the arrival ATSU will commence a search for you. This is called *alerting action*. If your flight cannot be located, SAR operations will be started. The upshot is that if for any reason you have to land at an airfield other than the specified destination, it is **your** responsibility as pilot in command to ensure that the flight-plan destination is informed within 30min of the ETA there. This is absolutely **vital**.

If you do not arrive at your destination because of some mishap, at least you can be sitting in your dinghy, or on the side of a hill, knowing that somebody is going to come looking for you using the route details from your flight plan. It follows that if you land elsewhere without telling the original destination, **you are putting lives at risk.** SAR resources are not unlimited, and searching for an non-existent "missing" aircraft might take the rescue services away from somebody who genuinely needs help. Several false searches are triggered each year, often by pilots flying cross-Channel who land somewhere *en route* without bothering to tell anyone. In some countries, the guilty pilot may be billed for an SAR operation falsely started in this way. At anything up to £11,000 an hour for a military reconnaissance aircraft, that could be the most expensive flight a pilot will ever make.

If your flight-plan destination does not have an ATSU, the concept of the 'responsible person' arises again. In this case, the 'responsible person' is informed of the flight by the pilot before departure, and is required to notify the parent ATSU if the aircraft fails to arrive at its destination within 30min of its ETA.

There is no strict definition of who can be a 'responsible person'. However, given the importance of their role, you will want to select someone with whom you can (literally) trust your life. In an extreme case, if you cannot find a responsible person at the destination – if it is a small airstrip with no permanent buildings, for example – you can contact the parent ATSU prior to departure and ask them to act as a 'responsible person'. In this instance you *must* contact this parent ATSU within 30min of landing at the destination. If the ATSU does not hear from you, it will automatically initiate alerting action.

These requirements may seem a little complicated and indigestible if you read and try to absorb them all at once. But you should not be put off filing a flight plan just because doing so seems a little daunting at first, especially if you are planning to fly over a remote area. From the ground, most of Europe can seem very crowded and it is difficult to imagine a forced landing not attracting lots of onlookers. Nevertheless, there have been many instances where aircraft have force-landed in a 'densely inhabited' area – such as the south-east of England – and then waited for over an hour to be located by people who already knew the aircraft's approximate position! In truly remote areas, a much longer wait could be in prospect if nobody had the details of your flight...

▶ Revision

80 You are planning a VFR flight and intend to file a full flight plan. If you plan to taxy at 1100Z, what is the latest time that you can file the flight plan?

81 The flight-plan destination is Birmingham (EGBB). You departed Le Touquet in France (LFAT) at 1410Z, with a flight plan EET (Estimated Elapsed Time) of 1hr 20min. For weather reasons you divert to Cranfield (EGTC) and land there at 1515Z. Who needs to be informed of the diversion, by what time, and who is responsible for this action?

Answers at page NAV 207

Time

Navigation

Time

▶ **UTC and Local Time**

▶ **Revision**

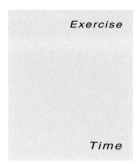

Exercise

Time

▶ UTC and Local Time

The standard time reference used in aviation is UTC (universal co-ordinated time), also known as 'Z' or 'Zulu'. For all practical purposes UTC is the same as GMT (Greenwich Mean Time). Time is given using the 24-hour clock, where 0100 is one o'clock in the morning and 2300 is 11 o'clock at night. UTC is fixed, and does not alter with location or season. When it is 1537UTC in the UK, it is 1537UTC all over the world (and *vice versa* of course!).

On the other hand, local times vary by location and season, being based primarily on the passage of the sun overhead. The world is divided into 24 *time zones*. The local time within each zone is set by reference to UTC. For example, winter local time in the UK is the same as UTC but summer local time (British Summer Time) is one hour ahead of UTC (UTC + 1 hour). So 1600 UTC (Z) is 1700BST.

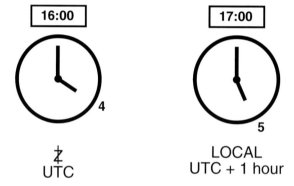

Comparison of UTC and local time

The potential for confusion is obvious – so when discussing times, always establish whether they are in local or Zulu (UTC). Some smaller airfields give their opening hours in local time rather than UTC, so **CHECK** to be **SURE.** If you are flying across more than one time zone, the whole business can become confusing; in these circumstances it is best to calculate times by working through UTC.

Example: You want to fly from Fairoaks, near London, to Clermont Ferrand in France. It is summer, so local time in the UK is UTC+1hr. Local time in France is UTC+2hr. If official night at Clermont Ferrand is 2030 local and the expected flight time is 3hr 30min, what is the latest time (UK local) that you can leave Fairoaks and still arrive at Clermont Ferrand before dark?

Working through UTC, 2030 local French time equals 1830UTC. Deduct the 3hr 30min flight time to give 1500UTC. Add one hour for UK local time and the latest departure time from Fairoaks becomes 1600.

Time

DATE	EGAA Belfast Aldergrove SR/SS	EGBB Birmingham SR/SS	EGPF Glasgow SR/SS	EGLL London Heathrow SR/SS	EGCC Manchester SR/SS	EGSH Norwich SR/SS	EGHD Plymouth SR/SS	EGPB Sumburgh SR/SS
Jan 1	0847/1610	0817/1604	0847/1555	0807/1604	0824/1602	0806/1551	0816/1624	0905/1512
Jan 15	0840/1628	0811/1621	0838/1615	0800/1621	0816/1620	0759/1619	0810/1649	0852/1536
Feb 1	0814/1702	0748/1653	0812/1650	0740/1651	0754/1651	0737/1640	0751/1709	0818/1619
Feb 15	0750/1728	0726/1716	0740/1723	0713/1718	0725/1721	0710/1708	0725/1720	0740/1659
Mar 1	0712/1800	0655/1742	0710/1750	0650/1740	0654/1748	0640/1734	0658/1759	0700/1735
Mar 15	0640/1828	0622/1811	0631/1822	0614/1811	0623/1815	0605/1800	0628/1823	0620/1808
Apr 1	0556/1902	0540/1840	0529/1831	0535/1836	0540/1845	0527/1830	0551/1849	0528/1850
Apr 15	0523/1928	0510/1905	0546/1857	0535/1836	0527/1830	0527/1830	0551/1849	0528/1850
May 1	0446/1958	0436/1931	0424/1922	0432/1926	0433/1939	0421/1923	0450/1937	0401/2004
May 15	0410/2041	0411/1956	0405/2024	0410/1948	0409/2004	0357/1946	0428/1957	0329/2036
June 1	0355/2050	0350/2019	0340/2052	0349/2010	0346/2027	0336/2009	0409/2019	0254/2114
June 15	0348/2102	0344/2030	0332/2104	0344/2020	0340/2038	0330/2020	0404/2029	0308/2110
July 1	0352/2104	0348/2032	0337/2104	0349/2021	0346/2039	0336/2020	0409/2030	0249/2127
July 15	0407/2053	0400/2022	0352/2052	0401/2011	0400/2029	0348/2010	0422/2021	0310/2107
Aug 1	0434/2025	0426/1959	0420/2025	0425/1949	0425/2004	0413/1947	0444/2000	0345/2034
Aug 15	0457/2000	0450/1930	0450/1950	0449/1923	0445/1939	0437/1921	0501/1936	0422/1955
Sept 1	0528/1920	0516/1858	0519/1914	0512/1849	0515/1900	0503/1844	0530/1900	0457/1910
Sept 15	0552/1841	0539/1826	0550/1832	0538/1814	0543/1822	0532/1808	0552/1828	0535/1822
Oct 1	0625/1803	0605/1747	0620/1757	0559/1740	0610/1743	0559/1730	0615/1753	0608/1730
Oct 15	0650/1728	0631/1711	0650/1715	0552/0626	0637/1711	0621/1659	0643/1723	0645/1655
Nov 1	0724/1651	0659/1640	0721/1639	0651/1635	0705/1638	0650/1620	0705/1651	0725/1610
Nov 15	0753/1623	0727/1615	0755/1609	0721/1611	0735/1611	0718/1600	0731/1630	0804/1534
Dec 1	0823/1603	0751/1557	0823/1550	0745/1556	0800/1555	0742/1544	0755/1615	0840/1509
Dec 15	0840/1558	0810/1553	0842/1543	0801/1553	0818/1550	0800/1540	0811/1612	0902/1459

Sunrise and sunset times from the UK VFR Flight Guide

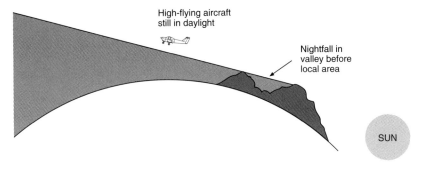

High-flying aircraft still in daylight

Nightfall in valley before local area

SUN

Nightfall comes first in deep valleys and in the shadow of high ground, and latest to high-flying aircraft

Unless you hold a night rating, a flight must be completed in daylight. Daylight is defined by the Air Navigation Order as being from 30min before sunrise to 30min after sunset (sunrise and sunset being defined at the surface). Most flight guides publish sunrise and sunset times for several major airfields and you can use these as a guide to sunrise and sunset elsewhere, although many airfields have their own sunrise and sunset tables at the ATSU or FBU. During your training you should always plan to complete your flight not less than one hour before official night, remembering that in overcast conditions, or in the shadow of high ground (e.g. in a valley), it may effectively become dark some time before official night. Conversely, nightfall occurs later at altitude than on the ground. It is possible to be cruising in daylight at high altitude whilst the airfield directly below is in darkness. This is no time to start wishing that you'd done that night rating, or that your destination had lights!

▶ Revision

82   It is winter, and in the UK local time is the same as UTC. French local time is UTC+1hr. You are departing from France to a UK airfield which closes at 1700 local time. If the expected flight time is 1hr 45min, what is the latest departure time from the French airfield (in French local time)?

83   The sunset time at a UK airfield is 1635Z. It is summer, and local time is UTC+1hr. What time (local) does official night begin?

Answers at page NAV 207

Flight Planning: Summary

▶ **Flight Planning – A Practical Example**

▶ **Route Selection**

▶ **Chart Selection**

▶ **Minimum Safety Altitude**

▶ **Chart Preparation**

▶ **Weather Considerations**

▶ **Daylight**

▶ **Completion of the Flight Log**

▶ **Fuel Planning and Mass Calculation**

▶ **Take-off and Landing Performance**

▶ **Alternate Airfields**

▶ **Radio Frequencies**

▶ **Pre-flight Information Bulletins**

▶ **Aircraft Documentation**

▶ **Flight Notification**

▶ **Conclusion**

*Flight
Planning
Summary*

▶ Flight Planning – A Practical Example

Flight planning is an integration of several skills and knowledge areas, particularly those concerning meteorology and navigation.

What follows is an example of flight planning for a simple VFR flight within the UK. A route has been chosen that can be planned on either the Southern England or Northern England 1:500 000 CAA aeronautical charts. Actual met. and AIS information has been taken from a specific day. You can follow through the flight-planning process, comparing your own calculations and conclusions against those here.

The plan is to fly a PA38 Tomahawk from Liverpool Airport (N5320 W00250) – assumed to be the 'home' base – to Sturgate (N5322 W00041) north-west of Lincoln. Two adults will be on board and the flight is to be conducted under VFR, departing Liverpool at around mid-day local time.

▶ Route Selection

The first step is to look at a straight line between the departure and destination (since this will be shortest route) then work from there.

The straight line from Liverpool to Sturgate passes through the Manchester Control Zone and directly over Manchester International Airport. You could try asking for such a clearance, but you are rather more likely to win the National Lottery than to have that sort of request granted. So it will be necessary to route around the Manchester CTR, either to the north or south. Routing to the south looks to be the shorter path, and has the advantage of avoiding the highest (and most remote) parts of the Peak District.

We therefore plan to leave the Liverpool zone at the VRP of Chester (nine miles south of Liverpool Airport) and route via at least one turning-point to 'dog leg' around the Manchester CTR. One possible choice is the town of Leek (N5306 W00201). However, the track from Chester to Leek runs closely parallel to the Manchester CTR (within 1nm) for some distance. A small deviation north of track could be embarrassing! A better choice is the town of Ashbourne (N5301 W00144). Although a smaller town than Leek, the route to Ashbourne has enough landmarks

The area around the Chester VRP, with the intended turning point

to aid map-reading and the town itself has a number of characteristics including rivers, roads and valleys leading into it. There is also a disused airfield just to the west and a large reservoir to the north-west (which will make a good landmark for establishing ourselves on the leg to Sturgate). A routing via Ashbourne also takes the flight clear of the highest and remotest regions of the southern Peak District, with the option of a 'bolthole' to the lower terrain and airfields to the south if there is a weather problem. Routing via Ashbourne instead of Leek only adds 4nm (which amounts to about 2.5min) to the flight.

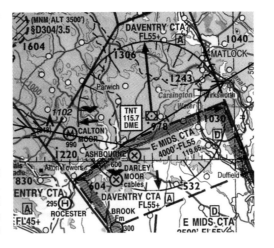

The turning point at Ashbourne

▶ Chart Selection

We decide to use 1:500 000 charts, principally because the entire flight can be planned on one map. Carrying both Northern and Southern England 1:500 000 charts will give the maximum coverage

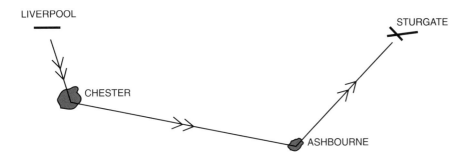

Overview of the route Liverpool (EGGP) to Sturgate (EGCS) via the Chester VRP and the town of Ashbourne

either side of the planned route. Because of the high ground over which part of our flight will take us, 1:250 000 maps are ruled out for primary use; the upper limit of these charts is 5000ft and we are likely to be flying higher than this.

A quick check of the latest chart catalogue AIC (green pages) confirms that the charts carried are current, the Southern England chart having changed edition about five weeks earlier. A check of the map key confirms the new portrayal of airspace boundaries.

NB: CONTROLLED AIRSPACE IS NOT DEPICTED ABOVE FLIGHT LEVEL 245 IN THE UK ALL CLASS [B] AIRSPACE IS ABOVE FL245. NO AIRSPACE IS DESIGNATED CLASS [C] IN THE UK. AIRSPACE RESTRICTIONS MAY BE SHOWN ABOVE FL 245.

The legend note on a UK 1:500 000 chart showing the vertical limits of the chart

▶Minimum Safety Altitude

Using a distance of 5nm each side of track and around the departure, turning points and destination, the following MSAs are calculated:

LEG	HIGHEST POINT	MSA CALCULATION
Liverpool – Chester VRP	Obstruction 533ft.	533ft rounds up to 600ft; + 1000ft = 1600ft. **But,** the lowest MSA on a UK 1:500 000 map is 1800ft (see Vertical Navigation chapter) so MSA = 1800ft.
Chester VRP – Ashbourne	Spot height 1519ft (3nm NE of Leek).	Rounds up to 1600ft; + 300ft for possible obstacle = 1900ft; + 1000ft gives an MSA of 2900ft.
Ashbourne – Sturgate	Spot height 1243ft (2nm N of Carsington reservoir).	Rounds up to 1300ft; + 300ft for possible obstacle = 1600ft; + = 1000ft gives an MSA 2600ft.

LEFT> The highest point on the leg Chester – Ashbourne, terrain with a spot height of 1519ft AMSL

RIGHT> The MSAs entered for the flight Liverpool to Sturgate

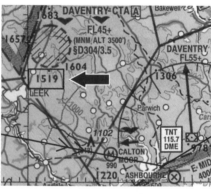

The highest point on the leg Ashbourne – Sturgate, terrain with a spot height of 1243ft AMSL

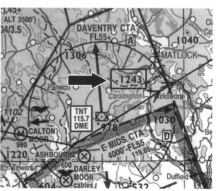

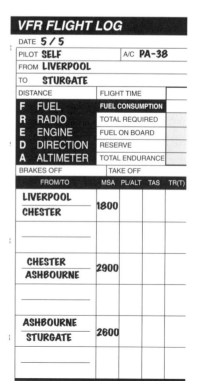

VFR FLIGHT LOG

DATE **5 / 5**

| PILOT **SELF** | A/C **PA-38** |

FROM **LIVERPOOL**

TO **STURGATE**

DISTANCE	FLIGHT TIME	
F FUEL	**FUEL CONSUMPTION**	
R RADIO	TOTAL REQUIRED	
E ENGINE	FUEL ON BOARD	
D DIRECTION	RESERVE	
A ALTIMETER	TOTAL ENDURANCE	
BRAKES OFF	TAKE OFF	

FROM/TO	MSA	PL/ALT	TAS	TR(T)
LIVERPOOL **CHESTER**	1800			
CHESTER **ASHBOURNE**	2900			
ASHBOURNE **STURGATE**	2600			

Flight Planning Summary

▶ Chart Preparation

The route is now measured on the map, and directions and distances entered onto the flight log. Out of personal preference, 10° track-error fan lines and quarter-way, half-way and three-quarter-way distance markers are added (using a different colour from the track lines). Variation is taken at the mid-point of the route as being 5°W.

The map is folded so that it will open out along the route.

VFR FLIGHT LOG

Airplan Flight Equipment
1a Ringway Trading Est. Manchester M22 5LH
Tel: 0161 499 0023 Fax: 0161 499 0298
www.airplan.u-net.com

DATE 5 / 5

PILOT SELF		A/C PA-38		ALTERNATE			
FROM LIVERPOOL				DISTANCE		FLIGHT TIME	
TO STURGATE				SUNSET		VAR. 5°W	

DISTANCE	FLIGHT TIME		2000' w/v			TEMP.
F FUEL	**FUEL CONSUMPTION**		5000' w/v			
R RADIO	TOTAL REQUIRED		DEPARTURE INFO.			
E ENGINE	FUEL ON BOARD					
D DIRECTION	RESERVE					
A ALTIMETER	TOTAL ENDURANCE					

BRAKES OFF		TAKE OFF			LANDING			BRAKES ON			

FROM/TO	MSA	PL/ALT	TAS	TR(T)	W/V	HDG(T)	HDG(M)	G/S	DIST	TIME	ETA	ATA
LIVERPOOL CHESTER	1800			177	/				9			
					/							
CHESTER ASHBOURNE	2900			103	/				41			
					/							
ASHBOURNE STURGATE	2600			060	/				43.5			

Tracks, distances and variation added

▶ Weather Considerations

The general weather situation is a settled one, which will have been evident to anyone keeping a weather eye open during the preceding days. The synoptic charts confirm a stationary high-pressure area (anticyclone) centred over the UK. There is a weak front to the north of the flight route, but all the indications are that it is not a significant feature. Settled high-pressure areas often imply haze and the METFORM 215 and AIRMET confirm that the biggest problem is likely to be the visibility, although this is expected to improve as the day goes on.

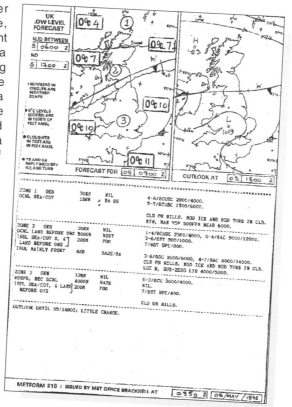

The METFORM 215 chart issued on the morning of the proposed flight. The route is in Zone 3. Note also the outlook for the afternoon

```
PART 1 OF 2 PARTS

AIRMET AREA FORECAST, NORTHERN REGION,
VALID MAY 5/0500Z TO 1300Z.

MET-SITUATION: HIGH PRESSURE WILL REMAIN OVER THE REGION, WITH A
               WEAK SLOW MOVING FRONT, FROM SOUTHERN IRELAND TO
               TYNE.

WINDS:
  1000FT: VRB/05KT PS15.
  3000FT: 230/05KT PS11.
  6000FT: 220/15KT PS07.
FREEZING LEVEL: 10000FT.
```

The winds at altitude from that morning's AIRMET forecast

The Liverpool TAF and METAR show the same story. Sturgate does not issue METARs or have a TAF provided. However, there is a military airfield – RAF Scampton – just 6nm from Sturgate (note: this airfield has since closed). Although Scampton's met. information is not distributed on services such as METFAX or the recorded TAF & METAR telephone service, its TAFs and METARs can be obtained from a forecast office. A local-rate phone call to the Manchester Weather Centre provides the Scampton TAF and METAR.

The TAFs and actuals for Liverpool (EGGP) and Scampton (EGXP). The term 'WHITE' in the Scampton actual refers to the weather state, as used by the RAF.

The TAFs and actuals for Liverpool (EGGP) and Scampton (EGXP). The term 'WHITE' in the Scampton actual refers to the weather state, as used by the RAF

```
EGXP  050834Z 050918 VRB04KT 4000 FU BECMG 0912
7000 TEMPO 1218 9999=
EGXP  050950 050950Z 01004KT 5000 HZ BKN025 20/11
Q1023 WHITE NOSIG=
EGGP  050607Z 050716 VRB05KT 5000 NSC BECMG 0709
CAVOK=
EGGP  050950 050950Z 12002KT 8000 BKN250 19/11
Q1023=
```

Looking at the METFORM 215 and AIRMET forecasts, the synoptic situation and the TAFs and METARs, the only significant weather problem is the possibility of haze. In the TAFs, the visibility is forecast to improve and is assessed as being acceptable in relation to licence limits, personal weather limits and VMC minima. Given the validity times of the forecasts, we decide to recheck the latest forecasts and actuals just before departure, with particular regard to visibility. We also bear in mind that the route will be slightly 'down sun', which should improve visibility. Flying higher above the haze layer should also improve air-to-ground visibility.

Flight Planning Summary

▶ Daylight

With a planned departure time of 1200 local, the approximate sunset time of 2000 local is not a problem for the flight. For the return, provided departure is before 1830 local there should be a safe margin to land back at Liverpool about 30min before sunset (and therefore one hour before the start of official night).

▶ Completion of the Flight Log

Headings and groundspeeds are calculated on the flight computer, using the W/V and temperature figures from the AIRMET forecast. The aircraft's cruising CAS is taken from the flight manual as 89kts, and this is used as the basis for calculating TAS.

Intermediate temperatures are used for the calculation of TAS (e.g. +13°C at 1500ft for the first leg to Chester). Not knowing which runway will be in use for departure, the first leg is drawn from the centre of Liverpool airfield and an extra 2min is added to the leg time to allow for the climb and turn on to track. The leg is planned to the east of the Chester VRP, where a railway line crosses the dual-carriageway bypass. This avoids flying directly over the 'congested' area of Chester, and increases separation from restricted area R311 – by staying east of the M53 the aircraft will automatically remain clear.

VFR FLIGHT LOG

Airplan Flight Equipment
1a Ringway Trading Est. Manchester M22 5LH
Tel: 0161 499 0023 Fax: 0161 499 0298
www.airplan.u-net.com

DATE 5 / 5

PILOT SELF		A/C PA-38	ALTERNATE		
FROM LIVERPOOL			DISTANCE		FLIGHT TIME
TO STURGATE			SUNSET **20:00**	VAR. **5° W**	

DISTANCE	FLIGHT TIME		2000' w/v **230 / 05**		TEMP. **+11**
F FUEL	**FUEL CONSUMPTION**		5000' w/v **220 / 15**		**+7**
R RADIO	TOTAL REQUIRED		DEPARTURE INFO.		
E ENGINE	FUEL ON BOARD				
D DIRECTION	RESERVE				
A ALTIMETER	TOTAL ENDURANCE				

BRAKES OFF		TAKE OFF		LANDING			BRAKES ON		

FROM/TO	MSA	PL/ALT	TAS	TR(T)	W/V	HDG(T)	HDG(M)	G/S	DIST	TIME	ETA	ATA
LIVERPOOL — CHESTER	1800	1500	90	177	230/05	179	184	88	9	8		
					/							
CHESTER — ASHBOURNE	2900	2400 / FL35	89	103	230/05	105	110	92	41	27		
					/							
ASHBOURNE — STURGATE	2600	FL50	90	060	220/15	064	069	104	43.5	25		
					/							

Winds, planned altitudes, TAS, headings, groundspeeds, leg-times and sunset time

Planned altitudes are input at this stage. For the first leg, the standard Liverpool VFR clearance is expected, which will be not above 1500ft QNH.

On the second leg, altitude is initially constrained by the base of the Manchester CTA (2500ft altitude). On the basis that height is safety, an initial cruising level of 2400ft is selected. This also puts the aircraft clear of traffic entering and leaving the Low-Level Route at 1250ft. After passing Alsager, the base of controlled airspace rises to FL45. On the basis of the magnetic track for this leg (108°M) we select quadrantals at odd FLs + 500 and decide that the obvious level to climb to is FL35. Having established from Manchester Weather Centre that the QNH is 1018 (i.e. more than 1013) we know that this flight level is available above the transition altitude. Furthermore, by converting the difference in millibars between the QNH and 1013 to feet, we can calculate the actual altitude at FL35. The sum is (1018 - 1013) = 5mb = 150ft. Since the QNH is greater than the ISA standard, 150ft is added to FL35 to give an altitude of 3650ft. This is comfortably above the MSA of 2900ft.

The magnetic track on the third leg is 065°M, giving quadrantals of odd FLs. Overhead Ashbourne the base of controlled airspace is FL55, although the East Midlands CTA is very close with a base of 4000ft QNH. We obviously need to consider our options carefully. Passing the canal and railway line in a valley south of Matlock, the base of controlled airspace becomes FL105. Past the M1 motorway there is no controlled airspace below FL245 (the upper limit of the CAA 1:500 000 chart). The obvious level to choose is FL50, which is available after passing Ashbourne provided the aircraft is clear of East Midland's CTA. This Flight Level is below the Daventry CTA and not so high that a prolonged climb will complicate the groundspeed calculations; however it is high enough to be comfortably above the MSA (FL50 + 150ft = 5150ft; MSA is 2600ft). Flying higher should also improve visibility through the expected haze. Clearance can be requested through East Midland's Class D airspace (which we will pass close to at Ashbourne) when approaching this turning point. If this clearance is not forthcoming, or if cloud prevents the climb to FL50, a descent can be made to FL30. This is still above the MSA, on the correct quadrantal and below East Midland's Class D airspace.

▶Fuel Planning and Mass Calculation

– Initial fuel plan. A planned flight time of exactly one hour is taken from the flight log. With a fuel consumption of 5 imp. gal/hr and a 2 imp. gal allowance for taxying and power checks (there is a long taxy to the runway at Liverpool) it does not need a flight computer to calculate a fuel required of 7 imp. gal.

– Weight Check. If possible, plan to take full fuel because happiness is full fuel tanks! To check whether this is possible, given the aircraft weight and other payload, a short calculation is necessary (using the actual aircraft documents):

Flight Planning Summary

Aircraft Weight

(including unusable fuel)	1182lb
2 x Pilots	310lb
Baggage	15lb
Total	1507lb
Maximum Authorised Weight	1670lb
Therefore weight available for fuel =	163lb

– Fuel/weight calculation. At a specific gravity of 0·72, 163lb = 22·6 imp. gal. This is unfortunately a little less than full tanks. Therefore the fuel load will be 22·6 imp. gal. and the fuel plan is calculated from this figure.

– Final Fuel Plan. The fuel plan based on a departure fuel of 20·6 imp. gal.(i.e. 22·6 minus 2 imp. gal taxying allowance) shows a reserve of 13·6 imp. gal on arriving overhead Sturgate. This is obviously pretty generous, giving just over 2·5hr reserve for diversion and holding. The total endurance (based on the departure fuel load of 20·6 imp. gal) is 4hr 7min.

VFR FLIGHT LOG

DATE 5 / 5			
PILOT SELF		A/C PA-38	
FROM LIVERPOOL			
TO STURGATE			
DISTANCE **93.5**	FLIGHT TIME		**1:00**
F FUEL	**FUEL CONSUMPTION**		**5**
R RADIO	TOTAL REQUIRED		**5+2**
E ENGINE	FUEL ON BOARD		**22.6**
D DIRECTION	RESERVE		**15.6**
A ALTIMETER	TOTAL ENDURANCE		**4:07**

The fuel plan

▶ Take-off and Landing Performance

The graphs for the calculation of take-off and landing performance are found in the aircraft's POH/FM. Detailed information on calculating take-off and landing distances is outside the navigation syllabus; nevertheless the principles are not difficult.

Given that Liverpool is the 'home' base and has a runway in excess of 2000m in length, the calculation of take-off and landing distance here for a PA38 is pretty much an academic exercise. We will concentrate on Sturgate instead.

The landing-distance calculation is done on the basis of the Sturgate elevation of 58ft, an anticipated temperature of about +20°C and nil wind. On this basis, the landing performance is calculated as 675m including a 43% safety factor.

The take-off performance, in the same conditions, is 530m including a 33% safety factor.

The runway dimensions and surface at Sturgate are found in the AIP AD section. Runway 04/22 is 460m long and therefore too short for either take-off or landing. The main runway (09/27) has different take-off and landing distances available in each direction. For landing the worst case is 09, with a Landing Distance Available (LDA) of 705m. For take-off the worst case is 27, with a Take-Off Run Available (TORA) of 790m – although a 30m 'starter extension' is available by day, making a total of 820m. Therefore Runways 09 and 27 are within the aircraft's performance capabilities for take-off and landing, but Runways 04 and 22 are not – either for landing or take-off.

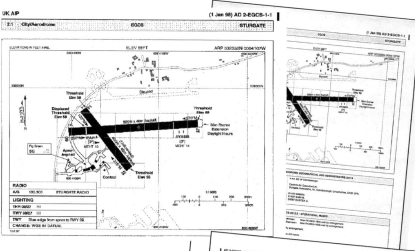

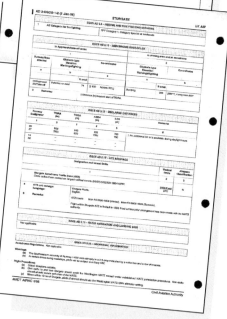

The Sturgate entry in the AD section of the AIP

The Sturgate page in the AD section of the AIP contains other valuable information, including the fact that Sturgate is PPR (Prior Permission Required). We must therefore make a telephone call to the airfield operator without further ado. The information gleaned from the conversation includes advice on liaison with the military ATC units nearby, the present runway in use (27) and today's closing time (1700 local). Furthermore, it is ascertained that the A/G frequency may be unmanned for short periods during the day – as is quite common at airfields with an A/G service – and that sea breezes may well affect the airfield from mid-afternoon onwards. These may reverse the runway in use from 27 to 09.

All this demonstrates once again the value of a telephone call to a PPR airfield. If we are unable to make contact on the A/G frequency we will know why. We will also pay particular attention to the surface wind and its effect on the runway in use. Finally, we will keep a sharp lookout for the local military traffic. A close encounter with a passing AWACS, a marauding Tornado or the Red Arrows *en masse* would not make our day.

▶ Alternate Airfields

Retford/Gamston is chosen as an alternate because:

1 It is just 11 miles from Sturgate. The runway is long enough to accommodate a PA38, and the airfield is notified to be open and available for use.

2 The diversion from Sturgate to Retford is essentially a reversal of track, making navigation simple, and Retford has good landmarks around it to help identifications. What's more, Retford has a VOR/DME (GAM) on the airfield which will also aid navigation to it.

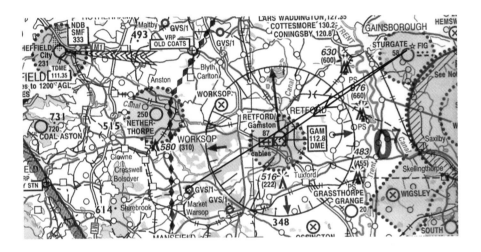

The route from Sturgate to the alternate airfield – Retford

3 Retford will be overflown *en route* to Sturgate, and is therefore an easy diversion. If returning to Retford from overhead Sturgate, the weather situation at Retford and what it looks like from the air will already be known.

The route from Sturgate to Retford/Gamston is now planned and added to the flight log. A mental calculation shows that a diversion from Sturgate to Retford plus 45min holding overhead Retford will still leave plenty of reserve fuel (at least 2hr) for diversion to numerous other suitable airfields, or even a return to Liverpool.

PILOT SELF		A/C PA-38		ALTERNATE **RETFORD**				
FROM LIVERPOOL				DISTANCE **11.5**		FLIGHT TIME **8**		
TO STURGATE				SUNSET		VAR. 5° W		
DISTANCE 93.5		FLIGHT TIME 1:00		2000' w/v 230 / 05			TEMP. +11	
F FUEL		**FUEL CONSUMPTION** 5		5000' w/v 220 / 15			+7	
R RADIO		TOTAL REQUIRED 5+2		DEPARTURE INFO.				
E ENGINE		FUEL ON BOARD 22.8						
D DIRECTION		RESERVE 15.6						
A ALTIMETER		TOTAL ENDURANCE 4:07						

BRAKES OFF			TAKE OFF			LANDING				BRAKES ON			
FROM/TO	MSA	PL/ALT	TAS	TR(T)	W/V	HDG(T)	HDG(M)	G/S	DIST	TIME	ETA	ATA	
LIVERPOOL CHESTER	1800	1500	90	177	230/05	179	184	88	9	8			
CHESTER ASHBOURNE	2900	2400 FL35	89	103	230/05	105	110	92	41	27			
ASHBOURNE STURGATE	2600	FL50	90	060	220/15	064	069	104	43.5	25			
STURGATE RETFORD	1800	2000	90	240	230/05	239	244	85	11.5	8			

DISTRESS 121.50	TRANSPONDER	DISTRESS 7700	COM FAIL 7600	CONSPICUITY 7000
STATION	SVC	FREQ.	CLEARANCE/OBSERVATIONS	

The alternate (Retford)

▶Radio Frequencies

These are found in the ENR and AD sections of the AIP. Those noted include some frequencies we do not actually expect to contact. Although the route is outside Manchester's airspace, a 'listening watch' on the Manchester Approach frequency will be useful for information on traffic entering and leaving the low-level route and VRPs. The London FIR FIS frequency is also noted, although it is not expected to be used – East Midlands Approach will be a more useful unit to contact for a radar service and possibly clearance through their airspace.

The radio frequencies added

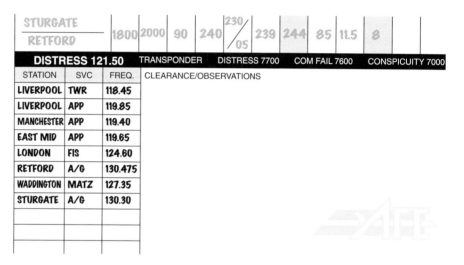

STURGATE			1800	2000	90	240	230/05	239	244	85	11.5	8			
RETFORD															

DISTRESS 121.50 TRANSPONDER DISTRESS 7700 COM FAIL 7600 CONSPICUITY 7000

STATION	SVC	FREQ.	CLEARANCE/OBSERVATIONS
LIVERPOOL	TWR	118.45	
LIVERPOOL	APP	119.85	
MANCHESTER	APP	119.40	
EAST MID	APP	119.65	
LONDON	FIS	124.60	
RETFORD	A/G	130.475	
WADDINGTON	MATZ	127.35	
STURGATE	A/G	130.30	

Restricted Area R313 (Scampton) is checked in the ENR section of the AIP for general details, and any specific information that may be relevant to the arrival at Sturgate. This reveals that the restricted area applies whenever Scampton is open; that it is established for the benefit of the Red Arrows; and that in-flight information can be obtained on the Waddington MATZ frequency. We naturally make a note of the latter.

Although our planned flight does not take us into a MATZ, we will clearly be flying very close to the Scampton MATZ and, of course, our plans may change in the light of circumstances. Therefore we should bear in mind the general advice to contact a MATZ 15nm or 5 minutes flying time (whichever is greater) before the ETA at the MATZ boundary.

Flight Planning Summary

▶ Pre-flight Information Bulletins

The AIRACs, AIP supplements and AIP amendments are checked for any change to the information found in the AIP.

The pre-flight information bulletins reveal nothing significant regarding the departure, destination or diversion airfields.

Two en-route items are identified:

1   A Royal Flight from RAF Northolt to Newcastle, which will cross the route at some point.

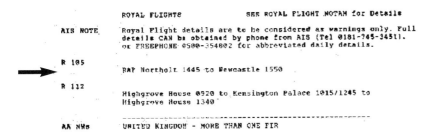

Notification of the Royal Flight (R105) in the A8 Pre-flight Information Bulletin

2   A low-level air exercise involving fast jets, near the turning point at Ashbourne, with an upper limit of 2500ft.

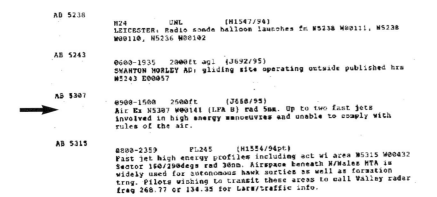

Notification of the fast-jet air exercise north of Ashbourne in the A8 Pre-flight Information Bulletin

More details of the Royal Flight are available from the FBU at Liverpool. These reveal that the Royal Flight will pass over Trent VOR at an ETA (UTC) of 1515, between FL100 & FL290 (i.e. inside controlled airspace). Both the level and timing of the Royal Flight mean that it will not affect our own. However, as a final check, we call the freephone number (0500 354802) for details of Royal Flights, Temporary Restricted Airspace, Emergency Restrictions of Flying etc. The recorded message contains details of the Royal Flight that we already know about, but nothing else to affect our flight.

▶Aircraft Documentation

A quick check of the aircraft documentation (particularly the Certificate of Maintenance Review and hours to next check) reveals that all is in order.

▶Flight Notification

Details of the flight are entered on the booking-out/tech log sheets. 'Booking-out' can be done by telephone, and a final weather check is made with particular regard to the visibility.

The visibility is improving as forecast and our planning is complete. All that remains is to pre-flight the aircraft and fly!

▶Conclusion

All in all, the whole flight-planning process described will take somewhere between one and one and a half hours. With the flight planning completed, you are now in a very good position to complete a professional and relaxed flight. Most reasonable eventualities have been covered, and most of the nasty surprises which can really ruin a flight have been considered. With routes, MSAs, headings, altitudes/flight levels and frequencies planned, you can concentrate on flying the aircraft. With pre-flight information bulletins and the AIP checked (and the PPR phone-call made) you know what to expect *en route* and on arrival. With the met. forecasts and actuals thoroughly researched, you know about any potential weather-related problems. And the price of all these benefits is about an hour and a half's work. As a matter of fact, if the flight has been planned in advance – with items such as route selection, MSAs, chart marking, radio frequencies, performance and the basic flight log completed before arriving at the airfield – you can probably complete the job in under forty minutes.

And if you choose (or "elect", as the accident reports put it) not to do proper flight planning? Well, consider the alternatives. Would you be expecting haze near the destination, or the possible sea-breeze effect? Could you plan a safe altitude over the high ground without a proper MSA calculation? And what about that low-level military exercise near Ashbourne? Do you really fancy a close encounter with a fast jet? And if you arrived overhead Sturgate, without PPR, would a lack of response from the radio worry you? Should you land, or is it better to divert – and if so, where? Could you land on a 705m runway in zero wind conditions? Could you use 04/22?

It's no coincidence that well-planned flights have the best chance of being successfully completed. Flights that haven't been properly planned are the standard fodder of accident/incident reports and 'I Learned About Flying From That' stories. The idea of having a Private Pilot's Licence is to enjoy your flying. Making a first-class job of navigation and flight planning is the best possible way to maximise that enjoyment.

Revision Answers

▶The Earth

1 – N5031 E00047.

2 – A great circle.

3 – Compass north.

4 – 135° M (magnetic).

5 – 68nm.

▶Aeronautical Maps

6 – A: Hucknall to Strubby   070°(T)   074·5°(M)   52·5nm

     B: Hawarden to Manchester/Barton   050°(T)   055·5°(M)   27·5nm

     C: Valley to Netherthorpe   088°(T)   093°(M)   119·5nm

     D: Finningley to Caernarfon   259°(T)   265°(M)   121nm

     (answers should be within 1nm and 2°)

7 – It is a great-circle track, which is the shortest distance between two points.

8

True	Variation	Magnetic	Deviation	Compass
184	5W	189	2E	187
300	3W	303	2W	305
004	5E	359	2W	001
355	10W	005	3E	002

9 – 50nm (as measured against the latitude markings)

10

Nautical Miles	Statute Miles	Kilometres
17	19.5	31.5
225	259	417
379	436	702
130	150	241
95	109	176
39.5	45.5	73

(answers should be with 1nm/2km)

11 – Yes. 1635ft = 498m

12 – 298ft (AMSL). The airfield is Woodford

13 – 500ft

14 – 1050ft

▶Navigation principles 1: The Triangle of Velocities

15 – TAS	TR(T)	W/V	HDG (T)	HDG (M)	G/S
80	167	280/20	180	185	86
97	242	280/20	249	254	80
101	330	300/30	321	326	73
110	010	090/15	018	023	107

(Headings should be within 2°, groundspeed within 2kts)

16 – 20kts tailwind component

17 – TAS	TR(T)	W/V	HDG(T)	HDG(M)	G/S
95	107	165/14	115	119	87
104	325	200/20	315	319	115
86	178	315/17	186	190	98
120	004	290/30	350	354	107

(W/V should be within 10° and 5kts)

▶Navigation principles 2: Airspeed, Groundspeed, Time and Distance

18 – 40kts IAS

19 – CAS (Knots)	Pressure Altitude (feet)	OAT	TAS
89	3000	+20°C	95kts
120	9000	+10°C	162 (Statute mph)
75	5000	-10°C	145km/hr
102	7500	0°F	110kts

(answers should be within 2kts/mph/kph)

20 – G/S	DIST	TIME
95	49	31mins
79	89	1hr 8min
113	9	4min 50s
89	124	1hr 24min

(time should be accurate to within 1min)

21 – G/S	DIST	TIME
170	139nm	49min
99	122nm	1hr 14min
56.5	34nm	36min

22 – 99kts.

23 – 1013.

24 – 145km/hr.

Revision Answers

▶ Vertical Navigation

25 – 3700ft

26 – 1500ft

27 – FL55

28 – 3960ft

29 – 991mb (Coal Aston elevation is 720ft, which equals 24mb. Subtracting, 1015-24 = 991mb)

30 – 255ft/min

31 – 245ft/min

▶ Aeroplan Magnetism

32 – Right; 330°.

33 – Right. If heading 020°, 110° will be in the 3 o'clock position (i.e. on the right wingtip).

34 – Left: compass reading will be about 020° as you begin to roll out.

35 – Left: compass will read about 120° as you begin to roll out. The clock-code position of 135° before starting the turn is 8:30.

▶ Practical Navigation:
– Dead Reckoning and Map Reading

36 – 1153

37 –

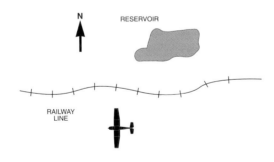

▶ Practical Navigation:
– Off-Track Calculations & Track Marking

38 – 7°

39 – 059° (TE = 9°, CA = 7°).

40 – 009° (TE = 5·5°, which is doubled so that aircraft will regain track in the same distance as it flew off-track).

41 – 1310. This can be worked out easily on the flight computer. Place 75 (representing 0·75 or $\frac{3}{4}$)under the time elapsed (21min). Above 1 read off the time – 28 minutes. Alternatively, divide time elapsed (21) by 3, then multiply by 4.

▶ Flight Planning: Fuel Planning

42 –

Flight Time/Endurance	Fuel Consumption	Fuel On Board/Fuel Required/Fuel Used
1hr 58min	12·2 imp. gal/hr	24 imp. gal
3hr 23min	47ltr/hr	159ltr
1hr 28min	17 US gal/hr	25 US gal
5hr 10min	8·5 imp. gal	44 imp. gal

43 – 206ltr

44 – 112ltr

45 – 200ltr

46 – 4hr 38min

47 – 2hr 48min

▶ Flight Planning: Performance

48 – 90ltr.

49 –175kg.

50 – Yes (up to 176ltr of fuel can be carried).

51 – No, the take-off distance required is 620m. It's really not worth trying it.

52 – 28.

53 – 26 and 32.

▶ Flight Planning: The Aeronautical Information Service

54 – Information relating to safety matters.

55 – The AD section.

56 – In the AD section of the AIP.

57 – In the ENR section of the AIP.

58 – The AIRAC system.

59 – Obstruction. Until 1600UTC on 14 July a tower crane will be sited on a bearing of 299° (magnetic) at a distance of 535m from the Aerodrome Reference Point. The top of the crane is 66ft above aerodrome level, the boom

Revision Answers

is 150ft long. The top of the crane and the end of the boom will be lit. Details in AIP supplement A585/95.

60 – Reference number AB5152. On 13 May between 1400 and 1430 UTC up to 12,000ft (AMSL). Location – Weston-on-the-Green, a Parachute Jumping Exercise centred on lat and long N5152 W00112. Radius from that point 2nm.

61 – The vertical limit between 0800 and 1800 UTC will be 40,000ft AMSL. The danger area designator is D115B.

62 – On a freephone number (0500 354802).

▶ Radio Navigation

63 – Night effect

64 – The magnetic heading to fly, assuming no wind, to reach the station: in other words the magnetic track to the station.

65 – Class B

66 – Increasing the height of the radar antenna above the surrounding terrain will increase radar range.

67 – No!

68 – A Plan Position Indicator (PPI)

69 – A transponder

70 – Where is SSR information normally displayed to an Air Traffic Controller?

71 – The aircraft's flight level (or altitude if the ground SSR is so configured)

72 – A Non Directional Beacon: a ground-based radio transmitter which transits in all directions

73 – On a fixed Radio Compass or Relative Bearing Indicator (RBI)

74 – Choose any three from:

Surface/terrain, precipitation static, coastal refraction, night effect, thunderstorm effect

75 – VHF Omni-directional Range

76 – Magnetic north

77 – H24 (that is, 24 hours a day)

78 – Groundspeed and Time To Station (TTS)

79 – No, it is the <u>slant</u> range

▶ Full Flight Plan

80 – 1000Z.

81 – Birmingham ATC, by 1600Z *at the latest*, and it is the pilot's responsibility.

▶ Time

82 – 1615 French local time.

83 – 1805 local.

Navigation, Meteorology and Flight Planning – Combined Index

index

B

C

D

index

index

F

I

J

K

L

index

M

N

O

index

P

index

I

index

S

index

T

n

index

O

index

U

V

index

W

Z

notes

notes

notes

notes

notes